SHIFTING CURRENTS

SHIFTING
CURRENTS

A WORLD HISTORY
OF SWIMMING

KAREN EVA CARR

REAKTION BOOKS

For Damian, who swam with me

Published by Reaktion Books Ltd
Unit 32, Waterside
44–48 Wharf Road
London N1 7UX, UK
www.reaktionbooks.co.uk

First published 2022, reprinted 2022
Copyright © Karen Eva Carr 2022

Printed and bound in Great Britain
by Bell & Bain, Glasgow

A catalogue record for this book is
available from the British Library

ISBN 978 1 78914 578 6

CONTENTS

INTRODUCTION

Most people today can't swim. This book explains why that is, and how we got there. After all, why not swim? All able-bodied people everywhere in the world could learn to swim. Swimming is not expensive; most people, including most non-swimmers, live within a few miles of an ocean or river. And it hasn't always been this way. At one time, most people in most parts of the world swam every day, from the time they were toddlers until they were old and frail. People swam together in convenient ponds, rivers or oceans, as a social occasion, to relax after lunch or in the evening. Children played swimming games, teenagers flirted in the water, young parents splashed their babies, older people soaked arthritic knees. But today, even adults who know how to swim are unlikely to swim socially, and people's ability to swim depends largely on their social identity: on race, income and education. The world's most powerful people are the most likely to know how to swim.

How did this happen? Why is swimming uncommon? Why is it associated with power and wealth? The story starts when people noticed that some groups of people enjoyed swimming and others didn't know how to swim. They seized on this difference as a line dividing 'us' from 'them'. Swimming is well suited to the establishment of cultural identity: it is fairly difficult to learn, especially as an adult, and impossible to fake. As a shibboleth, swimming is very effective.

Not that everyone wanted to be on the swimming side of that line. Many people throughout history have identified as proud non-swimmers. These non-swimmers tend to characterize swimming as sacrilege, displeasing to the gods, dirtying and disturbing the water. They often added that swimming was dangerous, not only because you could drown, but because of various health issues (swimming after eating, for example, was said to make you fat), and because of lurking sharks, water spirits, sirens, mermaids and sea monsters. Swimming was also said to encourage promiscuity, as you took off your clothes to dive in. Swimming was for fish or animals, not humans. Perhaps most importantly, non-swimmers simply saw swimming as something other people did.

On the other side of that line, swimmers felt just as strongly about their abilities. Swimming showed that you were properly brought up. Indeed, swimming was proverbially associated with reading as a way to identify people you would want to associate with. Swimming was important for safety, to prevent drowning, and for health. Social life, in some times and places, has depended on being able to play swimming games and splash in the water, and swimming has often been a passport into the avant-garde and the upper class. More ambitious swimming demonstrated courage and perseverance, and was often held up as an example of good character. On both sides of this line, people felt they had good sense and moral uprightness on their side.

And yet over the past several thousand years, whole groups of people have changed sides. Swimmers have become non-swimmers; non-swimmers have overcome (to some extent) their prejudices and fears and learned how to swim. Some non-swimming groups shift over to become swimmers when they meet more sophisticated, wealthy people who swim, in an effort to emulate their new neighbours. Others are inspired by meeting swimmers they see as living a freer, more natural life; they see swimming as a way to break free of old social constrictions. Swimming can be a means of moving from poverty to wealth, a way to identify with powerful groups, or a metaphor for revolution.

Societies of swimmers also cross the line in the other direction to become non-swimmers. They may be frightened out of the water by a specific well-publicized, traumatic drowning. Or swimmers may encounter powerful non-swimmers, so that swimming starts to seem old-fashioned and uncool or (if the swimmers have been conquered) even treasonous. Swimmers may also be forced out of the water by a variety of legal restrictions, from the proliferation of safety regulations to racist or sexist segregation of beaches and pools. They may even be told, incorrectly, that they are biologically incapable of swimming. Just as swimming can be aspirational, refusing to swim can also become a gesture of solidarity with the working class. On both sides of the line, though meanings and identities may seem immutable in the moment, over time they shift: the current pulls us this way and that, and we can never stay still in the moving water.

I love to swim, and both of my grandmothers were enthusiastic swimmers, but my more remote ancestors probably did not know how. Because of that, and because my academic work focuses on the ancient Mediterranean, this book foregrounds the non-swimmers. I began this book about eight years ago, when I first realized that there was no modern comprehensive history of swimming. Over the years, however, I have come to understand this project also as a way of making Whiteness visible, or strange, of learning to study Whiteness and White culture without normalizing it as neutral. This is a story about how we create identity. So although the story ranges over all the inhabited continents, it focuses on the line separating swimmers from non-swimmers. For the earlier periods, that line is mainly geographical. For more recent centuries, the line separates enslaver and enslaved, colonizer and colonized. There remains a whole separate history of Indigenous swimming still to explore, but Indigenous people are writing that themselves.

African American historians have already started on this work. There are a number of good accounts of the fight to end racist segregation of swimming pools, including those of Gilbert Mason and Lee Pitts, as well as the White historians Jeff Wiltse and Andrew Kahrl. Kevin Dawson's account of early modern African and African American swimming moves the story back a couple of centuries. The work early feminists did to get access to swimming pools has been chronicled by Glenn Stout and others.

Meanwhile, other historians have been circling the history of swimming without really diving into it. Garrett Fagan and Stefanie Hoss have done excellent work on medieval and ancient baths and bathing around the Mediterranean, joined by a number of more recent works. But bathing is not the same as swimming: bathers stay within their depth, where they can stand up, while swimmers brave the deeper water. In this book the focus is on swimming.

Another avenue by which scholars have approached the history of swimming is the terrible history of trial by water for witchcraft. Here, too, much excellent work has been done, from Russell Zguta in the 1970s to

Péter Tóth and Erika Gasser more recently. Their insights have contributed in no small measure to the argument I make here. But again, the forcible half-drowning that is trial by water is peripheral in this book in favour of voluntary swimming.

From Fernand Braudel in the 1920s to Emily Kneebone in 2020, scholars have considered Mediterranean attitudes towards the ocean. Chet Van Duzer and Vaughn Scribner have collected stories of ancient and medieval sea monsters and merpeople. Duane Roller and Steve Mentz have considered respectively ancient and early modern ideas about the Atlantic Ocean. Ships and shipwrecks have gained some attention, from Lionel Casson's work on ancient seafaring to James Morrison and Josiah Blackmore's work on shipwrecks and John McManamon's work on Renaissance salvage diving. McManamon's account of the transition from ancient to Renaissance swimming has, of course, also been very useful, as has Janick Auberger's suspicion that Greek swimming was not really so skilful. Clayton Evans has written on the history of lifesaving. Again, their insights into people's attitudes towards the water have shaped this story.

For the Pacific and East Asia, Shigeo Sagita and Ken Uyeno's *Swimming in Japan*, though published in 1935, did more than anything else to explain East Asian swimming. Bonnie Tsui's thoughts on samurai swimming were also illuminating. Most other work has focused on bathing. Edward Shafer's work on bathing in ancient China, now decades old, was still very helpful. For earlier periods, there is altogether less to go on. Prehistorians have given us João Zilhão and Paola Villa's innovative and timely (for me!) work on Neanderthal fishing and diving. Ashraf Abdel-Raouf Ragheb has written on diving in ancient Egypt, and Gina Konstantopoulos on Mesopotamian views of the ocean.

Modern books on the history of swimming from Nicolas Orme in 1983 to Eric Chaline in 2017 and Howard Means in 2020 have, for the most part, centred their attention on the glorious revival of interest in swimming in nineteenth-century Britain. For this period I am indebted to their much superior knowledge, as well as to more specialized work on British seaside resorts by Alain Corbin, Rachel Johnson and others, and on early swimming organizations by David Day and Margaret Roberts.

We are still in the opening stages of writing the history of swimming, and this book cannot hope to be the last word on anything. In addition to the work still to be done on Indigenous swimming, there is much cataloguing needed of local rivers and beaches, where dangerous currents, jellyfish, waterborne bacteria and parasites, sewage, pollution and predators may have had larger effects on people's decision to swim than I have been able to acknowledge. I am, however, convinced that further research will confirm the general outlines of the story presented here.

That story starts with the first swimmers in prehistory, even before the development of modern humans. (Indeed, the first definite evidence of human swimming is from a Neanderthal site in Italy.) The story continues as people spread out from Africa to the other continents, and then fewer people swam through the cold centuries of the last Ice Age. From the Ice Age the story moves ahead to the first written records in Bronze Age Egypt, Mesopotamia and China, and then to the much better-documented discussions of swimming from ancient Greece and Rome. Swimming reached a second low point in the global Middle Ages, as Mediterranean slave trading encouraged the racialization of swimming and the establishment of the Mongol Empire swept change across Eurasia. Then in the early modern period, Japan found a new enthusiasm for swimming, and European colonization brought European slave traders and settlers into contact with swimmers from all over Africa, Southeast Asia and the Americas. New knowledge gained from these swimmers, combined with European emphasis on their inheritance from the ancient Mediterranean, encouraged a wave of enthusiasm for swimming in the nineteenth and early twentieth centuries, which is only now beginning to subside.

From the last Ice Age to today, people have forgotten how to swim twice, and learned how to swim again twice, and now many of them have once again forgotten. This is the story of how and why that happened, and how we could get back in the water.

PART I

LEARNING
TO
SWIM

1 The first known image of people swimming, in the Cave of the Swimmers, Wadi Sura, Western Desert, Egypt, *c.* 8000 BCE.

1

ONCE EVERYONE COULD SWIM

Swimming was the first activity of the first living creatures on Earth. Four billion years ago, when the earliest one-celled living beings formed out of amino acids, they drifted through seawater in search of food. At first it was only the currents in the seawater that pushed the cells this way and that, but after half a billion years some cells used fine hair-like projections called cilia or flagella to swim towards food, or away from danger. When the cell senses the need for action, it sends energy to the cilia, and the cilia bend. In bending, the cilia push water behind them, and the cell moves forwards. This is the basis of all swimming: if you push the water behind you, then you will move forwards.

Five Ice Ages have come and gone since these first cells started to swim. In some eras Earth was so warm there was no ice even at the poles, and in other eras it was so cold that the whole planet may have been entirely encased in ice. About 600 million years ago, the first multicellular animals evolved. They, too, were swimmers. Jellyfish send electric signals through a nerve net to expand and contract their umbrella-shaped bodies, pushing the water behind them. Roundworms developed a different method to move through the water: they used their nerves to contract and relax two long muscles that ran the length of their bodies. As the worms contracted first one side of their body, then the other, their bodies bent back and forth, thrashing the water and pushing themselves forwards. Fish, with more energy from using jaws to chew food, waved fins to move faster. When the first ancestors of frogs and salamanders emerged from the water, they swam too. Up to this point, pretty much everything living on Earth was born into the water, knowing how to swim.

But here is the first big break: when reptiles and mammals evolved, they were not natural swimmers. All of the world's land was then grouped into one huge supercontinent. Rainclouds did not often reach the interior, where vast deserts formed. Mammals evolved in those dry deserts and they did not swim much.[1]

When that supercontinent broke apart and today's continents began to form, the climate became wetter and cooler. (Even today, though, the centres of the continents, Central and West Asia, the Sahara and the Great Plains, remain pretty dry places, and that's going to be significant for our story.) In these new wetter conditions, more mammals started to swim. Today most animals can swim at least a little. All they have to do is move their legs the way they normally do for running, and the paddling will get them across the pond. Mice and rats swim, dogs, pigs and horses swim, cows and goats swim. Tigers are good swimmers, and house cats will swim if they must, though they famously hate the water. Dogs may be afraid the first time, but they figure it out. Even desert animals like camels and giraffes can swim if they need to. The Roman natural historian Pliny thought elephants were 'unable to swim, because of their size', but a generation before Pliny, the Greek geographer Strabo knew that elephants could swim.[2]

Primates are weak swimmers, even for mammals. Some monkeys do learn to swim, and a few species of monkeys swim for pleasure. Proboscis monkeys, native to the Southeast Asian island of Borneo, swim with their heads out of the water, moving their hands and feet alternately in much the same way as swimming dogs. (Unlike mice, they do not use their tails.) These monkeys swim across deep rivers, just to climb trees on the other side. Rhesus monkey mothers, in India and across Southeast Asia, leap playfully from tree branches into rivers carrying their babies on their backs, and swim to the opposite shore. Their babies can themselves swim when they are only a few days old. But most species of monkeys – most baboons, most guenons and colobus monkeys – can't swim at all.

Our closest primate cousins – the great apes and orangutans, the modern gorillas and chimpanzees of Africa – swim even less well than other primates. None of the great apes likes to swim. Chimpanzees and gorillas will wade in shallow water, but they don't like to cross deep water. And yet, chimpanzees sometimes voluntarily cross wide rivers, moving the same way monkeys do, with their heads up and their hands and feet paddling. To sum up, most reptiles and amphibians are excellent swimmers, while most mammals swim less well. Primates are poor swimmers even among mammals, and the great apes have still more trouble swimming, and less enthusiasm for the sport.

Humans learn to swim

Humans are even worse at swimming than chimpanzees and gorillas. Like the other great apes, early humans evolved in the dry centre of a continent, in the forests and grasslands of the centre of Africa. But unlike the other great apes, early humans stood upright on two feet and walked. We do not know whether these early walkers could swim. Some researchers have suggested that early humans may have become fully aquatic, like dolphins, otters and seals (the 'Aquatic Ape hypothesis'), but this is very unlikely. First, no credible fossilized bones of aquatic early humans have been found, whereas a whole sequence showing the evolution of cetaceans has been documented. Second, humans are not comfortable enough in the water to have descended from an aquatic ape ancestor. A better suggestion has early humans standing upright not only to run after antelope in the grasslands, but to wade in rivers and lakes. Along the shores of lakes and on the banks of rivers, the first people could easily have collected mussels, freshwater shrimp, white lotus and other good food.[3]

If early humans spent a lot of time wading, they would have become used to the water at the same time that their increasingly upright posture made it harder for them to swim. Most animals, and to some extent even the great apes, can swim naturally because the natural movement of their legs for running will also keep them afloat in the water. But because humans run with their bodies upright, the natural motion of all four limbs will not keep them afloat. Many humans learn to crawl naturally, without ever having seen anybody crawl, and humans learn to walk even if they have never seen anybody walk. But if you toss a human child into deep water, even one who is already good at walking and running, even one who has seen people swimming, the child will drown.[4] Even adult humans who fall into deep water will drown if they have never learned to swim. (This is a major cause of drowning today: young men, especially if they have been drinking, wrongly think they will figure it out once they hit the water.) Once humans had evolved to stand upright and walk, they could only swim by learning and practising a different set of motions. This is the process we mean when we say that people can swim; a swimmer can manage well for extended periods in water where it is too deep to stand up, without boats or flotation devices.

So these early humans, wading in streams and lakes, collecting shell-fish and water plants to eat: did they learn to swim? Nobody knows. Early humans spent a lot of time in and around water. We would like to think that means they could swim, but many people still centre their lives on lakes and rivers and cannot swim a stroke. It's perfectly possible to live on the coast, paddle boats and catch fish without knowing how to swim. Our knowledge of the earliest fishing people, from South Africa, leaves that question open.

This is what we know: sometime around 165,000 years ago, a group of humans reached the southern tip of Africa and saw the ocean there. They lived right on the beach, at Blombos Cave near the southernmost point of South Africa. These people's Middle Stone Age descendants ate a lot of seafood. Inside their cave they left heaps of clamshells and fish bones dated to about 140,000 years ago, and traces of what may have been fishhooks carved from bone.[5] The ocean provided tasty, nutritious and above all reliable food: fish, crabs, squid, octopus, clams, mussels, algae and seaweed. These early Africans would certainly have known that other animals could swim, because they would have seen animals in the water all around them. Not just fish and otters but elephants, gazelles and hyenas would have been swimming near Blombos Cave. Did the people of Blombos Cave swim out to the fish, or did they bundle together reeds for boats? Or did they just stand in the surf and fish from there?

Recent evidence from Italy suggests that they swam. Neanderthals living in Italy about 100,000 years ago were diving 3–4 metres (10–13 ft) down to the bottom of the Mediterranean bay on which they lived. They dived to retrieve clamshells that, like the Blombos Cave residents, they shaped into tools. Their ear bones suggest that some of these Neanderthals swam enough to get 'swimmer's ear', an infection caused by getting water in their ears.[6] As we await similar reanalysis of clamshells and ear bones from other early archaeological sites, we are now justified in thinking that most early people – both modern *Homo sapiens* and Neanderthals – knew how to swim. In this chapter we will survey early swimmers across Africa, Asia and the Americas, before we turn to the non-swimmers in the next chapter.

Swimming in Africa

It is much later, after the last Neanderthals had died, and after the end of the last Ice Age, that we get the first pictures of swimming. Rock paintings depicting swimmers appear about 9000 BCE on cliff walls at Tassili n' Ajjer, in southern Algeria, far out in the Sahara Desert.[7] The Sahara might seem like a funny place to be splashing in the water, but when these pictures were painted it was not as dry as it is now. The world was still emerging from the last Ice Age. A wetter Sahara held meadows and forests, with creeks and ponds running through it. This was the kind of place early humans liked best. Painted images on the rock walls at Tassili n' Ajjer show people hunting, sitting and dancing. A few figures are painted parallel to the ground, with their arms outstretched. These painted figures may be swimming.

About a thousand years after that, and a little further east, somebody painted more such figures on another wall, in the Cave of the Swimmers at Wadi Sura in western Egypt (illus. 1). By 8000 BCE the people living near this cave were settling down in villages. They farmed wheat and barley, or herded cattle and sheep.[8] In their paintings, little red figures float more or less horizontally on the creamy background of the rock, holding out their arms in front of them. It seems pretty clear that the figures are doing the breaststroke, or a dog-paddle. Their legs are folded as if they are doing a frog kick, and they raise their heads to keep them out of the water. Although it is possible that these figures represent spirits floating in the air, or people sleeping on the ground, swimming is the most plausible explanation.

Swimming in ancient Egypt

African people were better swimmers 5,000 years later, at the time when Egyptians invented hieroglyphic writing and were able to leave us clearer information. An Early Dynastic seal from about 2900 BCE shows

2 Early Egyptian hieroglyph of a swimmer, *c.* 2900 BCE.

a person swimming (illus. 2). Early Egyptians used seals the way we use signatures today. An artist carved your name, or your official title, into a small stone cylinder, and you rolled that cylinder over a lump of soft clay to leave a mark that served as your signature. Although this particular seal shows a swimmer, the inscription is not about swimming. The swimmer is a hieroglyph, a way of writing a syllable in the owner's title that sounds like 'neb', the Egyptian word for swimming.[9] Now there is no question: this person is not floating, or sleeping, they are definitely swimming. The hieroglyph shows that by this time (and maybe earlier) Egyptian swimmers were alternating their arms and using a flutter kick with straight legs in something like a front crawl stroke.

From this point on there is plenty of evidence of swimming from ancient Egypt. The Egyptian nomarch Kheti, the powerful governor of a *nome* (province), thought it worth carving on the walls of his tomb that, when he was a child, he had swimming lessons with the king's children.[10] There must have been considerable prestige in having the right kind of swimming lessons. But poor people also swam in Old Kingdom Egypt, both for fun and for their work. On a tomb painting from Thebes, two fishers strain to hold a large fishing net full of fish. A third fisher dives down to the bottom to disentangle the net, braving the dangerous crocodiles that lurk in the water (illus. 3).[11] The idea of diving for work recurs in a Middle Kingdom father's letter urging his son to study hard, to 'plunge into the study of Egyptian learning, as you would plunge into the river.' The anxious father warns that without an education, work can be hard: 'the catcher of water-fowl, even though he dive in the Nile, may catch nothing.'[12] That is a recurring theme: people may swim for fun, but swimming can also be exploitative work.

By the New Kingdom, five hundred years later, with more literature, we can see a wider variety of uses for water skills. Diving contests can decide arguments. In one story, the Egyptian gods Seth and Horus change themselves into hippopotamuses and compete to see who can stay under-water longer.[13] Swimming proves your courage, as a young man swims across a crocodile-infested river in flood to reach his girlfriend ('sister' is a euphemism in this poem):

> My sister's love is on the far side.
> The river is between our bodies;
> The waters are mighty at flood-time,
> A crocodile waits in the shallows.
> I enter the water and brave the waves,
> My heart is strong on the deep;
> The crocodile seems like a mouse to me,
> The flood as land to my feet.[14]

It is a common story all over the world, as we will see: the young lovers separated by water who must swim across to be together. In this Egyptian poem the swimmer is confident that he will reach his lover safely. His love will sustain him through the dangers to the other side. That is how people tell this story in places, like ancient Egypt, where many are good swimmers. Where people are less sure of themselves in the water, the stories they tell have sadder endings.

3 Fisher diving for the net on a wall painting in the
11th Dynasty Tomb of Djar, Thebes, Egypt, *c.* 2000 BCE.

More than a thousand years after this poem was written, a joke involving swimming shows that Egyptians had not forgotten how to swim. As the Greek biographer Plutarch tells it, the pharaoh Cleopatra's partner, Mark Antony,

> was fishing with Cleopatra alongside him, and had no luck. So he ordered the seamen to dive down and secretly fasten to his fishhooks some fish that had been caught earlier, and he pulled up two or three of them. But the Egyptian [Cleopatra] wasn't fooled. Pretending to be impressed, she told her friends about it, and invited them to come see themselves the next day. Many of them came along on the fishing boats. When Antony let down his line, she ordered one of her own people, hurrying and swimming over, to stick a salted fish from the Black Sea on his hook. So Antony was convinced, and pulled it up, and everyone laughed at him.[15]

We don't know whether Cleopatra herself could swim, but some Egyptian women did. Artists tended to eroticize women's water activities, so that in one New Kingdom poem, a woman swims through a sexual fantasy:

> It is pleasant to go to the pond to bathe myself with you there, so I can let you see my beauty in my tunic of finest royal linen, when it is wet ... I go down into the water, and come up again to you with a red fish, which lies beautiful on my fingers.[16]

An Egyptian ostrakon dating to about the same time might illustrate the poem: painted on the limestone, a woman swims in the water, surrounded by plants, reaching for an egret with outstretched hands (illus. 4).[17] This connection between swimming and sex, the common nakedness of swimmers and lovers, was already a cliché in ancient Egypt. Sex runs all through the history of swimming.

Real women's swimming, however, was not so sexualized. Girls swam just for fun, like the enslaved twelve-year-old who went for a swim in the Nile with her friends in Roman Egypt in the third century CE. Sadly, we know about this child from a doctor's certificate confirming that she drowned after she was caught in a sluice gate. Aurelius Philantin, the

4 Egyptian woman swims to catch an egret, ostrakon from
Deir el-Medina, Egypt, *c.* 1300–1000 BCE.

doctor, apparently overcome by the tragedy, describes her 'twisted and lifeless body'.[18] But despite the sad circumstances, the Egyptian doctor's certificate shows that people were swimming in Egypt from the beginning of the Bronze Age right through to the later Roman Empire.

Swimming in North Africa

Outside of Egypt, other Africans were also swimming. Swimming was apparently common throughout North Africa and down the coast of East Africa. The Roman encyclopaedist Pliny the Elder – the same man who misinformed us about whether elephants could swim – tells several African swimming stories. In one story Pliny reports that boys used to swim in the bay of Hippo, in North Africa. (Hippo would later gain fame as the home of Augustine; today it is in Algeria.) As Pliny's nephew retells the story, these boys competed to see who could swim furthest out from the shore, meaning that they were good swimmers – they were not just playing in the surf, but swimming out well beyond their depth. One day a dolphin approached the swimming boys, one of whom then started swimming with it regularly. When word of the boy's dolphin friend got around, crowds of dignitaries started to come by to see it, and, in an unmistakably Roman approach, the city council ordered the dolphin killed in order to disperse the crowds.[19]

Floor mosaics found in Roman villas in North Africa also show people swimming. On a fourth-century mosaic from the villa of Pompianus in Cirta (also in Algeria), two men swim towards each other, with a border of waves around them (illus. 5). Like the Egyptian swimmer from Old Kingdom hieroglyphs, these men swim with one arm ahead and the other behind them in a front crawl stroke. How literally should we understand this image? Does it depict reality, or imagination? At a minimum, whoever drew the original sketch from which this mosaicist worked had seen swimmers. We usually see these black images as silhouettes, but we should resist the temptation to read White skin onto ancient artistic depictions.[20] Instead, we can recognize these swimmers as Black Africans.

An earlier Roman floor mosaic, this one from the House of Menander at Pompeii in southern Italy, also seems to show a Black man swimming (illus. 6). Other mosaics from the same building, which housed a large staff of enslaved people, also depict enslaved Africans.[21] But this particular man seems more explicitly African than the others, with short curly hair. His large nose, and his large erection, indicate that caricature is intended. Swimming may have been a skill that Romans explicitly associated with other stereotypes about Africans. Roman depictions of Black Africans, though not centred on skin colour, often featured ridicule, especially sexual ridicule.[22] Again, we cannot know what the artist intended, but this

5 Two swimmers on the mosaic floor of a bath from the
Roman villa of Pompianus in Cirta, Algeria, c. 4th century CE.

6 An African man, represented as a caricature, swims on the mosaic floor of a
Roman bath, from the House of Menander, Pompeii, Italy, before 79 CE.

Pompeii mosaic may be an early example of Europeans associating
African swimming with other demeaning traits.

Swimming in East Africa

Pliny also has stories to tell us about swimming in East Africa, outside the
borders of the Roman Empire. The further away from home they are set,
the more Pliny's stories grow into tall tales: if you believed that story about
the dolphin, he has some real whoppers for you. He tells us that in Sudan,
people swim in the Nile to hunt crocodiles, ride the crocodiles like horses
and when the crocodiles 'turn their heads up, with their mouths wide open
to bite, the riders shove a stick in crossways. Holding the ends with their
right and left hands, they use the stick as a bridle to bring their captives
to land.' A very similar scene is illustrated in a wall painting from Pompeii;
this painting, and others like it, also include hippopotamus hunts.[23] In
another of Pliny's fish stories, East African people catch huge tortoises
and use their shells for boats; hunters swim out and sneak up on these
tortoises when they're sleeping. Quickly the hunters flip the turtles over
so they are helpless, before killing them for their shells.[24] Apparently Pliny
and his Roman readers regarded East Africans as strong swimmers. In the

third century CE Roman writers were still discussing East Africans and their swimming, their crocodiles and their hippopotamuses, and Roman paintings were still showing them.[25]

An earlier hint that East Africans were swimmers comes from Egypt, where an ointment spoon dating to the New Kingdom, around 1400 BCE, takes the form of a swimming Black woman.[26] Traditional East African stories agree that East Africans were strong swimmers. In the Ethiopian story of 'Two Jealous Wives', for example, a jealous wife throws her co-wife's newborn twins into the river. Before they can drown, swimmers happen by and rescue the babies. In another story, a would-be husband has to show his courage by swimming out to a nearby island, spending the night alone there and swimming back. As in the earlier Egyptian poem from a little further north, the man swims successfully and wins the right to marry his lover.[27] These stories belong to a long oral tradition agreeing that swimming was common in ancient East Africa.

Swimming in West Africa

Traditional stories also show that West Africans were excellent, skilled, enthusiastic swimmers. In some versions of Mali's medieval *Epic of Sunjata* the hero's enemy Jolofin Mansa plunges into the Senegal River and swims into a cave, where he transforms himself into a crocodile, and a commander dives in after him and successfully brings Jolofin up.[28] Other West African folk tales also assume that most people are skilled swimmers and invoke the river gods for help. In these stories, people swim in the sea for fun. Girls foolishly swim with their mother's necklace on and lose it in the river. Women have babies that are really fish babies and lovers who are really snakes. Hunters assume that they can swim across rivers. Stingy women casually jump into the river and swim after a bean that got away. Distressed characters frequently appeal to rivers for justice, and often receive it.[29] Swimming must have been common in the Niger River, among the African fishing people who lived around Lake Chad and further south.

Medieval Africans swam mainly for fun, not because they lacked any other way to cross rivers. West African stories expect ferries and bridges in populated areas. A woman reserves her crossing in advance, paying in gold and silver.[30] And the traveller Ibn Battuta, visiting Mali

7 Person swimming with dolphins on a carved pebble from
the mouth of the Klasies River, South Africa, *c.* 400–300 BCE.

in the fourteenth century, uses a regular ferry service to cross even fairly
minor West African rivers without difficulty.[31] Swimming is generally
a pastime and a pleasure more than a practical skill.

Swimming in South Africa

A single early image shows that people were also swimming in South Africa.
This is a small carved pebble apparently depicting a person swimming with
four dolphins (illus. 7). The pebble, from the mouth of the Klasies River,
can be securely dated thanks to the piles of seashells that surrounded it
when it was found: it was carved circa 400–300 BCE.[32] The South African
swimmer uses an overhand stroke almost identical to the strokes depicted
in later North African mosaics. There is also a striking parallel to Pliny's
story of boys swimming with dolphins from the opposite end of the continent. Whether or not people actually swam with dolphins, stories about
the activity seem to have been widespread in ancient Africa.

FROM AS FAR back as we can look until the arrival of European slave traders in the 1400s, most people in Africa, rich and poor, men and women, knew how to swim. There are still big gaps in our knowledge. We have no information from before the last Ice Age. We know nothing about early swimming in West Africa or the Congo River basin, and from South Africa we have only a single carved pebble. Still, all the available evidence points in the same direction. Whether it was early Africans telling their own stories, or the Romans telling stories about Africans, Africans swam as a matter of course. Three different African stories about swimming expect the protagonist to succeed in proving his strength and courage. Africans swim not only in emergencies, but as part of their normal lives: to meet an approaching ship, while hunting, as a normal part of their employment or for a fun afternoon with friends.

2

~

LEAVING AFRICA

W
hat about the rest of the world? Could people swim on other continents? Yes, they could. Early people loved to swim, all across the southern part of Asia, in Australia and New Zealand and the nearby islands, and throughout North and South America. These swimmers were at least partly descended from people who left Africa around 100,000 BCE. Slowly moving along the coastlines, a little further each year, the migrants soon reached the Arabian Peninsula. Walking and paddling rafts or canoes woven from reeds, they eventually reached India, then Southeast Asia, then Australia. Some of them moved north along the Pacific coast of Asia to China, Korea and Japan. Eventually, maybe about 24,000 BCE, a few travellers crossed over to Alaska. Their descendants canoed along major river networks all across North America and south along the Pacific Coast to California, and then to Mexico, Peru and Argentina. By about 12,000 BCE their descendants reached Brazil and the Caribbean. In all of these places, archaeological remains, poetry, paintings and traditional stories show that people swam frequently and enthusiastically.

Pearl diving in the Arabian Peninsula

These travellers' first stop was the Persian Gulf, which became an early centre of swimming. As early as 5000 BCE Bahrain's principal industry was pearl diving. Skilled pearl divers were bringing up heaps of pearl oysters at Abu Khamis, as we can tell from the mounds of shells the shuckers left behind. Pearl oysters are not good to eat. They are only desirable for their pearls. A major local manufacturing industry produced pearl necklaces and earrings, and extracted mother-of-pearl from the shells, to sell to overseas traders as far off as Babylon and Ur in Mesopotamia.[1] These pearl divers may not have been very good swimmers. To dive for pearls, you tie a rope around you, grab a rock and a basket, and jump off a boat so that the weight of the rock pulls you to the sea floor. When your basket is full of pearl oysters, you drop the rock, tug on the rope and your partners pull you back up to the ship's deck. Still, you have to know something about swimming to manage in the water. You cannot be afraid of jumping into the ocean.

Persian Gulf divers (mostly men) were still bringing up pearl oysters 5,000 years later, when our friend the Roman encyclopaedist Pliny mentions Bahrain as being 'famous for having a lot of pearls'. Athenaeus of Naucratis, writing about a hundred years after Pliny, adds details: 'there are reed rafts surrounding this island, from which they dive into the sea to a depth of twenty fathoms [about 40 metres], bringing up double-shelled [oysters].'[2] The twelfth-century geographer al-Idrisi also gives a detailed description of the skilled pearl divers of Bahrain, who work in August and September and are rented by boat-owners.[3] Most pearl divers were employees of or enslaved by the powerful families that controlled the pearl beds. Like the Old Kingdom fishers pulling up their nets, these swimmers were exploited and poor. They continued to be so into the time of the Islamic Empire, when these same pearl beds were still in use.

Swimming in India

People were also swimming in places further east, in India. Probably people had been swimming in India since the Stone Age, but in the early years we know too little to be sure. Our ignorance may be due to changing sea levels in the Indian Ocean, so that some early coastal sites are now deep underwater, while others are far inland.[4] The only hint of swimming from India's Bronze Age is a public bath building from the Harappan town of Mohenjo Daro, along the banks of the Indus River in what is now Pakistan. This building was built in about 1500 BCE. It included a pool known as the Great Bath, built of mud brick and sealed with tar, with a drain at the bottom. Convenient stairs led down into the water, so people could get in and out easily. The Great Bath is about a quarter the size of a typical city pool today (12 × 7 metres or 39 × 23 feet) and about 2.5 metres (8 ft) deep. If it were filled with water, it would be too deep and wide to get across without lifting your feet off the bottom of the pool and swimming. But the dimensions are all we know, and, without any other information, we cannot be sure whether people were swimming in Bronze Age India. By the Iron Age, however, written texts assure us that Indian people were swimming.

Around 500 BCE the religious faith of Jainism took off in eastern India, and Jain priests collected their instructions for living, proverbs and rules into a manual known as the Jain Sutras. These Sutras assume that most of their readers know how to swim. What should you do, the Sutras ask, if you are on a boat, and you happen to hear the boatman ordering another crew member to throw you overboard? You should strip off your clothes and get ready to swim:

> If, on board, the boatman should say to another of the crew, 'O long-lived one! this Sramana is only a heavy load for the boat, take hold of him with your arms and throw him into the water!' hearing and perceiving such talk, he should, if he wears clothes, quickly take them off or fasten them or put them in a bundle on his head. Now he may think: These ruffians, accustomed to violent acts, might take hold of me and throw me from the boat into the water.

The same Jain Sutra goes on, sensibly enough, to warn Jain adherents not to use the water as a cover for sexual assault, and to practice water safety:

> A monk or a nun, swimming in the water, should not touch anyone else's hand, foot, or body with their own, but without touching anyone they should mindfully swim in the water.
> A monk or a nun, swimming in the water, should not dive up or down, in case water gets into their ears, eyes, nose, or mouth; but they should swim mindfully in the water.
> If a monk or a nun, swimming in the water, should be overcome by weakness, they should throw off their clothes and things, either all or a part of them, and not be attached to them.[5]

These people are clearly swimming, not wading or bathing, or their clothes would not endanger them. (The injunction against getting water in your nose is related to Jain ideas about not taking life: there could be living creatures in the water, and inhaling them might kill them.) The same Jain Sutra sternly warns monks and nuns against swimming for fun: 'A monk or a nun, wading through shallow water in a straight line, should not plunge in deeper water for the sake of pleasure or the heat; but they should mindfully wade through the shallow water in a straight line.' Another Indian religious code, the *Laws of Manu*, dates probably to the second century CE, not long after Pliny's time. This code, too, assumes that people in India know how to swim, and again forbids religious ascetics to swim for fun.[6]

In early medieval love poetry, on the other hand, Indian people do swim for fun. They enjoy going down the stone steps of the bathing ghat to the river and splashing around in the water with their friends. Third-century CE Tamil love poems from South India again associate swimming with seduction:

> Look at me, and live long!
> I will say to you, Lord,
> That I will bathe with you in the chilly freshets,
> Churning up the water's ripples
> Until gossip rises in the big town.
> Come along with us, why go home?

This poem makes the same association between water and sex, adding images of swelling and flowers into the bargain:

> That soft beauty with eyes like blue lilies
> Became my boon companion
> As we played in the freshets
> As the swelling flood came,
> Its waters crammed with flowers.[7]

Tamil hymns to the Hindu god Shiva also refer to swimming and diving. In one such hymn, 'women eager for water-play/ swim and dive, and splash about,/ and wash their hair'.[8] It is hard to tell whether these third-century lovers are swimming or only bathing, but the African traveller Ibn Battuta confirms that at least some medieval South Indian women were good swimmers. In the 1300s CE Ibn Battuta was sailing in the Indian Ocean with two enslaved Indian women. Suddenly their ship ran aground and foundered. Ibn Battuta could not swim, and neither could one of the Indian women, so, he tells us, 'the sailors made a wooden raft.' The raft could not hold everyone, but 'the other girl said, "I am a good swimmer and I shall hold on to one of the raft ropes and swim with them." So . . . [their possessions and] the one girl went on the raft, the other girl swimming.'[9] The next morning a boat picked up Ibn Battuta from his sinking ship, and all three made it safely to shore.

Pearl diving in Sri Lanka

People also dived for pearls around the island of Sri Lanka, off the tip of southeastern India. Again the divers were mostly men. In the Iron Age, in the 500s BCE, the *Mahavamsa* describes Sri Lanka's kings controlling great piles of valuable pearls.[10] Foreign visitors agreed that Sri Lankans dived for pearls. Megasthenes, the Greek traveller who served as Seleucus I's ambassador to the Indian emperor Chandragupta Maurya in about 300 BCE, reports that Sri Lankans 'leave the flesh [of the oysters] they catch to rot, but they consider the pits to be jewellery.'[11] Indeed, pearl oysters are not good to eat. Pliny, around 50 CE, also knew Sri Lanka as a source of 'pearls of great size'.[12] Seven centuries after the *Mahavamsa*, Sri Lankans were still diving for pearls: the *Rajavali* laments the '400 villages inhabited by pearl-fishers' that were destroyed by a tsunami in the 200s CE.[13] Muhammed al-Idrisi also reports that near Sri Lanka there are swimmers who 'can catch ships by swimming, even when the ships have a good tail-wind'; they sell pearls to the passengers.[14] As in Bahrain, despite the danger and discomfort of their work, Sri Lankan pearl divers did not share in the wealth they brought up from the depths.

Southeast Asian swimming

Southeast Asian legal texts also assume that most people know how to swim, at least by the Middle Ages. In Thailand, the king might make both the plaintiff and the defendant in a court case swim across a river, with the fastest swimmer winning. (Could disabled parties choose champions to swim for them?) Or both parties might dive underwater, and the one who stayed underwater longest won.[15] Muen Wai's (semi-fictional) trial by water in the 1300s CE, from Thailand's seventeenth-century epic poem *Khun Chang Khun Paen*, is an example of the second method:

> On the day of the ordeal, the two litigants are taken to the river. Khun Chang ought to have been put upstream, as he was the plaintiff, but the judge decided that since [the defendant] Muen Wai was a noble, Khun Chang should be put in downstream from him. Their heads are pushed down, but Khun Chang shoots right back up, claiming, 'This fellow Phra Wai has knowledge. He blew something onto me. The power of the mantra gripped my heart unbearably, and my hair stood on end. Giving the defendant the upstream side allowed him to blow a mantra down to affect me.'

After cursing Khun Chang as a loudmouth, the king redoes the trial, this time with Muen Wai downstream where he belongs. But the change does not help Khun Chang. Because Khun Chang is in the wrong, he feels imaginary snakes encircling him, and so he shoots back up to the surface,

8 Invading soldiers falling out of boats and drowning. Stone bas-relief from the south outer gallery, east wing of Bayon Temple, Angkor Thom, Cambodia, *c.* 1200 CE.

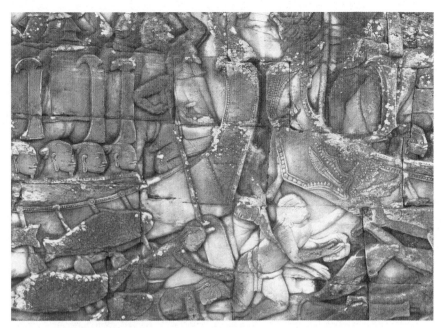

9 Cambodian men try to stave in the invaders' ships. Stone bas-relief from
the south wall of Bayon Temple, Angkor Thom, Cambodia, *c.* 1200 CE.

shaking with fear. The truth comes out, and Khun Chang loses his case.[16]
Thai water trials, or at least their representation in legal texts and epic
poetry, assumed that both plaintiff and defendant were good swimmers.

Chinese visitors to Cambodia saw medieval Cambodians as enthusiastic about getting in the water. Zhou Daguan, a Chinese official who
visited Cambodia in 1296 CE, marvelled that 'they are accustomed to bathe
many times each day and night: a family or several families jointly share
a pool, which they all visit together. Moreover the women there are fond
of bathing shamelessly in a river outside of town.' Chinese merchants
found this so striking that they would 'form parties to go and watch' the
women bathe.[17]

Now, bathing is not swimming. We do not know how deep the water
was in these pools or rivers, so the women and families may only have
been wading. And Zhou Daguan, writing a travelogue, may be intentionally exaggerating the differences between the Cambodians and the Chinese.
But medieval Cambodian images seem to confirm that Cambodians could
swim. The famous temple of Angkor Thom was built around 1200 CE. Its
carved stone walls display an image of a naval battle. Soldiers in armour,
possibly Chinese invaders, sit in small boats. Some of the invaders have

been shot with arrows, and are falling out of the boats and drowning (illus. 8). As we will see, it is no coincidence that in both of the examples here the Chinese are less enthusiastic about the water.

Meanwhile, the Cambodian defenders are swimming. Men stripped down to their loincloths swim underneath the invaders' boats, with big fish swimming around them (illus. 9). Probably the Cambodians are military sappers: soldiers sent to swim underneath the enemy's boats, bash in the bottoms and sink them. Similarly, a Vietnamese oral tradition set in the 1200s has the young peasant hero Yết Kiêu dive into the river and stay under long enough to drill holes in the hulls of the enemy's warships. Yết Kiêu is 'a faster swimmer, swift as an otter'. Many other traditional Vietnamese stories also involve swimming, from the fairies who take off their wings to enjoy a swim to the man who dives into the river to rescue his beloved, and swims back to the bank with her in his arms.[18]

For poor working people in East Timor, swimming was still more important, both as a living and as a lifestyle. Indonesian people were swimming at least by the first century CE, when the Indonesian seafaring nomads known as the Orang Laut became famous as great swimmers and divers. The Orang Laut, or 'sea peoples', dived mainly not for pearls but for shells, coral and edible sea slugs. In the Middle Ages, as both Chinese and Arab sources inform us, Orang Laut naval skills were crucial to the success of the Srivijayan Empire. Early European observers claimed that the Orang Laut 'leapt into the sea and swam underwater like fish, disappearing from view for about half an hour before coming to the surface as much as a thousand yards away from the place where they entered the water'.[19] Though each of these examples is slight in itself, and the reliability of each source dubious, taken as a whole they suggest that the early inhabitants of Southeast Asia knew how to swim.

Australia, New Zealand and Hawaii

Early Aboriginal Australians, Maori and Hawaiians were probably also swimmers. We know that the first people in Australia lived near the water, because they ate a lot of fish. On the shores of Lake Mungo, in central Australia, early humans discarded both fish bones and fishhooks. (In 40,000 BCE this was a much wetter and more nourishing environment than it is today; the lake is dry now.) Fishing does not necessarily imply swimming, but Aboriginal Australians' traditional stories assume that most people can swim. Bulpallungga's story, for example, recounts how 'Many and many a time he would go and swim in the pool where his mother had seen the vision.'[20]

Maori and Hawaiian oral traditions also celebrate swimming. In one popular Maori story, Tutanekai and Hinemoa fall in love at a party, but they cannot speak to each other because Hinemoa's father watches her and will not let her go, or let Tutanekai come to her. Every night Tutanekai plays his flute sadly from his island in Lake Rotorua, and every night Hinemoa hears it. She determines to paddle a canoe across the lake to him, but cannot find a canoe to take. So she uses gourd floats connected by netting to support her on a long-distance swim to Mokoia Island (about 1.5 kilometres away) to reach her lover. After Hinemoa finds Tutanekai, their parents relent, and the two lovers live together happily ever after.[21]

Much further east, in Hawaii, many traditional stories involve swimming. In one of these, the king of sharks sees a stunning woman swimming near the shore. He turns himself into a man with a beautiful feather cape and marries her. Eventually, though, he returns to the sea, and, later on, so does their son.[22] While these stories were recorded relatively recently, and were composed for very different purposes, all of them consider swimming to be an ordinary pastime, neither exceptional nor dangerous.

South China

Swimming was popular and widespread in South China by the Bronze Age, and probably earlier; we know this because writing also arrived in China during this period. Around 1200 BCE somebody scratched the first evidence of swimming in China into an animal bone shoulder blade. The shoulder blade is an oracle bone, one of the very earliest written records from China. Soothsayers used these oracle bones like Tarot cards to predict the future. But the prophecy does not concern us. We are interested in just one of the written characters: the one that means 'swim'. The character 泅 probably represents a person swimming, surrounded by water.[23] The long central stroke is the person, who has their legs together, perhaps with the knees slightly bent and their arms extended in front of them. The short strokes surrounding this swimmer represent the water.

Like the early Egyptian hieroglyph on the seal, this Chinese character was probably used here to represent the sound of the word rather than the concept of swimming, but it shows us that people in South China knew how to swim.

South Chinese people were surely still swimming in the Iron Age. Like their southern neighbours in Vietnam and Cambodia, South Chinese soldiers swam underwater to sink enemy ships. On an Iron Age bronze vase from near Chengdu, sappers swim beneath the ships to stave them in (illus. 10). In the centre, one soldier pulls his enemy's hair. The swimmers' arms show that they are using the front crawl stroke. A number of Sichuan bronze vases carry virtually identical versions of this naval scene. It was probably a common theme not just on bronze vases but in paintings and wall hangings during the Zhou Dynasty.[24] The similarities between these naval battles and those depicted on the much later temple at Angkor Thom suggest that the naval battle with underwater swimmers was a widespread and long-lived artistic theme throughout Southeast Asia. While we cannot know the intentions of the artists who depicted these battles, it is probable that Iron Age naval battles really did involve underwater sappers.

People in South China continued to swim throughout antiquity and the medieval period. At this point written accounts supplement the earlier images, and we can see people swimming as a way of making a living. In 139 BCE the scholar Liu An tells us that, 'To the south of the

10 South Chinese swimmers try to stave in the ships in a naval battle etched onto a Sichuan bronze vessel, 6th century BCE.

Nine Passes, tasks on dry land are few, while tasks on water are many. So the people cut their hair and tattoo their bodies in order to resemble scaly creatures. They wear short pants, not long trousers, in order to make swimming easier.'[25] The geographer Fan Chengda, writing more than a thousand years later in the 1100s, describes the lives of South Chinese fishing families who lived on their boats:

> When the baby began crawling, the mother would wrap a long rope around the waist and fasten the other end of the rope to a short wooden pole [on the boat]. Whenever the baby fell into the water accidentally, the mother could get him out by pulling the rope. When the baby began tottering, he would walk in the boat on water as easily as on smooth ground, and he learned swimming and walking at the same time.[26]

Though this baby's mother does not swim in Fan Chengda's account, the story of Lin Moniang, set in Fujian Province in the tenth century CE, suggests that she could. In one version of this story, Lin did not learn to swim until she was fifteen years old, but she became an excellent swimmer. When her father was lost at sea, Lin swam far out looking for him, and finally drowned, exhausted from her search. After her death, she became Mazu, the Chinese goddess of the sea and protector of sailors. Chinese women had always enjoyed sports and exercise; early medieval sources show elite Chinese women playing polo, swinging, flying kites, kicking balls, throwing balls and shooting arrows.[27] Apparently at least some South Chinese women enjoyed swimming too.

Early South Chinese swimmers were also diving for pearls. Pearl divers working the pearl oyster beds off Hainan Island and Hong Kong fell under the control of Han Dynasty speculators in the first century BCE, resulting in the same exploitation as elsewhere. By 150 CE irresponsible exploitation had exhausted the oyster beds, and the governor, Meng Chang, had to close pearl fishing down for years to rebuild the stock. Pearl diving was still under government control in the third century CE, when our sources claim that 'certain skilful robbers, crouching on the sea bottom, split open the oysters and get fine pearls, whereupon they swallow them and so come forth,' evading government fees and limits. A century later, South Chinese stories described *jiaorén*, mermaids, who wept tears of pearls. By the eleventh century, swimmers in South China told similar stories about the shark people, who 'live at the bottom of the sea, give lodging to pearl divers, and sometimes come ashore to wander about', paying their bills by weeping tears that turn to pearls.[28] (These South Chinese stories of the shark people may be related to similar Hawaiian stories; Polynesians probably left the Marquesa Islands for Hawaii around 400 CE.) Medieval Chinese pearling involved a ring of ten or more boats moored in place, with windlasses to bring the divers up faster. The poet Jia Dao describes the terrible effects this industrialized pearl diving had on the divers, often causing disabilities or ruining their health. He reproves people who buy and wear pearls for ignoring what divers went through to get them.[29]

In light of this exploitation, perhaps we can understand why some South Chinese swimmers turned to piracy and banditry. The medieval Chinese novel *The Water Margin*, set in the Song Dynasty (the 1100s) but first published two centuries later, features the outlaw brothers Zhang Shun and Zhang Heng, whose main identifying characteristic is their skilled swimming. Zhang Heng is 'a big muscular fellow, [who] can swim about fifteen *li* [about 7,500 metres] and can stay in the water for seven days at a time. In the water he swims in a straight line.' He tells this lively story about pretending to be a ferryman:

> I arranged for my brother to pretend to be a traveller, and also to come to our boat with his baggage. When the boat was full I would push off, but would soon drop the anchor, and taking a sword demand the fares. The proper fare was five hundred cash, but I would demand three thousand cash. I would first ask my brother, and when he refused to pay I would take his head in one hand, and the seat of his trousers in the other and throw him overboard. The other passengers would then willingly pay the amount demanded without raising the least objection. I would then row them to a quiet part of the bank, and they would quickly disembark and disappear. My brother would swim underneath the water to the side of the river, and emerge when nobody was about. We would soon meet, and divide the money. We earned a good living by this means for some time.

At least in fiction, South Chinese people feel that being tossed into the water fully dressed, swimming underwater and hiding in the water perhaps for quite some time is not at all problematic.[30] These are fictional heroes, but their skill in swimming seems characteristic of South China.

Surfing in South China

Another form of swimming or water play attested from medieval South China involved a tradition of *nong chao*, 'tide play', which we might call surfing. Around August or September every year, thousands of people left the Song Dynasty capital at Lin'an (modern Hangzhou) and went down to the mouth of the Qiantang River to see the tide play. As the tide comes in and meets the water flowing down the Qiantang River, it forms tidal bores. These are steep waves up to 30 feet high that can travel

11 Spectators watch people surfing the tidal bore at the mouth of the Yangtze River, China, woodblock print from *Amazing Spectacles Within* (*Hainei qiguan*, 1609).

as fast as 25 miles per hour. Professionals body-surfed these dangerous waves, holding up colourful flags (illus. 11). The Song Dynasty official Zhou Mi wrote a description of this surfing performance in about 1250 CE:

> The tidal bore on the Zhe River is one of the great sights of the world ... When it begins to arise far away at Ocean Gate, it appears but a silver thread; but as it gradually approaches, it becomes a wall of jade, a snow-laden ridge, bordering the sky on its way. Its gigantic roar is like thunder as it convulses, shakes, dashes, and shoots forth, swallowing up the sky and inundating the sun, for its force is supremely vigorous. Yang Wanli described this in a poem:
>
>> The ocean surges silver to form a wall;
>> The river spreads jade to gird the waist.
>
> As in every year, the governor of the capital appeared at the Zhe River Pavilion to inspect the navy ... There were several hundred youths of Wu who were expert at swimming. They had loosened their hair and had tattoos on their bodies. In their hands they held colored banners some twenty feet in size and raced against each other with the utmost exertion, swimming against the current, floating and sinking in the leviathan waves a myriad *ren* high. Their leaping bodies executed a hundred different movements without getting the tails of the banners even slightly wet – this was how they showed off their skill. Prominent commoners and high officials competed to bestow silver prizes.
>
> Up and down along the river for more than three miles, pearls, jade, gauze, and silk flooded the eyes; horses and carriages clogged the roads. Every kind of food and drink cost double the normal price, and yet, where viewing tents were rented out, not a bit of ground was left for even a mat.[31]

Song Dynasty sources show South China's people swimming for fun, as soldiers and spies, fishers and pearl divers, surfers, pirates, fraudsters and performers. Swimming was depicted as a normal part of many different ordinary activities. The same was true across the Pacific Ocean from China, in the Americas.

Native American swimming

Native American Indigenous people were probably also good swimmers. One image of swimming survives from pre-Columbian North America, from about 500 CE; it is from a rich family's house in Teotihuacan in southern Mexico. Inside this house a wall painting depicts a river flowing across a mountain. Several people are playing in the water, and one of them is definitely swimming (see illus. 39).[32] His arms are stretched out in front as if he is using a breaststroke, but his legs look more like he is using a flutter kick.

A strong oral tradition suggests that Native Americans were swimming throughout the rest of North America as well. Hundreds of Native American stories, from California to the Caribbean, centre on the water. Most of the time Native people are shown swimming in rivers. Their skill is evident in the custom of swimming competitions and their ability to swim against the current of the stream. In sunny southern California, Miwok people told the story of Tu-Tok-A-Nu'-La, about 'two little boys living in the valley who went down to the river to swim'. In the rainy Pacific Northwest, a Wasco legend about a wedding feast at Multnomah Falls involved swimming races on the river. A Haida story, from western Canada, has Salmon Boy go 'down to the river to swim with the other children'. Nearby Squamish people told a story where 'the chief had directed four of his young people, two boys and two girls, to go into the water and swim up the creek into the salmon trap.'[33]

Even the Inuit of the far north told swimming stories. In one story, Âtârssuaq taught his newborn son to swim.

> [He] came back from his hunting one day, and found that he had a son. Then he took that son of his and bore him down to the water and threw him in. And waited until he began to kick out violently, and then took him up again. And so he did with him every day for long after, while the child was growing. And thus the boy became a very clever swimmer.

Âtârssuaq's enemies killed him, but his son, thanks to his strong underwater swimming, was able to avenge his father, and he defeated the strangers by holding their kayaks underwater until they drowned.[34]

Fewer Native people lived in the Great Plains – cold, dry, lacking fuel and building materials – before they were crowded into them by the arrival of Europeans on both coasts. But along the great rivers of the Plains, the Missouri, the Mississippi and the Arkansas, Native American towns were linked in complex trading networks. People swam in these rivers too. The Blackfoot, for example, in the northern Plains, told the story of the Beaver Medicine, where a man 'ran to the bank, jumped in and dived, and came up in the middle of the river, and started to swim across'.[35]

Along the Atlantic coast of North America, and in the Caribbean islands, Indigenous people were also good swimmers. In Maine, the Passamaquoddy told the story of a young man whose enemies knocked him out of his canoe, reprising a theme we have already seen in the Inuit story above. 'The young man called for help. A Crow came, and said, "Swim or float as long as you can. I will bring you aid." He floated a long time,' and then the rabbit and the fox came to save him. In Virginia, Powhatan children dived for freshwater mussels.[36] Emma Pisatuntema, of the Choctaw people in the Southeast, told a story in 1910 about a plant that 'grew in the place where the Choctaw people went to bathe or swim'. The plant was poisonous, but it liked the Choctaw people and did not want to poison them. It gave away its poison to the rattlesnake and the spider. Then the plant was harmless, and, as the story concludes, the shallow waters of the bayou were safe for the Choctaw to swim in.[37] In the Caribbean islands, conch was an important food. Archaeology and oral history agree that diving for conch was a daily activity.[38] Thus throughout North America, the sources suggest that Indigenous people were good swimmers. Like swimmers in Africa, Asia and Australia, they competed in swimming races. They used swimming both to attack their enemies and to save themselves when attacked. They swam upstream and across rivers. Children swam and dived in groups, without adult supervision. In the North American oral tradition, swimming appears as an everyday, ordinary activity, useful for collecting food and in travelling, but also a normal part of people's exercise and entertainment.

Central and South America

As we wrap up this quick trip around the world, it will come as no surprise that people were also excellent swimmers in tropical Central America and in South America. Here we can combine images, texts and archaeological fieldwork to get a fuller picture. The earliest image of swimming in Central America dates to about 400 BCE–100 BCE, when a Maya stucco relief frieze from Guatemala includes a series of swimming figures around the edges (illus. 12). The frieze decorates a building that served as a Maya water-collection system, and this watery purpose is probably what inspired the designers to carve swimmers as part of the decorative ensemble. The angle of the swimmers' heads relative to their arms and legs suggests that they might be swimming with their heads held up out of the water, but perhaps the figures represent people diving. They probably represent the Hero Twins, Xbalanque and Hunahpu. Before the twins were born, according to Maya mythology, the Lords of the Dead called their father and uncle to the underworld, and there the two older men were defeated and sacrificed. The twins were born predestined to avenge their father and uncle, and the frieze shows them swimming down to the underworld to defeat the Lords of the Dead.[39]

The Hero Twins show up again a few hundred years later on a fairly common type of Maya pottery known as 'Swimmer Bowls' (illus. 13). The paired swimmers on these Maya bowls, one on each side of the bowl, keep their hands stretched out in front of them in a dog-paddle or breaststroke. Like the swimmers on the Maya water-collection building, they keep their heads up, and their knees are bent in what might be a frog kick.

12 A Mayan hero swimming, stucco decoration of a water-collection system at El Mirador, Guatemala, *c.* 400 BCE–100 CE.

But it is not just Maya gods who swim. Piles of abandoned shells from archaeological sites show that the Maya were diving for seafood. Tons of conch shells were found on Maya sites in Belize. The Maya were using conch shells as trumpets in the first century CE, and by the third century CE (if not earlier) they were diving in coral banks for conch.[40]

South of the Maya, swimming also seems to have been a normal activity in Panama. The oral tradition speaks of swimming races. In one Kuna tale, for example, the hero Tad Ibe and his rival the Iguana-Chief 'have a contest to see who could swim farthest underwater. Although Tad Ibe (who swam first) surreptitiously walked a bit farther after his swim so as to increase the distance he apparently had covered underwater, Iguana-Chief swam still farther and easily won.'[41] Swimming and not wading must be intended, or Tad Ibe's walking would not be against the rules.

Still further south, swimming was important early on as a means of collecting food. South American people were probably swimming as early as 6000 BCE, when the people living along the lower Amazon in what is now Brazil lived on the mussels, turtles and fish they caught by diving in the river.[42] Huge piles of seashells suggest that people were also diving for shellfish (probably both for food and for beads) along the Atlantic coast of South America. Archaeologists' analysis of human ear bones dating back to 4500 BCE suggests that early Peruvian men also did a lot of diving for

13 Another image of Hunahpu on a Maya Copador-style bowl,
El Salvador, *c.* 600–900 CE.

14 Swimmers dive from a boat for spondylus shells,
Late Chimu gold earspool, Ecuador, *c.* 1000–1450 CE.

mussels and other seafood – enough to cause bony growths in their ears, and alterations in their thighbones.[43]

Thousands of years later, another image shows people swimming in the Pacific Ocean, off the coast of Peru or Ecuador. An ear ornament hammered from gold, copper and silver was found in the Central Andes mountains, and can be dated to about 1000–1450 CE. In relief on the ornament, a boat with large sails waits on the surface of the Pacific Ocean, while underneath four divers collect spiky spondylus shells (illus. 14). A carved stone relief from a Peruvian palace bears a similar scene.[44] As with Asian pearl divers, this Ecuadorian industry was probably exploitative, often leading to disability or death. Spondylus shells were an important export item for Ecuadorians, who sold them for huge profits along river networks north to the Maya and south as far as Lake Titicaca in Bolivia. We see that people were swimming for shellfish and fish, to retrieve valuable shells and for competition, all over Central and South America.

THIS FULL CIRCLE around the world, from South Africa all the way to Brazil, shows that in our earliest records most of the people of the world, men and women, old and young, rich and poor, Neanderthals and modern humans, could swim. They swam all over Africa and on the Arabian Peninsula; they swam in Southeast Asia, and they swam in the South Pacific. South China and Japan had good swimmers too. Across the Pacific Ocean, the Indigenous people of North and South America were also enthusiastic swimmers, even in cold northern areas and far inland. They swam to retrieve shellfish from the ocean floor, in war or in athletic competitions, under compulsion or just for fun. All over the world people swam, with only one major exception, which we will see in the next chapter.

3

A NORTHERN SWIMMING HOLE

The previous chapter showed that most early people all over the world were strong swimmers. In this chapter we will see an important exception. Across Europe and northern Asia, people did not swim. They did not know how to swim, and they were afraid of the water. These people thought swimming was dangerous. They were so much afraid of drowning that they imagined the water teeming with giant crabs, dragons and sea monsters. They believed that rivers and streams had magical powers to detect wrongdoing, and that it was disrespectful to the gods for people to enter the water. They mocked and caricatured people – foreigners – who did swim. And, for good measure, they thought swimming was immodest, because you took your clothes off to do it.

Why did people in this northern zone not know how to swim? How did they develop their fear of the water? Hadn't their ancestors once been swimmers, like everyone else? It is certainly not a genetic difference. Physically they were completely capable of swimming. The most likely explanation is that northerners forgot how to swim because it was too cold during the last Ice Age. They lost the cultural habit of swimming. After the Ice Age some of these northern non-swimmers moved further south, into the warmer areas of southern Europe and northern India, but they carried their fear of the water with them. We know many of these migrants as the Yamnaya or Indo-Europeans; their descendants include the Greeks and the Romans, Scythians and Iranians. By the end of the Bronze Age, therefore, there were non-swimming cultures even in some places that had been warm during the Ice Age.

Before the Ice Age, people living in northern Eurasia probably knew how to swim. We have seen that Neanderthals were swimming in Italy 100,000 years ago. Most modern humans knew how to swim when they left Africa, and even if these people didn't, they had time to learn how to swim from Neanderthals when they arrived in the north, at least 42,000 years ago.[1] About 33,000 years ago, however, the climate changed. The great ice sheets started to grow again as Earth entered another cold period. To avoid previous Ice Ages, humans had migrated south where it was warmer. But not this time.[2] In the most recent Ice Age, early humans sewed themselves warm leather leggings and fur coats, built houses and fires, and stuck it out in the north.

The last Ice Age

The climate stayed cold for tens of thousands of years, more than long enough for people to forget how to swim. The last Ice Age reached its cold nadir about 23,000 years ago, when glaciers reached as far south as England, northern Germany, Poland and northern Russia. Then the climate slowly got warmer. But even towards the end of the Ice Age, in the height of summer, northern Eurasia probably did not generally get above 15–20 degrees Celsius (60s Fahrenheit).[3] For most of the summer it was too cold for anyone to want to go swimming, and even on the warmest days the water was still too cold. In addition, huge amounts of fresh water were tied up in glaciers. Less water for lakes and rivers meant fewer and smaller swimming holes. Though their bodies were still capable of swimming, people lost the habit. In Africa artists painted swimmers on rock walls, but although there are thousands of gorgeous Ice Age cave paintings from Altamira, Lascaux and many other cave sites across Europe, not one shows people swimming. At Lascaux, for example, there are images of stags swimming in a river from about 17,000 years ago, and there are a few images of people, but none is swimming.[4] By the time the last glacial period ended, in about 9700 BCE (11,700 years ago), the northerners who had lived under these chilly conditions for 20,000 years – six hundred generations – seem to have forgotten how to swim.

Around the end of the last Ice Age, these same northerners may have started to associate their lighter skin with their inability to swim. When modern humans first arrived in northern Eurasia, they had dark skin, like everyone else in the world at that time. But slowly people all across Eurasia developed lighter skin, mainly because they needed to absorb more sunlight. All humans synthesize vitamin D in their skin, using a chemical reaction that involves sunlight. In the north, sunshine hits the earth at a lower angle, so the sunlight had to travel through more of Earth's atmosphere before it reached their skin. The air attenuates the sunlight, making it weaker and less able to kick-start the necessary chemical reaction. Where the sunlight was weaker, people evolved paler skin so that they could make enough vitamin D for good health. Unlike the cultural shift that ended swimming, this shift to paler skin was an evolutionary process.

Genetic evolution of pale skin happened slowly. At first, many north-erners did not need to evolve lighter skin, because they ate a lot of fish and meat. Liver and fish both contain a lot of vitamin D, which is why Inuit people, despite living so far north, have kept their darker skin. They get their vitamin D from eating a lot of fish and liver, and their melanin protects them against sunburn from the glare of sunlight reflecting off the snow. During the Ice Age, when there was snow on the ground for much of the year, most northerners still had dark skin. But when people started farming most of their food, they ate a lot more bread and much less fish. From about 12,000 BCE people were growing wheat in the Zagros Mountains of Southwest Asia (now northern Iran and Iraq). In about 8,000 BCE they were growing millet in northern China. At this point many early farmers evolved to have genetically lighter skin, so they could make their own vitamin D.[5] And as they stopped fishing, the reduced damage to their ear bones from infections shows that they spent even less time in the water.[6]

Around 4000 BCE a large group of early farmers migrated from Southwest Asia into Europe. They brought their light skin to southern Europe. A thousand years later, pale-skinned Yamnaya cattle herders from the Caucasus followed the farmers west to Europe, while a related group of herders migrated east into China. A tipping point towards Whiteness seems to have been reached during the Late Stone Age, when many of those non-swimming northerners developed paler skin. All this is to say that the Late Stone Age may be when the connection between swim-ming and skin colour first began. Although the change in skin colour was genetic and the end of swimming was only a cultural habit, both came from living in northern Eurasia. By the end of the Stone Age most of the White people in the world lived in northern Eurasia, most of the people who lived in northern Eurasia were White and most of these White Eurasians did not know how to swim.

Mesopotamia: Land between the Rivers

At the beginning of the Bronze Age the development of writing and an increase in painted and carved images makes it possible to see that these northerners were not swimming. Our earliest information comes from the Sumerians, who lived in what is now Syria, Iraq and Kuwait. In the Bronze Age it was called Naharaim, the Land between the Rivers, which the Greeks later translated as Mesopotamia. As the name suggests, the Sumerians lived alongside two big rivers, the Tigris and the Euphrates. Sumerians started writing in around 3000 BCE, like the Egyptians, and they wrote a lot about the water. Sumerian poets write about dangerous flooding rivers. They write about barges and boats and rafts on rivers. They write about oxen and donkeys and fish in rivers, and they write about their admiration and respect for the life-giving rivers that irrigated their barley fields, but unlike the Egyptians they never jump in the river themselves. Despite the importance of their rivers, the Sumerians were not enthusiastic about getting wet.

When Sumerian storytellers reach for a water-related metaphor, it involves drowning or gasping for breath rather than swimming. The early Sumerian hero Gilgamesh associates water with death: 'I raised my head on the rampart, I saw a corpse afloat on the water. The mind despairs, the heart is stricken: the end of life being inescapable . . .'. When Gilgamesh takes a bath in the river, he neglects the plant of immortality and loses his chance at eternal life. The same epic tells the earliest version of the horror story we know as Noah's Flood:

> All day long the South Wind blew . . .
> blowing fast, *submerging the* mountain *in water*,
> overwhelming *the people* like an attack.
> No one could see his fellow,
> they could not recognize each other in the torrent.
> The gods were frightened by the Flood . . .

The gods were cowering like dogs, crouching by the outer wall.
Ishtar shrieked like a woman in childbirth . . .
'No sooner have I given birth to my dear people
than they fill the sea like so many fish!' . . .
Six days and seven nights
came the wind and flood, the storm flattening the land.
When the seventh day arrived, the storm was pounding,
the flood was a war – struggling with itself like a woman
writhing (in labour).
The sea calmed, fell still, the whirlwind (and) flood stopped up.
I looked around all day long – quiet had set in
and all the human beings had turned to clay![7]

Although Egyptian officials in Africa carved swimmers on their signatory seals, Mesopotamian people did not. No swimmers appear on any of the hundreds of types of Bronze Age or Iron Age cylinder seals. There are boats and rowers, but no swimmers. In Mesopotamia only ducks and fish swim on the cylinder seals. Dreams and stories repeatedly associate water with blood, vomit, famine and violence. The ocean is 'an obstacle to overcome or an opponent to battle', or the edge of the world. Only gods can cross the ocean, because 'the crossing is perilous, its way full of hazard'. Angry ocean waves tower over you, 'inspiring fearsome terror'. The chief god, Marduk, fights Tiamat, the Ocean.[8] When Sumerians envision more cheerful interactions with the water, they do not involve swimming, nor do they end well. If a poem about the goddess Nanshe envisages her 'laughing in the sea foam/ playing, playing in the waves', it is only against her mother's advice, and results in her being raped by the god Enlil. Again, a Sumerian proverb sees swimming as a waste of time, warning that 'while the donkey was swimming in the river, the dog was busy gathering food.' Despite another proverb suggesting that 'He who tosses his head succeeds in crossing the river,' Sumerians were not big swimmers.[9] (And the proverb suggests that even when Sumerians did swim, they did not put their faces in the water.)

Mesopotamian people saw water as scary and otherworldly, so magical that judges used water to finger witches and sorcerers. Trial by water for witchcraft shows up repeatedly in Mesopotamian legal texts from the Bronze Age.[10] In the most famous of these law codes, the Code of

Hammurabi, written by Akkadian rulers in about 1700 BCE, the second law jumps in:

> If a freeman has charged another freeman with witchcraft and he has not proved his charge, the accused shall throw himself into the river, and if the river overcomes him [and he drowns] then the accuser shall take his land. And if the river shows that freeman to be innocent and he comes out of the river safely, then the accuser shall be put to death, and the one who jumped into the river shall take his accuser's land.

If you are a witch, you will drown; if you do not drown, you are not a witch. Other cases, especially regarding women's misbehaviour, might also be settled with a water ordeal. Your wife moves in with another man while you are out of town? The Code of Hammurabi says to throw her in the river to drown. A Babylonian hymn to the river goddess Nungal tells the same story: the 'river ordeal' will separate the just from the evil-doers. If you are innocent you will be 'reborn' on the other side of the river. If you are guilty, though, Nungal the river will clamp on to you, and you will not escape; you will drown.[11]

This Mesopotamian version of the water ordeal is different from the versions swimming cultures used, in that only the accused person swims. In Thailand, both accuser and accused swam across the river, and the faster swimmer won his case. In Mesopotamia, the question is not who is stronger, but whether the defendant will drown. (None of these systems has much to do with a fair trial, but that's a different question.) This Babylonian version of trial by water took a lasting hold on judges' imaginations, so that Mesopotamian legal texts still recommended trial by water half a millennium later. Charles Horne, writing in 1915, took the popularity of this form of trial by water among the Babylonians and Elamites to mean that 'the art of swimming was unknown' in ancient Mesopotamia, and he was probably right.[12]

The eastern Mediterranean coast

Outside of Mesopotamia, other people living in Southwest Asia were no better at swimming. We can see this in the Jewish Torah, which Christians know as the first five books of the Old Testament. The Torah was probably written during the 600s or 500s BCE. In the aftermath of a failed revolt, many leading Jewish families were forced to move to Babylon, where the Babylonian king could keep an eye on them. Living in the big city, they developed literary ambitions. They combined their own people's oldest stories with the histories in the great Babylonian libraries, and wrote the Torah. Reflecting the concerns of its authors and their sources, the Torah is thoroughly permeated with uneasiness about swimming.

Nobody swims in the Torah. The closest approach to swimming is the prophet Isaiah's metaphor that God 'will spread out His hands in their midst as a swimmer reaches out to swim'. Then the prophet Ezekiel describes 'a river that I could not cross; for the water was too deep, water in which one must swim, a river that could not be crossed'. Why can't Ezekiel cross the river when the water is deep? Because the prophet cannot swim. Ezekiel can cross a river by wading, but if he is out of his depth, he is out of luck. King David voices a similar drowning metaphor in Psalm 69: 'Save me, O God: for the waters have come in even unto my soul. I stick fast in the mire of the deep and there is no sure standing. I have come into the depth of the sea, and a tempest has overwhelmed me.' Where he cannot stand, David cannot swim. Even Pharaoh's Egyptian daughter, as she rescues baby Moses in his basket, is 'washing' (יִרְחַץ) in the Nile, not swimming or bathing.

That is about it for swimming in the Old Testament – that, and the famous episode later in Exodus where God drowns the Egyptian army as they chase the fleeing Hebrews.[13] The Hebrews left Egypt 'with boldness', but when they reach the Red Sea they accuse Moses, 'Have you taken us away to die in the wilderness? Why have you so dealt with us, to bring us up out of Egypt?' Moses (brought up by Egyptians, and perhaps therefore knowing how to swim himself) soothes the Hebrews, and tells them not to be afraid. He stretches out his hand over the sea. God parts the Red Sea for the Hebrews, and then drowns the Egyptians.

> Then Moses stretched out his hand over the sea. The Lord drove the sea back by a strong east wind all night, and turned the sea into dry land; and the waters were divided. The Israelites went into the sea on dry ground, the waters forming a wall for them on their right and on their left. The Egyptians pursued, and

went into the sea after them, all of Pharaoh's horses, chariots, and chariot drivers . . .

Then the Lord said to Moses, 'Stretch out your hand over the sea, so that the water may come back upon the Egyptians, upon their chariots and chariot drivers.' So Moses stretched out his hand over the sea, and at dawn the sea returned to its normal depth. As the Egyptians fled before it, the Lord tossed the Egyptians into the sea. The waters returned and covered the chariots and the chariot drivers, the entire army of Pharaoh that had followed them into the sea; not one of them remained. But the Israelites walked on dry ground through the sea, the waters forming a wall for them on their right and on their left.

Thus the Lord saved Israel that day from the Egyptians; and Israel saw the Egyptians dead on the seashore.

This was the reverse of what readers might have expected, knowing that the Egyptians had always been strong swimmers and the Hebrews had never known how to swim. The parting of the Red Sea takes on new meaning when we realize that the Hebrews are non-swimmers, afraid of the water, being pursued by confident, experienced Egyptian swimmers.

Europe: The Greek islands

By the Late Bronze Age Europeans had probably also forgotten how to swim. Southern Europeans, living along the shores of the Mediterranean, may still have been swimming as late as the Stone Age. Stone Age fishers left their clay fishnet weights for archaeologists to find, and chemical analysis of their bones shows that they ate fish, so they were familiar with the water.[14] The pre-Greek language that people spoke in the Stone Age Aegean included the word κολυμβάω (*kolumbao*), 'to dive', probably because these people were, like the Neanderthals thousands of years earlier, diving for sponges and clams.

But during the Bronze Age non-swimming migrants came to Europe and convinced any remaining swimmers there to get out of the water. When Central Asian Yamnaya people migrated to Europe, starting in about 3000 BCE, at the beginning of the Bronze Age, they brought their pale skin with them. They probably also brought their fear of the water and their inability to swim. A second wave of Yamnaya migration arrived in Europe around 2000 BCE, driven by a terrible regional drought.[15] We call these travellers the Indo-Europeans, because they reached both India and Europe. The Yamnaya's homeland between the Black Sea and the Caspian Sea was known for its salt. They relied on salt to preserve meat, so they took their word for salt, *sal*, with them as they travelled, and they settled near salt mines. In Europe the Yamnaya took over the Hallstatt salt mines in what is now Austria, renowned then and now for salted pork sausage and ham.

Although they spread their word for 'salt' all over Europe, the Yamnaya did not even have a word for 'swim'. Their word *swem* meant something more general like 'move'. Much later on, German speakers gave *swem* the more specific meaning of 'swim', from which we get our English word. The Greek and Latin words for swimming, νάω (*nao*) and *nare*, both derive from a different Yamnaya word, *snā*, meaning 'wash' or 'bathe'. Nor did the Yamnaya have a word for 'ocean'. When the migrants first reached the Mediterranean, they used the locals' words for the sea, θάλασσα (*thalassa*), ὠκεανός (*okeanos*) and *mare*.[16] The Yamnaya took over κολυμβάω, the local word for diving, too. So when the Yamnaya arrived in Greece, it is safe to say they were not swimmers.

Late Bronze Age Greek paintings seem to confirm that the Greeks did not swim. Bronze Age Greeks were enthusiastic sailors whose main

15 Greek defenders drowning during a naval attack on their town, fresco from the West House at Akrotiri, Thera, Greece, *c.* 1650 BCE.

source of wealth was probably sea raiding. Many of them were pirates. Yet when their images show people in the water, they are not swimming; they are drowning. The earliest of these drowning figures appear on a fresco from the city of Akrotiri on the island of Santorini, ancient Thera (illus. 15). Around 1600 BCE a huge volcanic eruption buried the Bronze Age town of Akrotiri, just as the later eruption of Vesuvius buried the Roman town of Pompeii. A wall painting from one of the buried houses shows a sea battle. Since sea battles were a regular feature of life in the Aegean Bronze Age, they were also a favourite theme of Bronze Age Greek art: ships come to shore to attack a peaceful town, and the town's soldiers defend it. The same theme transposed to literature gives us the Trojan War, where the Greek ships attack Troy and the Trojan prince Hector defends it. On the Thera fresco, some of the defending fighters have fallen from their ships and are drowning, naked, in the ocean. Their crested hairstyles identify them as Mycenaeans, descended from the Yamnaya; the broken ship, the confusion of their limbs and their upside-down position makes it impossible to think that these men might save themselves by swimming.[17]

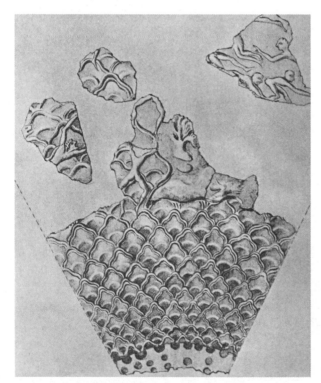

16 More Mycenaeans drowning in a similar attack, from the Siege Rhyton, a fragmentary silver cup found in Shaft Grave IV at Mycenae, Greece, c. 1550 BCE, drawing by Émile Gilliéron.

Drowning people are, it turns out, common in Greek Bronze Age images. Similar defenders drown on the Siege Rhyton, a fragmentary Minoan silver drinking cup from a grave at Mycenae (illus. 16). On this cup, once again soldiers are attacking a town. The bottom of the cup, very badly preserved, depicts people floating in the ocean. They are naked and their legs are bent. One at least is headed down towards the bottom. Probably these people, too, are drowning.[18] We can just catch a glimpse of a third such shipwreck scene on a set of fragmentary ceramic plaques from the Minoan palace of Knossos on Crete. On these ceramic plaques also, the Minoan attackers fall from ships. Their similarity to the Thera figures shows that they are not swimming, but drowning. There is a fourth example: the so-called 'Swimmers' Dagger'. Despite the name that optimistic archaeologists have given it, this, too, probably shows people drowning rather than swimming. A similar scene appears on a different silver rhyton from Mycenae, where shipwrecked sailors struggle to escape a dog-headed sea-monster.[19] All five of these Greek pieces, as well as other, even more fragmentary parallels, show several people drowning and nobody swimming. If we contrast these images with the slightly later Zhou Dynasty images of Chinese naval battles, where soldiers attack enemy boats by swimming underwater, we see what is missing here.

Probably the Minoans, despite living on the island of Crete and being great sailors, did not swim any better than the Mycenaeans. Thousands of representations of Minoan people survive from the buried town of Akrotiri and from the palaces of Minoan Crete. We see Minoan people walking, dancing, offering gifts to the gods, leaping over bulls (apparently as part of a game or competition), rowing boats, carrying fish, strumming lyres, boxing, wrestling and picking flowers. On their brightly coloured fresco paintings, dolphins and fish swim, and on their pottery vases, so do octopuses. But no paintings show Minoan people swimming, and we may conclude that despite living on a warm island ringed by beautiful sandy beaches, they did not do so.

The Sea Peoples

Egyptian artists noticed and emphasized this difference in their own representations of the Greeks. At the very end of the Bronze Age, when the Greeks and other Mediterranean people, collectively known as the

17 Sea People drown as the Egyptians repulse their attack, relief carving
from the wall of Rameses III's temple at Medinet Habu, Egypt, *c.* 1175 BCE.

Sea Peoples, were attacking Egypt, Egyptian artists made it clear that
these invaders could not swim. A large relief in stone, representing an
Egyptian battle with the Sea Peoples in about 1175 BCE, is carved on the
walls of the pharaoh Rameses III's temple at Medinet Habu in southern
Egypt (illus. 17). Here the Sea Peoples are once again drowning. Amid
the confusion of the elaborate Egyptian battle scene, the iconography
is remarkably similar to the Greek representations: people fall out of
their ships headfirst into the water, where they drift helplessly down
to the bottom of the frame. The Egyptians are the ones with pageboy
haircuts in the ships; the Sea People have crested haircuts – exactly as
in the earlier Thera fresco. And, as in the Greek images, the Sea People
are drowning.

The Yamnaya in India and China

Yamnaya migrants – the Indo-Europeans – seem to have brought their
fear of the water to South Asia as well. Drifting slowly south from the
Caucasus, many Yamnaya arrived in what is now Pakistan around 1500
BCE. Again, they may have been seeking salt deposits, because they settled in the Indus valley near a large vein of pink Himalayan salt, still
being mined today. Moreover, the Yamnaya reached India lacking any
word for 'swimming'. Their word *snā* meant 'washing' or 'bathing', and
that shifted to mean 'swimming' in Latin and Greek. But in India and
Iran *snā* kept its original meaning. The word for 'swimming' in modern

Hindi, *tairna*, probably comes from a much older pre-Indo-European word, as 'diving' does in Greek.[20] The existence of this older word supports the idea that people were swimming in India before the Yamnaya arrived. But the arrival of these non-swimming northerners seems to have put a stop to swimming, at least in northern India.

Yamnaya interactions with local Indian people produced (among other things) a long religious poem, the central text of Hinduism: the Rig Veda. This poem was probably composed around the end of the Bronze Age, though it was not written down for another thousand years. Many of the Rig Veda's prayers and hymns are about water. They focus on springs, melting snows, streams and rivers, including a series of hymns to river gods. Men, women and gods bathe in streams. But they do not swim. Instead, water is magical, supernatural or divine: 'Onward [the river god] flows . . . excited by the prayer, the water makes him wild. He . . . bathes in streams to satisfy the worshipper.' Swimming is only for animals. Horses, cows and swans know how to swim, but not people. Just one hymn may hint at deeper water: some friendships, it says, are shallow, like ponds that only come up to your shoulder or chin; others are deep, like ponds you could bathe in. But when people in the Rig Veda get into deep water, beyond their depth, the god Indra has to save them from drowning: 'The mighty roaring flood he stayed from flowing, and carried those who swam not safely over.'[21] These early Indian poems seem to parallel the Mesopotamian attitude that rivers are both magical and dangerous.

In addition to heading west into Europe and south to India, the Yamnaya also migrated east into northern China, and if swimming had not already stopped during the Ice Age, the Yamnaya probably stopped it there as well. They settled in the Tarim Basin (today the homeland of the Uighurs) around a third salt mine. The salty ground around this mine preserved their bodies and mummified them in their graves. Today they lie in the Ürümqi museum, with their red hair and beards, their blue eyes and their pale skin. Many new ideas reached China during the Shang Dynasty, around 1200 BCE, including the use of bronze and the idea of writing, along with horses and chariots. All of these were known first further west, and may have come to China through a second wave of Central Asian migration, or through trade. Along with these other new ideas, the Yamnaya may have brought their fear of the water to northern

China. Under the Shang Dynasty, North Chinese people worshipped the Yellow River God, trying to control the river's often devastating floods. Chinese oracle bones recommend human sacrifices to the river: 'Reward the Yellow River with thirty cattle and a woman' or 'marry a young female to the Yellow River.' Later historians also tell stories of sacrificing women to the Zhanghe River. These stories assume that the victims would not have known how to swim.[22]

Later people in northern China were also not swimmers. Under the Zhou Dynasty, around 800–600 BCE, they composed proverbs along the lines of, 'Deep water: raft, boat; Shallow water: swim, float.'[23] To a good swimmer, it does not matter how deep the water is, so these swimmers must not be very confident. A famous Daoist story, told and retold for generations, uses a swimming metaphor to contrast Confucian philosophy with Daoism, but again the danger of swimming is emphasized:

One day Confucius, while he was travelling around with his disciples as holy men do, came to a famous and dangerous waterfall. The waterfall dropped straight down for two hundred feet; even fish could not swim there. But then Confucius saw somebody jump down into the foaming water. Thinking that the person must have been committing suicide, Confucius sent out his disciples to try to help, or at least to get the man's body. He was very surprised, then, to see the man climb out of the water and walk along the bank, singing to himself. Confucius rushed down to the bank to ask the man how he did it. Did the man have a special way (*dao*) of swimming? The man explained that he just let the water go however it wanted to go, and he went with it.[24]

North Chinese writers like Liu An and Fan Chengda described South Chinese swimming as an alien novelty, and even embarked on medicalized (though not genetic) explanations. By the first century BCE North Chinese writers were racializing swimming. They tied South Chinese affinity for the ocean directly to skin colour: 'The people of the East live near the ocean and eat much fish and salt. Fish and seafood are thought to cause an "internal burning", salt to injure the blood. These factors cause a dark complexion.'[25] South China's fun body-surfing looked reckless and dangerous to people in northern China. In the 1100s northern Chinese Song Dynasty authorities tried to ban body-surfing altogether:

> Every year, on the eighteenth day of the eighth month, when the tides were at their highest, all residents of the town, regardless of class, turned out in droves to amuse themselves at the dike. Those natives who were good at swimming repeatedly submerged themselves in the water and reemerged again, each holding ten banners above water level, in a game called 'playing with the tides'. An amazing sight it was. There were also some poor swimmers who tried to emulate the feat but ended up being engulfed in the waves and drowned. When the matter was brought to the attention of the prefect of Lin'an, he had notices put up banning the practice, but, despite the many times his order was repeated, the custom of playing with the tides continued to be observed. A poem titled 'Watching the Tides', by the academician Su Dongpo, bears witness:

> Men of Wu grow up playing with the waves,
> Lightheartedly putting their lives at risk.
> Had the East Sea God known what the king wanted,
> He would have turned the water into farmland.[26]

Though South China had many good swimmers, North China was part of the northern Eurasian non-swimming zone. Their northern neighbours in Japan and Korea may also have been non-swimmers.

Swimming in Japan

The story of swimming in Japan parallels that of other northern communities. The first modern humans reached Japan in about 35,000 BCE, when they were able to walk over from China on what was at that time dry land. Excavations of Yamashita Cave on the island of Okinawa show that these first Okinawans lived right along the coast and left huge piles of discarded shells from the mussels and clams they lived on. Probably, like the Neanderthals of the Bay of Naples, they dived to the bottom of the bay for clams. But, like other northerners, they abandoned swimming during the last Ice Age. There is little evidence of swimming from ancient or medieval Japan, with the exception of commercial diving like that performed in the Mediterranean.[27] Even most of the pearl diving was passed off to women of the minority Ainu people. The Japanese Lady Nakatomi, writing poetry in the 700s CE, describes the arduous training of these Ainu pearl divers as a simile for learning to love:

> No one dives to the ocean-bottom
> Just like that.
> One does not learn the skills involved
> At the drop of a hat.
> It's the slow-learnt skills in the depths of love
> That I am working at.[28]

Ainu pearl divers reappear in the poet Sei Shōnagon's *Pillow Book*, from about 1000 CE, when Shōnagon writes sympathetically about women diving for pearls:

> A stretch of water may seem terrifying, but your spirits sink still further at the thought of the fisher girls who dive for shells. If that thin rope tied to their waist ever snapped, whatever would they do? It would be all very well if it were men doing the diving, but it must feel miserable for women. The men are on board, singing away lustily, moving the boat along with the women's waist ropes dangling into the water. You'd imagine they'd be feeling full of anxiety and trepidation. Apparently, when the woman wants to come up to the surface she tugs on the rope, and you can quite see why the men should scramble to pull her up as fast as possible. Even an onlooker must weep salt tears to witness the gasp of the woman as she breaks surface and lays her hand on the edge of the boat – really, I find it utterly astonishing to see those men sending the poor women overboard while they float lazily about on the surface!²⁹

In both Japan and Korea communal steam baths like the Scythian ones (see Chapter Four) were culturally important. Steam baths (*iwaburo* and *kamaburo*) long pre-date immersion baths in Japan.[30] In Korea, the *hanjeungmak*, or traditional sauna, is described in the fourteenth-century *Annals of Sejong*. This interest in steam baths may connect Japan and Korea to other northern non-swimming cultures.

THANKS TO THE Ice Age, and subsequent migrations, people forgot how to swim across most of northern Eurasia. Bronze Age people were not swimming anywhere in Europe, in West Asia or Central Asia, in India or in northern China. They were probably not swimming in Japan. But in southern China, Southeast Asia and Indonesia, people were still excellent swimmers, just as they had been before the Ice Age. Everywhere else in the world – in Africa, the South Seas and the Americas – most people were skilled and enthusiastic swimmers.

Living in northern Eurasia caused many of these same non-swimmers to evolve lighter skin. In the north, sunshine was weaker. Once they were eating the grain-based diet of early farmers, people needed pale skin to synthesize enough vitamin D. That same weaker sunshine also caused cooler temperatures, so that people stayed out of the water and forgot how to swim. There is no biological connection: pale skin did not make it harder to swim, and swimming did not really make people darker. But there was a considerable overlap between the people who stopped swimming in the Ice Age and early farmers who developed pale skin, which would, centuries later, become significant in drawing lines between enslaver and enslaved.

4

DANGER, SEX, GODS
AND STRANGERS

Northern Eurasian people kept their suspicious attitude towards water well beyond the Bronze Age. As they moved south and came in contact with more swimmers, they asked themselves why they were different. Why did they not swim, while others did? The Ice Age was too long ago; nobody remembered that. So during the Iron Age and the time of the Roman, Sasanian and Han empires, the non-swimmers developed some convenient stock answers. The answers they came up with are still very much with us today.

Water is sacred

First, the northern non-swimmers said, water was sacred to the gods. People who entered the water would pollute it with their bodies. The Greek poet Hesiod, writing around 700 BCE, warns against defiling the sanctity of rivers:

> Never cross the sweet flowing water of ever flowing rivers on foot before you have prayed, looking into the beautiful stream, and washed your hands in the much loved clear water. Anyone who wades a river without washing the evil from his hands, the gods resent him and send him trouble later.

Hesiod admonishes his readers, 'Never urinate in rivers flowing to their mouths, or in springs; but be careful to avoid this. And don't defecate in them: it's not right.'[1] Two centuries later the Greek historian Herodotus claims that the Persians are even more careful about polluting the water. The Persians 'never urinate or spit into a river, nor even wash their hands in one; nor let other people do it; instead, they greatly revere rivers.' North of the Persians, Herodotus tells us that the Scythians, in what is now Ukraine, bathe in hemp-seed steam baths, 'for they absolutely will not wash their bodies with water'.[2] Agreeing with Herodotus, Zoroastrian Avestas from Central Asia are indeed concerned about the purity of water: the river spirits 'were dissatisfied by the defilement of still water, so that they would not flow into the world'. The Lord Ahuramazda 'will pour six-fold holy water into it and make it wholesome again; he will preach carefulness.' The prophet Ezekiel repeats this concern in the Bible, again associating Egyptians with swimming:

> Cry for Pharaoh, king of Egypt, and say to him, You think you are a lion of the nations, but you are like a dragon in the seas. You burst forth in your rivers; you trouble the waters with your feet, and foul their rivers. Thus says the Lord God: I will . . . water with your blood the land in which you swim . . . I will destroy all the livestock [of Egypt] from beside the great waters, so neither men's feet nor beasts' hoofs will trouble them anymore. Then I will let the waters run clear.[3]

Later Sasanian and Manichaean sources repeat this restriction on bathing, so that 'at the warm baths which many have frequented . . . the pious went in, and came out wicked.' They warn against entering rivers and pools, like 'that wicked man who, in the world, often washed his head and face, and dirty hands, and other pollution of his limbs, in large standing waters and fountains and streams, and distressed Hordad the archangel'. A particular prohibition forbids swimming, or even approaching water, during menstruation.[4] Still further east in Korea and Japan, steam baths like the Scythian ones were also common. China's *Liji*, a Han Dynasty book from about 100 CE that claims to describe ancient customs, is more moderate; it suggests that people should wash their hands and faces in a basin every morning, and take baths in tubs once or twice a week.[5] But there is this same sense that you should not overdo it. We may sympathize with what seem to be reasonable concerns about clean drinking water, but the germ theory of disease was not then known.

These ideas are only partially motivated by concerns about keeping drinking water clean. The restrictions on bathing suggest that fear of the water was uppermost in people's minds.

Swimming is indecent

Second, these non-swimmers claimed that they did not swim because they were too modest to take off their clothes and be seen naked. Swimming in the water, or even bathing in it, might lead to sexual transgressions. For Enkidu, in the Mesopotamian Bronze Age, simply going down to the water's edge to drink leads to his sexual fall from grace. In the early Iron Age, the Sirens entice Odysseus – still on his ship – with their bewitching voices.[6] The Bible gives us the tales of Bathsheba and Susanna, both of whom accidentally incited men's sexual desire by bathing. And in a Buddhist Jataka tale from India, a king saw some young boys throwing stones at a snake. He saved the snake, which turned out to be the king of the naga-snakes, and in return the naga-snake king gave him a naga-girl. So the king took the naga-girl to the garden and 'amused himself in the lotus-tank' with her. The couple are not swimming – just bathing and hanging out in the pool.[7] But sure enough, the naga-girl soon abandons the king and resumes her snake form to get with a water snake.

In China, too, a folk tale tells the story of a pregnant woman who told her father that when she was swimming, a beautiful bird flew over her head and laid an egg, which she happened to swallow. Unsurprisingly, after a few days she realized that she was going to have a baby. A second well-known Chinese story was set in the Country of Women, where women with long hair and pale skin get pregnant by bathing in a yellow pool. Mixed bathing of men and women had erotic overtones, and was considered 'a disgusting peculiarity of barbarians and peasants'. North Chinese modesty, at least in theory, discouraged nudity even in single-sex bathing. Men sometimes wore two pieces of coarse cloth (presumably front and back) into the bath. In one Chinese story, a young man was so modest that he refused to bathe with his grandfather in an outdoor pool, saying that it was indecent to expose your body in broad daylight.[8] Similarly in Babylon, Jewish custom prohibited men from bathing with their close male relatives, in case this might lead to sexual thoughts.[9]

Europeans also associated swimming with sex. At least in literature, Roman people were never comfortable with mixed nude bathing, associating it with promiscuity. The Roman senator Cicero and the historian Plutarch both tell stories in which Romans thought it wrong for grown sons to bathe with their fathers. Cicero even criticized Clodia for watching men swimming in the Tiber from a seat in her garden.[10] The poet Ovid claims to object to women swimming on the grounds of immodesty, though it is partly tongue in cheek: he is urging women to be more modest on the grounds that modesty will attract men. Ovid even more than once presents swimming as a prelude to rape:

> I was (she said) a nymph . . . I found some water, neither deep nor shallow, gliding silently, so calm that you could hardly see it flow, and right to the bottom the water was so clear that every little stone plainly appeared . . . I entered in, and first of all I just put in my feet, and then up to my knees. And not content with wading, I took off all my clothes, and hung them on a tree nearby, and threw myself into the stream. Then as I played, beating and drawing, and competing with myself in a thousand little ways, casting my arms wide and swimming carelessly, I felt a bubbling in the stream – I didn't know who or what it was – and I got back up the river's nearest bank in fear. With that, 'Arethusa, where are you running to?' cried Alpheus from his waves . . . I hid away, naked as I was, for my clothes were still hanging on the other bank. That made him hotter and more eager than ever, and with me naked as I was, I seemed readier than he was.[11]

Arethusa was saved when the goddess Diana hid her in a cloud, but Ovid's presentation of swimming as risky serves to justify non-swimmers' fear of the water.

Central Asians likewise deployed stories of sexual assault to justify their reluctance to enter the water. A tale in multiple medieval manuscripts from Central Asia tells of women swimming naked while Alexander of Macedon and a companion hide behind a rock to spy on them (see illus. 38). The women's nakedness emphasizes the invader's lasciviousness, so the swimming here is a source of shame and titillation. Again, in a medieval South Indian story, *gopis*, or milkmaids, are bathing in the stream and have left their clothes on the bank.[12] The god Krishna sneaks up while the women are bathing and steals their clothes (see illus. 40, though note that the women painted are actually swimming with their petticoats on). The women modestly stay in the water until they are cold and shivering, while Krishna teases them. But in the end they are forced to come out and stand naked in front of Krishna, who then gives back their clothes and praises them for loving their god more than their own modesty. The Hindu moral is that people must be prepared to give up all attachments to family and even their honour in order to become one with God, but the popularity of the story, which was a common theme for Indian painters, surely stems from the perception that swimming leads to trouble.

Swimming is dangerous

Non-swimmers also asserted that swimming was dangerous. For one thing, there were health issues. Concerns about getting ill from bathing appear in the *Guanzi*, an early Chinese work of political science that was already old when Liu Xiang edited it about 26 BCE: people should not wash on winter days because it is not good for the body. A man's friends might worry about whether he would catch cold when he washed his hair outdoors in winter. Bathing appears more as a medical treatment than as a pleasure. Both hot and cold baths (depending on the ailment) were commonly prescribed as Chinese medical interventions. Far away in the Roman town of Aquae Sulis (modern-day Bath) in England, bathing was also medically prescribed for centuries. The early medieval Babylonian Talmud suggests that, as a cure for heatstroke, you should first eat leeks, then go and stand in water up to your neck until you feel faint before swimming out and sitting down.[13]

This northern Eurasian medicalization of bathing stands in sharp contrast to the more usual practice of bathing daily, or even multiple times in a day, in the rest of the world. Early non-swimmers' reluctance to enter the water wasn't necessarily irrational: Roman baths (and probably other ancient baths) regularly spread diseases like dysentery and parasites such as whipworm, fleas and lice.[14] But in most parts of the world people bathed every day in fresh or salt water rather than in baths. Once more, the non-swimmers' reluctance to bathe demonstrates their general attitude towards water.

18 Elamite soldiers drown in the river under Assyrian attack in the
Battle of the River Ulai. Relief carving from the palace of the
Assyrian ruler Assurbanipal at Nineveh, Iraq, *c.* 650 BCE.

Eurasian non-swimmers' fear of the water also expressed itself in
literature and art as a fear of drowning, or being attacked by crabs or
turtles, or eaten by large fish or whales. The *Odyssey*'s story of Scylla and
Charybdis, from the 700s BCE, is an early example. In the ocean, there are
terrible monsters that will eat you alive.

> She has twelve dangling legs and six long necks
> with a gruesome head on each, and in each face
> three rows of crowded teeth, pregnant with death . . .
> No sailors ever pass that way unharmed.
> She snatches one man with each mouth from off
> each dark-prowed ship. The other rock is near,
> enough to shoot an arrow right across.
> This second rock is lower down, and on it
> there grows a fig tree with thick leaves. Beneath,
> divine Charybdis sucks black water down.
> Three times a day she spurts it up; three times
> she glugs it down. Avoid that place when she
> is swallowing the water. No one could
> save you from death then, even great Poseidon.

19 Ships sail in an ocean full of fish, eels, lizards and crabs,
on a relief carving (sadly now lost) from the Assyrian ruler
Sennacherib's palace at Nineveh, Iraq, c. 700 BCE.

20 Capsized ship surrounded by drowning people and large fish, painted on an Athenian wine pitcher, *c.* 725 BCE, possibly representing the shipwreck of Odysseus.

Assyrian relief carvings dating to about the same time as Homer's *Odyssey*, from the walls of the kings' palaces of Sargon II at Khorsabad and of Sennacherib and Assurbanibal at Nineveh, convey the sense of danger that Mesopotamian people felt around the water (illus. 18 and 19). Rivers were terrifying, full of dangerous animals: giant fish, crabs, eels and crocodiles. Carved mermen guard the doorways of these palaces, half man, half fish. The mermaid Atargatis, worshipped along the eastern Mediterranean coast, combined the danger of the sea with the danger of lust that could be aroused by swimming; her monstrosity contrasts with the Egyptians' affection for their goddess Isis, who controls the Nile. Around the same time, the writers of Genesis were retelling the old Babylonian story as Noah's flood:

> The waters swelled so mightily on the earth that all the high mountains under the whole heaven were covered; the waters swelled above the mountains, covering them fifteen cubits deep. And all flesh died that moved on the earth, birds, domestic animals, wild animals, all swarming creatures that swarm on the earth, and all human beings; everything on dry land in whose nostrils was the breath of life died.[15]

21 Frightening marine creatures on a Roman floor mosaic from Lod, Israel, *c.* 300 CE.

The terrible Leviathan mentioned in the Book of Job and elsewhere shows that eastern Mediterranean people also identified with the old Sumerian struggle between Marduk and Tiamat, or Baal and Lotan – between God and the ocean.[16]

A little further west, contemporary Greek Geometric vases depict overturned ships, with giant fish eating the drowned sailors (illus. 20), and later on, the Hellenistic poet Leonidas of Tarentum wrote two epigrams on the same subject. Pliny wrote about a sea man (*marinum hominem*) who sat on the sides of ships and sank them, perhaps taking a cue from the Indian river monsters and *naramakara*, water monsters with male torsos and split fish tails, carved into stone at Krishna's pilgrimage city of Mathura about the same time. In the later Roman Empire, the travel writer Pausanias mentions giant turtles, while the poet Oppian describes huge monsters 'bred in Poseidon's seabeds' and imagines a giant whale in a battle with men on ships.[17] A Roman mosaic pavement from the city of Lod, in Israel, shows the ocean full of huge fish and whales, some larger than the ships (illus. 21). Another mosaic, from a synagogue in Huqoq, imagines an Egyptian soldier being eaten by a big fish as he tries to cross the Red Sea in pursuit of Moses and the fleeing Israelites (see illus. 41). A second Huqoq mosaic shows Jonah being eaten by a fish, which is eaten by a bigger fish, which is eaten by a bigger fish, which ends up being eaten by a truly giant fish (see illus. 42). On the other side of Asia, the *Guanzi* includes flood dragons and water spirits 'like snakes, eight feet long', while the early medieval *Nihongi* in Japan similarly describes a snakelike water monster that kills travellers.[18] The Roman scholar Varro even tells a story, repeated by Pliny and by the Late Roman bishops Augustine and Isidore, in which water could turn people into monsters: Arcadians, he says, 'when their lot was drawn, would swim across a certain pond and would be changed into wolves'.[19] Lastly, the early medieval European story of Merovech's mother, raped by a sea monster when she went out to swim in the ocean, reprises the melding of sea monsters with sexual transgression.[20]

Even when it was not a question of sea monsters, these non-swimmers associated swimming with drowning. An Indian fable from the 300s BCE tells of a goat whose prospective mother-in-law wants him to swim out to an island in the Ganges River and get her the green grass that grows there, as the bride-price for her daughter. The goat angrily refuses on the grounds that he does not want to die yet, and reminds his prospective mother-in-law that there are many other girl-goats in the world.[21] What a contrast to the Ethiopian story where the young man eagerly swims out to the island in order to win the girl!

The Greek tragedy of Hero and Leander is also a story about how dangerous it is to swim. In this story, Leander falls in love with a priestess named Hero. As a priestess of Aphrodite, Hero cannot marry, so she is imprisoned in a tower across the Hellespont from Leander. But every night her faithful lover swims over to be with her, as she sets an oil lamp in her window to guide him in. One night there is a bad storm, but he insists on swimming across anyway. The wind blows out Hero's lamp, and Leander loses his way and drowns. Hero leaps from her tower to be with her lover, and drowns alongside him.[22] Again, compare this to the Maori story of Tutanekai and Hinemoa from New Zealand. The Greek story reverses the genders so it is the man swimming across to his lover instead of the woman. And while Tutanekai and Hinemoa marry, and live happily ever after, the Greek swimming story ends in tragedy and death. When the Iranian poet Firdawsi retold this same story in his medieval epic *Shahnameh*, he took swimming out of the story entirely. Although Firdawsi still calls his heroine Rudaba, or 'River Water Girl', she never goes near the water. Like Hero, Rudaba is locked in a tower, but her lover Zal no longer swims – he is only able to reach her by having her lower her rippling long hair out of her window so that he can climb up. You may know her as Rapunzel.[23]

Drowning appears over and over again in northern Eurasian stories.[24] In one popular Greek tale, a boy, Hermias, made friends with a dolphin and the two played together in the water every day. One day a storm blew up and the boy drowned. The dolphin brought the boy's body back to the beach, and stayed there until it died itself of grief and shame.[25] Centuries later, a vivid illustration of Noah's Flood from late antique Syria also depicts the horrors of drowning (see illus. 43). The Christian bishop Isidore of Seville, writing in the seventh century CE, tells us that drowning in water is an 'especially cruel' death. The Islamic Quran tells the sad story of Nuh's son, who refused to get into the Ark: 'the waves came between them, so he was among the drowned.'[26] And further east, a Kashmiri-inspired story painted on the wall of a medieval Tibetan temple shows a miracle: the Buddha saves a drowning fisherman with his arms helplessly outstretched, surrounded by giant fish and sea monsters (see illus. 44). No wonder people avoided swimming when they pictured it as so dangerous.

Swimming is for foreigners and fish

Swimming was also to be avoided as something other people did: foreigners, people who were different. We have already seen how Liu An, writing in 139 BCE, drew a line between non-swimming North China and the swimmers of South China, with their scaly tattoos and short breeches. Early Chinese literature shows us how the people of South China loved 'boating, seafaring, naval warfare, swimming, water festivals and mixed bathing'. Meanwhile, to those in North China the swimming and water play of the South seemed strange, and possibly immoral.[27] Western literature drew the same contrast: both the Torah and the Quran draw sharp distinctions between Jewish non-swimmers and the Egyptian swimmers who enslaved them. The Roman Pliny describes a race of magicians living near the Black Sea who were lighter than water and couldn't sink, 'even weighed down by their clothes'.[28] He contrasts the excellent swimming of East Africans with the lesser abilities of his own people. Europeans and West Asians marginalized swimming as the sport of weird or subhuman people living in faraway places. For centuries, northerners explained their inability to swim the way Aesop's fox explained his inability to reach the grapes, by claiming they didn't want to swim anyway.

If many people consigned swimming to foreign lands, others thought swimming was not for humans at all. Proverbially, swimming was for fish:

fish belonged in the water, birds in the air and people on land. This idea was widespread at least by the sixth century BCE. It is in the very opening of the Bible, in Genesis 1:26, and a little later on in Chinese Daoist texts: 'Fish live in water and thrive, but if men tried to live in water, they would die.' Aristotle's biological system divides living creatures similarly, separating those that live on dry land from those that live in the water. In the Roman period, a few centuries later, Philo, a Jewish philosopher, brings Genesis and Aristotle together (somewhat ironically) to reinforce the point. Early medieval Zoroastrian Avestas continue to divide the world so that 'four-footed animals walked forth on the land, fish swam in the water, and birds flew in the air'.[29] Science and religion constructed powerful logical systems that rationalized northern non-swimmers' fears.

GENERATIONS OF NON-SWIMMERS in northern Eurasia found ways to explain why they did not swim. The water was sacred, or it was dangerous. Swimming was immoral, or it was best left to foreigners and fish. Nevertheless, when they met people who were good swimmers at the end of the Bronze Age, some of these pale non-swimmers wanted to learn. In the next chapter, we will see how some northern Eurasians learned to swim.

5

LEARNING TO SWIM

Despite their mistrust of the water, many northern non-swimmers tried to learn to swim again. Their attempts were faltering and fearful, often complicated by changing fashions and beliefs, and never altogether successful. African influences from Egypt and Carthage starting in the Late Bronze Age may have encouraged the first northerners to learn to swim. Swimming became a way of displaying your upper social class, like glass beads, ivory dolls, papyrus scrolls and other imported African luxuries. Not much later, immigration from the South Chinese regions of Shanghai and Hong Kong to North China seems to have brought swimming along with it, probably for similar reasons.

In the Iron Age, a new wave of Central Asian Yamnaya invasions swept the non-swimming Medes and Persians into Southwest Asia. Their cultural dominance discouraged swimming throughout the Persian Empire, but it encouraged swimming in Europe. As Europe resisted Persian invasions, Europeans reimagined swimming as a statement of identity and independence from foreign rule. If the Persians were going to stop swimming, then Europeans would swim more, to emphasize their different identities. Europeans still swam awkwardly, often with their heads held high out of the water, and they preferred to swim in artificial pools rather than lakes or rivers. Rich people swam more than poor people did, but performatively, not as a normal part of everyday life. The same was probably true in China. Nevertheless, the general trend through the Iron Age, in the great empires of antiquity and well into the Middle Ages was more Eurasian people learning to swim.

African influence

The growing power of African empires at the end of the Bronze Age may have encouraged many Europeans and Southwest Asians to dip their toes into the pool. Starting about 1500 BCE, Africans increasingly dominated their neighbours to the north and northeast. Egyptian armies employing Sudanese mercenaries gained military control over much of the eastern Mediterranean coast. Throughout the Late Bronze Age, Egypt's New Kingdom was the most powerful empire in Afro-Eurasia. After the New Kingdom collapsed, those same Sudanese mercenaries took control of Egypt, carrying southern ideas and fashions north to the Mediterranean. At the same time, Phoenician colonizers worked with local Berbers to build the Carthaginian Empire along the North African coast, in Sicily and Sardinia, and in Spain. Carthaginian traders negotiated treaties not only with the Etruscans, Romans and Greeks in Italy, but all around the Mediterranean Sea.

African culture seemed like the path to success: the model to imitate. Greek scholars went to Egypt to study in the great universities there, as people said Solon had done.[1] Around the northern and eastern Mediterranean, people added African linen to their wool clothing, perhaps worrying traditionalist Jewish scholars writing the Bible. Egyptian traders sold linen to Republican Italy, and soon Italians were growing more linen for themselves.[2] Greeks and Romans imported Egyptian glass and papyrus, Kenyan ivory, and faience scarab amulets. The Greek historian Herodotus imagined the origin of the Greek gods in ancient Egypt, and admired the wonders of Egypt. Herodotus also noticed and relayed to his readers in Greece that the Egyptians bathed in cold water several times a day.[3] Even the Scythians, raiding southwards from Central Asia, met and negotiated with Egyptian leaders along the eastern Mediterranean coast. Late Bronze Age and early Iron Age Eurasians admired and emulated their southern neighbours.

Hittites and Megiddo

By the Late Bronze Age this strong Egyptian influence seems to have encouraged some of the northern non-swimmers to learn to swim. A southern Egyptian wall carving from Abu Simbel, near Sudan, oddly enough provides the first example of West Asian swimming (illus. 22). This commemorates the Battle of Qadesh (*c.* 1274 BCE), contested between Egyptians and Hittites over northern Syria, where the Turks, Kurds and Syrians are fighting now. Egyptian representations of the Battle of Qadesh show the Hittite soldiers flailing in the river, but not all of the Hittites are drowning. Some of them are swimming.

As in the earlier battlefield scene from Akrotiri, the attackers attack, the defenders panic and wave their arms, and the defeated drown in the water between them. On the left, the pharaoh Rameses II charges in his horse-drawn chariot. The Hittite fort of Qadesh, with its terrified defenders, stands on an island to the right. Hittite soldiers drown in the Orontes River. But Rameses's accompanying hieroglyphic inscription belies our first impression. He says the Hittites are not drowning after all. According to Rameses, the Hittite troops are fleeing back across the river, 'hurrying as fast as crocodiles swimming'. A second Egyptian record of the same battle, from the Ramesseum in Thebes, showcases the corpses of the drowned (illus. 23). Most of the Hittites are struggling. They hold on to their horses' legs, while their friends reach out their arms from the further shore.[4] But a few of them seem to be swimming, in the first hint of swimming from Southwest Asia. Now, these are both Egyptian versions of this battle. The Hittite swimming could be just the imagination of Egyptian stone-carvers. But other evidence suggests that the Hittites might really have been swimming.

22 Hittite soldiers swim the Orontes River to escape an Egyptian attack in the Battle of Qadesh, fought in northern Syria, *c.* 1270 BCE, from a relief carving on the wall of Rameses II's temple at Abu Simbel, Egypt.

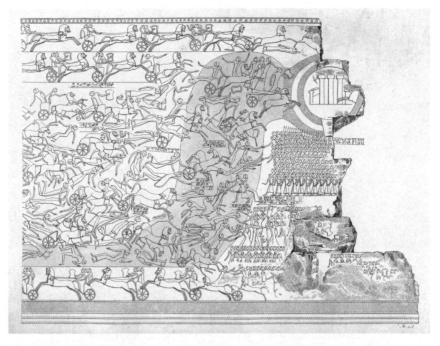

23 Hittite soldiers crossing the Orontes River, in a second Egyptian
image of the Battle of Qadesh from the Ramesseum in Thebes, *c.* 1270 BCE.

A series of Canaanite spoons also hints that Egyptians were sharing
their swimming skills with the eastern Mediterranean in the Late Bronze
Age. In Egypt, wooden spoons in the shape of a swimming woman, often
holding a bowl in the shape of a duck, were common in the 1300s BCE.
When Canaanite artists imitated this form, they usually left out the swimmer, carving only the duck-shaped bowl. Swimming may have seemed
too alien to their customers. But several (probably) locally made spoons
found at Megiddo in Israel and dated to the 1100s BCE do include the
swimmer.[5] The decision to include the swimmers on these spoons may
signal that New Kingdom domination of the eastern Mediterranean was
bringing with it an increasing familiarity with swimming.

Assyrians

As the Bronze Age ended and the Iron Age began, more West Asians
learned to swim. Egyptian cultural influence outlasted the collapse of
the New Kingdom in the 1000s BCE. With Sudanese kings ruling Egypt,
swimming may even have increased its cultural significance. Certainly

24 Assyrian soldiers swimming across a river, on a relief carving
from the palace of the Assyrian ruler Assurnasirpal II at Nimrud,
Iraq, *c.* 875–860 BCE.

25 Enemies attempt to escape Assyrian attack by swimming across a river,
on a second relief carving from Assurnasirpal II's palace at Nimrud.

by about 860 BCE some Assyrians were tentatively beginning to swim,
but they were not very good at it. Assyrian swimmers habitually used
flotation devices to keep afloat: goatskins called *mussuk*, with hollow
tubes inserted into them. Swimmers blew into the tubes continuously
to keep the skins inflated (illus. 25). Assyrians may have used the *mussuk*
not because they were awkward swimmers, but because rivers flow rapidly in eastern Syria and northern Iraq. It takes practice to use these
flotation devices.[6] But the absence of such tools outside northern Eurasia
suggests that they are not associated with skilled swimming.

Once again, in this Assyrian image, soldiers are attacking a town. The
defenders are in the river: in this emergency, they have not even stripped

off their long robes. The man furthest to the left is a eunuch, as we can see from his not having a beard (so he is probably a civilian, not a soldier). But this Iron Age scene deliberately disrupts the old Bronze Age iconography: the people on the walls of the city are not the panicked defendants, waving their arms around. Instead, the citadel has already fallen. And the defenders are not drowning, but swimming. One of the three men can swim on his own; the other two use flotation devices. Assyrian soldiers stand atop the walls of the conquered city, shooting arrows at the swimmers. One man has already been hit. His two companions assiduously blow into their goatskins and paddle for their lives, but their chances do not look good. A second Assyrian image also challenges the traditional iconography, this time by putting the attacking soldiers in the water, swimming underwater to escape the notice of the city's guards (illus. 24). As attackers, they have had time to strip off their clothes. But even so, only one of the men swims without his inflatable goatskin.[7]

By the 600s BCE, two centuries later, Assyrian images show men swimming in other contexts. A wall relief from Sennacherib's palace at Nineveh shows four men using flotation devices to help them swim, while one groom swims alone, holding the reins of the horses. By this time, apparently they can seal up the goatskins and no longer have to blow into them. In other scenes, Assyrian fishermen sit or lie on their *mussuks*. Swimming has moved beyond the military into commercial life, though nobody seems to swim for pleasure. A few years later, as the Jews were compiling their Torah in Babylon, they would envision immersion in the River Jordan as a cure for leprosy.[8] But the Torah also included a prohibition on eating shellfish. Fish, which you could catch from boats, were considered kosher.[9] Could the prohibition of shellfish have arisen from the need to dive for them?

Buddhism in China

North Chinese soldiers, far to the east, may also have been learning to swim in the Iron Age. The *Guanzi* presents Duke Huan as a military general of the Zhou Dynasty during the 600s BCE. When Duke Huan asked the clever prime minister Guanzi of the Li kingdom in northern China how to defend against a possible invasion, Guanzi suggested that Huan should dam up streams to make a large swimming pool, and then 'order people to take up diving and swimming for amusement', while 'stating that a thousand catties of gold will be awarded to those who can swim'. This is sometimes called a prize for a swimming competition, but there is no competition here. Guanzi and Huan are just paying Chinese soldiers to learn to swim. The pool provided for swimming seems to be a shallow one, in contrast to the deep one for boats. Guanzi adds, 'Before the thousand catties of gold could be spent, the swimming abilities of the people of Qi had reached a level no less than that of people from [the southern provinces of] Wu and Yue,' and that in the battle 50,000 Qi swimmers 'inflicted a major defeat on the men of Yue'.[10] South Chinese people never stopped swimming; North Chinese people may have been trying to catch up with them.

Contemporary proverbs from North China similarly suggest that people were learning to swim, but were concerned about safety. One Zhou Dynasty proverb reads: 'A swimmer uses his feet to kick and his hands to sweep. But if you have not mastered the technique of swimming, the more you kick, the more you will get into trouble. When you do learn to swim, it is not [just] a matter of hands and feet.' Another proverb opines, 'Someone who is swimming can't save [another] from drowning; his hands and feet are occupied.' Other proverbs warn of the danger of drowning. 'When crossing a river, if you lack the technique of swimming, you will assuredly drown despite your strength. If you possess the technique of swimming, you will assuredly cross to the other side despite your weakness.'[11] The *Shiji*, a later history of China from about 100 BCE, gets a little defensive about swimming: 'In bathing, we don't need a river or sea; we [only] require that it remove grime.'[12] Washing is enough to get clean. Swimming is difficult and unnecessary except in emergencies – there is no suggestion that people might swim for fun.

More North Chinese people seem to have learned to swim as time went on. During the Han Dynasty, many South Chinese immigrants moved north across the Yangtze River. They brought new fashions, including using feather fans to cool themselves and eating rice as part of their diet.[13] Swimming was one of these new trends, and Han Dynasty emperors built lavish swimming pools in their palaces. But in North China swimming still took on a different look. One Han Chinese emperor, for example, is said to have

dallied in the Western Garden, where he . . . had green moss
gathered to cover the stairs, and led water by an aqueduct to circle
about the flagstones, and it flowed round limpid and pellucid, and
he mounted a boat to idle on the waves. He had his Palatine Ladies
[board] them, choosing jade-complexioned and light-bodied
ones to hold the poles and oars, and they rocked and wavered in
the midst of the watercourse, whose water was clear and limpid.
At the season of the fullness of heat, he would have the boat
capsized and sunk, so he could admire these jade-complexioned
Palatines . . . Palatines who were above twenty-seven years and
below thirty-six, prinked and bedecked, would all undo their outer
clothing, and wear only their inner garments, and sometimes they
bathed naked together.[14]

This is not so much swimming as a mockery of swimming: an artificial
shipwreck in an artificial pool, closely tied to eroticism. Compare this to
a similar and apparently very well-known story from Bronze Age Egypt
(known to us from the Westcar Papyrus) in which King Sneferu has
beautiful women dress up and row around the pool for him to look at. In
this version, from a swimming culture, there is no shipwreck: only a hair
ornament falls into the water. The Chinese scenario allowed for swimming
while maintaining an ironic distance from it. As we will see, these erotic
games were emulated by later Eurasian autocrats as far west as Córdoba
and as far south as Madurai in South India.

By the early Middle Ages, Buddhist enthusiasm for ritual and medicinal bathing may have helped to coax North Chinese people into the
water. The geographer Li Daoyuan listed 38 different hot springs and mentioned that most of them could cure diseases, so presumably many people
were routinely submerging their bodies for their health.[15] Early medieval
wall paintings from Buddhist caves in western China provide the earliest
North Chinese images of swimming. Some of these, like earlier Egyptian
and Assyrian images, depict soldiers swimming or drowning as they try
to escape their enemies. But several other Buddhist paintings show
swimmers playing and having fun. Like other swimmers from this time,
they use an overhand stroke, though they hold their heads up out of the
water (illus. 26).[16] In the nearby Dunhuang Caves, reborn souls and
female figures, perhaps apsaras or fairies, swim in divine lotus ponds.[17]

26 Swimmers in Central Asia, wall painting by Buddhist artists
in the Kizil Caves, western China, *c.* 500–700 CE.

Buddhism reached Korea in the early Middle Ages, and may have
shifted bathing practices there as much as or more than in China. Buddhist
monks maintained medieval Korea's bathhouses (with both saunas and
tubs). Medieval Koreans seem to have been more comfortable than
Chinese bathers with nudity in the water. The Chinese emissary Xu Jing
reports that Korean people had a tradition of cleanliness and considered
the Chinese dirty. Koreans always bathed when they got up in the morning, and took two baths every day during the summer. Medieval Korean
people bathed naked together in the streams, regardless of gender.[18] If
Xu Jing's reports can be taken at face value, Buddhist influences may have
led medieval Koreans to add immersion bathing to their older tradition
of steam baths.

Similarly, in Japan, seventh-century myths emphasize the importance
the gods placed on bathing. Communal bathing was often linked to

Buddhism.[19] One later story set in the 1150s also involves swimming. In this story, Yoshinaka's father was in danger, and he took the precaution of hiding his pregnant wife in a peasant woman's hut. After Yoshinaka's father was indeed killed by his enemies, those enemies tracked his wife to the house of the peasant woman. As the women were running away, they split up to confuse the search, and the peasant woman ended up jumping into Lake Biwa and swimming towards some barges. But when she got near the barges, she was dismayed to find that they, too, were full of her enemies, who killed her. Yoshinaka's mother got away, and the hero was born safely.[20] This is not much to go on, but it suggests that, like West Asian people at the same time, East Asian people were slowly beginning to swim.

Odysseus and archaic Greece

Far away in Europe, African influence across the Mediterranean may also have encouraged Europeans to learn to swim. Europeans were not swimmers in the Bronze Age, at the time of the Trojan War. Bronze Age Greek images only depict people drowning. But in Homer's *Odyssey*, Odysseus knows how to swim. The *Odyssey* was first written down about 725–675 BCE, just a little later than the first Assyrian images of swimming. In Book 5, the hero Odysseus is shipwrecked and swims to shore:

> Cadmus' child . . . said . . .
> 'You seem intelligent. Do as I say.
> Strip off your clothes . . . With just your arms
> swim to Phaeacia . . . Here, take my scarf and tie it
> under your chest: with this immortal veil,
> you need not be afraid of death or danger.' . . .
> The hero . . . was troubled and confused . . .
> 'But when the waves have smashed my raft to pieces,
> then I will have no choice, and I will swim.'
> . . . he tied the scarf
> around his chest, and dove into the sea,
> spreading his arms to swim . . .
> Two days and nights he drifted on the waves:
> each moment he expected he would die . . .

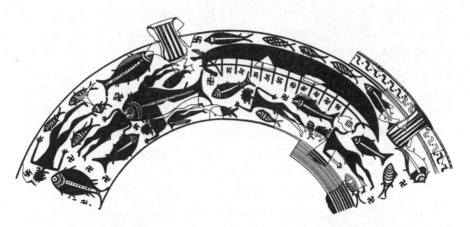

27 Another shipwreck scene on a ceramic vessel, but now one of the men in the water seems to be swimming an overhand stroke. The Pithekoussai Krater was made on the island of Ischia in Italy's Bay of Naples, 8th century BCE.

He swam until he reached a river's mouth
with gentle waters; that place seemed ideal.
... His legs cramped up;
The sea had broken him. His swollen body
gushed brine from mouth and nostrils. There he lay,
winded and silent, hardly fit to move.
A terrible exhaustion overcame him.[21]

Odysseus is pretty much the epitome of cool. If there was a new, trend-setting activity out there that Greek people were just becoming aware of, Homer's audience would of course expect Odysseus to be really good at it. And so he is – within limits. Even the hero Odysseus still needs a magic veil to help him swim.

Paintings on Greek vases agree that Southern Europeans learned to swim in the early Iron Age. As we have already seen, a Greek wine jug dated to about 725 BCE shows the same iconography of people falling off ships and drowning that we saw in Aegean Bronze Age frescoes. A ship has overturned and men – sometimes thought to represent Odysseus' men – have fallen off it and are drowning among the fish (see illus. 20). They are certainly not swimming; this is a disaster.[22] Many other more fragmentary Greek pots display versions of this shipwreck scene.[23] These scenes match what we know of the early Iron Age in Greece from Hesiod, who warned his readers against even urinating in the water.

But another Greek artist was already painting a slightly different shipwreck scene. This painter matched the *Odyssey*'s story by showing a person swimming. The scene was painted in the late 700s BCE in a Greek colony on the island of Ischia, in the Bay of Naples. Archaeologists found it there, buried in a rich Pithekoussan's tomb. (Pithekoussai is Ischia's ancient Greek name.) The krater, or wine-mixing bowl, is decorated with the familiar shipwreck scene. Underneath their overturned boat, the sailors are drowning. One on the right, perhaps already drowned, is being eaten by the usual giant fish. Some of the men may be missing their genitals – were they, too, eaten by the fish? But on the Pithekoussai krater, for the first time, one of the shipwrecked sailors is trying to swim. The man directly underneath the overturned boat has his arms going in different directions, as if he's performing a front crawl stroke (illus. 27).[24] Putting this together with Odysseus' swimming in the *Odyssey*, we can see that Europeans, like their Asian neighbours, first began to swim in the Iron Age. But how did they learn?

Just as with the Assyrians, Egyptian influences may have been the catalyst that convinced southern Europeans to enter the water. The late 700s BCE saw Egypt under the control of the Nubian king Piye, who energetically built new temples and reached out into the Mediterranean. The Greeks were paying attention. Homer tells us that Menelaus and Helen were eager to visit Egypt on their way home from Troy; they gathered amazing wealth and medicines there. The *Odyssey* itself may owe something to the Egyptian Middle Kingdom story of the shipwrecked sailor:

> A storm arose, which got more and more violent, and it blew up a wave eight cubits [high]. This wave drove a plank of wood towards me, and I grabbed it. As for the ship, those who were in it died. None of them escaped alive [except] me. And now you see me here by your side! A wave of the sea brought me to this island.[25]

People in the Iron Age Mediterranean were very much influenced by Egyptian trends, and these may have included swimming.

Another group of Africans could have taught Iron Age Europeans to swim. West of Egypt, Carthaginians were probably also good swimmers in the Iron Age. The arrival of colonizers from Tyre (in modern Lebanon) in the 800s BCE brought some non-swimmers to North Africa, but apparently not enough to change this habit. Roman historians emphasized Hannibal's swimming skills: he swims across unknown rivers. Stories from the Punic Wars describe how Carthaginian soldiers swam out in the bay to set Roman ships on fire, and how another troop of Carthaginians, defeated in battle, tried to swim back to their ships one night. Though many of them drowned in the darkness, they apparently knew how to swim.[26] Pliny's story about boys swimming with dolphins at Hippo shows that in the first century CE he still considered North Africans to be swimmers. We lack direct evidence for Carthaginian swimming in the early Iron Age, but probably, like other Africans, most of them could swim.

If so, Carthaginian traders may have brought their swimming skills across the Mediterranean to Europeans. The island of Ischia had been a small fishing town in the Stone Age, but by the Iron Age it had grown into a major Mediterranean trading centre. Both Carthaginian and Greek traders sailed to Ischia, to buy iron, timber, salt and enslaved people from Etruscans in Italy, the 'land of metal'. In exchange for these raw materials and captives, Carthaginian and Greek traders sold the Etruscans manufactured goods: Greek pottery, perfume and wine, Carthaginian glass beads and bronze pins, just as slave-trading Europeans sold rum and glass beads to West Africans centuries later. In the Iron Age, it was the Africans who were the sophisticates, and the Europeans who were being exploited.[27] Both the Greeks and the Etruscans learned a lot from their Carthaginian trade partners.

The Carthaginians, for example, seem to have taught Europeans to read. That Pithekoussai krater with the swimming sailor was made on the island of Ischia, by Greek potters and painters who lived alongside Carthaginian traders and their families. When Carthaginian babies died on the island, as babies too often did in those days, their families buried them in clay amphorae bearing funerary inscriptions in Punic, their parents' language. Archaeologists have excavated the tombs, so we know these inscriptions use alphabetic writing. The alphabet was still pretty new in the early Iron Age. It had been invented only a few hundred years earlier, probably in the Sinai Peninsula, and the colonizing Phoenicians had brought it west to Carthage. Now the Carthaginians seem to have taught the alphabet to their trade partners: the Etruscans and the Greeks.

The island of Ischia accordingly has a very early example of Greek writing. Of the two earliest known inscriptions in the Greek alphabet, one was found in Athens, and the other, the Cup of Nestor, on Ischia. The Cup of Nestor was probably made on the Aegean island of Rhodes in the 700s BCE and brought to Ischia by traders. At some time after the cup was fired, maybe after the wine cup came to Ischia, someone scratched on its side the oldest written reference to Homer's *Iliad*. The inscription, written from right to left like Hebrew or Punic, reads:

> Nestor's cup, good for drinking.
> Drink this cup empty, and right away
> You're seized with desire for beautiful Aphrodite.

The sentiment is familiar; wine still has that effect on drinkers today. The Cup of Nestor was buried in a Greek child's grave on Ischia soon after Homer wrote the *Iliad*, and about the same time that an unknown Greek potter on the same island painted a swimmer on the Pithekoussai krater.[28] Either the Carthaginians, or their Phoenician cousins, taught Ischia's Greek traders to write in the 700s BCE. They also taught the Etruscans, whose earliest writing follows the letter forms used on Ischia and was probably learned there. The Latin alphabet you are reading right now on this page is descended from this Etruscan form. Did the Carthaginians also teach their Greek and Etruscan trade partners to swim? The Carthaginians knew how to swim; the Greeks did not even have a word for swimming. The Pithekoussai krater with its swimming sailor encourages us to see the possibility.

Etruscans and Romans

Carthaginian traders may also have brought both swimming and writing to the Roman Republic. The Carthaginians carried on regular trade with the Romans during the early Roman Republic. Many Carthaginian traders and their families lived in Rome, mostly along the *vicus Africus*, Africa Street, on the Esquiline hill. Carthaginians also maintained trading bases along the coast a little north of Rome. These traders brought a variety of Mediterranean food to Rome: fish sauce (*garum*) and fish, pickled olives, garlic, nuts and fruit. They sold exotic African animals: monkeys, elephants, crocodiles, ostriches. They sold enslaved Black people from south of the Sahara. The Romans not only enjoyed Carthaginian luxuries and the service of enslaved Africans, but adopted Carthaginian customs, worshipping Carthaginian gods such as Melqart and Ba'al.[29] Roman families bought imported silver bowls from the eastern Mediterranean with Egyptianizing images of swimmers (or maybe drowning people) under the feet of the pharaoh. These are related to Assyrian battle images with swimmers from around the same time. Some of these swimmer bowls carry pseudo-hieroglyphic inscriptions; others bear words in Aramaic alphabetic characters.[30] So, like the Assyrians, Greeks and Etruscans, Romans may have also learned to swim from Africans.

Certainly the Romans, like the Greeks, thought their heroes should know how to swim. In Roman stories about the earliest days of the Roman Republic, heroes like Horatio are already swimming across the Tiber to safety. Another story has Gaius Mucius swim the Tiber in an attempt to assassinate the Etruscan king. In a third story, a young Roman woman named Cloelia and several other young women from powerful Roman families are sent over to the Etruscans as hostages. One night, Cloelia leads her fellow hostages in a daring swim across the Tiber to freedom. (But when the young women crawl dripping wet into their fathers' houses, their honourable fathers insist on sending them right back to the Etruscans.[31])

All of these stories are from the Roman historian Livy, writing hundreds of years later, but they tell us at least that later Romans thought their ancestors could swim. Diodorus Siculus, writing about the same time as Livy, agrees that early Romans could swim across the Tiber. He tells us that when the Romans were defeated by the Gauls, in the 300s BCE,

> Of the men who fled to the river the bravest attempted to swim across with their arms, prizing their armour as highly as their lives; but since the stream ran strong, some of them were borne down to their death by the weight of the arms, and some, after being carried along for some distance, finally and after great effort got off safe. But since the enemy pressed them hard and was making a great slaughter along the river, most of the survivors threw away their arms and swam across the Tiber.[32]

The Tiber River at Rome is about a hundred metres, or 330 feet, across, approximately four lengths of a standard swimming pool, and as Diodorus says, there's the current to consider. So swimming across the Tiber is not an astonishing swimming achievement, but it is far enough that you would have to really know how to swim.

More than their Assyrian neighbours, southern European artists soon moved beyond this sort of emergency swimming to depicting swimming as fun. On the François Vase, made in Athens about 570 BCE, one of Theseus' crew jumps spontaneously from the ship into the ocean, simply out of impatience to reach the shore (illus. 28). The sailor swims with a good crawl stroke and flutter kick, though he keeps his face out of the water. The giant fish of earlier shipwreck scenes have disappeared. This image might be a descendant, in a long line, of the Bronze Age drowning fresco of Akrotiri – there is still a boat in the scene – but there is no longer any sense of panic or disaster.

Similarly, southern Europeans liked to think of themselves as divers. In a sixth-century BCE Etruscan tomb painting, a boy strips off his cape and dives from a high cliff into the ocean; another boy climbs up behind him (see illus. 45). More divers appear painted on Etruscan vases.[33] The Etruscans' Greek neighbours in southern Italy also depicted themselves as divers, famously on a ceiling painting from the Tomb of the Diver, near Paestum in southern Italy, from the 400s BCE (illus. 29).[34] But were Iron Age Italians really skilled divers? The earliest Etruscan painted tombs date to the early sixth century BCE, not long after Europeans started to swim. The very existence of these painted chamber tombs, stocked with imitation goods for the afterlife, may show the influence of Egyptian ideas on southern Europe at this time. The tomb paintings may have symbolic

28 A man swims to shore from Theseus's boat using an overhand stroke, in a detail from the François Vase, Athens, *c.* 570 BCE.

29 A boy dives from a high platform, ceiling painting
from the Tomb of the Diver at Paestum, Italy, *c*. 470 BCE.

meaning, perhaps reflecting Egyptian ideas rather than embodying the
lived reality of the people buried there. Despite artists' depictions of artificial diving platforms in the Tomb of the Diver and on Greek red-figure
vases, archaeologists have not found any real diving platforms, so European
diving skills may have been mostly aspirational.

To sum up, in the Iron Age many non-swimming northerners, all
across Eurasia, were slowly learning to swim as they came into contact
with African and South Chinese swimmers. Carthaginians may have
taught southern Europeans to swim. Egyptians seem to have taught
Mesopotamians. Immigrants from South China may have influenced
North Chinese people to swim. Now some soldiers could save themselves
in an emergency by swimming across rivers, especially if they had inflated
goatskins to help them keep afloat. Some young people may have learned
to dive. Some of the more adventurous and athletic were even beginning
to swim voluntarily and enthusiastically, though they seem to have kept
their faces out of the water. But at this juncture, a new invasion of
non-swimming Central Asians disrupted matters, and chased many of
the new swimmers out of the water again.

Scythians and Thracians

Across northern Europe, in Russia, across Siberia and Mongolia, people
were still not swimming at all. They were too far north to be much

influenced by southern swimming cultures. They also were not yet using writing, which may not be coincidental. Because Central Asian northerners had not yet taken up writing, our knowledge of their swimming (or rather, of their reluctance to swim) comes not from Central Asians themselves but from their more literary neighbours, the Greek historians of the ancient Mediterranean. Herodotus is the first of these; most of the fourth book of his *Histories* describes the Scythian way of life. In Herodotus' time the Scythians were a powerful group who dominated most of Central Asia. Herodotus goes into exhaustive detail about them. He tells us accurately that the Scythians ride horses and keep herds of cattle, and that they practise archery, but he does not mention them swimming. As we have seen, Herodotus tells us that Scythians do not even bathe in water, but use steam baths or saunas instead. The Scythians' own images of themselves from this time confirm an extreme modesty. Scythian artists (and Greek artists) invariably depict both men and women wearing long sleeves and long baggy trousers, often with hats or hoods; Herodotus adds that even much further east, Central Asians 'wear Scythian clothing'.[35]

No other Central Asian people could swim either – not the Thracians, not Macedonians, or the Bithynians or Armenians. Thrace lies southwest of Scythian territory and closer to Greece, between the Black Sea and the Aegean. Like other Aegean people, many Thracians were pirates. In one story from the fifth century BCE, the Thracians sailed to Central Greece to raid the rich Greek city-state of Thebes. The Theban army, chasing the raiders off, drove the Thracians in panic back to their ships. But as the defenders forced the raiders into the sea, they found that the Thracians were drowning in the water. When the Thebans charged, the frightened crews on the Thracian ships had rowed the ships further out to sea, safely out of bowshot. The Thracian soldiers could not swim well enough to reach their ships.[36] This resembles the situation depicted by the Akrotiri fresco, and it contrasts with the Carthaginian troops who did swim out to their ships. Despite being pirates and having arrived on ships, none of the Thracians knew how to swim, not even enough to save their own lives in a crisis.

Next door to the Thracians, a little further west, the Macedonians also apparently could not swim. At least, Plutarch tells us that Alexander of Macedon bitterly regretted never having learned how. Alexander was a famous polymath. He made a point of learning everything that could possibly be useful to him in war. He knew all about hunting, riding, geography, the habits of the Persian court, medicine and history; if you could learn it in Macedon, Alexander was on it. If Alexander really could not swim, then swimming must have been pretty unusual in Macedon as well as among the Scythians and Thracians. Arrian does tell a story about Alexander swimming in the Cydnus River because he was hot and wanted to bathe, but even if that is true, and even if Arrian really meant swimming and not just wading, Plutarch certainly thought his readers would believe that Macedonian heroes might not know how to swim.[37]

Bithynians do not seem to have been able to swim either. Bithynia was a small country on the shores of the Black Sea in what is now northern Turkey, and the Bithynians were related to the Thracians to their northwest. Two centuries after Alexander's time, as the Romans were conquering West Asia, the Roman consul Sulla led a campaign against the Bithynian king Mithridates. History repeated itself: after the Romans beat Mithridates in battle, his Bithynian soldiers fled and the Romans drove many of the fleeing Bithynians into a neighbouring lake. Like their Thracian cousins before them, they could not swim, and they died (according to Appian) begging for mercy in their own 'barbarian' language.[38]

Jump forwards to the end of the Roman Empire, and Central Asians still could not swim. The Armenians lived between the Black Sea and the Caspian Sea, as they still do today. Their king, Para, escaped from Roman captivity with three hundred of his men. He was making his way back to Armenia when he encountered a river that he had great difficulty crossing because it was too deep to ford. His men, says the Late Roman historian Ammianus Marcellinus, 'were not skilful swimmers'.[39] People were learning to swim further south, but not yet in Central Asia.

The Persian Empire

In the sixth century BCE these Central Asians changed the new swimmers' attitudes. As they had in the Bronze Age, Central Asian non-swimmers migrated south into areas where people were starting to swim, and convinced them to stop. These invading Medes and Persians shared many of the customs of earlier Yamnaya migrants, including their religious restriction on entering the water. Now, as they assembled the Persian

Empire, the Medes and the Persians spread their fear throughout Southwest Asia, east to Pakistan and west to the Mediterranean.

Under Persian influence, swimming became unfashionable, and people gave it up. According to Xenophon's lengthy and hagiographic biography of the Persian king Cyrus, despite his heroism the king does not swim. Indeed, the *Cyropaedia* contains no mention of swimming at all. As among the Scythians, nudity was considered shameful to the Persians and an extreme modesty prevailed. Both men and women covered themselves in hats, long sleeves and patterned leggings. Women often wore long veils.[40] Herodotus opens his history with a reminder of the importance of modesty in Southwest Asia: 'since to the Lydians and most of the other barbarians near them it seems very shameful even for a man to be seen naked'.[41] Later Persian kings turned away from the sea, defining their empire in continental terms.[42] This Persian attitude ensured that swimming remained rare in Southwest Asia throughout antiquity.

Buddhism in India

Even as far south as the Deccan plateau in central India, stories speak of drowning rather than swimming. The important Indian epic poem the *Ramayana* was written down when the new alphabetic writing reached India about 300 BCE, four hundred years after it reached Europe. But unlike in Europe, the alphabet in India did not bring swimming in its wake. In the *Ramayana*, people bathe to be clean, and to be 'cleansed from sins', but nobody swims, not even animals. When Rama and Hanuman and their monkey army want to cross over the water to Sri Lanka to rescue Rama's wife, Sita, they build a huge bridge (it is actually a natural formation) instead of swimming.[43]

India's *Jataka Tales*, a collection of moral fables, funny stories and Buddhist parables, similarly include no human swimming. Indian Buddhist writers recorded the *Jataka Tales* about the same time as the *Ramayana*, using the same alphabet. (Many of the stories that Europeans know as *Aesop's Fables* are also found in the *Jataka Tales*; the relationship between the two collections remains unclear.) Shifting from the Hinduism of the Rig Veda and the *Ramayana* to the Buddhism of the *Jataka Tales* does nothing to abate Indian avoidance of water. In the *Jataka Tales* other animals swim: fish, elephants and crows, but not humans. Even the crow ends up being swept out to sea and drowned. In Indian stories people bathe, but they do not swim. Some bathe for health, like King Bimbisāra, an early Buddhist convert. The Buddha is said to have used hot springs medicinally, to relieve the pain from arthritis.[44] Others bathe to cool off: many stories describe bathing in springs or artificial bathing tanks, 'great tanks made for people to play in'. But nobody swims in the *Jataka Tales*, and the Buddha himself walks on water rather than swims. A first-century CE relief carving of a river crossing features scary river monsters.[45]

Most significantly, consider the Jataka story of Prince Mahajanaka, which parallels the Greek story of Odysseus, surely not coincidentally. Mahajanaka's uncle has usurped the throne, so when Mahajanaka grows up he takes a ship to get back home and demand his birthright. As with Odysseus, the ship is wrecked on the way. Prince Mahajanaka ties himself to the mast, because, unlike Odysseus, he does not know how to swim. He floats in the ocean for seven days, and then is rescued by a goddess. When he arrives, the hero reclaims his birthright by stringing a bow nobody else can string and solving riddles nobody else can solve. While Odysseus swims to shore when he is shipwrecked, his Indian counterpart Mahajanaka has to be saved.[46] Despite the apparent influence of Buddhist monks in encouraging bathing and perhaps swimming in East Asia, the same thing does not seem to have happened in India.

SLOWLY, STARTING IN the Late Bronze Age and extending into the Iron Age, most of the people who had lost the cultural practice of swimming in the Ice Age began to pick it up again. Their inspiration may have been the Egyptians and Carthaginians, Africans who knew how to swim, and who were at their most powerful at this time. But as the power of Persia and Rome grew and eclipsed the older African empires, these new swimmers shifted their perspective.

6

ANCIENT GREECE AND ROME

U p to this point we have been considering all these Central Asian northern non-swimmers and their descendants essentially as one group. But in the fifth century BCE there is a split: the Greeks and the Persians start to underscore their cultural differences and downplay their similarities. Greek men go naked while Persians cover up, they say. Greeks build temples, but Persians do not. Greeks have one wife, but Persians have many.[1] And the Greeks can swim, but the Persians cannot. This is not (yet) a racial distinction: they're not saying that the ability to swim is genetic or inborn, as indeed it certainly is not. The distinction is cultural, but it's nevertheless strong.

The Graeco-Persian Wars

What inspired this desire to emphasize cultural differences? A long, bitter war. When the Persians finished conquering Southwest Asia, they turned their attention to Europe. Under their kings Darius and Xerxes, the Persians first demanded that the Greeks submit to them, and then made a series of attacks on Greece, apparently hoping to extend their power into the Aegean Sea. The Persians succeeded in taking control of Thrace and Macedonia, but then, to everybody's surprise, the Greeks repelled the Persian attacks and succeeded in keeping their independence. As part of this struggle, Greek writers drew sharp lines dividing Greek culture from Persian culture, emphasizing among other things that the Greeks knew how to swim, and the Persians did not. Again, this was not yet a racial distinction, but a cultural divide.[2]

Greek accounts of the Persian Wars (as the Greeks called them) stress the Persian troops' inability to swim. Herodotus tells us about the First Persian War, in 490 BCE, that the Persian admiral Mardonius' wrecked fleet were not swimmers. When Mardonius' fleet was wrecked in a storm, 'some were dashed against the rocks, and others died because they did not know how to swim; and others of the cold.' Pausanias' later account of the Battle of Marathon, in the same war, may indicate that many of the Persian soldiers drowned as they fled the battlefield: 'At Marathon there is a lake that is very swampy. Not knowing the roads, the fleeing foreigners fell into the lake, and people say that this accident caused their great losses.'[3] It is not quite clear whether the Persian soldiers drowned or were slaughtered in the water, but Pausanias agrees with Herodotus that the Persians are culturally different from the Greeks, who do know how to swim.

The inability of the Persians to swim is even more central to the Greeks' version of the Second Persian War, ten years later. During Xerxes' attack on Thermopylae in northern Greece, a Greek diver named Scyllias is said to have cut the anchor cables of the Persian fleet, so that many Persian ships were wrecked on the rocks. Or, in a slightly different version, Scyllias dived to recover the treasure that was lost with Xerxes' pontoon boats.[4] Nevertheless, the Greeks lost the land battle of Thermopylae, and had to defend themselves again at the Battle of Salamis, near Athens. Salamis was a naval battle, and this time the Greeks won. Many Persian ships were wrecked. Their crew and the soldiers on the ships were forced into the water. Herodotus tells us that the Greeks involved were able to swim to save themselves, but the Persians drowned:

> Many other famous men of the Persians and Medes and other allies also died, but only a few Hellenes [Greeks], since they knew how to swim. Those whose ships were sunk swam across to Salamis, unless they were killed in action, but many of the barbarians drowned in the sea since they did not know how to swim.[5]

Herodotus' non-swimming barbarians were not primarily Persians, but they were West Asians. The Persians were no sailors, so the Persian fleet was built and crewed partly by Persian allies and partly by Greeks who were Persian subjects. Herodotus draws a cultural distinction between the ethnically Greek crew on the Persian ships, who knew how to swim, and the Persians and their other allies, who did not.[6]

The Roman story of Horatio at the bridge, which is set about the same time as the Persian wars, seems similarly to use swimming as an ethnic marker differentiating the Romans from their enemies. Horatio heroically holds off the Etruscans as his Roman comrades destroy the bridge over the Tiber. Once the bridge is down, Horatio swims across the river, but his enemies cannot follow. Do these fictional Etruscans not know how to swim? Centuries later, a Roman relief similarly shows Dacian soldiers from northern Europe drowning in the Danube. Whether this scene is fact or fiction, the drowning soldiers on Trajan's Column in Rome reinforce the ethnic distinction that swimming is for Greeks and Romans, and not for 'barbarians'.[7]

Sophisticated swimmers

Greek and Roman authors drew a second cultural distinction around swimmers as well: almost as soon as they learned to swim, they considered swimming to be an elite activity, suitable for rich, powerful people and not for their subordinates. In the *Iliad*, swimming may still appear as a lower-class skill. The hero Achilles cannot swim out of the river, but Patroclos taunts one of the Trojans as he falls headlong from his chariot, saying, 'By the gods, what a nimble man! How smoothly he dives! If only he were on the fish-haunted sea, he could support a large family by diving from a boat and bringing up oysters, even in a storm. Apparently there are divers even among the Trojans.'[8] Why is this funny? Because oyster-diving is a low-class occupation. But already in the *Odyssey*, swimming is identified with social class: it is a skill Odysseus has, and his crew lacks. Possibly this idea stemmed from Europeans' having learned to swim from sophisticated Egyptians and Carthaginians. Maybe it was reinforced when only rich traders and ambassadors and their children learned to swim. Certainly by the time of Herodotus, in the fifth century BCE, swimming, despite requiring no expensive equipment or clothing, was a marker of the upper class. When Herodotus describes Persian customs, he claims that the Persians 'teach [their sons] only three things: riding and archery and honesty.'[9] Herodotus does not need to remind his readers, but a

Greek proverb of his time described people who were uneducated as 'not knowing how to read or swim', the way we might say someone could not read or write. Plato mentions this proverb several times, and so do later writers like Aelius Aristides.[10] Herodotus seems to be suggesting that ignorant Persian barbarians teach their children *only* riding and archery. This sets the Persians apart from the Greeks, and from other civilized people like Egyptians.

By the late Republic, swimming seems to have been a fairly normal entertainment for the upper strata of Roman society. A friend of Cicero's was 'most studious of swimming'. The poet Ovid, exiled to the Black Sea, sadly remembered his happier days as a boy swimming in the cold waters of the Aqua Virgo in Rome; Seneca swam there too. Young men from rich families played and swam in the Tiber to impress young women.[11] In the second century CE, Greek festivals of Dionysos were even hosting swimming races with prizes alongside their boat races.[12] But not all Romans could swim: when Strabo describes Sicilian mineral lakes like Israel's Dead Sea, he mentions that 'even people who can't swim don't sink, but float on the surface like wood.'[13] Romans seem to have considered these non-swimmers to have been lower-class: note that the biblical Peter, though he is a fisherman, cannot swim.

In a society where many people cannot swim, swimming is a good class marker. Learning to swim well takes time, and you need access to clean beaches or pools. For upstarts, swimming is difficult and dangerous to fake. That is why Plato's proverb associates reading and swimming: swimming is something only educated people can do, the same few rich people who know how to read.[14] Centuries after Odysseus and Plato, Julius Caesar still used swimming to emphasize his status as a member of the most powerful class of Romans. When Caesar was travelling around Gaul, he often chose to swim the rivers he came to rather than go around to a ford, and as a result he often got where he was going ahead of his own (non-swimming) advance scouts. Even at 52 years old, Caesar was still a strong swimmer. When an Egyptian mob rose up against Caesar in Alexandria, he escaped by

> jumping into the sea and swimming two hundred paces [about 150 metres] to the next ship, with his left hand held up high, so the papers he was holding would not get wet. He clamped his

teeth on his general's cloak to drag it along, so it would not fall into the hands of the enemy.

If all Romans had known how to swim, Caesar's accomplishment would not have seemed so exciting.[15]

Women and swimming

As the wealthy Greek and Roman upper class began to swim for fun, a fair number of women also learned to swim. In the earliest representations, only men swim: Odysseus but not Nausicaa. By the time of the Persian Wars, Greek vase painters depicted women swimming, but they are probably not Greek women: they are Amazons, as we can see from their characteristic hats hanging from nearby hooks or branches (illus. 30). The two known examples are so much alike that they probably represent a familiar genre. In both images, one woman swims on the left, one dives from a platform in the centre and two other women stand by. A third Greek vase depicts a woman swimming above dolphins – or is she a sea nymph?[16] What does this mean? Athenians were well aware that Scythians – the usual real-life avatars of Amazons – did not swim, while Greeks did. Is the representation of these women as Amazons merely a fig leaf to propriety? Perhaps the safest route is to take these vases to represent imaginary scenes, but that may be playing it too safe: it is also entirely possible that some Greek women were swimming by this time.[17]

A few centuries later, at least some elite Roman women had learned to swim, perhaps as part of a more general change in women's status in the first century CE.[18] The collapse of the Roman Republic and the beginning of the empire took power from the senators and gave it to the family of the emperor Augustus. Women in that family – Julia, Livia, Messalina, Agrippina – gained access to power in ways that would have been unthinkable a generation earlier. The Christian apostle Paul of Tarsus was not the only powerful man who defended his privilege by telling women to sit down and shut up, though he may be the best known.[19] Possibly these New Women (as Elaine Fantham calls them) also marked their improved status by swimming. All we know is that Augustus' great-granddaughter, the Roman regent Agrippina the Younger, was said to be a strong swimmer. Both Suetonius and Tacitus report that Agrippina saved herself

30 Women, probably intended as Amazons, swimming an overhand stroke and diving, on an Athenian vase attributed to the Andokides Painter, *c.* 520 BCE.

from her son Nero's assassination attempt by swimming across a lake, even after having been stabbed in the shoulder.[20] For Roman women as for modern ones, feminism may have included the freedom to swim.

And yet Roman authors still associated swimming with sexual assault and rape. As we have seen, Ovid associates women's swimming with sex in his *Ars amatoria*, and he extends this idea in the *Metamorphoses* with many stories of women assaulted or raped while bathing. The Roman poet Propertius describes his lover Cynthia swimming while on holiday in southern Italy, where she flirts with men. Other Roman writers also hint at this association. One version of the story of Scyllias cutting the Persian anchor cables also includes Scyllias' daughter Hydna, whom he had taught to dive, and who came along on the adventure. This late version adds the improbable assertion that in order to dive, a woman has to be a virgin; this shimmer of virginity may have enhanced the erotic atmosphere of the Greek vases showing naked Amazons swimming and diving.[21] The Roman ruler Tiberius was said to train enslaved little boys, 'whom he called his "minnows", to chase him while he went swimming and get between his legs to lick and nibble him'. Domitian is said to have swum with sex workers. The Roman poet Martial also refers to sex in the pool, while the later emperor Elagabalus apparently hosted infamous pool parties.[22] Nilotic mosaics and paintings from the northern Mediterranean, set in Egyptian landscapes, frequently mock swimming by depicting drowning pygmies and sexualized scenes.[23] Swimming remained, for both Greeks and Romans, transgressive and likely to result in terrible consequences.

Still anxious in the water

As in Assyria and China, Europeans remained nervous and awkward swimmers, fearful of the water, associating swimming with drowning. Despite the modern desire to see ancient swimmers as confident and skilled models for us to emulate, Greek and Roman sources instead betray an ongoing concern with the dangers of swimming.[24] In Euripides' metaphor, you cannot save yourself from misfortunes by swimming.[25] Rumour had it that the Greek playwright Menander drowned while swimming in the ocean at Piraeus, the port of Athens. As a precaution against this danger, in case of exhaustion or cramp, Roman rescuers were instructed to hold tired swimmers up by their chins. Ovid pictures the sea in terms of shipwreck and drowning; he, too, in metaphor, is 'afraid of every sea'.[26] Jesus and Peter, like the Buddha, walk on the sea rather than swim in it. Tacitus describes the 'monster-filled sea'.[27] The Roman poet Oppian, though he advises fishers to learn to swim, contrasts the safer occupation of hunting with the dangers of fishing on the wild, unpredictable ocean. Rather than imagining fish men coming up on land and marrying swimming women, as Hawaiians did, Oppian sees the underwater world as a reflection or opposite of the terrestrial human world.[28]

Though some Greeks and Romans ventured into the water for fun, many others sought swimming's purported medical benefits. Swimming, whether in bathhouses, at warm springs or in cold water, was used to treat even the most serious medical situations. For paralysis, perhaps as rehabilitation after polio or a stroke, doctors suggested the patient should swim in mineral waters, preferably at warm springs, or in the sea. At first, 'an inflated bladder should be attached to the paralysed parts to reduce the effort required in swimming.'[29] Celsus recommends pouring cold water over the patient, and having them swim in cold water at medicinal springs. He even suggests water as a cure for rabies: in desperate cases, patients with hydrophobia (a symptom of rabies combining enormous thirst with an inability to drink) should be submerged 'by surprise' in a tank of water. If they cannot swim, let them sink to the bottom so they will drink water, he says, and if they can swim, hold them under to force them to drink.[30] Ancient doctors could do nothing effective to treat rabies, and of course this treatment would not work, but it does show that swimming was far from universally expected.

Roman doctors also assigned both ocean swimming and bathing as medical cures for less serious illnesses. This idea may derive from earlier Southwest Asian practices that we have seen in the Torah, and those in turn to the earlier Eurasian sense of water as sacred. The orator Aelius Aristides, chronically ill with a variety of shifting symptoms, often swam in rivers as part of his prescribed treatments; he mentions fifteen different visits to either hot springs or a river for medical purposes. He had a particular faith in rapidly moving cold water. At Pergamum (now in Turkey), Aelius swam in a stream so cold it was frozen over. Alarmingly, his prescription seems to have involved forgoing the warm towel or robe you might expect after such plunges, and instead sitting on the bank and air-drying in the cold.[31] Most people seem to have satisfied themselves instead with ordinary bathhouses. Roman baths could have special hours reserved for sick people; apparently, as at our swimming pools, these were the less busy mid-morning hours.[32]

Many healthy people also swam to maintain their health. The poet Horace, for example, mentions that healthy people should swim three times across the Tiber as a way to tire themselves out and get a good night's sleep. Horace followed many ancient medical writers in thinking you should 'grease up' before swimming: protect your skin by coating it with olive oil before diving into the water.[33] Both in Roman thought and in the early medieval Talmud, plunging in cold water, or taking cold baths, is morally and medicinally superior to warm or hot water, presumably because it feels worse, but ancient bathers also visited the hot springs at Thermopylae, Bath, Aachen and elsewhere.[34] Here, too, the anxiety lies just below the surface. In Hippocratic writing, medical opinion is pretty sure bathing will not hurt you, even if you bathe twice in the same day (a practice that was standard in much of the rest of the world).

Partly perhaps because it seemed safer, many Greek swimmers seem to have preferred artificial pools to natural ones. Andocides' red-figure vase painting of Amazon women swimming includes a slender column on the far right, and hooks on the wall where the Amazons have hung their characteristic hats, to show that this is an artificial pool and not a natural pond. Plato also mentions swimming pools metaphorically: 'the fact is that when a man is out of his depth, whether he has fallen into a little swimming bath or into mid-ocean, he has to swim all the same.'[35] Archaeologically, by the fifth century BCE a large swimming pool was associated with the ancient Greek Olympic Games. This pool was about half as big as a modern Olympic swimming pool, but only just over a metre and a half (5 ft) deep: shallow enough for most adults to stand in. No Greek athletic competitions included swimming events; this pool was to relax in after the foot-races and wrestling.[36] If the fresco painting of the Tomb of the Diver and the Greek vases depicting Amazons swimming are to be taken literally (though so far no archaeological evidence backs this up), Greek people may also have preferred artificial diving platforms to cliffs.

Swimming pools

The transition to artificial swimming pools accelerates with the transition from the Roman Republic to the Roman Empire. In the late Republic, as we have seen, Horace and Ovid swam in the Tiber, which ran along one side of ancient Rome, or in the canal formed by the Aqua Virga running along the Campus Martius. But in subsequent generations, due partly to the construction of new housing in this area as Rome's population grew, many Romans preferred artificial swimming pools. These were constructed and used throughout the Roman Empire.[37] The first such pools were ostentatious luxuries associated with dissipation. According to the historian Josephus, King Herod (the one who condemned John the Baptist and Jesus) enjoyed artificial diving pools in Jericho. Herod's patron, the Roman emperor Tiberius, had a lovely private pool on the island of Capri. A little later on, the wealthy politician Pliny the Younger had not one but two private swimming pools at his villa in Tuscany in northern Italy: a small indoor cold pool, and a larger and warmer outdoor pool.[38]

Public swimming pools soon followed. People swam in the water supplied by aqueducts to the *frigidaria* of famous Roman bath buildings.

The *frigidarium*, or cold bath, of the Baths of Caracalla in Rome covered the whole of a gigantic room in the front of the building. This large *frigidarium* measured 56 × 24 metres, which is more than twice as big as most city swimming pools today. Perhaps for safety's sake, or to save on water, this pool was only about 3 or 4 feet deep. You could swim in it, but it would be difficult for an adult to drown. The *frigidarium* at the Baths of Diocletian, also in Rome, was about the same size and the same depth. At the Stabian Baths in Pompeii, though the *frigidarium* was small, there was a large outdoor pool, the *natatio*, which would have been suitable for swimming, as the name suggests. Similar open pools were common throughout the Roman Empire, and many survive today, from the Baths of Gallienus at Volubilis in modern Morocco to the Public Baths of Odessos in modern Bulgaria.[39] There was a real lap pool, deep enough to dive in, at the *gymnasium* at Herculaneum, but lap pools were certainly much less common than shallow pools.[40]

This turn from rivers to swimming pools is sometimes said to have decreased the swimming ability of Roman soldiers. But as the accounts of writers like Aelius Aristides show, bathing in rivers was still possible long after the baths were constructed.[41] Modern historians often cite the Late Roman military historian Vegetius, who lamented that Roman soldiers no longer trained on the Campus Martius 'because it was near the Tiber, so the young men could wash off the sweat and dust in the river, and refresh themselves by swimming after their training'.[42] But Vegetius is writing centuries later, and (like too many modern historians) he is thinking of an idealized past; real Roman soldiers were probably always poor swimmers even before public baths became common.

Ancient swimming strokes

Swimmers in the ancient world pretty much universally used something like a front crawl stroke with a flutter kick. That's what we see Egyptians doing as far back as that early hieroglyph in the Old Kingdom, with separated straight arms and straight legs (see illus. 2). Hittite and Assyrian images also show swimmers with one arm ahead of them and the other behind them (see, for example, illus. 23, 24 and 25). The very first Greek swimmer on the Pithekoussai krater has his arms in a front crawl too. On the François Vase, the swimmer strikes the same pose. A first-century CE mosaic from the bath of a villa near Pompeii seems to show two figures using a rather inexpert crawl stroke as well (though with fingers spread). Ancient literature agrees: Propertius has his Cynthia swim 'arm over arm'. Throughout Roman literature, people swim *alternaque bracchia ducens*, 'with alternating arms'. A few ancient lines may hint at the breast-stroke: Manilius has a swimmer draw his hands apart underwater. Statius has Leander's arms 'striving like oars'; Silius Italicus has his Nereids 'rotate their white arms in the clear water'. But the breaststroke is completely absent from ancient imagery. Only one text hints at the backstroke: in the *Phaedrus*, Plato/Socrates suggests that a man 'swimming on his back against the current' is behaving foolishly, and this may be meant as an inversion of what he should be doing. The one figure lying on his back in a Nilotic wall painting from Pompeii may also be intended as a humorous inversion, or a comment on how different African swimming was. Manilius suggests that a swimmer might lie on his back 'keeping his limbs motionless', floating, but not swimming.[43] In the northern Mediterranean, the alternating overhand stroke was usual.

It may seem surprising, then, that unlike Egyptian and (perhaps) Assyrian swimmers, few Greeks and Romans ever brought themselves to swim with their faces in the water. The swimming woman on the Andocides vase keeps her head up, out of the water. On the François Vase, the swimmer also holds his head high up at an awkward angle. A small cupid on a fragment of a later cameo glass plate (illus. 32) seems to be holding his head up out of the waves. A fresco painting from a house in Pompeii, buried in the volcanic eruption of October 79 CE, has Leander swim across the Hellespont to his lover, Hero. Leander is clearly using the front crawl stroke, and his extended legs show us a flutter kick. But once again, Leander's arched neck suggests that his head is out of the water (illus. 31). Other images of Leander from wall paintings at Pompeii

31 Leander swimming across the Hellespont (Dardanelles) to his lover Hero, painted lunette from a tomb near Morlupo, *c.* 30 BCE.

32 Boy swimming, on a fragment of a Roman cameo glass plate, 1st century CE.

show him in a similar pose.[44] Ovid also seems to think that Leander's head only goes under when he is failing to swim, rather than as a natural part of swimming: 'the swollen water opposed my boyish attempt, and, swimming against the waves, my mouth was submerged.'[45]

Statius describes an embroidery of the Leander and Hero story in terms that may suggest that Leander's face is in the water: 'He is seen with one hand coming in to his side, and about to change arms; you would not believe that his hair in the picture is dry.'[46] But surely we should take this as hyperbole, in the service of Statius' point that the embroidery is extremely lifelike. One last instance clarifies that Romans preferred to keep their hair dry. Not long before the fall of Rome, when the empresses Pulcheria and Eudocia were sharing power, the southern Egyptian epic poet Nonnus wrote an account in Greek of how the priestess Semele met her lover Zeus. Nonnus tells us that Zeus first noticed Semele as she swam in the Asopus River to clean off the blood from sacrificing a bull to him. (Notice again the association between blood and water.)

> There the girl cleaned her body, and naked with her slaves, moved through the water with hands paddling like oars; she kept her

head dry, stretched well above the stream by her practised skill, under water only just to the hairline, pushing her chest through the stream and pressing the water back with alternating feet.[47]

Semele is clearly still swimming with her face out of the water, even in Egypt, and even at the end of the Roman Empire.

Swim lessons and gear

Because European swimmers thought swimming was hard to master and dangerous, they thought learning to swim required extensive, difficult lessons. While in Africa and the Americas children learned to swim informally as soon as they could walk, upper-class Roman children learned to swim with more formal lessons when they were older, sometimes from (often enslaved) professionals and sometimes, like African children, from their parents or grandparents. Plutarch tells us that the Roman politician Cato the Elder is said to have taught his son 'how to stand heat and cold and to force his way through the eddies and roughness of the river'. Cato was famously tough, and Plutarch's point here is that he is teaching his son to be tough too: to Cato, or to Plutarch, swimming is unpleasant and dangerous, and you have to be strong to do it successfully. Suetonius takes a slightly different tack, and describes how the emperor Augustus 'usually instructed his grandsons himself in reading, swimming and other rudiments of knowledge'.[48] Suetonius' description parallels, surely intentionally, Plato's old proverb that educated people know how to read and to swim. In their lessons, children learned to swim wearing chunks of cork wood or hollow gourds tied around them, until they could 'swim without cork', a common Roman metaphor for the ability to act independently. Alternatively, the Talmud envisions building a wooden 'swimmer's barrel' to help 'beginners' learn to swim. Or adults placed children learning to swim on a raft of woven wicker, and the children paddled the raft with their hands, as children today lie on a foam pad and kick their feet while the instructor tows them around the pool.[49] These methods were similar to those used in Africa (as we will see), and both the cork wood and the gourds may have come originally from there; these methods of teaching swimming may even have been learned from Africans. But the Roman conception of swimming as an arduous elite activity diverges from the swimming we have seen in other parts of the world, where all children learned to swim almost as soon as they learned to walk.

EVEN AS THEY continued to associate swimming with Europe and Africa, and to use their skill in the water to contrast themselves with the Parthians to the east, the Greeks and Romans also came to associate swimming with education and wealth. Most ordinary Europeans had not learned to swim, and those who had were the ones most in contact with international trade and diplomacy – the rich and powerful. But if swimming was now emblematic of the upper class, what did that mean for the decidedly plebeian Roman military?

7

SOLDIERS AND DIVERS

Much of what we know about Greek and Roman swimming comes from historians' accounts of military expeditions. From these we can see that soldiers entered the water reluctantly, and only for short distances. They considered swimming difficult and risky. Thus Xenophon, in the fourth century BCE, tells a story about soldiers wading across a river who stripped naked so they would be able to swim if necessary (though in the end they only waded). Again, some of Alexander's troops swam to safety from their wrecked ships, perhaps because they were 'sailing quite near the land'. On a third occasion, other soldiers swam to shore from boats within bowshot of the beach. As Arrian tells it, Alexander's admiral Nearchus planned an (unprovoked) attack on villagers along the desert coast of what is today Pakistan. He ordered those of his men who were the best swimmers to dive overboard and swim until they found their footing, then wait for the other soldiers, form up a phalanx and attack, which they did successfully.[1]

In Italy, people considered swimming to be even riskier and more dangerous than the Greeks did, and not everyone knew how to swim. Although the Greek historian Diodorus Siculus had the Roman troops retreating successfully from the Gauls in 387 BCE by swimming across the Tiber, his Roman contemporary Livy reports instead that many of these men drowned because they could not swim. During the Second Punic War, when Hannibal trapped Roman cavalrymen defending Naples, 'those who were good swimmers' escaped by swimming out to nearby fishing boats, but others, even among this group of young men 'from noble families', were killed. When one of the Carthaginian general Hasdrubal's captured Italian guides escaped by crossing a river, the guide performed this feat not by swimming (as many translations have it) but by wading across a ford: *per vada nota Metaurum flumen transavit*.[2]

Still further west, Hannibal's Spanish troops' frequent use of flotation devices to cross rivers suggests that few of them could swim. On their way to Italy in 218 BCE these soldiers used inflated skins to cross the Rhône. According to Livy, 'they threw their clothes on to [inflated] skins and placing their leather shields on the top they rested on these and so swam across.' That is, they 'swam' across in the same way that earlier Assyrians did, by sitting on inflated bags. Livy also reports a story that Hannibal's elephants swam the Rhône. Strabo knew, as we have seen, that elephants can swim, but, like Pliny, Livy does not believe it; he prefers another version of the story in which the elephants crossed on rafts. Livy is similarly sceptical of stories where Hannibal's army used their inflated skins again to swim the Po in northern Italy. Livy thinks it is more likely that they built a bridge. But Spanish soldiers were still using their inflated skins to cross rivers two centuries later. Julius Caesar, who usually relied on bridge-building to get his own troops across rivers, reports that whenever these Spanish troops were called up, they always brought their inflatable skins with them.[3] It begins to look as though swimming was less familiar as you moved further west. Many Greek soldiers could swim a little, though they avoided it. In Italy some cavalrymen could swim, though others could not. And in Spain nobody could swim, and soldiers carried flotation devices with them to cross rivers.

Lake Trasimene

We should not be surprised, therefore, to find that most Roman infantry soldiers could not swim. The famous example is the great battle of Lake Trasimene in the Second Punic War. In June 217 BCE Hannibal ambushed the Roman army in northern Italy and forced about 10,000 Roman foot soldiers into the lake. The trapped soldiers waded out until the water was up to their shoulders, but then were afraid to venture beyond their depth. 'An unreasoning terror drove some to try to escape by swimming,' but Livy portrays this as a last resort: 'in that vastness it was hopeless.' Soon 'their spirits failed them and they sank in the abyss.' Polybius (who was Greek and perhaps knew how to swim) blames the soldiers' failure to swim on their heavy armour, but in Livy it's the distance and the deep water. Most of the soldiers drowned, or waded back to the shallows, where Hannibal's cavalry killed them. None escaped.[4] Yet Lake Trasimene is only 10 kilometres (6 mi.) across, and swimming even a couple of kilometres would have taken them to one of several islands in the lake. Surely at least a few of these strong young soldiers in fear for their lives, if they had been good swimmers, would have reached the islands? Could they not have cut their armour off with their knives? In the Maori story, Hinemoa swam that far to reach her lover. Byron swam 5 kilometres (3 mi.) across the Hellespont in much rougher water just for fun, and fit swimmers today routinely swim 1.5 kilometres in swimming pools; ordinary triathlons require participants to swim the same distance in open water.

Later anecdotes confirm that many legionaries could not swim. In the Third Macedonian War, in 171 BCE, Roman troops panicked when they were forced to swim across a river at night. Appian has two of Lepidus' legions drowning in the ocean, with only a few soldiers apparently able to swim. In Spain, fleeing Roman soldiers again tried to swim out to their waiting boats and, while some succeeded, others drowned. Another of Caesar's soldiers 'plunged into the muddy current, and at last, without his shield, partly swimming and partly wading, got across'. Throughout Caesar's memoir, the *Gallic Wars*, the depth of rivers recurs as a military factor, apparently because shallow rivers can be forded, but Caesar preferred to build bridges over deep ones. When Caesar's ships approached the British coast, similarly, his men were reluctant to disembark because the water was too deep, and the higher-ranked standard-bearer had to rally them. Cicero riffs on this incident in a letter to his protégé Trebatius, joking that the aristocratic Trebatius may be an excellent swimmer, but he's no more eager to leap into the Channel than Caesar's ordinary troops. Thus despite the Roman military writer Vegetius' advice that 'every new recruit, without exception, should be taught to swim in the summer,' we may doubt whether this really happened.[5] Even if it did, the assumption that new recruits will not know how to swim, and will need to be taught, betrays the general tendency of the Roman populace.

Roman auxiliaries

Although Roman historians and modern ones alike tend to claim that northern European auxiliary troops were better swimmers than the regular Roman infantry, surely this was not the case.[6] We have already seen that European swimming skills declined sharply from east to west, and northern Europeans probably did not swim even as well as the Spanish with their inflated skins. More likely, Roman generals chose to protect their legions by deploying auxiliaries in dangerous situations, under the convenient pretence that the auxiliaries were excellent swimmers. Neither of the two early examples we have where northern Europeans get in the water suggests that they were good swimmers. In the first, Germans fleeing from a Roman attack try to swim across the Rhine, 'relying on their strength', apparently unsuccessfully. In the second, when fleeing Germans are pushed to the banks of the river, they despair instead of swimming. When they throw themselves in, it is suicide rather than escape: they all drown, 'overcome by fear, exhaustion, and the violence of the stream'.[7] This seems to refute the claims made by Cassius Dio and Tacitus that strong swimming was part of German culture (*ethos* in the Greek, *patrius* in the Latin).

Instead, the claim that auxiliary troops were good swimmers masks a tendency for Roman generals to risk the auxiliaries rather than the regular troops, given the poor swimming abilities of both groups. The Roman general Agricola used auxiliaries in just this way when he was invading Britain. His mission, in 77 CE, was to capture the island of Mona: today's Anglesey, just off the coast of Wales. When Agricola ordered a surprise attack, the British felt secure on the island as the Romans waited for their boats to arrive. They had some reason to think so, because in the first invasion of Mona some years earlier, Paulinus had indeed 'built flat-bottomed boats to cope with the shallows and uncertain depths of the sea. The infantry crossed that way, and the cavalry followed by fording, or, where the water was deeper, swam next to their horses.'[8] But in this second invasion in 77 CE, Tacitus claims that the Batavi, Agricola's auxiliary troops, surprised the British by swimming across the narrow Menai Strait.[9]

We can certainly see why Agricola did not want to risk his highly trained legions on a mission swimming into unfamiliar waters under enemy fire. Both Tacitus and Cassius Dio assert that the Batavi, from the northern Rhine delta in what is now the Netherlands, were famously good swimmers who could swim across even the roughest water while also managing their armour, their weapons and their horses.[10] But how true is this claim? Can even skilled swimmers successfully swim an ocean strait while wearing their armour and carrying weapons? Polybius did not think so when it was Roman legionaries at Lake Trasimene. The story seems fishy.

In fact, the Menai Strait hardly requires swimming. It is very shallow, and also tidal, and only about 400 metres (¼ mi.) across. You can ford the Menai Strait in the middle of summer, when the tide is right, and indeed Tacitus admits that it was midsummer, and that the Batavi 'knew where the fords were'. They probably rode their horses across the strait, just as Paulinus' cavalry had earlier. Agricola did not send his auxiliaries because they could swim. He sent them because the tidal currents in the narrow strait are fast and tricky, so the Batavi were riding under very difficult conditions into unknown danger.

Similarly, in his discussion of the Batavian revolt of 69 CE, Tacitus claims that while 'the Roman soldier is . . . afraid to swim,' the Batavian soldier is 'favoured by . . . the height of his stature'. Why does his height matter? Because the Batavians are wading and not swimming: they are taller, so they can better manage the 'hidden perils from the varying depth of the fords'. In 43 BCE, Britons 'knew where the firm ground and the easy passages in this region were to be found; but the Romans in attempting to follow them were not so successful'.[11] Both Batavians and British were wading, not swimming.

Professional divers

This false idea that auxiliaries could swim may owe something to Roman writers' awareness that many of the poorest Mediterranean workers, free or enslaved, swam for their work. Some were fishers. We have already seen that Oppian thought fishers should know how to swim, though probably not all of them did. He mentions divers who catch spiny fish and fishers who leap into the sea to poison nets. The fifth-century CE poet Ausonius also mentions fishers diving to retrieve their prey. Military divers swam across the bay at Sphacteria to bring food to the beseiged

Spartans, and sawed off wooden stakes blocking the harbour of Syracuse. They swam and cut the anchor cables of enemy ships, as when Alexander was besieging the city of Tyre.[12] Roman sources describe the *urinatores*, professional divers who helped with salvage operations for shipwrecks in shallow waters (the name refers to the oil they dribbled out of their mouths, and not to urine). These divers worked only in relatively shallow water and perhaps were not so badly off.[13]

But thousands of much more unfortunate Mediterranean divers descended to the deep ocean floor seeking pearl oysters, red coral for jewellery, murex shells for dyeing cloth and sponges used for padding, for bathing and as water filters. For these divers, swimming was unpleasant and dangerous. Sponge divers in particular sometimes had to dive so deep that their eardrums burst. The divers tried to save their ears through various means: they slit their ears and nostrils, they tied sponges over their ears or they poured olive oil into them. Greek sponge divers also sometimes deliberately (and painfully) punctured their own eardrums in order to reach the sea floor faster, without needing to wait for the pressure in their ears to equalize. The economic pressures on these divers outweighed the water pressure.[14] Oppian says there is 'no worse work nor any work more miserable' than sponge-diving:

> They are careful to prepare ahead to get good breaths before they work in the depths . . . A man has a long rope wound around his waist and, using both hands, in one he holds a heavy lump of lead and in his right hand he holds a pointed beak, while he holds shining oil in the jaws of his mouth. Standing on the ship's prow he looks at the sea's swells, turning over in his mind his heavy work and the unending water. The others use brave words to encourage him and urge him on to his work . . . when he leaps into the depths, the tug of the heavy grey lead drags him down. Now when he gets to the seabed . . . he sees the sponges stuck to the rocks; they grow on the flat shelves of the ocean floor . . . quickly he rushes to cut the body of the sponges, then he doesn't wait, but right away wiggles the rope, signalling the others to pull him up fast . . . So he is pulled up to the surface as fast as thought, and seeing him break free of the sea you feel both joy and pity, because his limbs are so weak and undone by fear and grievous effort.[15]

Sponge diving was a dangerous and poorly paid profession, perhaps done mainly by enslaved workers. They were brave and knew the water well, but it remains unclear how well they could swim. Like Bahrain's pearl divers, sponge divers used weights to reach the bottom quickly, picked the sponges and then were pulled back up on a rope. But even supposing that Mediterranean divers were good swimmers, diving remained a niche profession, and does not indicate that the general European population ever became comfortable in the water. As we see from medical, military and other examples, they did not.

Southwest Asia: Romans and Parthians

Despite the sharp cultural distinction that Herodotus draws between the swimming Greeks and the non-swimming Persians, we have seen that real Greeks were probably not skilled swimmers. By the same token, at least some real Persians were able to swim. Thus during Alexander's siege of Tyre, the crew of the Tyrian ships could 'swim off without difficulty' when their ships were captured.[16] A few more examples suggest that swimming was not unknown. The same book of the Bible that tells the story of Hanukkah also reports that some of the Maccabees fighting for Jewish independence 'leapt into the River Jordan, and swam over to the other bank'. Two centuries later, when Paul of Tarsus was shipwrecked, at least a few of his eastern Mediterranean shipmates also knew how to swim. The Roman government was conveying Paul to Rome for trial when his ship was wrecked in a storm. At first, 'the soldiers' plan was to kill the prisoners, lest any of them should swim away and escape': a solidly Roman approach to a problem. But 'the centurion, wanting to save Paul, kept them from their purpose, and commanded that those who could dive (κολυμβᾶν/ *kolumban*) should jump overboard first and get to land, and the rest, some on boards and some on parts of the ship. And so it was that they all escaped safely to land.'[17] Not all were able to swim, but some could.

The Jewish historian Josephus also claims that King Herod, the king of Roman-ruled Judea who condemned Jesus, drowned a young man who was swimming in his swimming pool:

So when the festival was over, and he was feasting at Jericho with Alexandra, who entertained them there, he was very nice to the young man, and took him aside where they could be alone, and played with him in a juvenile and teasing way. It was hotter than usual, so they went outside all together, suddenly, and in a crazy mood. As they stood by the swimming pools (there were large ones around the house) they went to cool themselves, because it was in the middle of a hot day. At first they were only watching Herod's household and friends swimming; but after a while, the young man, at Herod's urging, went into the water among them. Some of Herod's friends, as Herod had told them to do, dunked the boy as he was swimming, and held him under water, in the dark of the evening, as if they were just playing games. And they did not stop till he was completely choked.[18]

This story, even if true, does not necessarily imply that anyone was actively swimming, but the use of the Greek word for swimming, νέοντας (*neontas*), and the idea that there were diving pools, κολυμβήθραις (*kolumbethrais*), suggests that swimming was common enough. And yet the outcome of the story is, once more, drowning; water is still imagined as dangerous. Jesus, remember, like Buddha several centuries earlier, walked on water rather than swam through it.[19]

In a different passage, Josephus again associates swimming with drowning. Here Jewish rebels are fighting the Romans on the Sea of Galilee in northern Israel:

when they tried to come near the Romans, they ... were drowned, both them and their ships ... And those who were drowning in the sea, if they lifted their heads up above the water, were either killed by darts, or caught by the vessels. But if in desperation they tried to swim towards their enemies, the Romans cut off either their heads or their hands; and so they were destroyed this way or that way everywhere they went. When the rest were fleeing, they were forced to go up on the beach, while the ships surrounded them [on the sea]: but many of them were forced back when they were getting out of the water, and they were killed in the lake by the darts. The Romans jumped out of their ships, and killed many more on the beach: you could see the lake all bloody, and full of dead bodies. Not one of them escaped.[20]

We do not know how trustworthy Josephus' story is, but once again swimming is presented as an act of desperation, leading only to drowning and death. Even if some eastern Mediterranean people could swim, they were still mistrustful of the water. We see it in these texts, and also archaeologically: the ancient fish-goddess Atargatis, representing old fears of the water, reappears on Seleucid coins. And Roman public baths did not become common along the eastern Mediterranean coast until after the Jewish Diaspora, in the second century CE, long after they became common in Europe. One reason seems to be people's resistance to public nudity, an aversion that may itself have arisen as an excuse for not swimming.[21]

The same suspicion of water and swimming dominates Parthian sources further east. The Parthians represented a third wave of non-swimming invaders who swept down from Central Asia and settled in what is now Iraq and Iran during the first century BCE. As the putative successors of the Persians, the new Parthian rulers soon adopted the old Persian religion of Zoroastrianism, along with its respect for water. Like the Persians, the Parthians believed that swimming and washing in flowing water befouled the water. We have already seen the *Book of Arda Viraf*'s warnings against getting in the water. Many Parthians thought of rivers as dangerous, too. They worried about rivers' swiftness and strength. They imagined that only the pure of heart could cross rivers safely. The verses of Pahlavi texts credit Zoroaster with the miracle of helping people to cross a river, 'in the manner of a bridge'. It is a parable about 'providing a passage to heaven', but also shows how people still feared the water.[22] Although some Southwest Asian people clearly knew how to swim under Roman and Parthian rule, many others did not, and fear of the water was still widespread.

Fear spreads to North Africa

At the end of the Bronze Age and the beginning of the Iron Age, the Egyptians and the Carthaginians were the sophisticates whose love of swimming was emulated by their neighbours to the north and east. But once North Africa was conquered by the Roman Empire at the end of the first century BCE, the tables were turned, and the Roman Empire seems to have spread its fear of the water south across the Mediterranean

33 Cupids fish, swim and dive on the Lac de Bizerte, detail of a Roman floor mosaic from the baths of a villa in Sidi Abdallah, Tunisia, *c.* 400–450 CE.

to North Africa. Certainly people were still swimming in North Africa throughout the Roman period: we have seen the examples of the enslaved girl in Roman Egypt and the boy who swam with the dolphin in what is now Algeria. Strabo and Pliny also mention the people of Tentyra, in southern Egypt, who swam in the Nile and hunted crocodiles.[23] But northern fears gradually moved into Africa as well.

One reason for this was that northern immigrants moving south to Africa brought their fears with them. As soon as Alexander founded the city of Alexandria in Egypt, many Jewish families emigrated there; about one-third of the city's population was Jewish. These newcomers' scepticism about swimming seems to have mixed with local ideas. The Jewish philosopher Philo, writing not long after the Romans conquered Egypt, sometimes seems to think that swimming is natural to people, while in other passages he sees swimming as alien. On the one hand, he tells us, people can be at home in all four elements: land, water, air and sky. People live and move on the ground, so they are land animals, but because they often dive and swim and sail, they are water creatures.[24] That sounds like Egyptian thinking.

On the other hand, Philo also argues that swimming is unnatural for humans. God gave the water to fish, the air to birds and the land to people; they should each keep to their own kingdom, each getting 'the creatures appropriate to them'. Philo must be thinking of Genesis 1:20–22:

> Then God said, 'Let the waters abound with an abundance of living creatures, and let birds fly above the earth across the face of the firmament of the heavens.' So God created great sea creatures and every living thing that moves, with which the waters abounded, according to their kind, and every winged bird according to its kind.

To each his own: as we have seen, this was a common thought among non-swimmers.[25]

For the most part, this second idea dominates Philo's thinking. In repeated metaphors, Philo conveys that water is dangerous and swimming nearly useless. When people swim in the vast sea, they are tossed about. They are sunk under the water. Huge waves break over them, and they cannot swim or even get their head above water. They cannot reach the surface to take a breath.[26] This is the imagery of West Asia, transported south to Roman Egypt.

Roman immigrants moving south from Italy to Carthage in North Africa may also have brought their ideas about swimming with them. A floor mosaic from a Roman villa in the outskirts of Carthage (in modern Tunisia) provides a sense of the change in people's attitudes. This huge mosaic formed the floor of the villa's *frigidarium* (the swimming pool), so it is appropriate that it represents a swimming scene (illus. 33). But here again the scene is an odd mixture of positive and negative attitudes towards swimming. Of the eight cupids in the scene, four are safely in the fishing boat, pulling up the net. One is standing on shore, and another looks as if he is preparing to back dive into the ocean. (If he is, this is the only ancient evidence for a back dive.) So far, so good. But what's this? One of the cupids is being eaten by a large fish, just as in the eastern Mediterranean swimming scene we have already seen (see illus. 41). And around them the ocean teems with large, threatening creatures.

Perhaps Roman colonialism brought Roman fears of swimming to North Africa as well as to Egypt.

By late antiquity the European tendency to swim with your head held awkwardly high out of the water seems to have reached North Africa. On the *frigidarium* mosaic, one of the cupids is swimming, but he holds his head up out of the water just like the earlier cupid from Italy (see illus. 32). Similarly, the late antique Greek poet Nonnus imagined Semele keeping her face dry as she swam, even though he was writing in southern Egypt. A thousand years after Europe and Southwest Asia were taking their cultural cues from Africa and learning to swim, European and Southwest Asian colonizers seem to have brought their own non-swimming culture with them to Africa.

A COMMON SENTIMENT emerges during the Iron Age all across northern Eurasia, from China to Europe: people want to swim, but they are at the same time afraid of the water. They think of swimming not as a fun, natural activity that everybody learns, like running or jumping, but as a difficult skill that has to be formally taught. You need prizes to encourage people even to try. Swimming appears to these people to be so hard that many swimmers will need the support of artificial flotation devices. Because you need lessons and equipment, swimming becomes a class marker for educated, upper-class people. Homer thinks Odysseus can swim because he is intelligent; Plato on more than one occasion describes someone who is poorly educated as 'unlettered and unable to swim' and Suetonius also associates reading with swimming. Roman soldiers did not generally swim well; ordinary civilians probably swam even less, and outside the Roman Empire northern Europeans probably not at all. What started in the early Iron Age with northerners emulating African and Southeast Asian swimming turns in late antiquity to northern colonizers instead carrying their fear of the water south to Africa.

PART II

FORGETTING HOW TO SWIM

34 Swimmers compete for prizes in athletic games, Kaifeng, China, detail from *Games in the Jinming Pool*, attributed to Zhang Zeduan, 960–1127 CE, ink and colours on silk.

8

MEDIEVAL ASIA

Contrary to what is often assumed, the collapse of the great northern empires of antiquity – China's Han Dynasty in 220 CE, the western Roman Empire in 476 CE, the Sasanian Empire in 651 CE – did nothing to stop people from swimming. Well into the High Middle Ages, across Africa, Europe and Asia, people kept swimming. For many medieval people, the act of swimming showed that you were rich and powerful, connected with the glorious imperial past.

That is not to say everyone became a good swimmer. Northern Eurasian swimmers were still hesitant and awkward. A lot of people never learned to swim. But even without spending much time in the water, medieval people used swimming as a cultural marker. A thousand years earlier, Herodotus had distinguished the Greeks from their Persian enemies by their ability to swim. Now swimming delineated new, medieval cultural boundaries. Knowing how to swim, or not knowing, divided north from south, east from west, free from enslaved and civilized from barbarian. Even if people did not really swim much, they could identify with swimming by watching swimming competitions and performances, turning swimming into a spectator sport.

Swimming in medieval China

As medieval China was increasingly drawn into fractious relationships with Central Asia, and often ruled by Central Asian dynasties, Chinese people began to define themselves in cultural opposition to these outsiders, the Turks and the Mongols. In northern China, swimming became more important – in theory, if not in practice – in the tenth century, at the start of the Song Dynasty. The Song Dynasty's generals succeeded in wresting power away from a series of Turkic invaders and brought China back into Han Chinese hands. As one way to solidify the Song emperors' grip on power, their propagandist historian Xue Juzheng recalled (or invented) Tang Dynasty swimming from a century earlier. This shared swimming culture connected the Tang to the Song. In Xue's story, the Tang general Ma Wan sends his two brothers, both good swimmers, to carry messages secretly across open water from camp to camp, successfully breaking a Liang Dynasty siege. This story may have reminded Chinese readers that the Song, like the Tang, were Han Chinese and not Turkic invaders.[1]

In a second Chinese anecdote from the same century, the historian Sima Guang tells a similar story, this time about the early Song Dynasty general Zhang Yongde. He sent soldiers to swim across to enemy ships under cover of darkness and fasten them all together with a heavy iron chain. When Zhang Yongde's fleet attacked the next day, the chain held the enemy ships in place, and Zhang Yongde won the battle.[2] In antiquity North Chinese historians had disdained South Chinese swimming, but medieval China found unity as a swimming culture in opposition to Central Asian non-swimmers from still further north.

This does not mean that North Chinese people had learned to swim. Most of them were probably still very indifferent and reluctant swimmers. For professional salvage diving, Tang Dynasty China imported enslaved 'Kurung' swimmers from Cambodia.[3] Well-off North Chinese men still only took baths and washed their hair about every fifth day, contenting themselves with washing their hands and faces in a basin on most mornings. Eccentrics and philosophers sometimes failed to bathe for much longer periods. When North Chinese people did get in the water, it was often for medicinal reasons, using hot springs to ease the pain of arthritis.[4] Nobody swam for fun. Indeed, rather than swim at all, North Chinese people enthusiastically engaged professional performers and athletes to swim for them.

Starting in the eleventh century, Song emperors held regular swimming competitions in Jinming Pool, a large artificial pool in the imperial garden just outside the North Chinese city of Kaifeng. According to Men Yuanlao, an administrator at the Song court, Song Dynasty officials threw silver cups and other prizes into the pool on these occasions, and competing swimmers rushed to grab them. A contemporary painting of these games depicts the swimmers near the bridge in the centre of the image (illus. 34). Song emperors may have initially encouraged swimming competitions for military or dynastic reasons, but the events became popular spectator sports. Crowds of people, including the ruling empress or emperor, watched the frenzied competitors.[5]

These swimming competitions later evolved into an even more popular game called 'Run after Duck' or 'Catching Duck'. During the dragon-boat festival every year in June, right after the dragon-boat races, officials threw dozens of ducks into rivers. Crowds of spectators watched swimmers compete to catch the ducks, as they still do today; catching one is supposed to bring good luck.[6] Again, most people did not swim. They were satisfied to watch other people swim instead.

Building on these government efforts, professional swimming entertainments also took off during the Song Dynasty. Medieval China boasted a huge entertainment industry, and performers were happy to cater to this desire to watch people swim. Acrobats started doing *shui qiu qian*: fancy dives from wooden swings hung on boats. Two boats with *qiu qian* – swinging wood boards – floated at anchor on a lake. Divers stood on the swinging boards. They calculated when the swing would hang over the water, then dived into the water from their swings. The high swings allowed them time to do twists and somersaults in the air before diving into the water below:

> There are also two painted boats on which swings are erected; on their sterns the acrobats climb up a pole. The Overseer of the Left and Right Troops leads the activities, and the drums and flutes match with their sounds. Then someone climbs up on the swing, and when he is nearly level with the frame of the swing, he does a tumble and somersaults into the water. This is called 'water swing'.[7]

The danger and excitement lay in the dives themselves, but also in the possibility of miscalculating and landing on the wooden deck of the boat, or on the bank, instead of in the water. The huge audiences for these events still were not swimming themselves. They liked to imagine themselves as better, more comfortable swimmers in the water than they really were.

Swimming in the Islamic Empire

Swimming as a spectator sport was also popular in Southwest Asia, where there were again many non-swimmers who were eager to identify as swimmers, and enough wealth to support lavish performances. Already in the later Roman Empire, Syrian theatre performances featured 'lascivious aquatic displays'. Late fourth-century Christians in Antioch abandoned their prayers and ran down to the theatre to see women swimming in a mermaid show.[8] Spectator swimming continued into the Islamic Empire, where in the 900s there were apparently swimming competitions in the Tigris. According to a story that mocks the short-lived Abbasid caliph Al-Mustakfi, the caliph 'unduly encouraged wrestlers and swimmers, wherefore the young of Baghdad gave themselves up to learning to wrestle and to swim, so that a swimmer would swim holding in his hand a chafing dish upon which was a vessel and he would swim until the meat in it was cooked'.[9]

In promoting wrestling and swimming, the caliph may have intended to support early Islamic hadiths (collections of spoken advice from the Prophet Mohammed) that add swimming to the list of things fathers should teach their sons. Three different early Islamic hadiths meld the old Persian insistence on archery and riding with the Roman senator Cato's idea that parents should teach their children to swim.[10] The intermediary may have been the Talmud, a late antique compendium of rabbinical thought, which suggests that in addition to teaching your son Torah, and a craft or trade, 'there are some who say' you should also teach him how to swim.[11] The rabbis' attachment of swimming to reading Torah may indicate that they have heard the Greek proverb that an uneducated person can neither read, nor swim. Both they, and the writers of the medieval Islamic hadiths, may also have wanted to build a contrast with non-swimming Central Asian Turks and Russians to their north. Islam may have been more enthusiastic about swimming than Judaism: while shellfish (acquired by diving) remained forbidden to Jews, the Quran allowed shellfish to Muslims. Nevertheless, most medieval Muslims in the eastern Mediterranean did not eat shellfish.[12]

In practice, it is clear that many people in the medieval Islamic Empire did not know how to swim. The Talmud does not envision anyone frolicking at the beach or swimming for fun. Mostly the Talmud is concerned with the purity or impurity of water, and with the ability of people to purify themselves by immersing themselves in water, especially after sexual activity.[13] When the Talmud bans swimming on Shabbat, the rabbis' test case has Rabbi Abbahu standing in a tub of water in a courtyard. The question is whether Abbahu lifted his feet off the bottom and splashed in his tub, and so broke Shabbat rules about resting.[14] Old concerns about religious purity and water reappear in the Talmud, where immersion can wash away ritual impurity, but mourners are not supposed to bathe, perhaps out of a fear that they might pollute the water.[15] As in antiquity, swimming tended to be associated with immodesty: the sixth-century Justinianic law code condemns sexual activity at the public baths. Many Roman bath buildings along the eastern Mediterranean coast lost their *frigidaria*, their swimming pools, in late antiquity. The Talmud is also concerned about modesty when bathing; men cover themselves with their hands when anyone is looking.[16] John Moscus tells a story from sixth-century Alexandria, in Egypt, where a lustful nun (possessed by a demon) would enter baths and try to seduce laymen, and even priests, as they were bathing.[17] Stephanus Byzantinus, around the same time, revives the old story about the magicians living near the Black Sea who can kill with their breath and whose 'bodies, when thrown in the sea, do not sink'.[18]

Seventh-century Islam, sprouting in the Arabian Desert, was not a swimmer's religion either. The Quran's water stories involve drowning, not swimming. Pharaoh drowns crossing the Red Sea, and Nuh (or Noah)'s brother drowns as Nuh saves himself on the Ark. Like the Bible and the Avestas, the Quran sees water primarily in terms of danger. In the scholar al-Ya'qūbi's ninth-century *History*, nobody swims, but many people drown crossing rivers or falling off boats.[19] When the historian al-Baladhuri has his characters cross the Tigris, they wade at fords, or ride horses across, but they do not swim.[20] Similarly, the eleventh-century medical writer al-Ghazali warns that 'the unskilled swimmer must be kept away from the seashore, not the expert in diving,' and again that 'the slippery banks of a river are forbidden to one who knows not how to swim.'[21] Firdawsi's great eleventh-century Iranian epic *Shahnameh*, the Book of Kings, warns that 'no matter how great a man is, he can't . . .

survive the seas if he can't swim,' and Firdawsi eliminates swimming from the story of Rudaba and Zal, as we have seen. The water is dangerous; swimming is a matter of survival rather than socializing.

When Southwest Asians did get in the water, it tended to be for medical reasons. The Talmud prescribes bathing as a cure for fever, though the rabbis also worry about whether that activity is dangerous.[22] Similarly, the Islamic medical writer Ibn Sina, writing in the eleventh century, recommends swimming in cold water as a remedy for people travelling in hot weather, so long as they enter the water gradually. He envisions people bathing for fever, oedema (swelling), moisturizing, miscarriage, asthma and infected sores, but he is also concerned that bathing can cause harm: it is bad for your nerves and it can make you fat (especially if you bathe right after eating). Ibn Sina's list of healthy exercises includes wrestling, boxing, running, brisk walking, archery, dance, fencing and horseback riding, but not swimming.[23] Even as the Abbasid caliphs were trying to encourage swimming, other strong forces were pushing back against that trend.

One reason for this resistance may have been a nascent association between swimming and enslavement, due to the presence in the medieval Islamic Empire of tens of thousands of enslaved East Africans who did know how to swim. In the Middle Ages many East Africans were forced onto slave ships and carried across the Indian Ocean and up the Persian Gulf to Basra, where they did back-breaking work reclaiming swampland for farming. When these miserable, angry Africans rose up in a major revolt at the end of the ninth century, they used their swimming skills in guerrilla warfare, diving into the canals they had dug to intercept the troops sent to subdue them.[24] The Islamic Empire enslaved still more Africans starting in the eleventh century, after the Slavs converted to Christianity and their European coreligionists gave up enslaving them.[25] The presence of thousands of enslaved swimmers among them may have discouraged swimming among medieval Southwest Asians.

But at least some Muslims, perhaps mostly in wealthy families, followed the hadiths and taught their boys to swim. The most celebrated act of swimming of the Islamic Middle Ages is that of young 'Abd al-Rahman, the only member of the Umayyad dynasty to escape slaughter when the Abbasids overthrew his family in 750 CE. The twenty-year-old escaped by swimming across the Euphrates to safety, though his brother hesitated on the bank and was killed. (Five years later, al-Rahman made his way across North Africa to Spain, where he established the Caliphate of Córdoba and his descendants reigned for centuries.) Both 'Abd al-Rahman and his brother knew how to swim, and apparently their Abbasid pursuers also undressed and prepared to dive in when they reached the riverbank.[26]

The Abbasid caliphs, once they had established their new dynasty, built themselves luxurious swimming pools like the pools of contemporary Chinese leaders. The palace garden boasted an outdoor swimming pool for the caliph himself and another indoor pool for women.

> In the palace of the Caliphate to the north of present-day Samarra, so far very superficially excavated ... both the palace and its courts stand above the high river banks on a prominent platform, which may possibly have been a set of gardens. Further inland one passes through an immense door into a great ornamental garden court, which gets its water from a basin in the centre by means of a long canal stretching from the north down to south-west; that is in the direction of the river. At the end of the garden there is a large sort of square grotto with an underground tunnel on both sides. In each wall there are three specially constructed niches, dug out in each of the walls and richly ornamented with flowers and animal motifs. It was meant to be the Caliph's private swimming pool, probably to be used during the day, and the other one situated to the northwest of the first seemed to have been allocated to the Royal ladies and to be used during the night because the entire structure must have been roofed, a stately overture to the grandeur to follow: an esplanade of a completely walled garden.[27]

As in Song Dynasty China, these Abbasid pools may also have been used for swimming performances, sparing the caliph himself the need to swim.

Medieval Southwest Asian literature loves swimming metaphors as another way to identify with swimming without having to get wet. Tenth-century Sufi poetry uses the language of love, and the language of swimming, to express emotional commitment to God: 'I never stop swimming in the sea of love, up and down the waves are lifting me. Sometimes the waves lift me up and other times I sink underwater, then finally love bears me away where there is no shore to see.'[28] Like Ovid, these medieval poets repeatedly associated swimming with sexual desire, sin and knowledge: 'The few swim the sea on the water of understanding.' A few folk stories collected in the medieval *Alf Layla wa Layla*, the *One Thousand and One Nights*, include swimming: in one, a poor fisherman takes off his clothes and dives for his snagged net, just like Bronze Age Egyptian fishers. In another a fisherman befriends a merman, only to realize that they are too different to be able to get along, reminding us of West African and Hawaiian stories.[29] Firdawsi's *Shahnameh* cannot resist heroic swimming in the story of Rudaba and Zal's son Rostam:

> As he descended through the air toward the water, Rostam drew his sword and with this he kept off the sharks and sea monsters that made for him. With his left arm and leg he swam, and with the right he warded off attacks. He struck out immediately, as befits a man used to fighting and hardships, and after a short time, by going steadily in one direction, he caught sight of dry land.[30]

Rostam is not just saving himself from shipwreck, like Odysseus, and he needs no magic veil. Now the fictional hero can swim well enough to fight off monsters at the same time, though the water he swims in is still just as full of monsters as it was in the time of the Assyrians.

Swimming in medieval Central Asia

But if people were swimming more in Southwest Asia, they were still not swimming further north in Russia and Armenia. Rostam's swimming in the *Shahnameh* contrasts with the absence of swimming in medieval Central Asian epics like the eighth-century *Alpamysh*, where nobody swims, or even bathes, in streams. Central Asians probably were not swimming any more in the Middle Ages than they were in antiquity or in the Stone Age. In medieval epics, Central Asians wrestle and race horses and shoot arrows, and sometimes they fish, but they do not swim. Similarly, the Armenian polymath Ananais of Sirak leaves swimming completely out of his seventh-century *Geography*.[31]

Some translations of the twelfth-century *Tale of Igor's Campaign* use the word 'swim' (or Russian поплыл) in one anecdote, and this is often used to suggest that Central Asians liked to swim. But the so-called translation here is actually an interpolation for a missing word. In this verse, Prince Igor is crossing a river to escape from captivity. The verb is missing from the text: we do not know how Igor crossed the river. 'Wade' or 'ford' would be more in keeping with the rest of the story than 'swim'.[32] Russian versions of the *Tale* probably choose 'swimming' because it sounds more heroic, just as English translators do for Hannibal's Italian guide.[33]

In the Russian *Chronicle of 1113*, there is a single instance where a tenth-century boy escapes the siege of Kyiv by stripping, jumping into the Dnieper River and swimming across.[34] But more often when Central Asian poets let their characters get into the water, the stories are tragic. Fleeing Pechenegs drown trying to cross rivers. Two brothers dive into a river, and one of them makes it across, but the other one drowns. Christians, fleeing as their town is plundered and set on fire, drown in the river. When a storm wrecks the ships that people are travelling on, 'all the men and women with their children were perishing in the deep waters separating from each other and tumbling about at the will of the waves which left nothing living in the waters, but all drowned and put to death.'[35] Medieval Russian chroniclers feared and distrusted the water, as their ancestors had since the end of the Ice Age. Like the people of Song Dynasty China, the people of medieval Southwest Asia, though they were not, in general, skilled or enthusiastic swimmers, knew they were better at swimming than Russians and Turks. They used swimming, often as spectators, to emphasize their sophistication and disparage their Central Asian enemies.

Even bathing was not popular in Central Asia. Medieval Slavs, like the Scythians before them, preferred steam saunas to baths:

> I saw the land of the Slavs, and while I was among them, I noticed their wooden bathhouses. They warm themselves to extreme heat, then undress, and after anointing themselves with tallow, take young reeds and lash their bodies. They actually lash themselves so violently that they barely escape alive. Then they drench themselves with cold water, and thus are revived. They think nothing of doing this every day, and actually inflict such voluntary torture upon themselves. They make of the act not a mere washing but a veritable torment.[36]

The (fictional) speaker is Andrew, a Christian missionary from the Byzantine Empire to the Slavs, and his horrified reaction exemplifies the cultural distinctions between the two groups. Though the sauna process seemed like torture to outsiders, these saunas were foundational to Slavic culture. Slavs offered saunas to honoured guests, and built elaborate stone bathhouses if they could, but they avoided baths.

It is the same story in the later Middle Ages. In the *Secret History of the Mongols*, written about 1240, Mongols do not swim. Ibn Battuta, travelling in southern Russia in the mid-1300s, does mention that Turks liked to bathe in the hot springs at Bíshdagh (Pyatigorsk), but saunas remained popular.[37] In the Turkish *Book of Dede Korkut*, which was probably written no later than 1400, there is no mention of swimming. Like the ancient Persians, everybody rides horses, shoots arrows and wrestles, but nobody swims. The Central Asians were glad to think of their Chinese and Southwest Asian enemies as weak, sinful, promiscuous swimmers and to identify themselves by comparison as strong, clothed, horse-riding non-swimmers.

Western Europeans, on the other hand, liked to think of themselves as cleaner and more sophisticated than their Slavic enemies. Similar to the missionary Andrew's appalled reaction to Slavic saunas, when the eighth-century Austrian monk Sturm travelled to Mainz in southern Germany, he tells us that he was disturbed to encounter 'a great multitude of Slavs submerging themselves in the river to wash their bodies'. This upset the monk, he says, because the Slavs were all naked and smelled bad.[38] Even though Sturm's story has these Slavs actually in the process of bathing, he still identifies them as foul-smelling foreigners, and so the natural enemies of Western Europeans. Andrew and Sturm's cultural distinction between Slavs and Western Europeans rationalized the ongoing war between them. The unstable border between Eastern and Western Europe – still contentious today – provided an easy profit for both sides in capturing each others' people as prisoners of war and selling them into slavery through the slave entrepôt of Venice. The modern English word 'slave' and the Arabic term 'al-sakāliba' both derive from the medieval enslavement of Slavs.[39] On their side, the Slavs were equally enthusiastic slavers.[40] Emphasizing cultural differences, including differences in swimming abilities and cultural attitudes towards the water, helped to excuse the horrors of this slave trade.

BY THE HIGH Middle Ages it was possible even for people who did not know how to swim to identify as swimmers, or at least as members of a swimming culture, through the increasing deployment of spectator races, competitions and performances. At the same time, it became increasingly important to choose sides, as people began to use the line between swimmers and non-swimmers to separate free people from those destined for slavery. The fluidity of this categorization, however, appears in the different ways it could be deployed, depending on where you were getting your slaves. For Slavs and Muslims, who bought people to enslave mainly in Black Africa and Western Europe, swimming was a mark of barbarism, indicating that you were fair game for enslavement. For Western Europeans, who were capturing Slavs, Spanish Muslims and northern Europeans to enslave, knowing how to swim showed that you were naturally free, while it was not knowing how to swim that marked you as an ignorant barbarian fated for the slave markets.

9

MEDIEVAL EUROPE

Medieval Christians in Western Europe agreed that bathing and swimming placed you in an elite class of educated aristocrats, or at least in a civilized group that was not subject to being enslaved. They found support for this idea from respected Christian bishops: Tertullian in the second century, Clement of Alexandria in the early third century, Palladius in the fourth, Augustine in the fifth and Isidore of Seville in the seventh century all clearly approve of bathing (if not swimming). Rabanus Maurus, a ninth-century abbot, recommends swimming alongside horsemanship. Though Slavs preferred saunas to bathing, Western Europeans considered bathing to be healthy, clean and an appropriate part of a balanced, social life.[1]

In fiction, medieval Western Europeans were enthusiastic swimmers as well as bathers. Fictional heroes like Beowulf could be written as fantastic swimmers:

> Are you that Beowulf who struggled with Brecca
> in the wide sea swimming and fighting,
> Both for pride trying the waves
> And rashly in the deep water
> risking your lives? Nor could any man,
> friend or foe, stop you two
> from your sad striving, swimming the sound.
> Hugging the ocean currents with your arms,
> gliding over the sea.[2]

A similar tenth-century swimming competition appears further north in Iceland, in the saga of Cormac: 'Now one day the word went round for bathing in the sea. Said Steinar to Bersi, "Wilt try a race with me, Bersi?" "I have given over swimming," said he, "and yet I'll try." Bersi's manner of swimming was to breast the waves and strike out with all his might.'[3] In an eleventh-century story about the First Crusade, the heroic knight Tancred and his troops swim gloriously across a river to victory over the Turks. Western Europeans wrote their Crusader characters doing this heroic swimming, but they imagined barbarian Visigoths drowning as they tried to swim the Danube.[4]

When it came to real swimming, Europeans were less enthusiastic. The sixth-century chronicler Gregory of Tours describes people swimming a little in emergencies, but not for fun. When Leudast's boat sinks on the Loire, he swims successfully to the bank and climbs out. As other river-boats sink in Avignon, some of the passengers also swim to the bank, but others have to tear wooden planks from the boats and hang on to them, while 'a good many' who do not find planks drown in the river. (Is Gregory deliberately reflecting the Bible's account of the shipwreck of Paul? It's hard to say.) Again, when a rich young man and his enslaved servant must cross a river to escape, they need a wooden shield to support them, like a kickboard, as they swim across the river, as Caesar's Spanish troops had centuries earlier.[5] In contrast to Pliny's idea that evil magicians float, Gregory has two stories in which women wrongly condemned to death by drowning (for adultery) are saved because of their innocence; in the first, a saint helps the woman float.[6] In a similar vein, the Christian martyrs Crispin and Crispinian, first recorded as an eighth-century story, were miraculously able to swim across the Aisne River near Soissons even with millstones fastened around their necks. Also in the eighth century, Paul the Deacon has a greedy Lombard usurper drown when he tries to swim a river carrying too much gold.[7]

The best swimmers were still the most aristocratic: in another of Paul's stories, the rightful king of the Lombards is recognized by his ability to swim. The ninth-century biographer Einhard tells us that the emperor Charlemagne took pleasure in 'exercising his body by frequent swimming, in which he was so adept that none can rightly be said to have surpassed him'. Einhard's phrasing throughout this biography suggests that he's consciously channelling Suetonius' biography of Julius Caesar, also a famous swimmer.[8] Charlemagne swims, like Caesar, because, like Caesar, he captures barbarians and enslaves them. Already in the ninth century, powerful rulers used swimming to connect themselves to the Roman Empire, and used that connection to justify conquest and slavery.

Don't let Charlemagne fool you: even as Western Europeans were using swimming as a convenient cultural hook, they had not escaped their old fears. As Philo had in Egypt, the fourth-century bishop Ambrose of Milan contrasts fish with humans. Fish, Ambrose says, can swim naturally, but 'a person can swim only when they have learned how, for they could not do it unless they had learned.' Later Christian writers, such as Jerome, Paulinus and John Cassian, laid out the same line of thought in their letters and sermons.[9] Fish belong in the water, and people belong on land. Cyprian condemned men and women bathing together as 'polluting'; both Athanasius and Jerome invoked the old stories of Bathsheba and Susanna and the sexual harassment they suffered as a result of bathing.[10] Fears of sea monsters and sexual perversion survived into early medieval bestiaries like the *Physiologus*, which described mermaids, half-human and half-fish, luring men into the water to drown them. Raunchy images of mermaids spreading their tails, perhaps derived from earlier Indian merpeople, are common on Romanesque column capitals and in medieval manuscripts. (You know this mermaid today as the Starbucks logo.[11])

Swimming in Islamic Spain

Swimming also helped to define cultural boundaries in Islamic Spain. Throughout the early Middle Ages, Muslims in Spain generally presented themselves as swimmers, though like other Western Europeans they probably were not actually skilled or enthusiastic ones. The Umayyad caliph's court at Córdoba in southern Spain used swimming as one tool (among many) to demonstrate the continuity of power from the Roman past. Like Tiberius at Capri, or Herod at Jericho, Abbasid caliphs or Chinese emperors, Islamic caliphs in Spain built elaborate swimming pools for themselves, at the Medina Azahara near Córdoba, where they could splash with their courtiers and enslaved servants. By the tenth century (if not earlier), rulers were building and using these elaborate pools all the way from Kaifeng to Córdoba.

In accordance with the early Islamic hadiths recommending teaching your sons to swim, the twelfth-century Tunisian ruler Abdul-Mu'min is said to have trained his provincial administrators in swimming along with horsemanship and archery.[12] Did people also care about those hadiths in Islamic Spain? Apparently they did. Support comes from Petrus Alphonsi, a Jewish traveller (born Moses Sephardi) who fled Islamic Spain for England as Umayyad rule in Spain was collapsing in the early 1100s. Needing a way to support himself in England, Alphonsi leveraged his knowledge of the sophisticated Córdoban court to publish, among other things, a guide to correct behaviour for English aristocrats. Alphonsi declares that gentlemen should know 'riding, swimming, archery, boxing, falconry, chess and poetry writing'.[13] The first three items on Alphonsi's list echo the Islamic hadiths. (The last four items are newer favourites. Chess and falconry were relatively recent fads in the Islamic world at this time, just beginning to reach Europe; the addition of writing may again reflect Plato's proverb connecting reading and swimming.) These are ideals; even if children at the Caliph's court had swimming lessons, there is no reason to think that as adults they were skilled swimmers. But Umayyad Spain considered swimming to be a mark of urbanity and education.

The very Umayyad collapse that Petrus Alphonsi was escaping turned the tables on swimming in the Iberian Peninsula. By the mid-twelfth century Christians were conquering land, capturing defeated Spanish Muslims and selling them into slavery further north and east.[14] At least since Charlemagne's time, Europeans had thought of themselves as the natural heirs of Roman power and of Roman skills, including swimming. Now they doubled down on that and imagined their Muslim victims as ignorant non-swimmers.

The expert twelfth-century propagandist Abbot Suger, for example, presents his patron, the French king Louis VI (can we stop calling him Louis the Fat?), as a swimmer. In Suger's story, Louis' two-pronged attack on the castle of Gournay, near Paris, involved one group of soldiers in river boats and a second group that stripped off their clothes and swam across the Marne. Suger claims that Louis himself led the swimming group, though he may have been riding a horse.[15] Louis' swimming marks him as both civilized and aristocratic.

In contrast, the French *Song of Roland* imagines Spanish Muslims as non-swimmers. It is an epic poem about Charlemagne and his knight

Roland, but it was not written in their time; the poem rose to popularity during the time of Louis VI and Suger. In this poem, the Muslims drown when they hit the water:

> God wrought for Karl a miracle:
> In his place in heaven the sun stood still.
> The heathens fled, the Franks pursued,
> And in Val Tenebres beside them stood;
> Towards Saragossa the rout they drove,
> And deadly were the strokes they gave.
> They barred against them path and road;
> In front the water of Ebro flowed:
> Strong was the current, deep and large,
> Was neither sloop, nor boat, nor barge.
> With a cry to their god Tervagant,
> The heathens plunge, but help is scant.
> Encumbered with their armour's weight,
> Sank the most to the bottom, straight;
> Others floated down the stream;
> And even the luckiest drank their fill, I deem:
> All were in great anguish drowned.
> Cry the Franks, 'In Roland your fate you found.'[16]

The implicit contrast is with Charlemagne, who was a renowned swimmer. Was the *Song of Roland* a fair assessment of Spanish swimming abilities? Did Louis VI really know how to swim? For the purposes of French propaganda, it hardly matters. Swimming appears as a Christian skill, and not knowing how to swim justifies the capture and enslavement of Spanish Muslims.

Swimming strokes in the Middle Ages

Judging from both images and literary descriptions, the primary stroke of most swimmers worldwide at this time was still a kind of front crawl. It may have been the only stroke in general use in the Middle Ages, though few literary descriptions of swimming survive from this period. In the *Shahnameh*, the hero Rostam swims 'with his left arm and leg' as he

35 A woman or Nereid swimming, on a Romano-British gold bracelet, 5th century CE, found in Hoxne, Suffolk.

36 Krishna swimming with the Gopis in *jal krida* (water sport), Hindu manuscript folio from a Bhāgavata Purāna, *c.* 1525–50, Palam, near Delhi. Some women have their arms apart, representing the front crawl, but others are beginning to use the breaststroke.

37 A couple swim on a Sasanian silver vase from Southwest Asia or Central Asia, *c.* 500–700 CE.

wields his sword with his right arm. This could be a sort of sidestroke. We have seen that in a Scandinavian saga, Bersi's 'manner of swimming was to breast the waves and strike out with all his might', and that could be a description of the breaststroke, but it might not be. Images are perhaps not very helpful either; medieval artists from England to India had learned a standardized way to depict swimming, and they stuck to it. A gold bracelet from Late Roman Britain shows a woman swimming with her arms apart (illus. 35). A Sasanian silver bowl from Iran shows a man and a woman in a very similar pose (illus. 37). Late medieval Indian images also show the same way of holding the arms (illus. 36; notice how the swimming is sexualized as Krishna reaches out for a woman's breast). Insofar as we can gather a swimming stroke from these stylized images, it must be the front crawl.

Probably many Eurasians were still holding their heads out of the water. A phrase from the European Middle Ages describes a poor victim who was 'buried up to his face [in the dirt] (as a swimmer's body floats with its chin just clear of the water)'.[17] If this is the usual position of a swimmer, then their face would be clear of the water. The few available images, cited above, similarly seem to show heads cocked backwards, as if to keep faces out of the water. And Ibn Sina, in his eleventh-century discussion of bathing, warns his readers to keep their heads above the water, at least when bathing in certain types of water.[18] Nobody discusses side breathing, or depicts it, though the use of front crawl without side breathing would surely have been very tiring.

Against all this, we can set the Catholic priest Lambert's description of Petronilla's swimming. Petronilla was a Flemish aristocrat, a married woman living in northern Europe in the eleventh century. Lambert tells us that she swam for fun:

> Petronilla, a young God-pleasing woman, was simple and God-fearing. Sometimes she carefully did her duty to God in church. Often at other times among her girls she turned her young spirit to boyish jokes and songs and dolls and games like those. And many times in summer, moved by her great simplicity of spirit and lightness of body, stripping off her clothes down to only her undershirt or cami, she went down into the fish pond, not so much to wash or bathe as to cool off and really stretch out,

38 Swimming women are exposed to the spying eyes of Alexander of Macedon,
in Muhammad Musá al-Mudhahhib's manuscript folio, 1517/18, Iran.

39 Aztec swimmer, perhaps swimming to or through the underworld, from the mural known as the 'Paradise of Tlaloc', Teotihuacan, Mexico (now Mexico City), *c.* 450 CE.

40 Krishna steals the Gopis' clothing, leaving the women stuck in the water, Hindu manuscript folio from 'Isarda' Bhagavata Purana, North India, 1560–65.

41 Large fish swallows an Egyptian soldier in a depiction of the parting of
the Red Sea, on a Roman floor mosaic from Huqoq, Israel, *c.* 500 CE.

42 Roman floor mosaic depicting Jonah and the whale,
from Huqoq, Israel, *c.* 500 CE.

43 Sinners drown in Noah's Flood, folio from the *Vienna Genesis* (Codex Vindobonensis Theol. Gr. 31), illustrated in Syria, *c.* 500–550 CE.

44 The Buddha helps out a fisherman in distress during a storm in a Kashmiri-inspired image from Temple of Yeshe Ö, Tholing, Tibet, *c.* 1000 CE.

45 Boys climb a cliff and dive off, wall painting from the Etruscan Tomb of Hunting and Fishing at Tarquinia, Italy, *c.* 525 BCE.

46 Attendants drown while the crowd cries out, in Tara La'l and Amal Sanwala's
illustration of the Indian epic *Akbarnama*, India, 1590–95.

47 Sohni swims to meet her lover Mahiwal, who is Krishna in disguise, using a clay pot to keep afloat; painted in India, *c.* 1770–85.

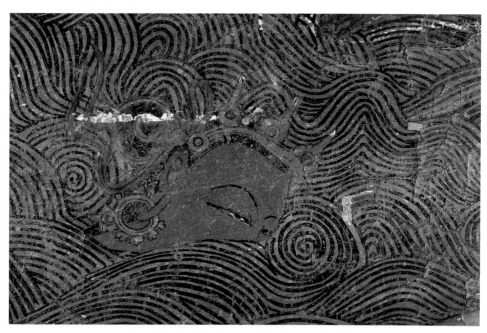

48 The Buddha wins a swimming competition in order to marry Gopa, detail of a mural painting in the Red Assembly Hall, Tholing Monastery, Tibet, 1436–49.

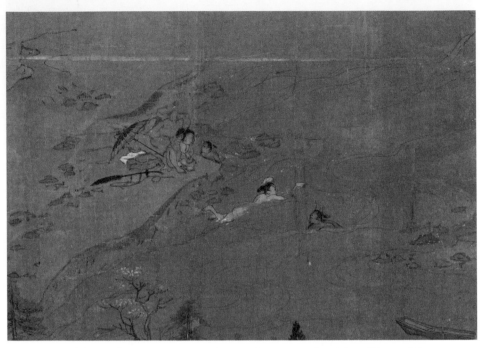

49 Men and women swim together at a hot spring, detail from Hogen En'i, *Illustrated Biography of Priest Ippen*, vol. VII (1299), colour on silk scroll.

50 Japanese pirates swim towards Chinese ships to sink them, detail from a Japanese Pirates scroll (*Wokou tujuan*) attributed to Qiu Ying, 16th century, handscroll, ink and colour on silk.

swimming here and there through the currents and swirls of the waters, now face-down, now on her back, now hidden under the water, now showing whiter than snow above the waters (or showing her super-white dry shirt), in sight of the soldiers no less than of her girls. So in these and other similar harmless ways and habits, she showed herself pleasant and deserving of love, as much to her husband as to the soldiers and the people.[19]

Lambert wants to make sure we understand that Petronilla is not just splashing here; she can swim on her back or face down, and she can swim entirely underwater. This may be the first mention or depiction of anyone doing the backstroke anywhere in the world. But we uncomfortably recall that Plato, too, mentioned someone swimming on their back, and we thought it was likely that he meant to ridicule them for not swimming correctly. Is Lambert playing the same game with Petronilla, whom he describes as 'simple'? Or is this the first indication of the backstroke?

IN THE MEDIEVAL period, even though not all people who considered themselves swimmers actually swam well, swimming served as a cultural identifier to divide one group of people from another. Africans, living the furthest south, were the best swimmers. Central Asians, in the north, generally did not know how to swim. Between these two extremes, the Europeans, Southwest Asians and Chinese were enthusiastic about swimming in theory, though that often meant watching people swim rather than actually swimming. But in the late Middle Ages, the Central Asian non-swimmers – the Turks and the Mongols – swept out of their homeland, bringing their own customs and encouraging others to adopt them. All across Europe, Asia and North Africa, people again forgot how to swim.

10

CENTRAL ASIAN POWER

After slowly beginning to dip their toes into the water during antiquity and the Middle Ages, people all over Europe and Asia backed
away from the pool around 1200 CE. Why did they stop swimming?
One reason was that new migrants from Central Asia, like earlier migrants,
brought their fear of the water with them. The military victories of the
Slavs, the Turks and the Mongols made it seem up to date to do things
the Central Asian way. From China to Morocco and Britain, late medieval fashion was Central Asian, and that meant staying out of the water.

Slavic migrations to Europe

Already during Charlemagne's lifetime, Slavic newcomers arriving in
Eastern Europe from Central Asia were shifting European attitudes
towards water and swimming. By the year 1000 Slavic Poland had become
the strongest political unit in Europe. The Polish Empire extended all
the way to Kyiv in the east and almost to Leipzig in the west, and it held
onto power for another century. This powerful empire naturally influenced
its neighbours.

Like earlier Central Asians, the Slavs were not swimmers. They used
trial by water, and believed in its efficacy for the identification of witches.
Slavic church liturgical formulae in tenth-century southeastern Germany
approve of trial by water:

> I adjure thee, water, in the name of the Father Almighty, who
> did create thee in the beginning, who also did order thee to be

separated from the waters above ... that in no manner thou receive this man, if he be in any way guilty of the charge that is brought against him; by deed, namely, or by consent, or by knowledge, or in any way: but make him to swim above thee. And may no process be employed against thee, and no magic which may be able to conceal that (fact of his guilt).[1]

That is, if the man is innocent, he will dive to the bottom; he was probably tied up to prevent easy diving. If he is guilty, he will be unable to dive and will float on the surface. Witch swimming probably went back centuries among the Slavs, and may be related to the Bronze Age witch swimming we saw in the Code of Hammurabi.[2]

On the few occasions when the Slavs do appear as swimmers, it may be due to imitation of contemporary heroic texts from Western Europe. The *Deeds of the Princes of the Poles*, the oldest European Slavic history, was written in the late twelfth century. Like other similar tales, the *Deeds* were commissioned to demonstrate how heroic Polish princes were, so they included examples of heroic swimming. King Boleslaw's brother Zbigniew, accused of treason, 'fled like a stag, swimming across the Vistula River'.[3] Boleslaw's soldiers swim 'swiftly across, one after the other'. Even Boleslaw's camp-followers can swim 'over the river' while carrying soldiers' weapons. In a fourth anecdote, the chronicler tells us that the Poles' Cuman (Turkic) enemies swim across the Vistula in a raid:

> vast numbers of Cumans assembled, planning in their wonted manner to raid Poland. Dividing into three or four groups they swam by night across the Vistula at quite separate points, and at the break of the next day broke off in different directions. Moving at speed, they seized booty beyond measure, and around evening returned laden with their spoils to the other side of the river. There, tired but feeling safe, they put up their huts for a night of rest.[4]

But could these Turks really have swum back across the Vistula holding their plunder in their arms? Could Slavic camp-followers have swum the river carrying weapons? By the twelfth century some Central Asians may have learned to swim, but it is more likely that they waded through the rivers, which are often low during the late summer fighting season.

The author of the *Deeds*, a French or Flemish monk invited to Poland for the purpose, seems to have inserted swimming stories to suit his own Western European ideas of heroic behaviour. The stories told here closely parallel those we saw in Suger's *Deeds of Louis the Fat* and the *Song of Roland*. Our monk may simply have paraphrased stories he already knew. (The *Song of Igor's Campaign*, written around the same time, may represent a still more distant echo of those French stories, and the dubious reference to swimming in it may be owed to that.[5]) In a more credible story from 1364, when the Ottomans fought off the Serbs' attack, many of the Serbian soldiers drowned trying to escape across the Maritsa River.[6] But if Slavic power may have begun to discourage swimming in Western Europe, it was not the main impetus: that was the Turkic and Mongol migrations that followed.

Turkish and Mongol influence

Later medieval Turkic and Mongol migrations seem to have been the main force behind the end of swimming throughout Eurasia and North Africa. These invasions started with the Huns in the 400s CE. By the 1600s Turks and Mongols controlled not only all of northern Asia, but North Africa and much of Eastern Europe (as the Ottoman Empire), North India (as the Mughals) and China (first as the Yuan Dynasty, and then as the Manchu). Central Asia saw a tremendous influx of wealth and a corresponding flowering of science and invention. Thanks to the Silk Road, the wealthy merchants of Samarkand could afford to endow research institutes, build great libraries and patronize scholars. Many new ideas came out of this effort, especially during the twelfth and thirteenth centuries, and people on the periphery, in Europe and China, received a steady flow of scientific ideas, recipes, music and fashions from Central Asia. The stream of novelties that reached Europe and China from Central Asia between 1100 and 1400 includes (among other things) Arabic numbers, smallpox inoculation, an explanation of fevers, steel swords and sewing needles, knitting, the spinning wheel, cotton clothing, coats and buttons, paper, printing and books, glass lenses, the ancestors of violins, sugary sweets and Persian carpets. Small wonder that, both in Europe and in China, people were inclined to adopt Central Asian ideas, including Central Asian fear of the water.

Not all of these new inventions were originally Central Asian, but they all reached Europe and China from the land between them, and so repeatedly reinforced the notion that Central Asia was the source of important new ideas. Arabic numbers were invented in northern India in the 600s CE; they reached China in the early 700s CE and Europe in the 1200s.[7] The twelfth and thirteenth centuries also brought Ibn Sina and al-Razi's medical texts to Europe. Eastern medicine was so respected that medieval French pharmacists kept their medicines in imitations of Islamic ceramic jars. Doctors throughout Europe used al-Razi's great compendium of medical knowledge in the later Middle Ages and the Renaissance. It was one of the most popular books printed on early printing presses. Central Asian medical knowledge also travelled east: Indian knowledge of inoculation against smallpox (by blowing powdered scabs up the patient's nose) seems to have reached China in the eleventh century. The new European invention of eyeglasses owed much to Central Asian scholarship; so did the *camera obscura* in China.[8]

Both Europe and China were also getting their best steel from Central Asia. Pliny calls this steel 'Seric iron', using the Roman word for East Asia.[9] Chinese written sources from the 500s to the 1300s CE refer repeatedly to imported *bin* iron from Persia and Ghazni.[10] When Charlemagne led his Frankish troops to raid the Muslim city of Saragossa in 778 CE, his followers already knew about special *spatha indica*, 'Indian swords', and were eager to seize them in plunder.[11] Viking river trade – selling enslaved people to the Abbasids for steel – brought much more crucible steel to Europe, from the Caspian Sea up the Volga River to the Neva, and from the Neva to the Baltic Sea.[12] Fashionable people adopted Central Asian trousers, lined cloaks, cotton, knitted socks and buttons.[13] Manufacturers adopted the new spinning wheel.[14] Around 1000 CE China adopted books from Central Asia; by 1250 European water mills were turning out good-quality rag paper.[15] Woodcut printing reached Europe from China, through Central Asia, about the same time, and by the 1300s Europeans were printing playing cards, also originally from China. (Chess had arrived a little earlier.) Sugar arrived in Europe and China in the 1200s as well, thanks largely to the efforts of the Mongol ruler Kublai Khan.[16] Spinach, garlic, mustard and peas also came to medieval China from Central Asia. Lemons from Central Asia were a health fad in southern Europe by the 1100s.

Persian carpets and early bowed instruments also served as ways for wealthy families in medieval Europe and China to associate themselves with powerful Central Asia. Persian carpets reached China by the 700s, as we can see in Tang Dynasty paintings.[17] With the rise of the Ottoman Empire in the 1300s, Europeans also became avid importers of Turkish carpets.[18] Families that couldn't afford real Eastern carpets bought cheaper woven tapestries made in Europe but with Eastern-influenced *verdure* or *millefleurs* backgrounds like those of Persian carpets.[19]

The ancestors of violins and cellos, bowed instruments roughened with rosin, also appeared first in Central Asia and spread quickly to Europe and China.[20] While today we can only trace the transmission and evolution of the instruments themselves, bowed instruments were made to play music, and Europeans must have been listening to Central Asian melodies just as they were eating Central Asian sweets and wearing Central Asian coats. At both ends of Eurasia, in China and in Europe, people were used to getting new ideas and inventions from Central Asia. In that atmosphere, any ideas coming out of the region seemed exciting and fashionable. The old Central Asian fear of the water spread easily all over Eurasia, and people in both Europe and China forgot how to swim.

West Asians give up swimming

Swimming lost its footing first and most completely in Southwest Asia, where Central Asian conquerors arrived earliest and stayed longest, and people had never been more than tentative swimmers. Starting in the eleventh century, Turkish mercenary soldiers dominated the Abbasid court. Soon Southwest Asian writers were shifting their focus from swimming to drowning. The great Jewish doctor Maimonides, the official doctor for the Kurdish sultan Saladin in late twelfth-century Cairo, does not mention swimming at all. But Maimonides explains that a person drowns when 'the cavities of his body are overfilled with water' and so 'breathing becomes impossible for him'.[21] Omar Khayyam's *Rubaiyat* (whatever parts of it may be authentic) includes no swimming. In the poems of Rumi, from the 1200s, only fish swim. When Rumi's characters are in the water, even metaphorically, they fall into whirlpools and cannot escape. The waves overwhelm them and they drown.[22] Swimming drifts away and becomes a vague memory.

From the thirteenth century onwards, swimming was mainly reserved for emergencies. In the *Secret History of the Mongols*, armies 'forced to throw themselves into the waters' mostly drown, though two heroes save themselves.[23] A century later, when two women fell off their horses crossing the Saqari River in winter, 'a group of men on the opposite bank, witnessing the accident, immediately swam into the stream and managed to drag both victims ashore'. (One woman died and one survived.[24]) When Amir Bakht and a group of co-conspirators absconded with their patron's fortune, the fugitives decided to cross the Indus by swimming, while 'those who could not swim' would use a raft. But when it came down to it, the crossing was too frightening, and they all decided to risk the official ferry. In another story, a boat sinks attempting to cross a river in Yemen and one man saves himself by swimming to the bank; the other occupants drown. Ibn Battuta, who tells us these stories, himself did not know how to swim in the mid-1300s.[25] These are only anecdotes, but they illustrate a shift in attitudes from a few centuries earlier, when the hadiths urged people to teach their sons to swim, and 'Abd al-Rahman actually did swim the Euphrates.

It's not that nobody could swim. Ibn Battuta, as a traveller who had met many people and heard many stories, does have some swimming stories to tell. He tells us about Ghazi Chelebi, the son of the sultan in Turkey, who

> was a brave and audacious man, with a peculiar capacity for underwater swimming. He used to sail out with his war vessels to fight the Greeks, and when the fleets met and everyone was occupied with the fighting he would dive under the water carrying an iron tool with which he pierced the enemy's ships, and they knew nothing about it until all at once they sank.[26]

This seems to have been a popular story in Sinop, possibly based on older tales like Herodotus' story about Scyllias. Another of Ibn Battuta's swimming stories concerns an underground irrigation canal or tunnel in Syria, where 'sometimes a daring swimmer will plunge into the stream at the upper end of the hill and, swimming with powerful strokes under the water until he makes the passage of the channel, will come out at the lower end of the hill'. The tunnel in question is

20 metres (66 ft) long, so we can well believe that this was, as Ibn Battuta says, 'a terrible risk'.[27]

It was not impossible for Southwest Asian women to swim in the late Middle Ages, at least in jokes, but it was not common. This Turkish story from the 1200s sometimes features Nasreddin and sometimes the Arabic trickster Juha:

> Juha had two wives. One evening, when he was sitting with them and enjoying their company, they decided to trap him by asking which one of them he loved the best.
>
> 'I love you both the same,' he told them.
>
> 'Oh, no', they both said, 'you can't just slither out of it like that. You're in trouble this time! Now, there's a pool over there. Just choose which of us you'd rather drown in it. Which one of us are you going to toss in the water?'
>
> Juha hesitated, pondering his dilemma. Finally he turned to his first wife.
>
> 'I've just remembered, my dear,' he said. 'You learned to swim some years back, didn't you?'

Still, this is not a world where most people learn to swim as children; instead, it is a world where water is a murder weapon. Ibn Battuta himself was almost murdered by drowning along the coast of Yemen.[28] And anxiety around women taking off their clothes to swim and men spying on them probably left women few opportunities to swim.

In the medieval stories collected in the *One Thousand and One Nights*, people are often thrown overboard or shipwrecked. Strikingly often, they are saved by some device that avoids swimming. One woman's lover drowns, but she is cast up on an island and soon realizes that there is 'a dry strip of land connecting the island to the shore'.[29] A dervish escapes his island the same way: the water recedes until dry land appears and he can wade through shallow water to the mainland.[30] Again, when a man and his wife are thrown into the sea, his wife turns into a demon and carries him to shore.[31]

Under Turkish influence, most people in medieval North Africa also seem to have forgotten how to swim. Before the Turks reached Africa, they probably still knew how: along the Mediterranean coast of Africa, people had traditionally been swimmers. According to the North African economist Ibn Khaldun, in the late twelfth century Tunisian men 'threw themselves in the sea and fled by swimming' when the Almohad ruler al-Mansur attacked them. But in his own time, in the fourteenth century, Ibn Khaldun mentions 'those who know how to swim', as if most people do not.[32] And Esteban de Dorantes, who lived in Morocco until he was thirteen years old, nevertheless did not know how to swim when he was sold into slavery in Portugal just after 1500.[33] One unsurprising exception is Mubārak al-Ḥabashī al-Qābūnī, a Black man – Ibn al-'Imād describes him as 'very dark, black and very tall' – who led a Sufi temperance move-ment in the face of Mamluk corruption in late medieval Egypt. Mubārak's biographer Ibn Ayyūb describes him as a very strong swimmer, who 'would come up from the water with fish in his toes and fish in his fingers and in his mouth a bigger fish, and under each armpit, a fish'.[34] Presumably Mubārak was from further south in Africa, where people still knew how to swim, or so his biographer imagined him.

Like their earlier counterparts, Turkish rulers enjoyed swimming as a spectator sport: a favourite of people who do not want to get in the water. The Ottoman sultan Murad III is said to have built a swimming pool for the women of his palace inside the harem. Ottaviano Bon, the Venetian ambassador to the Ottoman court in 1607, tells us that the

51 Swimming pool of the Ottoman sultans, now empty, Topkapı Palace, Istanbul, 1460s.

sultan (probably Murad's son Ahmed I), like Han emperors in China, used his pool to abuse victims:

> [He had] an artificial square lake ... whose water came from about thirty fountains, which were built upon a kind of terrace or high platform of very fine marble ... and in the lake there was a little boat, into which (as I was told) the Sultan often went with his mutes and buffoons, to make them row up and down, and to sport with them, making them jump into the water, and many times as he walked with them on the walkways above the lake, he would throw them down into it, and plunge them over head and ears.

The unattractive pastime of throwing disabled people into the water is not swimming, but in any case, the pool seems to have been, like Roman *natatoria*, only a few feet deep (illus. 51). Ahmed was not the only sultan who liked to throw struggling people into the water. Mehmed IV, about fifty years later, used to throw women from his harem into a pool in his gardens, 'on the pretext of making them swim', and 'take great pleasure in their pretence of screams and cries'.[35] Indian rajahs built a similar swimming pool in the 1500s, and a fresco from the 1700s shows a mythical

52 Queen's swimming pool in the Vijayanagara palace at Hampi, India, *c.* 1520.

53 Indian king Vijaya Raghunatha swimming with women, wall painting from the upper chamber, Ramalinga Vilasam, Ramnad Palace, India, 1720s.

Indian king swimming surrounded by women, eating and making love, in just such a pool (illus. 52, 53).[36] We can relate this to the simulated shipwrecks in the swimming pools of Han Dynasty emperors and the 'minnows' of the Roman emperor Tiberius' pool on Capri: they associate swimming with eroticism, transgression and danger.

India and the Mughals

In northern India people had not been swimmers even in the early Middle Ages. Stories of the life of Buddha, such as the (probably) third-century CE *Lalitavistara*, involve competitions in 'swordsmanship, archery, elephant guiding and wrestling', but not swimming. Later Hindu sacred texts from medieval India continue to express the sense that anyone in the water is in serious danger. In the early medieval Puranas, for example, the god Krishna's father, Vasudeva, escapes with his infant son across the Yamuna River in northern India. But no version of the story convincingly describes swimming. Usually Vasudeva's crossing requires a miracle, the same sort of parting of the waters that the non-swimming Hebrews needed in order to cross the Red Sea. One version has Vasudeva wading, but even then his feet remain on the bottom of the stream.[37]

When the Mongols arrived they only confirmed an already existing fear of the water. Northern India was more or less under Turkish or Mongol control from the year 1000 until the 1700s: first under the Turkish Ghaznavids, then successively under the Mongols and the Mughal Empire. (The name 'Mughal' is just an Indian version of the word we know as 'Mongol.') Swimming remained alien to northern Indians throughout this period. In the 1300s Ibn Battuta tells us that suicidal Indians often drown themselves in the Ganges River.[38] A richly illustrated biography of the achievements of the Mughal ruler Akbar, the *Akbarnama*, from about 1590, shows Akbar helplessly watching two of his followers drown as they try to swim their horses across the Ravi River in Lahore (see illus. 46). Although a crowd stands on the banks of the river, excited and upset, waving their arms around, none of the bystanders plunges in to save their companions.[39]

In Indian fiction, too, swimming people often drown. In a Mughal miniature from the 1700s, Sohni swims across the river towards the cowherd Mahiwal, an atavar of the god Krishna (see illus. 47). This was a popular Hindu allegory, often retold and represented in many contemporary paintings, and the point of the story is that Sohni does not swim well. Sohni loved Mahiwal, a cowherd, who tended his herd across the river from her father's house, but her father would not let her marry him. Instead, he made her marry someone she didn't like. Every night Mahiwal would swim the river to be with his lover secretly. Then one day Mahiwal injured his leg and could not swim. Sohni decided she would swim to him instead. Because Sohni was not a strong swimmer, she brought along an empty pot to help her float, and in this way Sohni crossed safely.

But one day her sister-in-law (her husband's sister, who did not appreciate Sohni cheating on her brother) secretly replaced Sohni's pot with a pot that had not been fired yet, and as she swam it turned back into mud. Sohni drowned as Mahiwal watched in horror. But when he jumped in to try to save her, he could not swim with his injured leg, and the lovers drowned together.

Like the story about the bathing milkmaids, the story of Sohni and her pot served Hindus in India as an allegory about devotion to Krishna.[40] But surely this is an Indian version of the Maori story in which Hinemoa used gourd floats to help her swim to her lover? That story, told by swimmers, has a happy ending. The Mughal Indian story, told by non-swimmers, ends in tragedy, like the similar story of Hero and Leander. Under Mughal rule, the people of India, like the people of Southwest Asia, were not swimmers.

China stops swimming

This late medieval cultural turn against swimming reached China as well. Mass conversions to Buddhism in the early Middle Ages, together with the new Central Asian luxuries, made people in China very enthusiastic about Central Asian influences. The Tang emperor Taizong's son, in the 600s, even took up speaking Turkish, and built a Turkish camp where he could play at being Turkish himself. Artists painted and carved statues of Central Asians and their horses. Painters adopted Iranian artistic conventions, such as the use of one long line of unvarying thickness to outline figures. Despite a backlash against Buddhism and other Central Asian influences in China in the 800s, by the tenth century many people in China were again openly Buddhists. Buddhist monks brought many new Central Asian ideas to China, while traders, as we have seen, brought others.

The Mongol invasion of China in the 1200s developed these new products – cotton clothes, sweets – but it also brought renewed fear of the water. As if it were a portent, Yuan Dynasty Mongol rule in China began with the drowning of the last Song Dynasty emperor, a small child, clinging to the back of his prime minister Lu Xiufu as Lu jumped off a cliff into the ocean. The Song Dynasty's light-hearted 'Run after Duck' games and the divers turning somersaults off wooden swings into the water vanished. They were replaced by archery, horse-riding and wrestling, the 'Three Manly Sports' in Mongolian tradition.[41]

As in West Asia and India, under Mongol rule drowning replaced swimming in popular Chinese images and stories. In a Chinese story from 1292, for example, a rich merchant is crossing a river near Lake Tai on the Yangtze delta. Halfway across, his boat runs aground and the boatman's pole becomes stuck in the mud at the bottom of the river. The merchant orders his servant to get into the water to try to lift the boat free. Diving down, the servant finds that the boat is stuck on the spine of a dragon. The merchant panics and jumps overboard, but he doesn't know how to swim. Though his servants rescue him, he dies when he gets home.[42] Instead of swimming being an elite achievement, it is an activity that has been relegated to the servants. After this story, swimming disappears from Yuan Dynasty Chinese literature. There is no swimming, for example, in the *Twenty-Four Paragons of Filial Piety*, a popular Chinese text of that time. In a Southern Song painting from the mid-1200s, a Daoist immortal walks on water, like the Buddha and Jesus before him.[43] In Yuan Dynasty poetry, only fish and geese swim.

In the medieval Chinese novel *The Water Margin*, set in the Song Dynasty but written probably under Yuan rule, many of Huang An's North Chinese soldiers, fighting in the south, are captured when they do not know how to swim. Similarly another North Chinese character in the same novel, Lu Junyi, is 'unaccustomed to swimming', and when his boat is overturned his captors have to rescue him from drowning.[44] Set in opposition to the northern non-swimmers, *The Water Margin*'s South Chinese characters Zhang Shun and Zhang Heng can swim. Another set of characters, the rebel Ruan family, are also known for their swimming.

> Ruan the Seventh said, 'On the other side of the river there are many boats. My two brothers and I will swim across, and get the boats to come here so you can all embark [as pirates].' Chao Gai thought this was a good plan, and the three Ruan brothers stripped off their clothes, armed themselves with a dagger each, and plunged into the water.[45]

The Ruan brothers do not come from South China, but they are professional fishermen from near Liangshan Marsh in northern China. The novel's author may be emphasizing Chinese identity against the non-swimming Mongols who were ruling China in his lifetime, leading up to the Red Turbans rebellion and the Ming Dynasty. The novel's title, variously rendered as *The Water Margin* or *Outlaws of the Marsh*, ties the theme closely to water, so the swimming rebels are surely an important concept here.

Even after the Mongols lost power in 1368, and the Ming Dynasty took over, most people could not swim, or could not swim well. In Ming Dynasty painting, Daoist Immortals still walk on water.[46] As in India, drowning remained a common method of suicide in China; the poet

Chang Yü, for example, drowned himself in 1385.[47] Wu Cheng'en's *Journey to the West* (*Hsi yu chi*), a collection of traditional Chinese tales from the 1500s, includes a story where travelling scholars who fall into the water with their books have to be saved by magic, or they would have 'sunk straight to the bottom'; when these same travellers need to cross a river, they build rafts or ride magic turtles. When a ferryboat overturned in Yangzhou, 'even a few of the people on the shore who knew how to swim jumped into the water for the relief effort'. Most of the bystanders, presumably, did not know how to swim.[48] In an account of the popular annual dragon-boat races, one Ming Dynasty chronicler boasts that 'the boatmen are all familiar with the water and are expert swimmers', but then admits that 'the headman, flagman, drummer, and clapper need not be able to swim, as the oarsmen are responsible for their lives'. South Chinese visitors remarked on this difference between southerners and northerners: a South Chinese narrator in a Ming Dynasty story explains that, 'Yue men, being all northwesterners, were not accustomed to battles on water ... But I am a southerner. I learned to swim at an early age and can stay underwater for three days and nights in a row.'[49]

In 1644 Manchu forces from Central Asia took power again in China, this time as the Qing Dynasty. They, too, rejected swimming on ethnic grounds. In 1696, when Yen Yuan wanted to reject the intellectual pretensions of the Ming Dynasty and bolster Chinese sports and practical crafts, he opened an academy in Hopei that taught 'military training, strategy, archery, riding, boxing, mechanics, mathematics, astronomy and history'. Swimming was not included.[50] The Manchu government required Chinese men to participate in fencing, archery and horse-riding – Central Asian sports. Other popular competitions involved wrestling and lifting and throwing heavy kettlebells. Even civilian candidates for political office were tested on their ability to shoot arrows from horseback. Ice-skating became newly popular.[51] But Qing dynasty officials ignored swimming.

Instead, Qing dynasty literature is dominated by stories about drowning. In a story from the 1600s, Shap Nong was forced into sex work at thirteen, and had earned enough money already to be rich at nineteen. When she meets a young man named Lei, they fall in love. But on their way home to Lei's father, the lovers meet a rich acquaintance of Lei's, Sun Fu. Sun Fu plays on Lei's poverty and his fear of his father, and persuades Lei to sell Shap Nong to him. The next morning, when Shap

Nong is told to leave her lover's ship for Sun Fu's ship, she brings a box with her. On Sun Fu's ship, in front of the two men, she opens the box and shows them the expensive jewels within it. Then, reproaching Lei for his cruelty and greed, she holds the box, jumps into the river and drowns.[52] In an earlier era, Shap Nong might have swum away to freedom, but the mood had changed.

Swimming in Tibet

In the 1200s CE the Mongols conquered Tibet along with China; they left Tibet when they left China, in the 1300s. This traumatic experience may have left Tibetans more interested in swimming than they had been before, as a political statement of their independence. Thus Tibetan stories of the Buddha's life from the 1400s include swimming among the competitions the Buddha won to gain the hand of his wife Gopa (see illus. 48). When the Manchu (re)conquered China in the 1640s, they did not succeed in capturing Tibet, which remained independent into the 1700s. In this period of political independence, and possibly as a political statement, Tibetans appear to have been enthusiastic swimmers. One Tibetan image of men diving and swimming in the Kyichu River in 1695 comes from a wall mural in the Potala palace, the traditional home of the Dalai Lama (illus. 54). People dive, swim and float on their backs. The occasion seems to be a swimming competition, like those that were popular in China under the Song Dynasty, before the Mongol conquests. In short inscriptions, the swimmers egg each other on; one reads 'Go deep,' and another, perhaps related to the southern Chinese surfing event, which also involved flags, reads, 'Carry the flags to the middle of the river.'[53] The three flags are visible at the bottom of the image.

Tibetans also continued in the 1600s to list swimming among the *pho rtsed sna dgu*, the 'Nine Different Games of Men'. The first three games are talking, writing and maths. The second set are archery, lifting and carrying stones, and jumping. But the last three games are foot racing, swimming and wrestling.[54] Tibet is centrally located in the middle of Eurasia, and it shows: from the west, the Tibetan list takes the wrestling, archery and swimming of the Islamic hadiths; from the east, the Tibetans took three of the Confucian Six Arts – archery, calligraphy and computation. The sport of lifting and carrying stones must be related to the Manchu

54 Swimming contest in the Kyichu River in Tibet, detail of a mural painting in the Potala Palace, Lhasa, *c.* 1695.

passion for kettlebells. And, although swimming is not one of the Confucian Six Arts, the Tibetans apparently preserved that part of Chinese culture too, even as the Chinese themselves, under the Qing Dynasty Manchu, let swimming go.

Swimming in Japan

In Japan, as in China, people seem to have learned to swim around the end of the first millennium CE. But although Chinese people mostly stopped swimming in the thirteenth century, people in Japan stayed in the water. The Mongols tried and failed to conquer Japan, and, at least in later Japanese retellings, swimming played a significant role in Japan's naval defence. Stories describe how thirty samurai swam out to a Mongol ship, cut off the crew's heads and then swam back.[55] From then on, while swimming declined in China, it was encouraged by the emperors in Japan. Possibly, as in Tibet, they wanted to drive home the point that

Japan was independent and China was not. On a Japanese scroll painted not long after the Mongol attack, men and women swim together at the local hot springs (see illus. 49). Communal bathing seems to have come to Japan with Buddhism in the early Middle Ages, but it really took off after the Mongol conquest of China. The fourteenth century yields the first evidence of paid public hot water baths in Japan, and of the central importance of purificatory bathing to Shinto worship. At first these were used mainly by families or small groups. Starting in the Edo period, perhaps in the 1600s, Japanese bathers used the baths communally with strangers, and also stopped wearing loincloths and began to bathe naked, in contrast to Chinese and Korean practice. Koreans visiting Edo Japan commented on the immorality of communal bathing.[56]

In the long late medieval war between China and Japanese pirates over trade rights, the Japanese pirates did most of the swimming. In a typical attack on China in 1554, 'several hundred pirates swam ashore from their ships.' Confirmation comes from Chinese scrolls painted about 1600; in one, Japanese pirates climb back into their boat after swimming, while in the second, three of the Japanese pirates swim towards the Chinese ships to attempt to sink them by staving in their sides (see illus. 50 and 55). In the aftermath of the Battle of Han-San between the Japanese and

55 Japanese pirates swim to a boat and climb in, detail from a Japanese Pirates scroll (*Wokou tujuan*), 16th century, handscroll, ink and colour on silk.

the Korean navies, in August 1592, when several ships were set on fire, four hundred men were able to swim to safety on a nearby island.[57] If we compare that to the catastrophic reports of drowning of Persians at the Battle of Salamis, or Romans at Lake Trasimene, or Jews in the Sea of Galilee, we can see that Japanese attitudes towards swimming, and probably their real swimming abilities as well, must have been very different.

In early modern Japan, as in Tibet, swimming was included on lists of important skills. Japanese lists of the eighteen martial arts that samurais should know resemble Central Asian ones with their archery, fencing, horse-riding and wrestling, but the Japanese lists added swimming.[58] This was not just theoretical: Japanese samurai distinguished military swimming, *nihon eiho*, from ordinary recreational and sport swimming. Trained instructors taught soldiers very specific swimming techniques that were useful for attacking the forts of their enemies. Because many Japanese forts in the turbulent Edo period had defensive moats around them, ninjas learned how to swim while holding their weapons, how to swim silently and how to swim long distances underwater.[59] In June 1575, during a siege, the samurai Torii Suneemon, to get help for his besieged castle, slipped into the river in the middle of the night and swam past the besiegers with his message. While he was at it, he also cut the cable blocking the river to ships.[60]

Competitive swimming was also popular in Japan, but as a participatory event, not a spectator sport. When Tokugawa Ieyasu reunited Japan under his leadership in about 1600, he kept the peace by turning his warriors' attention towards sports and sporting competitions, including swimming. In place of the old attacks on warlords' castles, Tokugawa ordered in 1603 that all samurai boys should learn to swim. He held regular swimming competitions among different schools to replace the old battles.[61] These popular swimming competitions enjoyed a long life in Japan. Government support for swimming in Japan and Tibet contrasts, perhaps intentionally, with the decline of swimming in China and Korea. To Japanese and Tibetan people, swimming showed their strength and independence. But to the non-swimming people of northern China, the swimming abilities of their Japanese, Tibetan and South Chinese neighbours signified only barbarism and backwardness.

FOR 2,000 YEARS most Eurasians had associated swimming with sophistication and power. Now increasing Central Asian power, with Turkish irruption into the Islamic Empire and the establishment of the Mongol Empire, forced a reassessment of that line of thought. Wealth and power were centred in the trade cities of Samarkand, Merv and Baghdad. The best new music, the most fashionable clothing and the highest-quality weapons poured out of these non-swimming areas and spread across the continent. From China to North Africa, people turned to wrestling and polo, and left the water. Even as far west as Western Europe, which remained politically independent of Turks and Mongols through the Middle Ages, Central Asian influence still discouraged Europeans from swimming.

11

A FAMOUS DROWNING

f the explosive growth of Central Asian power and influence was not enough to discourage Europeans from swimming in the later Middle Ages, they also had before them a forceful example of the water's dangers. In 1190 CE all of Europe was shocked by the sudden drowning of Frederick Barbarossa, the most powerful man in Europe – who was not only drowned, but drowned while he was on Crusade to the Holy Land. In the early Middle Ages Europeans had considered drowning to be something that happened mainly to Muslims, since God would save drowning Christians. Now Barbarossa's drowning seemed to suggest that God wanted Christians to stay out of the water. We can see this feeling developing as medieval retellings of Barbarossa's story shift their focus.

In the earliest versions of the tale of this catastrophe, eyewitnesses reported that on 10 June 1190, as the army of the emperor Frederick Barbarossa marched through Anatolia to Jerusalem to fight the Third Crusade, Barbarossa insisted, despite warnings, on trying to swim his horse across a rapid and unfamiliar river.

> The vanguard that marched forth that day, 10 June, had made camp in the plain of Seleucia. All the members of the army of the Holy Cross, both rich and poor, sick and those who seemed still healthy, were now toiling one and all because of the difficulty of the way, through rocky crags that were accessible only to the mountain goats and birds, and also the warmth of the sun and the raging heat. The emperor, who was unruffled by any danger,

wanted to alleviate the dreadful heat and to avoid the mountain peaks by swimming across the fast-flowing river of Seleucia. But since, as the wise man says: 'nor should you struggle against the force of the river', that man who was wise in other matters tried in vain to pit his strength against the flow and 'the force of the river'. Even though everyone warned him against this, he entered the water and was swept away by the flood. He who had so often escaped great dangers died miserably . . . The other nobles who were with him hastened to his aid, albeit too late; however, they got hold of his body and brought it to the bank.

Everyone was deeply upset by his death, and so keenly stricken by grief that some people, torn between fear and hope, finished their lives with him; others indeed despaired, and, seemingly thinking that God had abandoned His care of them, renounced their Christian faith and went over to the heathen.[1]

Frederick Barbarossa's drowning was such a horrendous catastrophe, Ansbert tells us, that many of the remaining soldiers of the emperor's army, dispirited, soon turned around and walked home to Germany.[2] The Third Crusade failed to retake Jerusalem from the Turkish sultan Saladin, and the Christians never held Jerusalem again. A manuscript

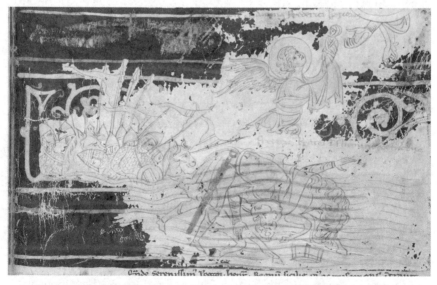

56 Emperor Frederick Barbarossa drowns in the river as an angel carries his soul up to Heaven, miniature from Peter of Eboli, *Liber ad honorem Augusti* (c. 1197).

57 Possible early breaststroke in a later version of Frederick Barbarossa's drowning, miniature from the Gotha manuscript of the *Saxon World Chronicle*, 1270–79.

illustration painted less than a decade after the drowning gives an idea of the catastrophic feel that this event had for Europeans (illus. 56). In this early depiction of Barbarossa's death, the bearded old man drowns with his clothes and his sword on, after trying to swim his horse across the river. This image matches the eyewitness account of the events above, and has little to do with the act of swimming itself. The emperor was just riding his horse across the river when he fell off and drowned because of the weight of his armour.

But two later illustrations of the same tragedy over the next couple of generations show how memory altered people's ideas about Barbarossa's drowning. In one later version, the emperor was simply swimming to cool off:

The lord emperor had crossed these valleys and mountains through a short cut: and on this same day he traversed this fast-flowing river and reached the other side in safety. He had lunch there, and, after the many and terrible exertions that he had undergone in the previous month and more, he decided to bathe in that same river, for he wanted to cool down with a swim. But by the secret

58 Different version of Frederick Barbarossa's drowning, miniature from the Berlin manuscript of the *Saxon World Chronicle*, 1301–25.

judgement of God there was an unexpected and lamentable accident and he drowned.[3]

This second story seems much less likely: what 68-year-old man goes for a casual dip in a dangerous and unfamiliar river? But it was this version that caught the popular imagination. The Muslim chronicler Ibn al-Athir, a member of Saladin's court, gives the same version: the 'emperor entered [the river] to wash himself and drowned at a spot where the water did not reach a man's waist'.[4] Later illustrations no longer show the horse or the armour. Instead, Barbarossa appears alone, beardless and young, naked except for his crown (illus. 57). The *Saxon Chronicle*, about fifty years later, mixes the two stories: 'The Emperor attempted to swim through a river and was drowned, and there was great mourning throughout Christendom.'[5] By 1250, in a third representation, Barbarossa is more flailing than swimming (illus. 58). Just as the Mongols were conquering Asia and Eastern Europe and spreading their fear of the water, Europeans were also changing Barbarossa's drowning into a moral warning against swimming.

Europeans give up swimming

Frederick Barbarossa's catastrophic drowning, on top of Central Asian cultural influence, caused a sharp decline in swimming in Western Europe around 1200 CE. Rather than being a marker of class and character, swimming began to be taken for recklessness. Only a decade after Barbarossa drowned, the French theologian Jacques de Vitry told a moral story about drowning: a man warned his wife to stay away from the riverbank. The disobedient wife went there anyway and drowned in the river.[6] And in the German *Niebelungenlied*, also from around 1200, when the priest gets thrown overboard he is 'no swimmer' and is only saved by his faith in God:

> [Hagen] hastily threw him out of the skiff. Plenty of them called out, 'Catch hold now, sir, catch hold!'...The priest swam urgently – he wanted to save his life, if anyone could come to his aid. That could not be then, for mighty Hagen was in a very angry mood. He thrust him down to the riverbed – no one thought well of that. When the poor clergyman saw no help forthcoming, he crossed back over, suffering great distress. Although he was no swimmer, God's hand helped him emerge onto land again, safe and sound.[7]

Drowning stories remained common throughout the thirteenth century. King Louis IX's French Crusaders, on their way to the Battle of Mansurah in Egypt's Delta, got too close to the muddy, slippery banks of the Nile. They and their horses slipped into the water and drowned.[8] On the same Crusade, as the French soldiers leapt into the sea to join battle, one was killed by a sword, but 'two or three' drowned, 'having plunged into the sea too hastily in their fervent eagerness to fight and thus perished'.[9] In 1268 in England, when a river boat sank and the people on board fell into the water, one man drowned and the others 'barely escaped to land'.[10] Even simple horseplay and fun might lead to drowning. In 1273 a chronicler in Scotland tells the sad story of two men who drowned in the River Tay:

> There was present among the rest a dashing squire with his groom ...When they sat down on a summit by the shore, he went down

[to the river] to wash his hands, which he had stained with mud while larking about. As he did so, standing up and half bending over, one of the maidens . . . came up behind him unobserved and pushed him into the bed of the river. He, making a joke of the thing and taking pleasure in it, said, 'What do I care? I can swim, even if I go further out.' Thus moving in the river with the others applauding him, he felt a whirlpool unexpectedly drag down his body, and shouted and wailed, but he had no one who could help him except his servant, who was at play nearby. At the clamour of the bystanders, he rushed impetuously into the depths, and both men were swallowed up in a moment, before the eyes of all.[11]

Jacobus de Voragine's *Life of St Martha* (1275) includes the story of a young man who, having no boat, tried to swim across a river to hear the holy Martha speak. He strips off his clothes and starts across naked (the text points out his immodesty), but is caught in the current and drowns; his 'body was found the next day'. Martha, proving that she was a saint, raised her admirer from the dead.[12]

Swimming is not absent from stories of the late Middle Ages. In the 1200s Martin of Genoa lived at the end of a rocky peninsula on the coast, and apparently many local boys would swim out there to visit him.[13] Thomas Malory escaped from prison in July 1451 by swimming across a moat.[14] But Jacobus's collected saints' lives contain repeated references to drowning and few to successful swimming. A schoolboy from Mainz was fishing and 'carelessly' fell into the river and drowned. Mary Magdalene saves a pregnant woman from drowning, holding her up by the chin as Ovid recommended. Demons threaten to drown chattering monks. There are sea monsters, river monsters and pond monsters. With all this danger, it's not surprising that when people come to a river, they do not dare to try to cross it. St Christopher, famously, does help travellers to cross the river, but he does it by wading rather than swimming. Some people can swim across, but others who do not know how to swim try to cross a river that way and drown. There is only one expert swimmer, 'a man named Frederick', also from Mainz, who makes fun of a man and splashes water in his face, and as a result is cursed. Frederick doesn't care, and swims away into the deep water, but 'suddenly lost all his strength, could not help himself, and sank to the bottom like a stone'.[15] Where swimming had been celebrated, if not common, in antiquity and the early Middle Ages, in the course of the thirteenth century it was marginalized. By the late fifteenth century, a British manuscript illustration shows a boy falling off London Bridge; he has to be rescued by boatmen, because he cannot swim.[16]

Swimming in literature

Fictional characters continued to swim in medieval European literature, perhaps because authors were modelling their stories on earlier works, where swimming identified the hero. But considering that they are heroes, these medieval characters don't swim very well. Boccaccio, in the mid-1300s, modelled his shipwrecked sailor Landolfo in the *Decameron* on the Arabic story of Sindbad the Sailor, who in turn had been modelled on Odysseus. Boccaccio's story requires Landolfo to swim:

> Landolfo . . . was terrified now that he saw death at hand, and got hold of a plank, like the rest . . . Bestriding the plank as well as he could, and driven to and fro by the wind, he supported himself till daylight . . . at length a great blast of wind sent [a chest] with such violence against the plank on which he floated, as to overset it, and plunge him over head and ears into the water. He rose again, however, and swimming with the strength of fear rather than with his own, he found himself at such a distance from the plank that he was afraid he could not recover it. Getting therefore to the chest, which was nearer, he laid his breast upon it as well as he could, and used his arms for paddles. In this manner was he carried up and down, with nothing to eat, but drinking more than he desired, neither knowing where he was, nor seeing anything but water for a day and a night.
>
> The next morning [he] drew near to the island of Corfu, at a spot where, by good fortune, a poor woman was scouring her dishes with salt water and sand . . . Moved by compassion, she stepped a little way into the sea, which was now calm, and seizing the half drowned wretch by the hair of his head, drew both him and the chest to land, where, with much trouble, she unfolded his

arms from the chest, which she set upon the head of her daughter, who was with her.[17]

Landolfo swims with his wooden chest the way Sindbad swims with his plank, or Homer's Odysseus swims with his magic veil, and he meets a girl the way Odysseus meets Nausicaa in the land of the Phaeacians.

Boccaccio's next story recycles the Greek myth of Hero and Leander. In this version, Gianni rows over every night from his home on the island of Procida in the Bay of Naples to see his girlfriend Restituta on the nearby island of Ischia. But sometimes when he cannot get a boat he swims over, even if it is only 'to please himself with a sight of her house'.[18] As we saw with the *Shahnameh*'s story of Rudaba, you can retell Hero and Leander without the swimming, and so it is here: Boccaccio lets Gianni row a boat. Gianni only has to swim when the boat is not available. (Unlike the sad end of Hero and Leander, Gianni's story ends happily with the two lovers married.)

Even this limited literary swimming diminishes in the late 1300s. Although Chaucer's *Canterbury Tales* were partly inspired by Boccaccio's stories, none of Chaucer's characters swim. Nor did Thomas Malory mention swimming much in his fifteenth-century adventure stories about King Arthur, even though he himself knew how to swim in an emergency. As Europeans came to have more contact with enslaved Africans who were good swimmers, Europeans' disinclination to swim may have been strengthened by a desire to disassociate themselves from their enslaved victims. As we have seen, this had happened centuries earlier in the Islamic Empire.[19]

Further north and west, away from Mongol or African influence, late medieval stories still included more swimming. In Orkney, north of Scotland, about 1200, the hero Kali and the brave farmhand Havard went out in search of treasure and swam across the lake holding ropes, torches and tools. Swein and Margad swim in the ocean, along the cliffs. A character in *Njal's Saga* repeatedly swims 'like a seal'. About 1240, in the Icelandic *Egil's Saga* or *Egla*, not only can the heroes swim, but three Irish slaves escape by swimming from the mainland to some small islands offshore. One of these slaves is a woman who evades pursuit by jumping off a cliff and then swimming away.[20] (Despite frequent suggestions in modern swimming books that medieval women could not swim, medieval authors present swimming women alongside swimming men.) The Icelandic *Saga of Grettir the Strong*, written circa 1400, describes how the outlaw Grettir swam in contests against his friend Bjorn. Later in the same saga, Grettir

> threw off his clothes and his weapons and swam out to the nets. He gathered them together, returned to the shore and cast them up on to the bank. Just as he was about to land Thorir quickly seized his short sword and drew it. He ran towards Grettir as he stepped on to the bank and aimed a blow at him. Grettir threw himself down backwards into the water and sank like a stone. Thorir stood by the shore intending to guard it until he came up. Grettir swam beneath the water, keeping close to the bank so that Thorir could not see him, and so reached the bay behind him, where he landed without letting himself be seen. The first Thorir knew of it was when Grettir lifted him up over his head and dashed him down with such violence that the sword fell out of his hand.

In the second story Grettir can swim well enough to swim underwater, and it is not just Grettir, the hero, who can swim, but also his victims, like Gisli, who 'thought that he would sooner not learn anything from Grettir than have another such flogging, nor did he do anything more to earn it. Directly he got his feet under him again he ran off to a large pool and swam across the river.'[21] But outside of these northern sagas, Europeans weren't swimming much in the late Middle Ages: they had never been very enthusiastic swimmers, and now they were much more reluctant than before.

From crawl to breaststroke

As the status of swimming changed in the late Middle Ages, Eurasian swimming strokes also disintegrated. By the late Middle Ages, swimmers all over Eurasia stopped using an overhand crawl stroke and shifted to a dog-paddle or the rudimentary beginnings of the breaststroke. As far back as the Roman Empire, Seneca had complained about excessive splashing in the water, and Ibn Sina also recommends bathing calmly and quietly. A sense that splashing was undignified may have been one reason for shifting from the crawl to the breaststroke. Or possibly people swam the breaststroke because, as later swimmers observed, most of your body could stay underwater, shielded modestly from view, with only your head on display above the surface.[22] The new stroke suited people's sense that water was sacred and should not be disturbed, and their conviction that swimming was immodest.

The earliest example of the European breaststroke dates to the 1260s, when a manuscript of the extremely sophisticated Hohenstaufen emperor Frederick II's book *On the Art of Hunting with Birds* shows us a falconer swimming in a pond (see illus. 71).[23] The falconer needs to know how to swim in order to retrieve his falcon. (As swimming became a less important sport in thirteenth-century Europe under the influence of the Mongol Empire, falconry was becoming more important for the same reason.[24]) Like earlier swimmers, the falconer is swimming naked; he has left his clothes by the side of the pool. He keeps his hat on, so probably, like other medieval swimmers, he is not planning on putting his face in the water. But the falconer does not use the ancient overhand stroke. He swims dog-paddle or possibly breaststroke, like the drowning Barbarossa.

A generation later, neither of the two swimmers in a scene from the English Queen Mary Psalter, probably made in London between about 1310 and 1320, seems to know the crawl stroke (illus. 59). One is treading water, and the other, like the falconer, has both arms extended ahead of him. In 1375 we get our last hint of a European memory of the

59 Two very inexpert swimmers, miniature from the Queen Mary Psalter, 1310–20.

overhand crawl stroke in the 'swyngyng of armys' mentioned in the anonymous *Gest Hystoriale of the Destruction of Troy*, which describes the Greek hero Ajax,

> Himselvyn in the sea sonkyn belyve,
> Swalprit and swam with swyngyng of armys,
> Yet he launchet to lond, and his lyfe hade,
> Bare of his body, bretfull of water . . .

After that, all over Eurasia, everyone did the breaststroke or backstroke.

The backstroke also makes its first definitive appearance in the later Middle Ages. We have seen possible European references to it already, in Plato, at Pompeii and in the medieval story of Petronilla, but the first image of the backstroke appears not in Europe but further east. In a manuscript illumination from fourteenth-century Iran, two peris (fairies) talk on the bank while a hidden man swims in the stream, perhaps eavesdropping on them (see illus. 72). The swimming man appears twice; once floating on his back and a second time doing the breaststroke, possibly with a frog kick.[25] The next backstroke image is from Europe, in the famous medieval calendar of the *Très riches heures du duc de Berry*, painted in Paris about 1415. For the month of August, the artist gives us a group of people swimming in the Juine River, with the Château d'Etampes in the background (see illus. 73). The lower-class swimming of these peasants contrasts with the falconry of the rich riders in the foreground. Their lack of concern about nudity may convey the same message. Some swim breaststroke, others backstroke. The one on his stomach doing the breaststroke has his head out of the water, as usual. And in the *Très riches heures* the swimmers are again using the frog kick instead of the scissor or flutter kick that was common in antiquity.

A contemporary manuscript illumination by the Boucicaut Master, also from Paris, illustrates Suetonius' story of how Julius Caesar swam to a boat while keeping precious documents dry by holding them over his head (illus. 60).[26] For the first time since the Assyrians, the swimmer is fully clothed. But the Boucicaut Master has more serious problems with his illustration: how can Caesar hold his documents out of the water while swimming the breaststroke? If ever you needed a sidestroke it is here, in this military emergency, with a difficult, heroic mission being

60 Julius Caesar swims while holding a letter over his head, miniature
from *Des cas des nobles hommes et femmes* (*c.* 1413–15).

carried out by a champion swimmer.[27] And yet it is still the breaststroke:
the Boucicaut Master must not have known of any other swimming
stroke.

Just as the Boucicaut Master depicted Caesar fully clothed, in a late
medieval illustration of the Roman story of Cloelia, three girls fully dressed
in contemporary Italian clothing swim across the Tiber towards Rome
(illus. 61). Two of the girls have both arms outstretched. The third swings
her arms in a way that might once have indicated the crawl stroke, but
here she is only reaching out for the riverbank. Again on an Italian plate
illustrating the story of Hero and Leander (see illus. 74), from about 1525,

61 Cloelia and her fellow hostages, fully clothed, escape by swimming across the Tiber River, in Guidoccio di Giovanni Cozzarelli, *The Legend of Cloelia*, *c.* 1480, tempera and gold on wood painting.

first Leander swims with his hat on and both hands extended in front of him, and then he lies drowned under the water.

Southwest Asian and Indian artistic representations of swimming maintain the crawl stroke longer, but they, too, switch to the breaststroke in the late Middle Ages. A 1435–6 illustration of Baghdadis escaping a Mongol attack by swimming across the Tigris shows the swimmer using a crawl stroke, but by 1540, some of the *gopis* swimming with Krishna may be using the breaststroke (see illus. 36).[28] An illustration in the Mughal *Akbarnama*, about 1590, shows a man swimming the breaststroke in the water (see illus. 76). Far to the east in Japan, traditional swimming strokes of the samurai period resemble the breaststroke and the sidestroke: 'the swimmer made the body turn sideways and if he were left-handed he drew out his left hand only and kept the right hand always in the water.' One traditional stroke, known as the Chimba-Nuki, in which 'the swimmer used the right and left hands alternately, with feet fluttering', may be the alternating stroke of early medieval swimmers. At least as described by later authors, the backstroke was not known.[29] Some descriptions of these strokes explicitly describe the swimmer's face being out of the water; none of them describe breathing techniques. And as in medieval Europe, Japanese writers emphasized serenity and grace in swimming.

FROM CHINA TO WESTERN EUROPE, the rise of Central Asian power in the Middle Ages encouraged people to cross the line and identify with non-swimmers instead of swimmers. In Europe this shift was reinforced by the shock of Frederick Barbarossa's death by drowning in 1190. In the course of the thirteenth century, people stopped swimming, or they became much worse swimmers, replacing their overarm strokes with the new breaststroke and backstroke. In addition, just as the great Ice Age had forced northern Eurasians out of the water thousands of years earlier, the Little Ice Age that started around this time also played a part in the late Middle Ages' disinterest in swimming.

12

THE LITTLE ICE AGE

For this second decision to get out of the water, written sources survive to speculate about what caused the change. As in antiquity, most medieval writers attribute this new dislike of the water to the fear of dangers lurking within it, or to a new sense of moral propriety. More recent writers on swimming have followed the same line of thinking, updated for their own time. But most of these explanations fail to hold water. Along with Central Asian cultural dominance, the significant and widespread climate change of the late Middle Ages is likely to have played a more important role.

Swimming as a metaphor for danger

In later medieval literature all across northern Eurasia, with the exception of Norse sagas, swimming tends to represent danger. As in antiquity, medieval swimming stories involve shipwrecks, drowning and monsters. In China a whole genre of Tang Dynasty poetry (so-called 'seeing-off poetry') deals with sea monsters that threaten travellers sailing from China to Japan:

> The rude sails of your ship are set towards your distant retreat. On the voyage you will recite powerful mantras assiduously; While holy relics will leap to defend you from sea monsters. Though menaced by storms, you will perfect your composure; In the midst of the Sea King's demesne you will meditate calmly. Where will you go first when you reach your home?[1]

The sea monsters of medieval Chinese poetry find their parallel in the prolific sea monsters and mermaids of medieval European maps: 'Here there be dragons.'[2] We have already seen the dragons and sea monsters of Jacobus's lives of Christian saints. The same association between swimming and danger appears in a medieval European bestiary illustrated with a mermaid dragging a man out of his boat by the hair.[3] Jonah appears in the whale's mouth, half-eaten. Between Europe and China, the Southwest Asian *One Thousand and One Nights* has a fisherman find in his net 'a demon, with his feet on the ground and his head in the clouds. He had a head like a tomb, fangs like pincers, a mouth like a cave, teeth like stones, nostrils like trumpets', and so on.[4]

Even without sea monsters, the medieval sea is dangerous. In the *One Thousand and One Nights* swimmers meet 'a great wave as tall as a mountain'.[5] The late 1200s saw a number of European manuscript illustrations of Psalm 69 (see Chapter One), showing King David naked in the rising water, begging God to save him from drowning. Similarly, the Dominican philosopher Catherine of Siena, circa 1370, uses a swimming metaphor to describe the monk who fails to follow the rule of his order, rather than staying safely in the ship of his rule:

> Such a man thinks like a fool to navigate this tempestuous sea, with the strength of his own arms, trusting in his own miserable knowledge, and will not navigate it in the arms of his order, and of his superior. Such a one . . . swims in the tempestuous sea, tossed to and fro by contrary winds, fastened only to the ship by his clothes, wearing the religious habit on his body but not on his heart . . . he does not see that he labors more swimming with his arms, than the good religious in the ship, or that he is in danger of eternal death; for if his clothes should be suddenly torn from the ship, which will happen at the moment of death, he will have no remedy.[6]

Seafarers must expect to be storm-tossed and shipwrecked, at the mercy of the waves. In the *One Thousand and One Nights* story of Jullanar of the Sea, King Badre rides one of the planks of his wrecked ship for three days and nights, drifting 'helplessly' with the wind, before being cast up on shore.[7] After another shipwreck, a dervish climbs on a floating plank and the wind immediately throws him up on land.[8] Then the *Little Flowers of St Francis of Assisi*, a collection of mostly apocryphal stories about Francis written in Italy around 1390, remarks that, 'Some men who cannot swim cast themselves in the water to save others from drowning, and so all of them are lost together.' Lurid images of the drowned are common in European art of the later Middle Ages: a pink crow pecking at the eyes of the drowned in a stained-glass window at Chartres, an ocean with pale greenish corpses floating in it from the Holkham Bible.[9]

And when it is not a question of monsters or storms, even Egypt's Nile is dangerous:

There once lived in Egypt, on the banks of the Nile, a washerman, by name Noah, who was – like an atom – all day in the sun, and – like a fish – all the year round in the water . . .

This man had a darling son, who was headstrong, good-for-nothing, and foolish; and who, as soon as he saw his father in the water, would seat himself on his father's ass, and drive it into the river. The father was in constant terror lest the boy should fall into the water and be drowned, or lest a crocodile should seize him.

One day, the boy, as usual, mounted the ass, and rode with such fury into the river, that at once the water reached his head. At one moment he was, like an oyster, under water; the next, like a bubble, on its surface.

As soon as the father learned that his son was drowning, he rushed into the water, in the hope of saving him, and caught him by the hand. The lad grasped at his father, and seized him by the hair. Both sank, and were drowned together.[10]

Swimming and sex

Not surprisingly, swimming in the late Middle Ages also intensified its earlier correlation with sexual transgression, in that both usually involve taking your clothes off. Central Asians in particular had always been squeamish about showing skin. Classical Greek vase painters imagined Scythians and Persians as covered from head to toe, with leggings or trousers, long-sleeved shirts and hats or hoods, in contrast to the Greek characters, who were often shown nude or wearing short tunics.[11] West

Asians also usually covered themselves, as Adam and Eve did in the Garden of Eden; Noah's sons were shocked when he got drunk and passed out naked in his tent. Central Asian and West Asian people continued to cover themselves throughout the Middle Ages. They wore trousers and shirts, and often turbans or hats. Women, when they were not riding horses in trousers, wore long sleeves and skirts to the ground, and often veils as well. In place of classical tunics and togas, Byzantine men and women wore high-necked, long-sleeved robes that reached their ankles. The Quran similarly urged both men and women to cover their bodies and not to look directly at one another, in the interest of morality.[12] And as both Chinese and Europeans copied Central Asian fashions in coats and trousers, they, too, covered their skin more and more completely.

Among people who lived so covered, the association between undressing, swimming and sex must have seemed obvious. The thirteenth-century *One Thousand and One Nights* story of the 'Porter and the Three Ladies' shows us the kind of behaviour people now associated with swimming:

> They drank for a while, and then the eldest and fairest of the three stood up and began to undress . . . the girl stripped naked, threw herself into the pool, and immersed herself. The porter looked at her naked body, which looked like a slice of the moon, and at her face, which shone like the full moon or the rising sun, and admired her figure, her breasts, and her swaying heavy hips, for she was naked as God had created her . . . When the girl heard his verses, she came quickly out of the pool, sat in his lap and, pointing to her slit, asked 'O light of my eyes, O sweetheart, what is the name of this? . . . Then the porter stood up, took off his clothes, and, revealing something dangling between his legs, he leapt and plunged into the middle of the pool.[13]

Iranian miniaturists also used the excuse of swimming to undress their subjects. A typical illustration of swimming from Safavid Iran in the early 1500s shows people swimming naked and embracing, while Alexander the Great spies on them (see illus. 38). As in northern Indian images of *gopis*, these women are really just standing in the water, even though one spreads her arms apart in an awkward rendition of the crawl stroke. And, like the *gopis*, when bathing women lose their clothes in the sixteenth-century Chinese novel *Journey to the West*, they too are ashamed to come out of the water, and are sexually victimized by their tormentor.[14] On the other hand, decent swimmers begin to be clothed: the swimmer in the Indian *Akbarnama* has a cloth wrapped around his hips, and the swimming *gopis* are also more or less fully dressed as they swim.

The same associations between swimming, sex and shame were beginning to reach out of Islamic North Africa even as far as West Africa. Images of sexualized mermaids spreading their tails reached West Africa in the tenth century, probably coming from India. We see them reproduced on the Benin bronzes. By the late Middle Ages, North African travellers such as Ibn Battuta were letting West Africans know how scandalized they were by nudity of all kinds.[15]

Europeans similarly associated swimming and sex. Boccaccio describes an adulterous friar in Venice, who escapes discovery by throwing himself out of his lover's bedroom window into the Grand Canal: 'As the water was deep, and he was a good swimmer, he received no harm.'[16] The ability to swim, as in classical antiquity, is associated with sexual desire and promiscuity. In the later Middle Ages Christian bishops began more and more to be concerned about morality in bathing. Around 1400 John Lydgate warned people against indulging the body at the expense of the soul. Bathhouses and baths became closely associated with brothels in medieval literature and art, and as a result many public bathhouses gained a bad reputation and were closed. By the 1500s 'mermaid' and 'siren' were common euphemisms for sex workers.[17]

Changes in bathing habits

As this concern about public baths suggests, the old northern non-swimmers' idea that even entering pools of water was risky also regained its power in the late Middle Ages. Towns made new regulations intended to safeguard river water, and ideas about appropriate bathing changed in similar ways all across northern Eurasia and North Africa. People became reluctant to bathe in public. Where people continued to use public pools, it was often in the context of sickness, where people were visiting hot springs ostensibly for their health. And increasingly, even in the hot springs, bathers kept their clothes on.

Public baths were considered to be bad for morals and possibly bad for your health.[18] Twelfth-century doctors in Southwest Asia and North Africa warned against spending too much time in the bath. Where Ibn Sina, in the early eleventh century, urged his patients to bathe regularly and 'stay for a good amount of time', Maimonides, a century later, suggests bathing only once a week. Both, however, warn their patients not to remain 'too long' in the bath: 'as soon as you perspire and your body becomes supple, rinse your body and leave the bath.'[19] In China, people regarded mixed bathing (men and women together) as 'licentious in the extreme'.[20] Many old communal baths of the Song Dynasty, the Abbasids and the Romans were replaced by newer public baths with individual bathing tubs in private or semi-private rooms. Ibn Sina in the eleventh century clearly envisioned communal bathing, but Ibn Battuta's description of the bathhouses in Baghdad shows that by about 1350 Islamic *hamam* baths no longer involved either public nudity or big swimming pools:

> The baths at Baghdad are numerous and excellently constructed, most of them being painted with pitch, which has the appearance of black marble. This pitch is brought from a spring between Kufa and Basra, from which it flows continually. It gathers at the sides of the spring like clay and is shovelled up and brought to Baghdad. Each establishment has a large number of private bathrooms, every one of which has also a wash-basin in the corner, with two taps supplying hot and cold water . . . In no town other than Baghdad have I seen all this elaborate arrangement, though some other towns approach it in this respect.[21]

By the late Middle Ages public baths in Europe, like the ones in Baghdad, were being built with private, individual tubs.[22] People who could afford it constructed bathing spaces in private homes, or bathed in wooden tubs in their own houses or gardens. Even these wooden tubs could be surrounded with bathing tents for privacy (and perhaps warmth).

The exception was health spas, where people continued to bathe communally. After a decline in the popularity of healing baths in the seventh century, the late Middle Ages saw a resurgence of the idea that water could be healing, reviving ancient ideas about the power of water.[23] The *Regimen sanitatis*, a thirteenth-century European medical advice pamphlet, strongly recommends hot and cold bathing as a means of regulating humours and restoring health.[24] In late medieval China as well, public baths were especially for sick men. The Italian traveller Marco Polo saw large heated public baths in Hangzhou in the 1200s, where a hundred people could bathe together. Chinese sources agree that Hangzhou was a centre of big public baths with brick-walled pools, and add that public baths were common across medieval China.[25] (This idea that many people with different contagious diseases should bathe in the same water demonstrates that bathing is not necessarily healthy even when people do it for their health.)

All across northern Eurasia, people who used public baths increasingly wore clothes into the water. In China, this had been true at least since the Zhou Dynasty: a man covered himself with 'two coarse kerchiefs about his body', front and back.[26] In medieval Baghdad, you used three towels: one to wrap around your waist on your way in, a second to wear on your way out and a third to dry off.[27] Europeans wanted even more coverage than Asians. At the Baden hot springs in Germany in the spring of 1416, Poggio Bracciolini reported that both men and women were wearing clothes to bathe there. He disapproves: 'the men wear only a pair of drawers. The women are clad in linen vests, which are however slashed in the sides, so that they neither cover the neck, the breast, nor the arms of the wearer.'[28] Not only were people wearing clothes to bathe in, but Poggio thought they were not wearing *enough* clothes.

Then in 1449 the proprietors of the old Roman hot springs at Bath in England tried to stop people from wearing their underwear in the pool, enforcing an old rule. But people were outraged. Customs had changed: people were not comfortable in their skins anymore. They wanted to wear clothes into the water. When the proprietors insisted, the bathers asked the local bishop, Thomas Beckington, for support, and Beckington forbade naked bathing in the hot springs as immodest. He ordered that everyone – men and women – over the age of puberty should wear clothes.[29] Not long afterwards, European bath-keepers began, as in China, to separate men and women bathers.

Europeans and Southwest Asians continued to go to the baths in the late Middle Ages. Many people associated the cleanliness of bathing with the cleanliness of baptism.[30] Nevertheless, most people seem to have leaned increasingly towards keeping their clothes on in public, using individual tubs, separating men from women and, starting in the thirteenth century in western Afro-Eurasia, installing bathrooms or tubs in their own homes.[31] None of this was conducive to swimming, and indeed by 1599, as part of the same prudish movement that put fig leaves over the genitals of ancient Greek statues (some of them still in place today in the Vatican Museum), Pope Clement VIII promulgated a law forbidding people from swimming naked in the Tiber in Rome.[32]

Swimming and strangers

Like earlier non-swimmers, medieval Eurasians also constructed ethnic and cultural distinctions dividing swimmers from non-swimmers. Swimming was not yet seen as an inborn genetic or biological ability, but it was increasingly a choice associated with cultural or religious identity, or even legal identity. In the 1250s, for example, the law codes of Alfonso the Wise, in Spanish Castile, forbade Jews and Christians from bathing together.[33] In China, swimming became a trait attributed to South Chinese and Japanese people, not for anyone in northern China. Like the choice of what language to speak, the ability to swim divided one people from another. Like their ancient forebears, late medieval non-swimmers justified their reluctance to get in the water in cultural terms, or in terms of danger or personal modesty.

Early modern explanations

By the early modern period, however, these traditional explanations seemed insufficient. In the 1700s the French editor of Melchisédech Thévenot's early swimming manual proposed some new explanations for why people had given up swimming. These reflected the concerns of that time:

> False sophistication caused a softness, which soon destroyed this healthy institution [of swimming]. The lords left the countryside, where they could have spread abundance and happiness, and moved to the towns. There they learned new customs and new tastes. Other citizens, aping these knights, abandoned their old ways, and the country games, the innocent amusements, like the art of swimming, were left to peasants and people like that. Since

this revolution, a fatal time when good customs were inverted, the better-off looked down on the pleasures that ordinary people could share with them. The dangers that they might find themselves exposed to in the course of their life, the pleasure they might make out of the necessity of a bath, to strengthen their limbs and keep themselves healthy, the delicious emotions that a tired man feels when he dives into running water – nothing could convince them to take up the old simple ways. And, if from time to time there have been some whose spirits were strong enough to dare to go against the national prejudice, those were exceptions to the rule, and not of any importance. Good swimmers, today, are only to be found in those climates where our luxuries and fastidiousness have not yet penetrated.[34]

Poncelin's class-based observation is astute. Indeed, in the early Middle Ages Eurasians had considered swimming to be a marker of elite status: hence Charlemagne's emphasis on his swimming, and the swimming of the Iranian heroes Rustem and Sindbad. In the late Middle Ages people associated swimming with servants, as in the Chinese story above, and with peasants, like those depicted in the *Très riches heures*. Poncelin blames this shift on urbanization, and growing medieval cities may indeed have played a part, but equally urbanized polities in Japan, South India, Indonesia, East Africa, South China and Mexico nevertheless maintained a lively interest in swimming. Urbanization is not a sufficient explanation.

More recent explanations

Nineteenth- and twentieth-century historians suggest that people stopped swimming because they were worried about spreading disease. Did they hold their heads out of the water to keep from drinking dirty water?[35] But northern Eurasians seem to have always swum with their heads out of the water, even in antiquity. And no medieval source mentions concerns about getting ill. Few if any people in medieval Afro-Eurasia were even aware that diseases could be caught from dirty water. And the timing does not match up: by the time the Black Death hit in the mid-1300s, Afro-Eurasian swimming had already been in decline for over a century.

There is no basis for any relationship between disease and the end of swimming. This idea probably goes back to nineteenth-century scholars, who were simultaneously absorbing the new idea of germs spreading diseases such as cholera and beginning to wonder why Europeans had abandoned swimming. Naturally they would have combined the two. But the Black Death does not explain the end of swimming.[36]

Attempts to tie the end of swimming in medieval Europe to a supposed decline in medieval shipping are equally unhelpful. This supposes that people learned to swim mainly to save themselves in case of shipwrecks. But swimming had never been primarily a question of water safety. Furthermore, people also stopped swimming in the Indian Ocean, where medieval trade was more, not less, lively than in antiquity.[37] And we now know that the early medieval Mediterranean carried far more shipping than had been thought, with correspondingly more shipwrecks. Similarly, John McManamon's recent attribution of the medieval decline in swimming to 'the ethos of chivalry and the Christianization of Europe' is too Eurocentric to be useful.[38] A change that affected all of northern Eurasia requires an explanation of similar breadth: the Central Asian conquest is one of the two changes that fits that charge. The other, to which we will now turn, is the Little Ice Age.

The Little Ice Age

In the late Middle Ages a significant climate change known as the Little Ice Age made swimming less attractive, just as the more serious Ice Age had thousands of years earlier. In Europe summers became colder and rainier, bringing frequent crop failures and forcing wine-making further south. The consequences of the Little Ice Age outside of Europe are just beginning to be understood. Nevertheless enough data has now emerged on the serious droughts that affected India and Africa to suggest that people's attitudes towards water may have changed at this time in the south as well as the north. The combination of climate change and Central Asian cultural dominance led people all over Eurasia and North Africa to stop swimming by the end of the Middle Ages.

Unlike changes in shipping patterns or urbanization, the Little Ice Age, like the Mongol conquests, affected all of Eurasia in the late Middle Ages. We should be wary of our generation's inclination to find climate change at the root of all historical events, but the serious, prolonged changes in global temperature and rain patterns that make up the Little Ice Age must have affected people's interest in swimming. Just as the last major Ice Age convinced many northern Eurasians to give up swimming in the Stone Age, so the Little Ice Age convinced them to stop swimming in the Middle Ages.

The Little Ice Age started in the 1200s and ended in the 1850s. Across northern Eurasia it brought colder weather. One cause may have been a spate of huge volcanic eruptions that spewed out enough ash to block sunlight. The eruption of Samalas volcano on Lombok Island in Indonesia in 1257 may have started the cooling trend.[39] Eurasia's average temperatures only cooled by one or two degrees, but (as with climate change today) that was enough to matter.[40] Summers became much rainier, causing widespread crop failures when wheat and barley went mouldy. Millions of people in China starved. In Europe many people had to switch to eating rye bread, or a mix of rye and oats. This was the much maligned 'black bread' of the peasantry, which they only stopped eating in the nineteenth century after the end of the Little Ice Age.[41] Small surprise that these wet, cold, hungry people also lost interest in going swimming.

Meanwhile, across most of Africa and India, the Little Ice Age instead brought a long, terrible drought. So much of the world's water was tied up in glaciers, and in the rainy weather up north, that there was not much left to fall as rain in Africa or India.[42] Massive monsoon failures occurred throughout the second half of the 1500s and the 1600s. Setbacks in the Mughal Empire may be associated with the drought, too.[43] In places where people had always been tentative swimmers, this drought may also have had an effect on people's swimming. Droughts associated with the Little Ice Age in South Asia may have caused people to feel yet more strongly that water was sacred, perhaps discouraging people from entering it. Where in the Middle Ages water rituals had required Krishna's Hindu pilgrims in Braj to touch or drink the water of the sacred river, by the mid-1500s it was enough to look at the Yamuna's water, even out of the window of a stone tower that may have been constructed for this purpose, or simply to look at paintings of the Yamuna River (Sugata Ray calls this 'hydrolatry').[44] Though the Central Asian Mughals' fear of the water must have played a part, the regular and disastrous failure of the monsoons in this period apparently did as well.[45] Thus the Little Ice Age may have discouraged swimming in Iran and India owing to drought, and across northern Eurasia on account of the cold and rain.

BY THE END OF the Middle Ages distinctions between swimmers and non-swimmers were almost as stark as they had been at the end of the Stone Age. Across northern Eurasia, swimming had faded away. Most people were scandalized at the idea of naked swimmers, and the over-arm crawl stroke had disappeared. Those few who continued to swim substituted dog-paddle or breaststroke. From Europe to China, the combination of Central Asian expansion and the Little Ice Age caused most people to stop swimming. This fear of the water even extended to North Africa, where people had previously been swimmers. In the rest of the world, where the Mongol influence did not reach, in Japan, in Australia, in South Asia, in Africa and in the Americas, people were still good swimmers, still using overhand strokes. Northerners had all but forgotten that there were people in the world who knew how to swim. But the same climate phenomenon – the Little Ice Age – that had encouraged northern Eurasians to give up swimming also impelled them to cross the oceans and colonize new places. In the next chapter we will see what happened when the non-swimming Eurasians encountered the swimmers everywhere else.

PART III

STILL SWIMMING

62 Somali men diving for money at Aden, Yemen, illustration from *The Graphic*,
27 November 1875. Note the use of an overhand stroke on the right.

13

~

AFRICAN SWIMMERS

When Bishop Beckington was banning nude bathing at Bath in the 1440s, more adventurous Europeans were already heading out into the Atlantic Ocean in their caravels. In the 1300s Europeans colonized the Canary Islands, off the coast of West Africa in the Atlantic Ocean. In 1443 they reached Mauritania. The next year they captured and enslaved people along the coast of Senegal. In 1471 Europeans reached Ghana, and eleven years later the kingdom of Kongo. In 1492 Columbus arrived in the Caribbean, where he enslaved Native Americans for the first time. A few years later Vasco da Gama reached the important trading zone of the Indian Ocean. By 1512 Europeans were trading in Indonesia, and the next year China; they arrived in Japan less than a century after they reached West Africa. Everywhere these European traders arrived, they were astonished to discover that most of the people they met were excellent swimmers – better swimmers even than the best swimmers of Renaissance Europe. While even good swimmers in Europe could only use the breaststroke, Africans, Southeast Asians and Native Americans all used an overarm crawl stroke. European swimmers used a frog kick, but other people all used variants of a straight-leg kick. Most could swim with their faces in the water, and many could execute elegant dives. People swam carrying children on their backs (see illus. 75). Though some Europeans were intrigued, many of them reacted to this discovery by asserting that swimming was an activity unsuited to civilized people, appropriate only for animals and subhumans.[1] Swimming now became racialized. Knowing how to swim divided Black from White, and the ability to swim was twisted to support the pretence that the people of Africa and the Americas were natural slaves.

This justification is not surprising, because Europeans set out for Africa precisely in search of people to enslave. The reduced crop yields of the Little Ice Age may have helped drive Europeans to explore the Atlantic Ocean, but they were not sailing to find new land to farm; they wanted new peoples to farm; they wanted salable captives. Countries did not pay to outfit fleets of expensive ships out of an interest in science or a sense of adventure.[2] As far back as the Roman Empire, European maps showed India and Africa, and so did medieval European maps. Geographers knew that sailing west from the Canary Islands brought you to a big patch of seaweed in the ocean, and they would not have had to strain to see that there might be islands near there: the Caribbean.[3] European sailing fleets knew where they were going: places where there were people for sale, a good climate for growing sugar cane and markets with money to buy the products of colonial slavery.

Europeans expanded their slaving voyages to West Africa in the late 1400s because their usual sources of victims had dried up. To the east, the Polish and Ottoman Empires now defended their borders against Western European slavers.[4] In Spain, gradual European conquests of Muslim territory during the 1300s had flooded southern Europe with enslaved Muslims. Their labour boosted European manufacturing. But by the mid-1400s, with Spain mostly Christian, that source had also evaporated.[5] Now the slave trade mostly meant Islamic slave-dealers whose camel caravans crossed the Sahara Desert.[6] So Henry the Navigator's Portuguese ships' captains began to explore ways of circumventing the camel caravans, first by conquering Ceuta, in Morocco, and then by exploring south by ship along the Atlantic coast of Africa. Magnetic compasses (from China), better astrolabes (from Iran), better clocks and improved shipbuilding technology made it less risky to sail on the open ocean, out of sight of land, and against the current and the prevailing wind. Like the Spanish and Portuguese, the Venetians and Genoese had been slave-dealers for centuries, and Venetians like John Cabot and Genoans like Christopher Columbus were deeply invested in these early slave-dealers' efforts. European slavers' intentions shaped their understanding, so that when they saw their prospective victims swimming, they registered swimming as a skill suitable only for animals, monsters, foreigners and the enslaved.

Africa

When the first Portuguese slave traders sailed down the Atlantic coast of Africa to Senegal in the 1440s, they immediately noticed that Africans could swim better than Europeans. Many of the Portuguese sailors, despite making their living on the ocean, could not swim at all. After an unsuccessful Portuguese slave raid in the 1440s off the coast of Senegal, when the Portuguese had to scramble to retreat to their boats, they reported that, 'some of the men who knew how to swim, seeing danger so near at hand, threw themselves into the water and saved their lives by swimming.' But the others 'who did not know that art' were killed by the angry Senegalese.[7]

Africans had been good swimmers in antiquity, and they were still swimming when Europeans arrived. Zamba Zebola, who grew up along the Congo River in the 1700s, reports that as a child he was 'quite used to the water in Africa and could swim like a seagull'.[8] Along the Niger, people swam for 'pleasing amusement' as well as in fishing or boating, wearing amulets against drowning.[9] In Ghana, the Asante were also expert swimmers, diving with reed nets to catch fish.[10] Divers brought up oysters and cowrie shells, salvaged property lost overboard when canoes overturned and even 'fished' for underwater gold.[11] (However, most cowrie shells were retrieved by wading, as on the Maldive Islands.[12]) Like Roman children a thousand years earlier, West African children learned to swim 'on bits of boards, or small bundles of rushes, fasten'd under their stomachs'. They could swim very fast, dive very deep and stay underwater for a long time.[13] And like Song Dynasty body-surfers, West African children rode surfboards through the waves along the Atlantic coast. Swimming included 'both men and women, from their infancy'.[14] South African Indigenous accounts describe swimming as part of a raid to recover a woman who had been kidnapped by a neighbouring group:

> They had a river to cross, which was deep; they were wrong to try and get across; they ought to have fought on this side. Before they had gone over half the water, we had assagied two of them. They soon sank, and were eaten up by the alligators. The other two got over. We all jumped into the water, and swam after them.[15]

In East Africa, off the coast of Mozambique and Kenya, early accounts describe many good swimmers in the late 1400s, some able to swim away from Vasco da Gama's ship even after torture, and with their hands tied.[16] The Ethiopian priest Aba Gorgorios describes how Ethiopian Christians celebrated Epiphany in the 1600s:

> The King with all the Nobility of the Court, the Metropolitan with the Clergy, Nobles and Plebeians, Old and Young, before Sun-rise, throng into the Rivers and Ponds, and there delight themselves in the Water, plunging and diving over Head and Ears. As they meet any of the Priests, they crave a Blessing from them . . . it is frequent for the Young men upon this day to leap, and dance, and swim and duck one another . . . a day of Jollity.[17]

Gorgorios here is defending his people from a dangerous Portuguese Catholic charge that they engage in the heresy of multiple baptism, so it is not clear whether Ethiopians really celebrated Epiphany with swimming. But even if the specific ceremony is fabricated, Gorgorios knows rivers and ponds as places for having fun and socializing. All around Africa, people were still good swimmers.

The ancient African sport of leaping on animals in the water and fighting them, known from the Roman encyclopaedist Pliny's description and from Pompeii's Nilotic wall paintings, also continued into the colonization period. In the late 1600s Senegalese swimmers killed sharks by waiting until they 'see him turn on his side to attack them, and then diving under him and splitting his stomach as they swim under him'.[18] East Africans fought hippopotamuses: they 'hurled their harpoon, and swimming for some distance under water, they came to the surface and hastened to the shore'.[19] As Pliny says, Africans hunted huge sea turtles weighing 130–180 kilograms (300–400 lb).[20] And, again as in Pliny, African swimmers fought crocodiles:

> they surprise [a crocodile] in a place where it can't hold itself up without swimming. They attack it with a cow leather around their left arm, and a bayonet in the right hand. They put the leather-covered arm down his throat and hold it open, and since he has no tongue he fills up with water like a barrel and drowns. To hasten

his death, they give him blows in the throat with the bayonet, or put out his eyes, and so by skill they manage what they could not do with a much greater use of force.[21]

These battles may have been connected to ritual demonstrations of masculinity, but African women fought crocodiles too, and proudly displayed the scars.[22]

Swimming was not universal in Africa. Pieter de Marees claims that people further inland did not swim, and in the 1700s Olaudah Equiano apparently did not know how to swim when he was kidnapped into slavery in Nigeria. As he was marched through different areas on his way to the slave ships he was 'often very much astonished to see some of the women, as well as the men, jump into the water, dive to the bottom, come up again, and swim about'.[23] West African conversions to Islam, the faith of a non-swimming culture much concerned with bodily modesty, may have discouraged swimming, introducing motifs like the Indian *naramakara* split-tailed mermaid. These appear in African art starting around the time of the arrival of Islam, in the ninth century CE. The mermaids were still current in West Africa when Europeans arrived; one appears on the famous Benin Bronzes.[24] But Equiano's report in itself confirms that most West Africans could swim.

Non-swimming Europeans were enormously impressed with African swimming. One Venetian slave trader reported that West Africans were 'such good swimmers that they can swim from one bank to the other, and they are the most perfect swimmers that you can find in any region of the world, that I know of'. Senegalese people bathed their children every day and taught them to swim as soon as they could.[25] Like other good swimmers, these West Africans used a crawl stroke, and not the European breaststroke, 'throwing one [arm] after another forward, as if they were paddling, and not extending their arms equally, and striking with them both together, as Europeans do'.[26] They could swim 'very fast, generally easily outdoing people of our nation in swimming and diving'.[27] Alvise Cà da Mosto recalled an example of strong swimming he had seen in 1455 in the land of Budomel, near Senegal:

> Desiring to send a letter to those in my ship to let them know that they should come to that river, to which I would have to go

by land, I asked the blacks if there was anyone who knew how to swim well and who had sufficient courage to take my letter to the ship, which was about three miles away.

At once many of them said yes, but because the sea was high and there was a lot of wind, I said that I did not think such a thing was possible for a man to do. The principal reason was that about a bow-shot off shore, there was a reef and bank of sand and other banks two bowshots farther still, and between these banks such a current ran now one way and now another, that it was a very difficult thing for any man swimming to withstand it and not to be carried away. So great a sea broke over these banks that it appeared impossible to pass them.

In spite of this, two blacks offered to go and when I asked what I should give them, they said that they should be given two manilhas of tin each, which is something they greatly value. So for sixteen marchetti each, they took on themselves to bring the letter to the caravels and went into the sea. I cannot describe the difficulty they had in passing those sand banks in such a sea. Sometimes they remained for so long without being seen that I thought they had drowned.

Finally one of them could no longer withstand the force of the sea which broke over him and turned back. The other struggled on bravely across the bank for the space of an hour. Finally he passed it and took the letter to the ship and returned with a reply, which seemed to me to be a remarkable thing. From this I conclude that the blacks of that coast are the greatest swimmers which there are in the world.[28]

Along the Atlantic coast of West Africa (now Liberia), about 1600, a skilled diver used swimming to escape with valuables from a European trading ship:

They can swim below the water like a fish, as they proved there. One of them, who had a pewter tankard of beer in his hand and a soldier's helmet on his head, jumped into the water with them and swam thus a great distance underwater; then he re-emerged and jumped into his little boat, which his companion had to bring to him. Thus he got away with the helmet and tankard, and no-one could overtake him.[29]

In 1656 the first Dutch governor of Cape Town, South Africa, saw local people swimming across the river with their cattle.[30] And in 1795, when the Scottish explorer Mungo Park crossed the Senegal River in Mali, a 'few boys swam after' his horses. The following year, 800 kilometres (500 mi.) inland, Park saw a fisherman dive underwater to collect and set fish traps. When the man stayed underwater for several minutes, Park was so surprised and concerned that he 'thought he had actually drowned himself'.[31] The expedition ended when Park himself drowned in the Niger River, partly because, like most Europeans at this time, he did not know how to swim.[32]

When these Europeans saw how well Africans could swim, they might have been inspired to take swimming lessons. But instead they twisted African swimming into an excuse to exploit and enslave Africans.[33] In this they were following earlier Islamic stories that also contrast Muslim swimming with the excellent swimming of East Africans and racialize the distinction. The late medieval Southwest Asian stories of Sindbad the Sailor have Sindbad, like Odysseus, needing 'a piece of timber' to swim when he is shipwrecked in the Indian Ocean; his companion drowns because he 'could not swim'. But when Sindbad meets 'a multitude of ape-like savages' (probably meant as a slur on East Africans), they 'appeared on the beach and began to swim out towards the ship'.[34]

Like the anonymous author of the Sindbad stories, European slavers presented African swimming skills as evidence that Africans were more like animals than humans, and therefore undeserving of human rights. This inexcusable spin on swimming was only one small strand of the huge hairball of racism that Europeans were developing, but it fitted into the larger context of enslavement. Europeans seized on any and all cultural differences as evidence that Africans were natural slaves.[35] Slave owners named the African people they owned 'Jumper, Juno, Fido, and so on', the same names as pets and farm animals, 'in a sustained attempt to deny the obvious fact of their humanity'.[36] And as everything about Africans justified slavery in European slavers' eyes, so it was with Africans' ability to swim.

Europeans used swimming to dehumanize Africans in at least two ways. First, Europeans assumed (or pretended to assume) that African skill at swimming was natural and inborn. They claimed that, like dogs or horses, Indigenous children were practically born knowing how to swim – very much unlike civilized English or Portuguese children. Early slave traders claimed that African toddlers learned to swim without adult assistance or supervision. In 1602 one wrote that 'Once the [West African] children begin to walk by themselves, they soon go to the water in order to learn how to swim and to walk in the water.'[37] In the early 1700s they claimed that 'the [West African] Mother gives the Infant suck for two or three Years; which over . . . they [are] able to go . . . to the Sea-side to learn to swim . . . nobody looks after it.'[38] Jean Barbot, in the 1730s, understood that it was practice that made Africans into good swimmers. When he saw (or claimed to have seen) 'several hundred of boys and girls sporting together before the beach [at the terrible slave fort of El Mina in Ghana] and in many places among the rolling and breaking waves, learning to swim', he reported that Africans' strong swimming abilities 'proceed from their being brought up, both men and women from their infancy, to swim like fishes; and that, with the constant exercise, renders them so dexterous'.[39] Indeed: fish are born knowing how to swim; humans are not. But even modern writers repeat the idea that 'along the coasts of South America, Africa, and India, versions of the trudgen stroke . . . had been swum naturally for time immemorial'.[40] When William Percey acknowledged in 1658 that 'man doth not altogether naturally Swim as other creatures do, but immediately descends towards the bottom,'[41] he meant White people: Indigenous people and Africans did not count.

Slave traders' false suggestion that Africans swam innately, like fish, found a corollary in the idea that Africans could swim because, like animals, they were incapable of rational thought. As late as 1840, swimming books repeated this canard:

> Man cannot swim with the same faculty as many of the inferior animals, which seem to be led by instinct to use the proper action for their preservation, while rational creatures, being aware of their danger, grow fearful or impatient, and begin to struggle, which has the effect of making them sink in the water.[42]

If rationality made swimming more difficult, then plainly the reason Africans could swim so much better than Europeans was that they were less rational. This emphasis on Africans learning to swim as babies also usefully reinforced a widespread belief that African children grew up faster than Europeans – again, like monkeys, fish, dogs or horses.[43] In this way Europeans used African swimming to justify not only enslavement, but the widespread sexual abuse and rape of African children.[44]

A second way Europeans dehumanized Africans was to turn African swimming into a spectator sport like cock-fighting, bear-baiting or dog-fighting, all of which were common in Early Modern Europe. Eighteenth-century European slave traders encouraged Ivory Coast West African people to perform for them:

> You are probably acquainted with the expert Swimming and Diving of these Negroes, which I have several times seen with Surprize. Whenever they were on Board, and I threw a string of Coral, or any thing else into the Sea, one of them would immediately dive after it, and tho' almost got to the bottom fetch it up again. This they seldom missed of, and were sure of what they brought up as their Reward.[45]

When an American traveller threw coins from his ship, West Africans dived from the yardarm, about 7.5 metres (25 ft) up, to retrieve them.[46] Slavers were playing the same game in Somalia as late as 1875 (illus. 62).

Africans were not immune to racial distinctions; African people also dehumanized Europeans upon first encountering them. The first time Equiano saw White people he fainted. He thought he would be eaten 'by these white men with horrible looks, red faces, and long hair'.[47] Another West African captive reported that his people 'generally imagined, that all who were sold for slaves, were at least eaten or murdered, since none ever returned'.[48] Both groups found each other funny-looking, weird and impious.[49] Africans, like Europeans, counted swimming among the differences they noticed. Many Africans believed Europeans drowned when they fell into the water, or that sharks were attracted to them, because the gods were punishing Europeans for shooting and enslaving Africans.[50] But Africans could not convert their fears into economic profits as Europeans did. Not only in Africa but all over the world, as European trading ships reached each new group of people, captains and passengers repeated this pattern of astonishment, rationalization and exploitation.

Europeans reach India

Europeans had been travelling back and forth to India for at least 2,000 years before Vasco da Gama reached Goa in the late 1400s, so they cannot have really been astonished by Indian customs. Europeans knew and valued Indian medicines, pepper, steel, cotton and sugar. They used Indian numbers, and played the Indian game of chess. Roman trading ships had been sailing from Egypt to Gujarat and South India since the time of Augustus, and Roman mercenaries fought in India. Before the fall of Rome, Roman ships reached Burma, and possibly even Thailand and Vietnam.[51] This trade continued through the Middle Ages; in 1291, for example, a Franciscan missionary sent letters home to Italy describing the East Indian coast.[52] European sea captains and traders knew what to expect from India before they set out to sail there via the Horn of Africa.

But now for the first time Europeans arrived in India as conquerors, determined not just to trade but to control the Indian Ocean. Europeans were quick to profit from the swimming abilities of the people of the Indian Ocean. By 1521-2 the Portuguese navy had seized control of Bahrain in order to profit from the pearl-diving industry there.[53] Pearls became hugely popular among the wealthier classes in Europe, and in European portraits from this time everybody is wearing ropes of pearls, from Ottoman sultans and Venetian grandees to Queen Elizabeth and Sir Walter Raleigh. Then a few years later, the pearl fisheries of Sri Lanka, off the eastern coast of India, also fell under the control of the Portuguese navy.[54] Tens of millions of pearls were extracted and brought to Europe.

Europeans seized control of trade in the Indian Ocean by force. In 1502 Vasco da Gama captured a ship carrying more than four hundred Muslim pilgrims returning from the hajj, their pilgrimage to Mecca. He removed some of the children to enslave them, then set the ship on fire. It exploded with the pilgrims still aboard.[55] One way the traders justified this at home, of course, was to lean on the religious distinction between Christians and Muslims. But another way to dehumanize Indians, as with Africans, was to emphasize their swimming abilities. Soon after reaching India, for instance, Vasco da Gama attacked Indian boats anchored at Goa, on the southwestern coast. His confederate Gaspar Correa reported that the Indians who had been on board these boats 'were swimming about in the sea'.[56] Further south in Kozhikode, the local resistance made plans to set the Portuguese ships on fire and then, as Correa has it, to 'throw themselves into the sea, and escape by swimming in the boats which they would take equipped for that purpose'.[57]

European attempts to portray Indians as swimmers were not very convincing. Indians, like Europeans, swam only for work or in emergency situations. There are no parallels to the accounts of African children paddling about joyfully on the beaches, or swimming curiously out to the ships. Indians were clearly not able to swim the way Africans did. Yet even if imaginary, this contrast between swimmers and non-swimmers underlined emerging racial distinctions, and helped to justify for Europeans back home the sickening violence with which European traders seized control of Indian Ocean trade.

NEW DISTINCTIONS were being forged. No longer would Europeans consider swimming to be a mark of education and sophistication. Instead, Europeans now re-imagined swimming as something animals did. When people swam, Europeans took it to mean that the swimmers were practically animals themselves, and could be treated as such. Conveniently for European colonization, for the slave trade and for the European project to dominate world trade, there could be no objection to buying and selling them, renaming them, beating them or slaughtering them. This same expedient view would also assist Europeans in their conquest of the Americas.

14

IN THE AMERICAS

After a few years in the Portuguese slave trade in West Africa, the Genoese slave trader Christopher Columbus headed west across the Atlantic Ocean, sponsored by Spain.[1] When Columbus reached the Caribbean in 1492, he, too, professed himself amazed at the swimming abilities of the people he met there. Arawak people 'came swimming to the boats, bringing parrots, balls of cotton thread, javelins, and many other things'.[2] Five years later, another expedition reported that,

> before we reached the land, many of them jumped into the sea and came swimming to receive us at a bowshot's length [from the shore], for they are very great swimmers, with as much confidence as if they had for a long time been acquainted with us: and we were pleased with this their confidence ... they swim [with an expertness] beyond all belief, and the women better than the men: for we have many times found and seen them swimming two leagues out at sea without anything to rest upon.[3]

(If this letter is a forgery, as appears likely, it is only the more striking how much emphasis Europeans wished to put on Indigenous swimming.) Most Native Americans were certainly excellent swimmers, but, as in Africa, the slave trade lurked beneath the Europeans' admiration.

To heighten the contrast between Native Americans and Europeans, early European chroniclers also emphasized their own inability to swim. In the early 1500s Spanish slave traders reported that they could only keep afloat in the water by clinging to their boats:

as we made a simultaneous rush to our boats, they soon sunk or capsized, so that we were forced to cling to them as well as we could; and in this manner by swimming we strove to make the best of our way to the small vessel, which was now in all haste coming up to our assistance.[4]

Another Spanish slave trader reported that in 1540 his companions 'did not know how to swim, and that they greatly feared the rivers and inlets they had to cross, which in that land are many'. Again, 'The reason I stayed so long was to take with me a Christian who was on the island . . . In the end I . . . carried him across the inlet and four rivers that are along the coast, because he did not know how to swim.'[5]

Some of the Europeans in this party of adventurers did know how to swim: 'we also agreed that four men, who were the most able-bodied, should go to Panuco . . . They were all good swimmers and took with them an Indian from the island.' And in 1544 a Spanish Dominican friar recalls that when they were becalmed in the Atlantic Ocean on the way to Mexico, 'the young neophytes went diving in the water and swimming around the motionless vessels.'[6] But most European explorers in early North America emphasized their inability to swim. In 1565 five European explorers were so eager to get from the ship to the coast of Florida that they tried to swim ashore from their anchorage. The soldiers stripped and dived in, but the 'distance was greater than it appeared . . . and, the current being very rapid, two out of the five were drowned'.[7] In this account, as in many others from this period, stories of drowning, shipwreck and danger allow Europeans to present themselves as the ones courageously undertaking risks, unprepared for danger, even as they cross the oceans expressly to despoil and enslave strangers.[8] Europeans' ignorance of swimming is presented as heroic, while the vastly superior swimming ability of Indigenous people is used to justify their enslavement.

As in Africa, Europeans in the Americas overlaid Native American swimming with imagery of brutish unreason and animal behaviour. Columbus's expedition wasted no time in kidnapping a number of Arawak people to sell into slavery in Spain (or in claiming to have seen a mermaid).[9] In 1519 the Scottish theologian John Major justified the sale of Indigenous people on the grounds that Native Americans 'live like beasts on either side of the equator . . . the first person to conquer them, justly rules over them because they are by nature slaves . . . this is the reason why the Greeks should rule over the barbarians, because the barbarians and slaves are the same.'[10] (Major's association of Renaissance Europeans with the ancient Greeks is an early example of a trend that would have serious implications for the history of swimming.) In 1578 a French colonist published a description of Brazilians swimming that served to further the idea that they were near to animals:

> the men and women of America all know how to swim, so that they can go get their game and their catch in the middle of the water, *like spaniels*; even the little children, as soon as they begin to walk, get into the rivers and the water along the seashore, and are already splashing around in it *like little ducks*.

The same colonist recounts a second story of Brazilian swimming, again with animal parallels:

> While we were strolling around on a bulwark of our fort, we saw a bark boat . . . turn over in the sea; in it were more than thirty savages, adults and children, who were coming to see us. Thinking to rescue them, we made toward them with great speed in a boat. We found them all swimming and laughing on the water; one of them said to us, 'And where are you going in such haste, you Mairs?' (For so they call the French.) 'We are coming', we said, 'to save you and pull you from the water.' 'Indeed', he said, 'we are very grateful to you; but do you think that just because we fell in the sea we are in danger of drowning? Without putting foot to ground, or touching land, we could remain a week on the surface, just as you see us now. So', he said, 'we are much more afraid of some big fish pulling us to the bottom than we fear sinking.' Thereupon the others, who were, indeed, all swimming *as easily as fishes*, having been alerted by their companion to the cause of our swift approach, made sport of us, and began to laugh so hard that we could hear them puffing and snorting on the water *like a school of porpoises*. And indeed, although we were still more than a quarter of a league from our fort, there were only four or five of them who wanted to come into our boat, and that

was more to talk with us than from any fear of danger. I noticed that the others who were ahead of us not only swam as smoothly and steadily as they wished, but also would rest on the water whenever they pleased.[11]

The emphases in both stories are mine. The second story, pleasant and amusing, seems to make fools of the French, but it may have been intended more to emphasize the strangeness of the Native Americans.

Pearl diving

Though Europeans forced a few Indigenous Americans across the Atlantic to sell into slavery in Europe and Asia, most Native Americans ended up being enslaved right where they were, in the Americas. The huge profits Europeans reaped from pearl diving off the coast of West Africa and in the Indian Ocean in the early 1500s encouraged slavers to try the same business in the Caribbean. Pearl diving provides an easy way to monetize violence against swimming people. Rather than expensively shipping the enslaved people to Asia, these slave traders forced enslaved Native Americans to dive for pearls in the Americas, and then brought the pearls across the Atlantic to sell. European governments took a fifth of the (enormous) profits as their share.[12]

Diving for pearls was not new to Native Americans. Even before the arrival of European slavers, Native American people took boats out and dived for oysters and other molluscs, pearls and valuable shells. European explorers reported in 1516 that:

> The caciques had nets near the coasts where they fished for pearl oysters. The caciques have skilful divers trained from infancy to this profession, and who dive for these oysters as though in fish-ponds, but they only do so when the sea is calm and the water low, which renders diving easier ... It is necessary to dive three and sometimes even four times a man's height to find the more deeply embedded shells; but to get the daughters and grandchildren [the smaller oysters] it is not required to go deeper than the waist and sometimes even less.[13]

Along the Gulf Coast, French missionaries saw 'villages where the inhabitants have pearls, which they go to seek on the seacoast, and find, they say, in oysters'.[14] In Brazil, as in Japan, women rather than men may have been the primary divers. In the 1940s, at any rate, Kawésqar women in Chile were diving for marine mussels.[15] Elsewhere in Central America, as in Sri Lanka or Bahrain, the principal divers seem to have been men. Pearl diving had long been a favoured method of exploitation in the Indian Ocean, and so it was a natural choice for European traders like Vasco da Gama, who came to the Americas from India. Vasco da Gama himself was in Panama, forcing Indigenous swimmers to dive for pearls, just after 1500:

> Vasco determined to have that part of the sea where Chiapes obtained his pearls explored by swimmers. Although the weather was bad and a storm threatened, the cacique, to please him, ordered thirty of his divers to repair to the oyster beds. Vasco set six of his companions to watch the divers, but without leaving the shore or exposing themselves to risk from the storm. The men set out together for the shore, which was not more than ten miles from the residence of Chiapes. Although the divers did not venture to the bottom of the ocean, because of the danger from the storm, nevertheless they succeeded in gathering, in a few days, six loads of pearls, including the shells gathered near the surface or strewn by the violence of the storm on the sands. They fed greedily on the flesh of these animals. The pearls found were not larger than a lentil or a little pea, but they had a beautiful orient, for they had been taken out while the animal was still alive. Not to be accused of exaggeration concerning the size of these shells, the Spaniards sent the King some remarkable specimens, from which the meat had been removed, at the same time as the pearls.[16]

The friar Bartoleme de las Casas describes how this 'cruellest and most damnable' industry developed soon afterwards in the West Indies. Like Oppian a thousand years earlier, and like Sei Shōnagon, de las Casas tells us that 'the life of a pearl-fisher in these conditions is worse than any other on the face of the earth,' even worse than the lives of enslaved gold miners. While later pearl divers worked for only two to four hours a day,

63 Enslaved African pearl divers in the Caribbean, miniature from *Histoire naturelle des Indes*, known as the Drake Manuscript, *c.* 1586.

these early Indigenous divers were 'in the water from dawn to dusk'. And while later divers, despite being enslaved, often got wine to revive them after their dives, early Indigenous divers were, he says, fed nothing but the oysters they brought up themselves and some cassava bread, and were 'kept perpetually hungry'. They die quickly, he says, often choking on their own blood from haemorrhages, and we can see why.[17] As the more sympathetic tone of this account suggests, not all Europeans thought that Indigenous swimming abilities justified their enslavement and abuse. There were many like Las Casas who condemned the slave trade.

Nevertheless, the slave traders won the day. By the time Las Casas published his account in 1552, European traders had worked most of the trained Native American divers to death, and were already beginning to enslave West African divers and ship them to the Americas to dive for pearls (illus. 63). De Marees explained in 1602 that West Africans were a good choice for this task, because they

are very fast swimmers and can keep themselves underwater for a long time. They can dive amazingly far, no less deep, and can see underwater. Because they are so good at swimming and diving, they are specially kept for that purpose in many Countries and employed in this capacity where there is a need for them, such as the Island of St. Margaret in the West Indies, where Pearls are found and brought up from the bottom by Divers.[18]

Not all African pearl divers worked in West Africa or the West Indies; many others dived off the coast of nearby Venezuela (illus. 64). Both men and women seem to have worked as divers.[19] Pearl divers pushed deeper and deeper, reportedly reaching as deep as 36 metres (120 ft) on a single breath. Slavers, who usually held about a dozen divers but might have up to about fifty, paid pearl divers a small percentage of what they brought in, as an incentive, and, though many still died, now some pearl divers were able to earn enough to buy their freedom. By the 1600s these trained divers were also working as salvage divers when Spanish treasure galleons sank offshore.[20]

The objections of some Europeans to this mistreatment of Africans show that we should not absolve the slave traders on the grounds that times were different and they did not know any better. In the early colonial Caribbean of the 1600s, Black, White and Indigenous children often swam together, 'blissfull in swimming', and many White colonists

64 Enslaved Indigenous and Black pearl divers in Venezuela, illustration from John Hamilton Moore, *A New and Complete Collection of Voyages and Travels*, vol. II (1785).

became good swimmers as a result.[21] In addition to Las Casas, the French publisher Poncelin complained in 1780 that 'This skill of people whom our European delicacy calls barbarous procures for us a great deal of help . . . It is through their skill that we enjoy sponges, corals, pearls, and a lot of other precious baubles, which our luxuriousness prizes.' Poncelin rejects the European tendency to consider these swimmers 'barbarians'. In Genoa, White people hired African swimming instructors for their own children.[22] The idea that Europeans might treat Africans and Native Americans as humans was available, even though it did not prevail.

African American swimming

By the 1700s, as worse motivations came to the fore, swimming became for many Europeans increasingly a symbol of barbarism and irrationality. Swimmers and non-swimmers regarded each other as intrinsically different. They even seemed, increasingly, racially distinct. European slavers shipped West Africans across the Atlantic not only as pearl divers but to grow rice on farms in South Carolina and Georgia. Africans had been growing rice for generations in West Africa, while rice farming was new to most Europeans; European colonists in the Americas needed African knowledge of rice farming. But on the waterways that ran between the rice paddies, African swimming abilities also turned out to be useful to their enslavers as African American divers regularly cleared stumps and debris out of the way of fishing nets. Swimming abilities brought a premium when enslaved Africans were sold, and yet Europeans still considered swimming to mark Africans as less than fully human.[23]

As rice farming gave way to cotton in the late 1700s, African Americans continued to swim, and slave-holders still expected swimming of them in the course of their work. Enslaved African Americans dived to clean barnacles off ships, served as lifeguards for White swimmers (as Harriet Beecher Stowe has Tom save Eva in *Uncle Tom's Cabin*), recaptured people who tried to escape slavery and salvaged lost goods from shipwrecks.[24] Solomon Northrup, born free in New York State in 1808, learned to swim as a child working on rafts on the rivers and lakes of upstate New York. He became 'an expert swimmer, and felt at home in the watery element'.[25] In the Caribbean, both men and women swam in their free time to gather shellfish, sea urchins, lobster, octopus, sponges and coral to sell.[26] Yarrow

Mahmout, a Black Muslim born in Africa, was said to be the best swimmer ever seen on Washington's Potomac River. The formerly enslaved
Bill Crump, in North Carolina, remembered swimming during the
dinner break from field work, and sometimes after work.[27] Some enslaved
African Americans successfully swam to freedom or, sadly, drowned
themselves to escape enslavement.[28] Indeed, Andrew Kahrl suggests that
many enslaved African Americans thought of swimming as a metaphor
for freedom. To people who dreamed of re-crossing the ocean and going
home, getting into the water and then out of it symbolized freedom.
African American rituals, especially at funerals, used (and still use) water
to suggest returning home.[29]

Swimming may also have helped African Americans maintain ties
to traditional African culture. Aquatic competitions to kill sharks and
crocodiles had a long history in Africa. Enslaved Africans brought that
sport with them to the Americas. In the Carolinas in 1700, a British traveller saw 'some Negro's, and others, that can swim and dive well, go naked
into the Water, with a Knife in their Hand, and fight the Shark, and very
commonly kill him, or wound him so, that he turns Tail, and runs away'.[30]
Games involving shark-fighting or alligator-fighting, or (less dangerously)
duck-chasing, were common in the Caribbean and the American Deep
South as well.[31] These fights served to connect African Americans to
African culture, or to assert enslaved men's physical and economic dominance over women and weaker men (partly by providing needed food).
But the sport was also twisted by White observers to justify enslavement.
African American fights against sharks and alligators were taken to prove
that enslaved people were savages or primitives, that 'primitive people
were unafraid of primitive creatures.' Thomas Jefferson, for example,
surmised that African Americans' courage 'may perhaps proceed from
a want of forethought, which prevents their seeing a danger till it be
present'.[32] These arguments helped American slave-holders justify
enslavement.

Right up through the Civil War, Southern slave-holders admired
how well African Americans could swim. In a tendentious conversation
among Civil War Confederate soldiers in the 1860s about how happy their
enslaved workers were and how much worse off Northern wage-earners
were, for example, one soldier claimed to have been taught to swim as a
child by an African American mentor his father had enslaved, who 'taught

him the first use of a gun, how to swim, how to catch and ride a horse, and a thousand other things'. (Notice the parallel to the old Islamic trilogy of archery, swimming and horse-riding.[33]) White Americans followed the pattern laid out by the earliest Portuguese explorers. They did not swim, or did not swim well, and they admired the swimming of Native Americans and African Americans, but they twisted their admiration into a rationale for mistreating and enslaving people of colour. A slave-holder in 1774 compared African Americans to animals:

> In hot climates, bathing is one of the highest luxuries; it is no wonder then that we find their inhabitants universally adopt this agreeable practice, especially as cattle, wild beasts, and other quadruped animals, use it for their refreshment. The Negroes teach their children to swim at a very tender age; hence they become expert divers, and are able to continue an incredible length of time under water . . . In these climates the brute creation fly to shelter from the rain; the Negroes likewise avoid it with extreme anxiety . . . Their women are delivered with little or no labour; they have therefore no more occasion for midwives, than the female oran-outang, or any other wild animal. A woman brings forth her child in a quarter of an hour, goes the same day to the sea, and washes herself.[34]

In 1804 a British doctor saw a Black man swimming in Barbados, and again was quick to see the similarities between Africans and animals:

> In one of our late walks we . . . met with a slave who was amusing himself by exercises of uncommon agility in the sea. Not an otter, nor a beaver, nor scarcely a dolphin could appear more in his element. He was quite at play in the water, and diverting himself in all kinds of antic tricks, and gambols. He dived to the bottom – swam in a variety of ways – walked or paddled along like a dog – concealed himself for a long time under water – laid himself at rest upon the surface, and appeared as much at his ease, in the ocean, as if he had never breathed a lighter, nor trodden a firmer element.[35]

Not satisfied with one animal, the doctor compares the swimming man to one animal after another. In quick succession, he becomes an otter, a beaver, a dolphin and a dog.[36] Positioning African Americans as not human, based on their skill at swimming, made it easier for Europeans to treat them like animals, or as slaves.

Colonialism

Elsewhere in the Americas, European colonizers also emphasized Indigenous swimming, and their own inability to swim, to justify colonization. Like the Portuguese before them, a few of these French and British colonizers could swim, but not willingly and not well. Some Europeans could swim short distances in calm water in the 1600s: one Jesuit missionary

> sprang into the water to catch the branch of a tree, and then was unable to get back to the raft. He ... soon after appeared on our side, having swam ashore ... The Sieur de la Salle sent two men to swim out and help us push the canoes in, and they brought us safely in.

But then one of the men drowns: he 'sprang into the water and immediately disappeared. It was an abyss, where he was in a moment swallowed up. A few hours afterwards his body was recovered.'[37] An abyss swallowed him up? Did he drown as soon as he was in over his head? Most of the European traders and settlers could not swim, or at most could dog-paddle a few strokes in an emergency.[38]

Native Americans, on the other hand, were good swimmers, as we have seen. In the 1600s they swam across a river while a French fur trader crossed in a canoe. Similarly in the early 1700s a French missionary's Native American guides pushed his raft across deep rivers while swimming themselves (for which he rewarded them by calling them 'savages'). Again in 1724 Native Americans fled 'part by the ford and part by swimming' when British troops killed yet another French missionary in the Mississippi valley.[39]

When the Lewis and Clark expedition travelled west in 1805, many of the Europeans, including Sacagawea's husband, the trapper Charboneau, still could not swim, but both the African American man York and the Shoshone woman Sacagawea were probably good swimmers. According to Clark's journal, Sacagawea saved many important items that had fallen in when her husband accidentally capsized their pirogue in May 1805, including scientific instruments, trade items and the journals of the expedition:

> the articles which floated out was nearly all caught by the Squar who was in the rear. This accident had like to have cost us deerly; for in this perogue were embarked our papers, Instruments, books, medicine, a great proportion of our merchandize, and in short almost every article indispensibly necessary to further the views, or insure the success of the enterprize in which, we are now launched to the distance of 2,200 miles.

(Although, *contra* many sources on the expedition, the journal entry does not really say that Sacagawea was swimming; she may have caught the items from the canoe.[40]) York definitely could swim: on 5 June he swam to a 'Sand bar to geather Greens for our Dinner'.[41] Even in the early 1800s White colonists identified swimming as a useful skill for Indigenous and African American underlings, but not for themselves.

Gender and swimming

To further dehumanize their victims, many European colonists and slave-holders emphasized Native American and African women's swimming. The sexualization of Native American and African American women who swam served not only to justify sexual abuse and rape, but to further distance colonized people from civilized Europeans. Not incidentally, these colonial accounts, which were widely read in Europe, also reminded European women what happened to women who rejected their assigned gender roles, and so reinforced women's oppression in Europe. Europeans found it convenient to be shocked by mixed bathing and transgressions of gender boundaries, because how could people who did not even understand Christian moral codes deserve freedom?

This connection began with Muslim slave traders, who associated Central African nakedness with promiscuity and not being fully human.

In the twelfth century they scorn these 'people of the Sudan, who are naked and do not cover themselves with anything at all'. In the thirteenth century they complain about the nakedness and promiscuity of women in Mali. In the fourteenth century they explicitly associate Africans with the Slavs: they are both 'dumb animals . . . remote from humanity'.[42] In the sixteenth century it's that Africans 'spend all their days in most lewd practices . . . they don't wear shoes or clothes . . . [It is] a beastly kind of life.'[43] Like these earlier accounts, European swimming stories reinforced both racism and patriarchy. As early as 1512 a Spanish proclamation criticized Native Americans for living in a sinful way 'where everyone went naked and the men took several wives', in which the women 'gave themselves readily considering it shameful to deny themselves'. Native Americans were 'so inept and foolish that they do not know how to rule themselves', and therefore must be enslaved: they were 'called slaves as those who are almost born to serve and not to rule'.[44]

By the 1600s, if not earlier, this pretended concern regarding nudity and promiscuity had grown to include swimming. In 1605 de Marees reports that West Africans 'spend their time in the water every day, girls as well as boys, without any distinction or Bashfulness'. He still wants to see African women as less good swimmers than the men; 'they are not able to dive or stay under water for a long time,' and 'there are some who are to swim well, but not many,' but this distinction soon vanished.[45] On the Caribbean island of Barbados in the 1640s, a slave-holder reported that, 'Excellent Swimmers and Divers they are both men and women', and then he provided an illustrative anecdote:

> Colonel Draz (who was not so strict an observer of Sundays, as to deny himself lawful recreations) would sometimes, to shew me sport, upon that day in the afternoon, send for one of the Muscovia ducks, and have her put into his largest pond, and calling for some of his best swimming negroes, commanded them to swim and take this duck; but forbad them to dive: for, if they were not barred that play, they would rise up under the duck, and take her as she swam, or meet her in her diving, and so the sport would have too quick an end. But that play being forbidden, the duck would make them good sport, for they are stronger ducks, and better divers by far, than ours.

The enslaved Africans know swimming strokes unknown to Europeans, and they are excellent swimmers, but so is the duck. (Whether this game owes anything to China's 'Run after Duck' games remains unclear.) He seems to intend us to gather that the Africans are more like ducks than human beings, and can be treated like animals. So far, this is like other swimming contests we have seen organized by European slave-holders. But as he continues his story, he suggests another reason for thinking that Africans are bestial, and therefore natural slaves:

> while we were seeing this sport, and observing the diversities of their swimmings, a negro maid, who was not there at the beginning of the sport, and therefore heard nothing of the forbidding them to dive, put off her petticoat behind a bush, that was at one end of the pond, and closely sunk down into the water, and at one diving got to the duck, pulled her under water, and went back again the same way she came to the bush, all at one dive.[46]

This common justification for slavery builds on the ancient non-swimmers' association of swimming with indecency and promiscuity. Although to us the girl's swimming shows her subversion of the game, the slave-holder means the girl's swimming to show that Africans lacked morals, and therefore needed White supervision in order to make them behave decently.

In South America the slave-catcher John Stedman tells us that although wrestling and other land-based games had their place, 'swimming is their favorite diversion, which they practice every day at least twice or thrice.' He describes a game played on Dutch Guiana's Suriname River in the 1770s, where Indigenous South Americans and African-descended people had a mock swimming battle using only their feet and legs to kick each other. This apparently looked like so much fun that Stedman and his friends stripped and joined the swimmers in the water. But the community-building aspect of traditional swimming games and competitions must have been undermined by the presence of White, slave-holding spectators.[47]

Stedman also claimed to be shocked to find 'groups of naked boys and girls promiscuously playing and flouncing, like so many tritons and mermaids, in the water'. Again, later in his trip, he saw children swimming promiscuously, in groups of boys and girls, and both sexes exhibit astonishing feats of courage, strength and activity. I have not only seen a negro girl beat a hardy youth in swimming across the River Comewina . . . but on landing challenge him to run a two mile race, and beat him again, naked as they were; while all ideas of shame on the one side and of insult on the other, are totally unknown.[48]

Part of Stedman's problem is the promiscuity of mixed bathing, but he is also eager to add other gender policing: he is outraged that a girl would race a boy, that a girl would beat a boy in a race and that the boy could fail to resent it. Stedman thinks such people could hardly be human. They are more like 'tritons and mermaids' who do not, of course, have legal rights.

Nearly a century later, about 1850, a young American diplomat travelling along the Amazon River again acted both shocked and titillated when he encountered mixed naked swimming:

The first spectacle which arrested our attention on landing was that of a number of persons of both sexes and all ages, bathing indiscriminately together in the waters of the river, in a state of entire nudity. We observed among them several finely formed Indian girls of exceeding beauty, dashing about in the water like a troop of happy mermaids.

Despite his unconcealed sexual interest in the Indigenous children, the young diplomat congratulates himself on being more civilized than the swimmers. He is not promiscuous, as the 'mermaids' are. He, and White people generally, can control his baser impulses to live by a moral code: 'The heat of the sun was so intense, that we ourselves were almost tempted to seek relief from its overpowering influence by plunging precipitately amid the joyous throng of swimmers. But we forbore!'[49] Travellers also dehumanized Native Americans by treating their swimming skills as freaks of nature. In a 1924 photograph from Panama, the Indigenous child swimming is also an albino. The girl, naked, swimming and perceived to have a disability, is triply, the photograph seems to imply, in need of European colonialism.[50]

AFRICAN AND NATIVE American swimming looked to Europeans like promiscuity and genderbending, and so it played comfortably into European notions that the people they met had no more morals than animals. And if Africans and Native Americans were animals, or practically animals, then Christians had not only a right, but a moral duty, to enslave them for their own good. Hadn't God placed Adam on Earth to rule the animals? All across Africa and the Americas, European explorers regularly used people's swimming skills against them, creating a narrative that justified slavery, exploitation and expropriation.

15

CHINA AND THE PACIFIC OCEAN

Meanwhile, on the other side of the world, the new ocean-going ships brought non-swimming Europeans to still more places where people knew how to swim. In Southeast Asia, and then in Australia, New Zealand and the Pacific Islands, Europeans first marvelled at local people's swimming, and then used it to justify colonization and enslavement. About 1520, when the explorer Ferdinand Magellan's wooden flagship sprang a large leak, the king of Malaysia (or someone the European colonizers saw as the king) sent over 25 of his own divers to stop the leak and fix the problem. But European accounts added another story, where an Indonesian attempt to assassinate another colonizer was foiled by 'a woman of Java, who by night swam off to the ships to warn one of the mariners who was her lover'.[1] As in Africa and the Americas, women appear in these colonialists' stories as swimmers, and again European story-tellers insist on that close connection between women, swimming and sex.

As in Africa and the Americas, so in the Pacific, Europeans first admired, then racialized and sexualized local swimming. In the Philippines, in 1604, a Jesuit missionary marvelled at how Indigenous people 'take to the water as soon as they are born. Men and women, even as very small children, swim like fish. To cross a river they have no need of a bridge. They bathe at all hours both for comfort and cleanliness.'[2] In New Zealand, Maori children were taught to swim at a young age and sometimes used floats when they were learning; hollow gourds stood in for Roman cork and African bundles of reeds. In eighteenth-century Hawaii, a canoe being overset, in which was a woman with her children, one of them an infant, who, I am convinced, was not more than four years old, seemed highly delighted with what had happened, swimming about at its ease, and playing a hundred tricks, till the canoe was put to rights again.[3]

Similarly, in 1817 an American sea captain claimed,

the children of the Pacific Islands are all taught to swim very early, the girls as well as the boys. I have seen the mothers throw them into the water twenty times in succession, when they were not more than two or three years old, and catch them up again, after they had paddled a while with their hands and feet, and were about sinking. In this manner the art of swimming is acquired incredibly early, and affords them complete protection against drowning, since they can all swim like dolphins.[4]

In the 1770s the British captain James Cook and his crew were unapologetic about their sense that swimming was for people of colour. Cook was sailing to Australia and the South Seas, the last part of the world still untroubled by European colonization. Neither Cook nor his crew knew how to swim, and they were all nervous around water.[5] One of Cook's crew members, for example, when sent out on a search party in 1777, 'attempted the lagoon, and waded nearly across, without the water rising higher than his middle, but all at once plunged overhead in deep water, and it was next to a miracle that he saved himself from drowning'. When Cook arrived in Hawaii in 1778, he found good swimmers there as well. Again, he emphasized that women were swimming:

They are vigorous, active, and most expert swimmers; leaving their canoes upon the most trifling occasion, diving under them, and swimming to others, though at a great distance. It was very common to see women with infants at the breast, when the surf was so high that they could not land in the canoes, leap overboard, and without endangering their little ones, swim to the shore through a sea that looked dreadful.[6]

Eighteenth-century scientists echoed these same opinions. In 1792 a French naturalist drew and described Tasmanian women who 'dived for abalones and other species' (illus. 65).[7] Tahitian swimmers (both boys and girls) surfed in water 'impossible for any European boat to have lived in', as an eighteenth-century British botanist exclaimed, 'and if the best swimmer in Europe had, by accident, been exposed to its fury, I am confident that he would not have been able to preserve himself from drowning.'[8] Even in the 1820s a British colonialist drew a picture of an unnamed Tasmanian man swimming and pushing a thick log, on which the colonialist himself comically sits, pulling up his legs to keep his shoes dry (illus. 66).

Still more than these travelogues, the new fiction adventure market of the eighteenth century allowed European authors to emphasize the contrast between the poor swimming of Europeans and the skilled swimming of Indigenous people. Daniel Defoe's *Robinson Crusoe* and Jonathan Swift's *Gulliver's Travels*, both written in the early 1700s, owe a good deal to Odysseus, and probably even more to Islamic stories of Sindbad the Sailor, which had recently been translated into English. Crusoe tells us that he 'swam very well', and when he finds himself cast away on his famous island, he strips down to his breeches and stockings (he's an

65 Tasmanian people diving for shellfish, illustration from Jacques Labillardière, *Atlas pour servir à la relation du voyage à la recherche de La Pérouse* (1799).

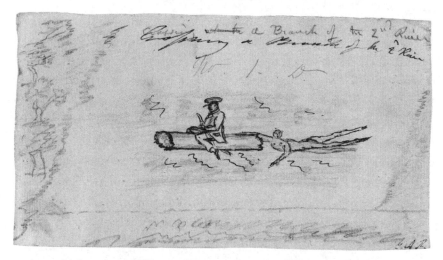

66 An unnamed Tasmanian swimmer pushes European colonialist
George Robinson across the Forth River, seen in a sketch from
George Robinson's journal, 15 September 1830.

adventurer, but he's not a savage who swims naked!) and swims out into
the bay to the wrecked boat to get supplies. Gulliver, like Odysseus and
Sindbad, manages to reach shore after a shipwreck:

> What became of my companions in the boat, as well as of those
> who escaped on the rock, or were left in the vessel, I cannot tell;
> but conclude they were all lost. For my own part, I swam as fortune
> directed me, and was pushed forward by wind and tide. I often
> let my legs drop, and could feel no bottom; but when I was almost
> gone, and able to struggle no longer, I found myself within my
> depth; and by this time the storm was much abated.

A few pages further on, Gulliver manages to swim 30 metres (100 ft) out
to the fleet, and again a short way in order to get a boat, but 'being out
of my depth', he cannot tread water well enough to fasten a rope to the
boat when he gets there. Later on, he can barely swim well enough to
keep afloat in a Brobdingnagian cream pitcher for a few minutes, until
he is found nearly drowned.

Indigenous swimmers in both books are much more skilled. In
Robinson Crusoe, which was an immediate runaway success in Britain,
going through four editions in the first year, an Indigenous Moroccan
'swam like a cork, and . . . swam for the shore, and I make no doubt but

he reached it with ease, for he was an excellent swimmer'. Again, when Africans land on Crusoe's island they 'made nothing of [swimming], though the tide was then up; but plunging in, swam through in about thirty strokes'. Defoe represents Crusoe as a much less able swimmer than the people he meets.[9]

Jonathan Swift's *Gulliver's Travels*, published seven years later in 1726, mocks Indigenous people, personified as the Yahoos, precisely for their excellent swimming. The Yahoos look human but are uncivilized (and some of them have dark skin). Swift tells us that they 'swim from their infancy like frogs, and are able to continue long under water, where they often take fish, which the females carry home to their young'. A Yahoo woman terrifies Gulliver by jumping into the water and embracing him when he is bathing naked: thus Swift again encourages his readers to believe that Indigenous women are hypersexual and promiscuous.[10] In Southeast Asia and the South Pacific, just as in Africa and the Americas, Indigenous people were excellent swimmers, and Europeans who could not swim so well found in this difference an excuse to colonize and enslave them.

The crawl stroke

As they observed Pacific Ocean, Native American and African swimming, Europeans were particularly struck by the differences between Indigenous swimming strokes and European breaststroke. Defoe highlights how Crusoe's companion Xury can swim while holding a gun up out of the water, presumably using the Indigenous swimmer's crawl or sidestroke, and this contrasts with Swift's Gulliver, who must stop swimming in order to push a boat ahead of him. Most Native Americans from Chile to Canada still swam a front crawl stroke. In the 1700s an English settler in Virginia described it: 'They strike out not both hands together but alternately one after the other.'[11]

Africans, and African Americans, also used an overhand stroke. In 1605 West Africans swim 'in the manner of the Portuguese, with their arms above the water, one forward and one backward'.[12] Also in the 1600s, African Americans chasing ducks in Barbados swim 'some the ordinary ways, upon their bellies, some on their backs, some by striking out their right leg and left arm, and then turning on the other side, and changing both their leg and their arm, which is a stronger and swifter way of swimming, than any of the others.'[13] (This may be the first description of backstroke or breaststroke among African Americans.) The West African swimmers are also said to kick their legs with one forwards and one backwards, 'like Frogs', which may mean they were using a sidestroke. Though no descriptions survive from this early period, Pacific islanders also used an overhand stroke.[14] Europeans noticed how the crawl or side-stroke allowed swimmers to use their arms to carry objects or push canoes, and that the crawl was substantially faster than the breaststroke. Yet they still saw the breaststroke and backstroke as more civilized, and considered the overhand crawl stroke to be the mark of the savage and the natural slave.[15]

China and Japan

Along the Pacific coast of Asia, the mental image of swimmers that Europeans were forming did not map so well on to the reality they found. By the time Rafael Perestrello, a cousin of Christopher Columbus, sailed to China in 1516, Europeans had long known China and Japan both by reputation and more directly through visits. They already knew what they thought of East Asia: old civilizations, respected and respectable. Jesuit missionaries came to Japan in the 1540s, and these Jesuits, too, initially identified Chinese and Japanese people more or less as White north-erners, unlike the southern, darker-skinned people of Africa, India and Southeast Asia. Francis Xavier, who visited Japan in 1552, reported that, 'The Chinese whom I have seen in Japan and elsewhere, and whom I got to know, are white in colour, like the Japanese, are acute, and eager to learn.'[16] In 1584 an Italian Jesuit wrote admiringly that the Japanese 'excel not only all the other Oriental peoples, they surpass the Europeans as well'.[17] Here were White people, with impressive docks and cities, emperors and court ceremonials.

The discovery that people in China could not swim must have further reassured European traders that China was a respectable trade partner. Mongol influence from Central Asia had had the same discouraging effect on swimming in China as in Europe, and most Chinese people, like Euro-peans, had forgotten how to swim. There were still many public baths in China, but there was little swimming.[18] To northern Chinese writers, southern Chinese swimming now seemed unnatural. They disdainfully remarked that on Hainan Island – so far south it is off the coast of modern Vietnam – in the mid-1600s two servant children 'could swim incredible distances under water and preferred raw seafood to cooked food'.[19]

Only the pearl divers and river people of South China were still at home in the water. Ming Dynasty pearl diving would have seemed familiar to Europeans coming from the Indian Ocean. Here, too, pearl diving was hard, dangerous and poorly paid work for people from the lowest social classes. Some 'found a tomb in the bellies of fishes', while others died of cold. Perhaps Europeans and Chinese communicated about methods: European divers were experimenting with breathing tubes and diving bells as early as the 1190s, and in 1637 a Chinese encyclopaedia describes a new development in Chinese pearl diving, where divers wore airtight leather masks and breathed through a long curving pipe, reinforced with rings of tin, which led to the surface.[20] But that was South China. The northern Chinese people whom Jesuit missionaries met at the imperial court in the 1600s, many of them Manchu aristocrats, were just like the Europeans in regarding swimming as an activity for barbarians.

And yet Europeans soon saw that Japan was a different story. In Japan, unlike in China, many people were strong swimmers. Swimming was a part of the Japanese national identity, perhaps as a rejection of Central Asian power and a reaction to the non-swimming Mongol and Manchu conquests of China and Korea. To sixteenth-century Chinese writers, swimming identified the Japanese as barbarians and pirates. European missionaries, similarly, when they noticed how well and how enthusiastically Japanese people were swimming, tried to suppress swimming and bathing there. The missionaries banned swimming in the boarding schools they founded to educate Japanese boys as Catholics, but the children were so shocked and miserable that their teachers soon were forced to allow the children 'to swim in the river or sea in suitable weather'.[21] European interaction with Japan did not last long. The missionaries hardly had a chance to look around before Japan's shogun Ilidéyoshi heard reports of what Portuguese colonists had done to India. In the 1630s, following the example of India's Mughal emperors, Ilidéyoshi banned all Europeans from Japan. Still, the discovery that Japanese people, who seemed so civilized, were also excellent swimmers may have made an impression on non-swimming Europeans that they carried home with them to consider.

IN THE LATE Middle Ages, many people across northern Eurasia associated swimming with poverty and ignorance. Swimming was dangerous, weirdly old-fashioned and disfavoured by God. It led to indecency and promiscuity, and it was best left to foreigners. As European slave traders and colonizers began to exploit the people of Africa, the Americas and the Pacific, they used these prejudices to justify their own brutality. In the journals and chronicles these slave traders published, as well as in contemporary fiction, swimming appeared as the mark of the pagan and the savage. The discovery that people in China also could not swim helped to reinforce these ideas among Europeans, and perhaps also among the Chinese. In both Europe and China, free, civilized, self-respecting people stayed well away from the water.

16

FLOATING FOR WITCHCRAFT

Just as European slave dealers in Africa and the Americas were justifying their iniquities with claims that swimming was for foreigners and slaves, a new wave of concerns around water and swimming also reached Central Europe from Russia and Ukraine. These concerns grew out of the ancient feeling that water was magical and sacred. People entering the water risked defiling it and angering the gods. As the idea that swimming was barbaric met the idea that water was sacred, Eurasia's sixteenth and seventeenth centuries saw sharp increases in the use of drowning as a punishment, and of trial by water, especially for witchcraft. Yet again, fear of the water spread from the northern steppe west through Europe. Between the 1500s and the 1700s, the practice of floating women for witchcraft slowly spread west from Ukraine to Germany, then to England, and across the Atlantic to the British colonies in the Americas.

Trial by water has a long history. We have seen it in the Bronze Age Code of Hammurabi from Iraq, and it appears in many subsequent West Asian law codes. But trial by water formed no part of Roman law, and, even though we tend to think of the swimming of women for witchcraft in England, France and Germany as belonging to the Middle Ages, water trials were not much used in medieval Europe.[1] Most Western European water trials for witchcraft belong to the 1600s and 1700s – to the early modern period, not to the Middle Ages. Certainly there were a few medieval examples of trial by water for heresy; we have already seen one from southeastern Germany from the 900s CE.[2] Trial by water was also used at Soissons in France in 1114, in England in the 1170s and again at Vézelay about the same time. But by the time Frederick Barbarossa drowned in 1190, trial by ordeal had fallen into disrepute.[3] In 1215 the Fourth Lateran Council condemned trial by ordeal and forbade clergy to participate in ordeals. The influential Italian scholar Thomas Aquinas also rejected trial by ordeal as itself being too much like witchcraft.[4] In the Valais witch hunts of the mid-1400s in eastern France and Switzerland, and in the Val Camonica witch hunts of the early 1500s in northern Italy, although hundreds of women were convicted of witchcraft and burned or tortured to death, none of them underwent trial by water.[5] In the sixteenth century, however, northern Europeans began again to turn to the water for justice.

Russian and Ukrainian origins

In Russia and Ukraine, where swimming was always rejected, trial by water seems to have always remained popular, usually but not exclusively for witchcraft. Our first evidence of trial by water in Russia and Ukraine after the ancient law codes dates to 1094, but the local practice of swimming women for witchcraft probably goes back long before that. It may be continuous from the Bronze Age.[6] Certainly in medieval Russia and Ukraine, trial by water seems to have been common, especially for women. Even early accounts include the elements known from later witch trials in Western Europe. A Syrian merchant who visited Kyiv in 1153 described a trial by water he saw there:

> Every twenty years the old women of this country become guilty [or suspected?] of witchcraft, which causes great concern among the people. Then they seize all those they find in this area and throw them, feet and fists tied [together], into a big river that passes through . . . Those who stay afloat are considered to be witches and are burned; those who, on the contrary, go under are declared innocent of all witchcraft and are set free again.[7]

The trial focuses specifically on women, who are accused of vague or unspecified wrong-doing. They are tied up in a specific way, with their feet and hands fastened together so that they are curled into a ball, and then thrown into the water. And it's not floating, but sinking, that proves your innocence. All these details are identical to later European practice, and suggest a Russian and Ukrainian source for Central European trial by water for witchcraft.

Contemporary Russian sources substantiate this trader's story. Drought affected Suzdal, northeast of modern Moscow, in 1024, followed predictably by crop failure and then famine. As in the Syrian trader's account, the town blamed a number of old people and eventually executed them. In 1070 and 1071 famine hit nearby Rostov, and this time the town executed a number of women of various ages.[8] A third, more serious famine lasting from 1271 to 1274 inspired more witch trials. This time a local bishop, Serapion, specifically condemned the floating of women for witchcraft as heresy and superstition. Serapion thundered,

> And you still cling to pagan traditions; you believe in witchcraft and burn innocent people and bring down murder upon the earth and the city . . . Out of what books or writings do you learn that famine on earth is brought about by witchcraft? . . . In the past three years there has been no harvest not only in Rus' but among the Latins as well. Are witches responsible for this? . . . You make water the witness and say: if she begins to sink, she is innocent; if she floats she is a witch. Is it not possible that the devil himself, seeing your weak faith, supported her so that she would not sink, thus contributing to your own perdition? For, you prefer the testimony of an inanimate substance to that of a created human being.[9]

This too is typical of later trials further west: in general, Church officials thought witch floating was nonsense if not heresy.

A similar story about ordeal by water was being told further south in West Asia about the same time as these, again involving tying the accused up, and floating indicating guilt. We have it from a Syrian courtier in 1175:

> They installed a huge cask and filled it with water. Across it they set a board of wood. They then bound the arms of the man charged with the act, tied a rope around his shoulders and dropped him into the cask, their idea being that in case he was innocent, he would sink in the water and they would then lift

him up with the rope so that he might not die in the water; and in case he was guilty, he would not sink in the water. This man did his best to sink when they dropped him into the water, but he could not do it. So he had to submit to their sentence against him – may Allah's curse be upon them! They pierced his eyeballs with red-hot awls.[10]

The courtier did not see this himself, but he claims that he heard this story from the blind man's lips, and he claims that it is a Frankish punishment; that is, something that Europeans did. Apparently at least some Crusaders knew the same theory of ordeal by water that the Russians were using, and that we later see in Western Europe. Medieval trial by water reverses the ancient Babylonian method, in that floating, rather than sinking, proves your guilt. In ancient Babylon's law codes, officials tested women for witchcraft by throwing them in water to see if the water would drag them to the bottom: Nungal the river god, they said, would clamp on to you and you would drown. In West Africa, as well, successful floating or swimming proved your innocence. Willem Bosman reports that among the Ouidah, in Benin, a particular river had 'the strange Quality of immediately drowning all the Guilty Persons which are thrown into it'.[11] But Bosman emphasizes that drowning the guilty is 'contrary to the European manner of trying Witches', and indeed the view that the guilty would float had been slowly taking hold in Europe since ancient times. The Hellenistic scholar Phylarchus (in a text that is now lost) assured his readers that some magicians were lighter than water and could not be made to sink. The Roman geographer Pliny repeated Phylarchus' notion. The second-century CE travel writer Pausanias adds some possibly related ideas about water and floating; he relates a custom of the Greek city of Epidauros, where worshippers threw loaves of barley bread into a fountain. If the offering was accepted it sank, but if the offering was rejected the bread floated, which was 'a very bad sign'. Pausanias also mentions that 'The Dead Sea has properties that are opposite to all other water; for the living float without trying to swim, and the dying fall into the depths.'[12] In other words, in normal water, Pausanias expects normal people to sink.

Geographers in sixth-century Byzantium repeated the idea that magicians were lighter than water, and in the ninth century the French archbishop Hincmar explains that liars will not sink in holy water, because 'the pure nature of water' rejects them. A related idea may have led to the medieval Ukrainian practice where officials threw women accused of witchcraft in the water to test whether the water would reject the women and float them. They believed that water – clean, pure, used for baptism – would refuse to receive criminals or heretics.[13] By the Middle Ages it was commonly accepted all across Europe, from Russia to the Atlantic Ocean, that (except in the Dead Sea) the guilty float, while the innocent sink to the bottom.

Drownings

As Central Europeans forgot how to swim in the late Middle Ages, they also began to think of the water as a practical, efficient and appropriate way to kill people, especially but not only in cases where they had offended God. This, too, may have started in Russia, where in 1497 Tsar Ivan III ordered women suspected of witchcraft to be drowned in the Moscow River.[14] In Central Europe the two great Protestant reformers of this period, Martin Luther and John Calvin, do not mention swimming at all, even metaphorically, in any of their essays and sermons. But they wax enthusiastic about drowning. Like other Europeans of his time, Luther thought drowning was an appropriate way to get rid of disabled children. He describes one child who 'did nothing but feed', cried on being touched and laughed when anything bad happened in the house; Luther suggested that the prince should 'throw it into the Moldau River'.[15] In 1526, in Switzerland, Ulrich Zwingli thought Anabaptist heretics should be drowned, too, and at least some Anabaptists were.[16]

Not long after this, Catholics drowned heretics in France and England as well. In 1593 Christopher Marlowe wrote a scene in his play *The Massacre at Paris*, in which French Catholics forced Protestants into the Seine to drown:

GUISE
My Lord of Anjoy, there are a hundred Protestants,
Which we have chaste into the river Sene,
That swim about and so preserve their lives:
How may we doe? I feare me they will live.

DUMAINE

Goe place some men upon the bridge,
With bowes and cartes to shoot at them they see,
And sinke them in the river as they swim.[17]

Though Marlowe was writing a play, the heartless dialogue in this scene was based on a real event, the St Bartholomew's Day massacre of 1572, which had recently happened in Paris. Many Protestants had drowned in the Seine on that terrible day. The drowning in Paris was not an isolated incident. In 1641 Catholic mobs in Ireland killed a hundred or more Protestants by forcing them into the River Bann, south of Belfast, where most of them drowned, and the few who could swim were, as in Paris, shot from the bridges.[18]

Moving east from Russia and Ukraine towards China, we can glimpse similar concerns about witchcraft and water, and similar enthusiasm for drowning. Sixteenth-century river demons sink boats and drag the passengers under.[19] A Chinese novel published in the sixteenth century and expanded in 1620 revolves around a demon that escapes by leaping into wells.[20] And in 1768 China too was taken up by a fear of sorcerers who were soul-stealers. The Chinese government was working to rebuild a bridge north of Hangzhou, near the Yangtze River delta, and a rumour spread that the masons were using sorcery to construct the pilings in the river. Mendicant monks were said to be stealing people's souls to help the masons. Angry mobs wanted to burn or drown the putative sorcerers, and were restrained by higher government officials only with difficulty.[21] In this period, drowning seems to have been considered a respectable, normal way to kill heretics and witches all across Eurasia, from China to Ireland.

Floating witches

From drowning heretics, it was only a small step to trial by ordeal for witchcraft, and, as Central and Western Europeans began to think of swimming as something uncanny, that step was soon taken. Ordinary people could not swim. Therefore, if you could swim, you must have supernatural powers. And if you had supernatural powers, you were a witch, or allied with witches. Trial by water – *indicium aquae* – would show whether you could swim.[22] The increasing reluctance of religious leaders to get involved in questions of witchcraft and exorcism drew secular authorities into the business by popular demand. If your priest refused to come to your house and sprinkle holy water, you could use witchcraft charges to force the local magistrates into action.[23] Thus after being banned in the 1200s, the forcible near-drowning of women (it was mostly women) known as 'swimming witches' or 'floating witches' became hideously popular with Central and Western European crowds in the late 1500s and 1600s.

Poland and Hungary

The revival of trial by water came earliest and became most widespread in Poland and Hungary, where people were most influenced by Russian culture. We know that violent crowds in Ukraine were pushing suspected witches into rivers between 1271 and 1274. Then between 1274 and the 1700s, silence: there are no more anecdotes about witch swimming from this area.[24] Is this a gap in our sources, or a real change of heart? We don't know. But whether or not the practice of trial by water died out in Russia and Ukraine, it picked up in Poland and Hungary, starting with the southeastern areas closest to Ukraine. In Poland witch trials began in the 1570s.[25]

67 Unnamed women tied up for a witchcraft trial by water, one floating and one sinking, illustration from Hermann Neuwaldt, *Bericht von Erforschung, prob vnd erkentnis der Zauberinnen durchs kalte Wasser* (1584).

In Hungary witch hunts reached their first peak in the 1580s.[26] In 1588 a Hungarian official paid Romani people 24 denars to throw 'the woman from Monostor street' into the water, because she was 'suspected of putting a spell on a little girl'.[27] And the way people swam women for witchcraft in Hungary – feet and fists tied together – exactly parallels the practice we have seen from medieval Ukraine. As in Ukraine, the proceedings of Hungarian witch trials imply that people used witch swimming as a form of collective weather magic during droughts, to bring the rain.[28]

From Poland and Hungary, trial by water for witchcraft soon moved to Germany. The connection between witch trials and weather magic weakened as the custom moved west.[29] But all across Europe into Germany, England and the American colonies, we see the persistence of the medieval Russian and Ukrainian habit of tying the woman's thumbs to her opposite toes. This habit surely did not arise independently, and must show a Russian or Ukrainian origin for the Western European practice of floating women for witchcraft.

Germany

Witch-swimming became popular in Germany during the sixteenth century, despite considerable resistance from both Church and secular authorities who knew it was nonsense. In 1532 Charles v's criminal law code prohibited trial by water in no uncertain terms – no *Wasserprobe* or *Hexenbad* – but this is an indication that officials were beginning to come under pressure to float women for witchcraft. Sure enough, by 1563 a German scholar published a clear description of the process, including the traditional Russian and Ukrainian method of tying the victim's left thumb to her right toe, and her right thumb to her left toe, though he condemned it as irrational.[30]

In 1583, as the debate intensified in Germany, the philosopher Wilhelm Schreiber certified trial by water as legal and Christian, and in 1584, just as witch trials were reaching their first peak in Hungary, the first definitely known early modern trial by water took place in Germany.[31] All through the seventeenth century German officials continued to use trial by water, and to tie women up in the approved manner (illus. 67).[32] The sexual availability suggested by the pose is not accidental. Witches were marginalized outcasts (or marginalized outcasts were witches), and so were promiscuous women, so it was easy to conflate the two. Early modern Europeans increasingly associated swimming with outsiders, and bathing with promiscuity, and so sexuality, witchcraft and water trials fell in together.

Throughout this period, popular demand made floating women for witchcraft more and more common in Germany. Many intellectual and religious leaders spoke out against it: in 1584, as the first German witch trials were being held, a prominent German professor still rejected trial by water, and in 1598 a German Calvinist pastor again spoke out against it.[33] In 1592 a German legal scholar considered swimming women for witchcraft to be a superstition invented by the Devil.[34] But this became a minority view, and by 1643 Hermann Conring, a Leipzig doctor, considered trial by water to be an entirely legitimate way of identifying witches.[35] The rise of a desire for scientific, empirical tests also led to the revival of the swimming test for witchcraft at this time.[36] To give an idea of the kind of experiments people undertook, about this time the German military commander Johann von Sporck suspected that his own soldiers' wives were using witchcraft. He decided to check it out by floating them. Unusually for his time, von Sporck seems to have believed that innocent people would float, rather than sink. He tried out his theory scientifically (so to speak) by floating a volunteer, a Jewish man named Löb, and then tested suspected witches, many of whom sank and were subsequently executed.[37] But this sort of experimentation was unusual; most women were convicted if they floated (or 'swam'). In Westphalia, in western Germany, judges floated women for witchcraft throughout the 1600s. In circa 1630 local magistrates apparently hauled more than thirty women accused of witchcraft out of their beds one morning, tied them up in the usual way and threw them in the water. When they floated, they were arrested. Under torture, the women confessed, so they were all burned at the stake.[38]

Great Britain and Ireland

Despite the popularity of trial by water in early modern Germany, it never caught on in Italy, Spain, Portugal or France. Witchcraft trials were as popular in these countries as they were in Germany, but in the Catholic countries of western Europe, people suspected of witchcraft

68 The swimming of Mary Sutton, from the title page of the popular
pamphlet *Witches Apprehended, Examined and Executed . . .* (1613).

were generally tortured on dry land. The German fashion for swimming
suspected witches encouraged local officials in eastern France to give it a
try in 1587–8, but the national government in Paris quickly put a stop to
the practice.[39] That was pretty much the end of witch swimming in
southern Europe. Similarly in China, though there were many witch
trials in the 1700s, officials relied on breaking suspects' legs or crushing
their ankles in vises to torture them into confessing, rather than using
trial by water. Qing Dynasty officials also pushed back successfully against
popular panics.[40]

But in the northern European nations the Netherlands, Great Britain
and Ireland, the popularity of trial by water quickly overwhelmed official opposition, and even won rulers over to its side.[41] The first trial by
water in the Netherlands, as in France, took place in 1588.[42] Two years
later, officials were swimming women for witchcraft in Denmark, which
influenced Scotland's King James VI also to encourage trial by water. The
23-year-old James, with his fourteen-year-old Danish bride Anne, had

been on board a ship carrying the couple from Oslo to Scotland when a terrible storm arose. The Danish admiral of the fleet blamed the storm on witchcraft, and a number of prominent Danish women were convicted of raising the storm. James was impressed by this procedure, and soon wrote 'that God has appointed . . . that the water shall refuse to receive them in her bosom, that have shaken off them the sacred Water of Baptism, and wilfully refused the benefit thereof'.[43] As with Ukrainian witch trials, and in early modern Germany, so in Scotland again the pure water will reject a guilty witch, while an innocent person will sink.

The water ordeal arrived in Scotland freighted with Central Asian customs. Medieval English trial by water had involved women and men, but early modern witchcraft trials almost solely involved women. The new focus on women fitted well into an early modern British landscape of tense gender relations, but the emphasis on gender has deeper roots in Central Asian practice.[44] These women were stripped and tied hand to foot, as in Central Asian trial by water. King James's reference to baptism also reflects earlier Central Asian theories.[45] With the official imprimatur of the king, swimming women for witchcraft gained a legitimacy in Scotland that it never had in France – or, as we will see, in England.

A second edition of James's *Daemonologie* appeared in 1603, the year in which he took power in England, encouraging his new English subjects also to adopt trial by water. By 1612 for the first time women were accordingly being swum for witchcraft in England. An English pamphlet of 1613 had the title *Witches Apprehended, Examined and Executed, for notable villanies by them conducted both by Land and Water: With a strange and true triall how to know whether a woman be a Witch or not*. Inside, the pamphlet told the story of Mary Sutton and her mother, who were accused by a Master Enger of cursing his pigs and horses so they died. The pamphlet assured readers that, 'being throwne in the first time shee sunke some two foote into the water with a fall, but rose againe, and floated upon the water like a planke'. On their second swimming, Sutton and her mother both had their thumbs tied to the opposite toes (illus. 68). Eventually both women confessed to having worked spells, and in 1612 they were hanged.[46] In the same year, justices in Northamptonshire floated a man and his parents, and the man was again hanged.[47]

As in Russia, Germany and the Netherlands, local authorities tried to resist: in 1616 a well-respected English physician rejected trial by water as 'uncivil force and lawless violence', and in 1653 the political writer Sir Robert Filmer also wrote that trial by water was 'none of the best evidence'. Filmer knew that trial by water came to England from Germany, and he warned that 'It concernes the People of this Nation to be more diligently instructed, in the Doctrine of Witch-craft, then those of forraigne Countries.' He scorned the popular belief that 'the Devill being most light, as participating more of Aire then of Water, would hold them up above the Water, either by putting himselfe under the Witch, and lifting her up, as it were with his backe, or by uniting himselfe, and possessing her whole body.'[48] But the popularity of the exciting drama overcame these principled objections.

As the 1600s wore on, swimming women for witchcraft became increasingly popular and common in Britain. Filmer described the general method: a man or woman (but usually a woman) accused of being a witch would be stripped naked and tied up with ropes, often thumb to toe, and then thrown three times into a pond or a deep stream. If she sank, she was considered innocent (but sometimes she drowned). If she floated, she was guilty and could be hanged for witchcraft. In one typical case:

> This old woman was had to a great river near the town, to see whether she could sink under water; her legs being tied, she was put in, and though she did endeavour to the uttermost (by her hands) to get herself under, yet she could not, but would lie upon her back, and did swim like a piece of cork: There were present above twenty persons to attest the truth of this, yet could not gain credit in the minds of people: Therefore, she was had to the water a second time, and being put in, she swam as at first; and though there were present above two hundred people to see this sight, yet it could not be believed by many. At the same time also, there was put into the water, a lusty young woman, who sunk immediately, and had been drowned, had it not been for the help that was at hand. To satisfy the world, and to leave no room for doubting, the old woman was had down to the water the third time, and being put in as before, she did still swim.[49]

The size of the crowd shows why this kind of trial took place: witch-floating became a form of popular entertainment. And again in Leicester, in September 1717, an accused mother, son and daughter 'had severally their thumbs & great toes ty'd together & that they were thrown so bound into the water, & that they swam like a cork, a piece of paper or an empty barrell, tho they strove all they could to sinck'.[50] In 1718 Francis Hutchinson, then a minister in Bury St Edmunds, Suffolk, objected to the practice, remarking, 'our Country-People are still as fond of [floating women for witchcraft], as they are of Baiting a Bear or a Bull.' A sense of the ribald and riotous atmosphere of these trials – very much like a bear-baiting – can be gathered from one held in 1734:

> the Worcestershire justice, John Goodere, was removed from the bench after his highly unusual attendance at a swimming. After the alleged witch had been swum, Goodere stripped, jumped into the water, and 'swam about it on his back, exposing his nakedness to the Men and Women that were present'. On emerging from the water he pulled on his breeches 'before several women that were present and asked which of them would be kn——kt'.[51]

There were several witchcraft panics in the late 1500s in Scotland, and one big witch hunt in England in the 1640s, but in Scotland and England the scale of these events stayed considerably smaller than the massive witch hunts of Central Europe. There were only about 5,000 executions for witchcraft in England in the early modern period, as against four or five times that many in Central Europe.[52] These numbers, again, suggest that witch swimming was a Central Asian tradition that swept westwards over Europe in the sixteenth century.

The American colonies

Trial by water took longer to cross the Atlantic Ocean to the British colonies in North America, and so it arrived later, and was never common there. Even when the idea of swimming women for witchcraft was known to them, American colonists tended to be sceptical of its worth. In 1662, almost a century after the first trials by water in Germany, judges in Hartford, Connecticut, threatened to float Elizabeth Seager, but they did not go so far as to actually do it.[53] In 1684 the well-known Puritan minister Increase Mather mentioned, in relation to the same Hartford witch hunt, that

> there were some that had a mind to try whether the stories of witches not being able to sink under water, were true, and accordingly a man and woman . . . had their hands and feet tied, and so were cast into the water, and they both apparently swam after the manner of a buoy, part under, part above the water. A bystander imagining that any person bound in that posture would be so born up, offered himself for trial, but being in the like manner gently laid on the water, he immediately sunk right down. This was no legal evidence against the suspected persons; nor were they proceeded against on any other account.[54]

Like Richard Filmer a generation earlier, Mather is (rightly) sceptical of the efficacy of trial by water. Eight years later, in September 1692, officials in Fairfield, Connecticut, floated another two accused witches. Mercy Disburrow and Elizabeth Clauson were 'bound hand and foot and put into the water, and they swam like a cork, and when one labored to press them into the water, they buoyed up like cork'. (This was the same year as the Salem witchcraft trials, but Salem did not use trial by water.) But educated Puritan ministers objected, on the basis of Increase Mather's arguments, that 'ye endeavour of conviction of witchcraft by swimming is unlawfull and sinfull & therefore it cannot afford any evidence'. Both women were acquitted.[55]

Scepticism about the efficacy of swimming witches, not only among ministers and officials but among bystanders, continued into the eighteenth century in the American colonies. When Virginia officials subjected Grace Sherwood to trial by water in July 1706,

> She could not make any excuse or Little or nothing to say in her own Behalf only Seemed to Rely on what the Court should Doe and there upon consented to be tried in the water & Likewise to be Serched againe which experiants being tried & She Swimming when therein and bound contrary To custom & the Judgment of all the spectators.[56]

Once again, despite having floated during her ordeal, Sherwood was freed in the end. Swimming women for witchcraft, though it was attempted here and there, never gained any real foothold in the American colonies.

People in the Caribbean islands seem also to have remained more or less unfamiliar with the idea of trial by water. European colonists on Martinique subjected a local (unnamed) woman to the water ordeal about 1650:

> The judge . . . followed the counsel of a Mr. Jacques, a surgeon, an Italian by birth, and called the Roman, who told him that he had seen the trial by water practiced in Germany and in Italy, and that he was allowed to use it . . . The next day they carried her to a tolerably deep river near the 'Carbet', where they stripped her. M. Jean . . . tied her two thumbs to her two great toes, and having fastened a great rope round her waist, which was across the river, she was pushed into the water, and hauled to the deepest part, where she floated like a balloon, without their being able to sink her, although she herself made several efforts to go to the bottom![57]

Even more in Martinique than in North America, the local people do not consider trial by water to be normal. They would not have thought of it themselves; they are only trying it out on the advice of a visitor who has seen it done in Germany. (Despite this reference, I know of no examples from Italy. But in the seventeenth century, the line between southern Germany and northern Italy was still fluid.)

TRIAL BY WATER never became more than a passing experiment in the Atlantic colonies. The popular enthusiasm for swimming women for witchcraft, emerging from Russia and Ukraine and sweeping westwards across Europe in the 1600s, remained too foreign for most American colonists. But as in the Stone Age and the Middle Ages, once again in the early modern period this association between danger and water spread west from the steppe. In a wide belt across Europe from Ireland to Ukraine, all through the centuries we like to call the Enlightenment, trial by water was a real threat for anyone whose neighbours did not get along with them.

17

DUCKING STOOLS

The ducking stool (also called the cucking stool) was another mani-festation of the renewed European fear of water in the early mod-ern period, and of its association with women. Ducking was a form of waterboarding: a wooden stool was attached to a crane or a long lever. People might be sentenced to be tied to such a stool and forcibly plunged into a nearby pond or river, sometimes repeatedly, to the point of choking and near-drowning, or, not infrequently, actual drowning.[1] The origins of ducking stools remain uncertain. The earliest known in-stance of ducking is an informal one. In the early 1200s, just as people were forgetting how to swim, Philip Augustus of France ordered people who blasphemed in public to be thrown into the river. Similar duckings took place in Avignon in 1243, in Verona, Italy, in 1228, and in Vicenza in 1264. By 1286 Zürich seems to have had an arrangement to hoist people up in a basket and leave them hanging over a pond. They could only get out by jumping into the dirty water while the crowd laughed at them.[2]

In Britain, too, local authorities seem to have started to duck people around this time. An English manuscript illustration painted about 1250, with a woman seated up high on a sort of ladder and a man standing down below, may be an early reference to this practice, but the water is not shown (illus. 69).[3] In putative references from as early as the eleventh century, the cucking stools are more like movable pillories and do not involve water. The first definitive example of a ducking in water comes only with this verse written in the early 1300s, just at the time that the crawl stroke had definitely fallen out of use in Europe:

69 Earliest likely illustration of a ducking stool,
miniature from the Rutland Psalter, *c.* 1260.

Hail to you the brewsters with your gallons,
Pottels and quarts, over all the towns.
Your thumbs bear much away, shame have the trickery;
Beware of the cucking-stool, the lake is deep and dirty.[4]

As this verse suggests, early ducking stools seem to have been mainly used to punish fraudulent brewsters – women who made and sold ale. This continued to be the case in mainland Europe, where the victims were mainly fraudulent men. By the fifteenth century, however, as English alewives lost their business to public houses owned by men, ducking stools came to be thought of in England and Scotland as an appropriate punishment for all specifically female offences. By 1423 Coventry's 'cokestoole' on Chelsmore Green was used to punish 'scolders and chidders'.[5] At this point ducking stools became much more common. Women who refused to submit to their town's expectations for their behaviour (they fought with their husbands or neighbours, or called their parents 'thieves and whores') were the usual targets, though the 'punishment of harlots' was also mentioned.[6] Ducking reinforced male privilege by force, both in breaking the power of the female brewsters in favour of male beer-sellers and more generally.

Though the earlier pillory kind of cucking stool was clearly still in use, ducking women in water became increasingly common in early modern Europe. In Germany and the Netherlands, the old basket arrangement had now been adjusted to tip its victims out on cue. (They were still generally bakers and other men.) In France, women were forced inside large iron cages and dunked.[7] There were classic ducking stools in England at Sandwich in 1534, beside the Fye Bridge in Norwich in 1562 and at Lincoln in 1576, among many others.[8] In 1602 a magistrate in northern England ordered Katherine Hall and Margaret Robinson to be 'soundly ducked'. In 1657 another set of magistrates, also in northern England, sentenced Margery Watson to the same penalty.[9] There are dozens of other examples from around the same time, along with illustrations (illus. 70). We do not yet have any clear sense of how common ducking was. Could most women expect to be ducked at some point in their lives? Would most European women have known another woman who had been ducked? Some evidence suggests that the practice varied regionally, perhaps, as with witchcraft trials, being more common in smaller villages, where the poor had less power and the powerful were more conservative.[10] Certainly the ducking stool was a

70 Ducking stool in use in Shropshire, illustration from an 18th-century chapbook, reproduced in William Andrews, *Old-Time Punishments* (1890).

real threat used to silence women throughout the early modern period, as 'an instrument to cool Hot Fiery Tongued Women, which have their Tongues set on Fire by the Devil, which nothing can Tame except it be well ducked'.[11] The ducking stool at Grimsby remained in use until 1780, but its success rate in silencing women was questionable, as evidenced in this example of circa 1680:

> A woman named Jane Dutch . . . was repeatedly subjected to the ordeal, without deriving the least benefit from the application. It is recorded of her that the frigidity of the wave, even in the depth of winter, was insufficient to cool the fervour of her tongue. Between every dip she favoured the spectators with abundant specimens of her exhaustless eloquence; and when the watery castigation was at an end, though dripping wet, she saluted her persecutors with such an overpowering volley of high-sounding tropes and rhetorical flourishes, as convinced them that her weapon of offence was unconquerable.[12]

Ducking was also used in a few of the British colonies in the Americas. New England seems to have rejected ducking completely, but further south in Virginia women were ducked throughout the 1600s and 1700s. Local court records show that, in 1626, Margaret Jones was 'toughed or dragged at a boates Starne in ye River from ye shoare unto the *Margaret & John* and thence unto the shoare againe', and that in the following year Amy Hall was similarly 'toughed round aboard the *Margaret and John*' and then ducked three times.[13] In both cases, the town seems to have lacked an actual ducking stool. Local officials were improvising with boats and ropes.

Over time, ducking became less impromptu, so that by the late 1600s towns both in Britain and in some British colonies were required to have actual ducking stools. The archives of British towns document many payments to carpenters for the construction or repair of ducking stools throughout the seventeenth and eighteenth centuries, and there are references to ducking in early modern plays and popular literature as well.[14] Similarly in the Americas, a Virginia law of 1662 ordered local authorities to erect 'a ducking stoole in such place as they shall think convenient'.[15] The following year, Maryland followed suit.[16] In 1717 officials in Elizabeth

City County, Virginia, ordered the construction of a ducking stool 'according to the pattern of them in Williamsburgh'. In 1746 Frederick County built a ducking stool, and in 1751 Augusta County did. In King George County, Virginia, as late as 1767, the magistrates built a ducking stool on a wharf.[17] We still lack a good understanding of how common this abusive punishment was, but it remained in use throughout the eighteenth century. Unsurprisingly, by the later part of this period, people seem to have come to associate the ducking stool with witches as well as scolds. The Italian writer Giuseppe Baretti, in 1760, reports that 'the superstitious inhabitants of Honiton used formerly to place on [the stool] those old women whom they thought to be witches, and duck'd them unmercifully several times; sometimes to death.'[18] Indeed, a Nottingham woman apparently drowned in 1731 while being ducked (for which the mayor was prosecuted).[19] Thus from the thirteenth to the eighteenth century, non-swimmers' fear of the water led people both in Britain and in the American colonies to reimagine water as a weapon of silencing and oppression.

Demons and medicine

The same fear that led Eurasians to use water to silence outspoken women, identify witches and dispose of unwanted heretics and disabled people also suggested other related uses for water. Thus the German doctor Hermann Conring, whose enthusiasm for swimming women for witchcraft we have already seen, also evidently believed that there was an old practice of throwing newborn babies into the Rhine to determine if their parents had been married. Apparently the babies sank if their parents were unmarried, and floated if their parents were married.[20] This idea reverses the view of the witch trials – shouldn't the water reject the unbaptized babies? – but his contemporary von Sporck seems to have shared the idea that water might also drag down the guilty.

The magical power of water could also be brought to bear in medical cures. Even in the early Middle Ages, cures for demon possession might involve splashes of holy water.[21] In the later Middle Ages, as people stopped swimming, they became newly enthusiastic about water cures. This enthusiasm continued into the early modern period, as Henry VIII's physicians, for example, recommended warm-water bathing for the recalcitrant leg ulcer caused by his diabetes, and Henry's daughter Elizabeth I also sent for healing water for leg pain.[22] Along with the swimming of purported witches and ducking of outspoken women, water cures became associated with magic, witchcraft and demonic possession. By 1653, at Oxford in England, a young man who had malaria 'was told that the disease was caused by a devil, and that the proper course of action was to jump into the river, and then run quickly out, leaving the evil spirit to drown'.[23] The European custom at this time of getting people possessed by demons to name the witch who had sent the demons, and then swimming the accused women, only introduces an extra step to the process.[24]

All across Eurasia, this renewed interest in water demons can be seen in collections of folk stories and images, from the Japanese kappa in the east to the Scottish kelpie in the west. Though there had been earlier stories about sea monsters, new stories and traditions around kappa took off in Japan in the 1600s and 1700s, not only in local legends but in popular illustrated stories and even as the subject of zoological studies. The habits of kappa are often sexualized (they like to rise out of latrines and grab your backside, and steal mythical organs out of drowned people's anuses), reflecting the continuing connection between swimming and promiscuity. In 1689, similarly, a Slavic story included a young woman enchanted by a water spirit called a *vodnik* and dragged away to drown in the river. The Scottish kelpie, a water-horse that drowns children and travellers, first appeared in print in the mid-1700s, and remained popular through the nineteenth century.[25]

Suicides by drowning

These changing attitudes to the water may have caused increasing numbers of Europeans, and especially women, to think of drowning as a method of suicide during the 1600s. Hanging had long been the most common choice among people who wanted to kill themselves, with drowning second.[26] But as people stopped swimming at the end of the Middle Ages, drowning became more common, especially among women. In Kent, more than half of women's suicides were by drowning. In London at the same time, while drownings were usually recorded as accidental deaths, the high numbers of drownings suggest that their proportion of the total number of suicides was about the same as in Kent.[27] In Sweden,

71 A falconer swims awkwardly to retrieve his bird, miniature from Frederick II,
On the Art of Hunting with Birds (1258–66).

72 First illustration of the backstroke, miniature from Ibn Abī al-Qāsim Shīrāzī,
Ṣadaqah, *Kitāb-i-Samak 'Iyār*, part III, Iran, *c.* 1330.

73 First backstroke in Europe, and a better example of the breaststroke, as August harvesters take a break to swim, miniature from *Les très riches heures du duc de Berry* (1411–16).

74 Leander drowns trying to reach his lover Hero,
ceramic plate from Faenza, Italy, *c.* 1525.

75 Arawak or Carib swimmers near Trinidad, miniature from
Histoire naturelle des Indes, known as the Drake Manuscript, *c.* 1586.

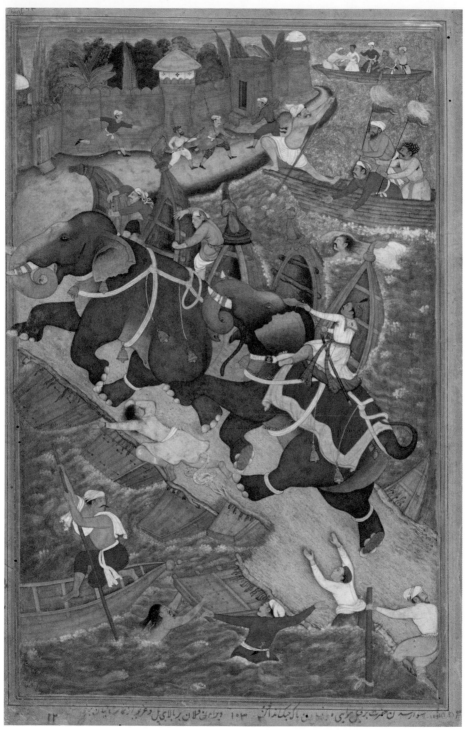

76 Servant swims with his arms straight out, in Basawan and Chetar's
illustration of the Indian epic *Akbarnama*, India, 1590–95.

77 Hursid, an imaginary Chinese ruler, watches his vizier's son swim in a pool,
miniature from an Ottoman manuscript (*Hamse-i Atâyî*), 1721,
painted by Heyrullah Heyri Cavuszade.

78 Boy swims with the help of an inflated bladder, detail from
Pieter Bruegel the Elder, *Children's Games*, 1560, oil on wood.

79 Poster for Pennsylvania Railroad, 1936, featuring a blonde woman
promoting the beach resort in Atlantic City, New Jersey.

80 Kawanabe Kyōsai, 'Children Swimming', from the series *One Hundred Pictures by Kyōsai* (Kyōsai hyakuzu), 1863–6, woodblock print.

81 People wading and relaxing in Chimelong Water Park,
Guangzhou, China, 30 August 2014.

82 Children from a displaced-persons camp swim in the Luhulu river
near Kitchanga, Democratic Republic of Congo, 2008.

though hanging remained the leading choice, drowning accounted for more than one-third of all suicides in this period, and this rose to 42 per cent of women's suicides.[28] Even in fiction, Samuel Richardson's early novel *Pamela* (1740) has the heroine plan to escape by faking her own drowning in a pond:

> So what will I do, but strip off my upper petticoat, and throw it into the pond, with my neckhandkerchief! For to be sure, when they miss me, they will go to the pond first, thinking I have drowned myself: and so, when they see some of my clothes floating there, they will be all employed in dragging the pond, which is a very large one; and as I shall not, perhaps, be missed till the morning, this will give me opportunity to get a great way off; and I am sure I will run for it when I am out.

This shift from hanging to drowning probably reflects increasing urbanization, with fewer opportunities for hanging from trees or in barns. Changing domestic architecture, so that fewer houses had large exposed beams to hang yourself from, probably also played a part.[29] But the general inability to swim may also have played a part in the rising popularity of drowning as a form of suicide. The figures, and the conclusions we draw from them, are uncertain partly because of the difficulty of distinguishing suicide by drowning from the many accidental drownings. Some drownings recorded as accidental were surely suicides, but on the other hand many people also died from accidental drowning during this non-swimming period. Children were especially vulnerable; boys, and especially poorer boys, who were less closely supervised, were both more likely to swim and more likely to drown, than girls, who were kept closer to home.[30] These increased rates of drowning, whether accidental or intentional, were high enough to cause alarm.

Swimming bans

Fears of drowning, and these associations of water with heresy, witchcraft, disability and suicide, led many early modern communities in Europe to ban swimming altogether. By the 1530s German schools banned all students from swimming, with whipping threatened for violators.[31] In 1567 a student at the University of Cambridge drowned 'while washing himself in a Place in the river Cham called Paradise'. Four years later the vice-chancellor banned swimming: scholars were 'not to enter any river, pond, or water within the county of Cambridge by day or by night for the purpose of swimming or bathing'. For a first offence, undergraduates were to be beaten; graduate students were to be placed in the stocks for the day and fined ten shillings. Repeat offenders faced expulsion.[32] The ban stood for the next 150 years, and typified a general tendency to legislate against swimming in the interest of public safety and public morals.

Renaissance and early modern European authors and artists reflected this attitude in their own pessimism around swimming. In 1518 the Dutch scholar Desiderius Erasmus wrote his influential *Naufragium* (Shipwreck), which uses a metaphorical fear of the ocean to mock religious superstition. William Shakespeare's *The Tempest*, of about 1611, takes up similar themes; his *Julius Caesar* reimagines Caesar's heroic swimming as a near-drowning ('But ere we could arrive the point proposed, Caesar cried "Help me, Cassius, or I sink!"'), while in the opening scene of *Two Gentlemen of Verona*, his modern stand-in for Leander cannot swim. *As You Like It*'s Rosalind mocks Leander:

> he would have lived many a fair year, though Hero had turned nun, if it had not been for a hot midsummer night; for, good youth, he went but forth to wash him in the Hellespont and being taken with the cramp was drowned and the foolish coroners of that age found it was 'Hero of Sestos'. But these are all lies: men have died from time to time and worms have eaten them, but not for love.

Marlowe's unfinished *Hero and Leander* similarly emphasizes Leander's pathetic drowning rather than his heroic swimming. Not long afterwards, the artist Peter Paul Rubens also depicted Leander drowning in a terrifying storm scene.[33]

THE SIXTEENTH AND seventeenth centuries saw the high point of Eurasian fear of the water. People stayed out of the water; they entered it only when they were forced to, and they got out as soon as they could. Swimming became illegal in many places. The practice of swimming women for witchcraft, like the idea of drowning heretics, started in Central Asia and spread slowly westwards across Europe. Trial by water reached Germany in 1584 and England in 1613, and by 1700 had crossed the Atlantic Ocean to the British colonies in North America. Ducking stools appeared in Europe in the 1200s, and were common in the 1600s and 1700s. Water demons and water magic proliferated. Water was not for sport or enjoyment, or even for cleanliness; it was the dangerous realm of spirits and death. And yet, at the same time, a counter-current was beginning to stir.

PART IV

CHANGING PLACES

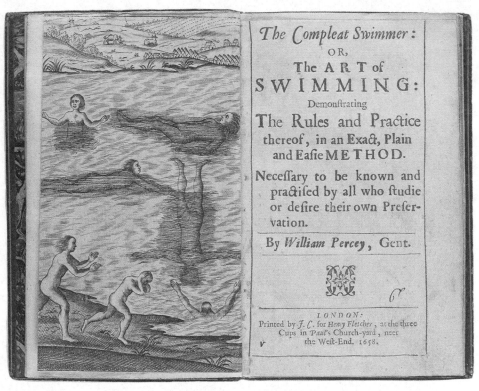

The Compleat Swimmer:
OR,
The ART of
SWIMMING:
Demonstrating
The Rules and Practice
thereof, in an Exact, Plain
and Easie METHOD.

Necessary to be known and
practised by all who studie
or desire their own Preservation.

By *William Percey*, Gent.

LONDON:
Printed by *J. C.* for *Henry Fletcher*, at the three
Cups in *Paul's* Church-yard, neer
the West-End. 1658.

83 Suggested ways to float to prevent drowning, frontispiece illustration to William
Percey, *The Compleat Swimmer; or, The Art of Swimming* (1658).

18

THE AVANT-GARDE

Even as the wave of regulations and prejudice against swimming crested in the sixteenth and seventeenth centuries, a counter-current was already working to convince northern non-swimmers to dip their toes in the water again. If these contrarians were inspired to swim mainly by seeing how much fun Indigenous swimmers were having all over the world, they didn't say so. Instead, Europeans attributed their desire to swim to a desire to emulate the Greeks and Romans. These ancients had built the first European empires, and now Europeans were building the first global empires. Just as Caesar had been a great swimmer, and Augustus had taught his grandsons to swim, so Europeans (or at least elite Europeans) would also learn to swim. Ottoman and Russian elites, who had imperial ambitions of their own, were also happy to play up their ancient connections to Roman swimmers. Han Chinese revolutionaries used swimming to symbolize rejection of Manchu rule. But Eurasians did not want to swim naturally, the way Indigenous swimmers did. Like the Romans, they would instead swim scientifically and modestly, for the exercise and medical benefits. They would swim safely, like civilized people.

Swimming and the classics

When the Greeks and Romans first learned to swim in the Iron Age, they associated swimming with the more sophisticated civilization of Egypt. Renaissance Europeans felt the same way. They wanted to swim to associate themselves with the sophisticated Greeks and Romans.

Already in 1513, not long after the first European slave ships reached West Africa, Niccolò Machiavelli repeated the Roman author Vegetius' admonition that soldiers should know how to swim.[1] Soon after that, the first European swimming manuals were published, and they, too, connected swimming to ancient Rome (illus. 83). In 1538 the Swiss scholar Nicolas Wynman quoted Propertius in his swimming manual's frontispiece. Wynman's preface reminds readers that Augustus had taught his grandsons to swim; later on Wynman points to Horatio's swimming the Tiber and again quotes Vegetius. For good measure, Wynman adds that the Germans had always been great swimmers. In 1555 Olaus Magnus agreed that military training should include swimming. Olaus adds that only animals swim naturally. For humans, swimming is an art (*arte natandi*) in, as he explains, the ancient Roman sense of the word. A generation later, in 1587, Everard Digby's swimming manual also played up swimming's connection to the Roman Empire, presenting his work as being in the tradition of Virgil, Vegetius, Galen and Justinian. In 1696 Melchisédech Thévenot, translating Digby into French, noted that Caesar was a great swimmer.[2] The connection between reading and swimming, already proverbial in Plato's time, was thus reinforced by a new elite practice of reading books about swimming; the first appearance of swimming in a Robin Hood story about 1660 may be related.[3]

This association with education and the ancient world encouraged Eurasians to associate swimming with wealth. Lists of what a man should teach his sons once again included swimming, as they had in the twelfth century. Thus in 1531 a popular list of the accomplishments of a gentleman included wrestling, running and swimming (mentioning in passing the new fad of tennis). The inclusion of wrestling owes something to Mongolian lists, but with regard to swimming this list-maker cites the Roman writers Vegetius and Galen, and the examples of Horatio and Caesar. Similarly, a fresco from the French king François I's palace at Fontainebleau (about 1535) shows the centaur Chiron teaching the young Achilles to wrestle, ride and swim. A generation later, a similar list included the Central Asian skills of riding, archery, wrestling, music and hawking, but again added swimming and tennis.[4] After the Russian tsar Peter the Great (called 'tsar' after the Roman title 'Caesar') visited nascent athletic programmes in England in the spring of 1689, he too added swimming to his navigational school's curriculum.[5]

The British philosopher John Locke, writing in 1692, quoted the ancient proverb: 'the Romans thought [swimming] so necessary, that they rank'd it with letters; and it was the common phrase to mark one ill-educated, and good for nothing, that he had neither learnt to read nor to swim: *Nec literas didicit nec natare.*' Locke insists that adults should teach elite boys to swim as soon as they are old enough to learn.[6] By 1721 an Ottoman artist, Heyrullah Heyri Cavuszade, represented the same notion in a startlingly modern image of an imaginary Chinese ruler watching his vizier's son swim in a tiled pool (see illus. 77). In July of the following year, when campaigning on the shores of the Caspian Sea, Tsar Peter ordered all of his officers who had not previously bathed in the Caspian to go for a swim. Some of the older officers, who did not know how to swim, were reluctant, but they all apparently obeyed. Peter, equally unable to swim but more accommodating to his own fears, had himself carried into the water sitting on a wooden board.[7] As in the Roman Empire, swimming signified elite status.

Most elites still could not swim, but by this time young men were beginning to be ashamed to admit it. About 1700 the teenaged King Charles XII of Sweden nearly drowned himself rather than admit to what seemed like cowardice:

> Horn leaped into the water and calmly swam around to the other side of the royal ship. Charles, leaning over the rail, shouted down to ask his friend whether swimming was difficult. 'No', cried Horn, 'not as long as you are not afraid.' Stung by the challenge, Charles immediately leaped into the water ... He was thrashing violently but sinking when Horn grabbed him by his clothes and towed him ashore.[8]

Like Charles, upper-class schoolboys throughout the British Empire tried swimming, sometimes with tragic results. A fifteen-year-old Harvard student drowned in July 1773; John Padock was splashing in Boston's Charles River when the current pulled him out of his depth. When he got in over his head, he was helpless, despite being only a few yards from the shore. He grabbed another boy and 'pulled him under water once or twice', but the second boy pulled free and saved himself, while Padock drowned. Padock could not swim, but some of the others did know how.

Padock's body was retrieved by 'Parker, a boy belonging to Welsh the painter' (so perhaps an enslaved African American) and two (presumably White) other students who knew how to dive.[9]

Back in Europe, boys were also beginning to swim. Though in 1571 Cambridge's vice-chancellor had threatened dire penalties for swimming, by 1794 it seems to have been normal for the boys at Eton College to bathe in the River Thames, and even sometimes to dive off a low wooden bridge. One young lord drowned, but as at Harvard some Eton boys knew how to swim, like the boy who dived into the river holding the hare he had poached in his mouth and reached the other side safely.[10] The future poet Lord Byron, soon to become a leader of the most avant-garde group of European trendsetters of his day, became a very strong swimmer while he was at Harrow in his teens in the first years of the nineteenth century.

Swimming became so popular among wealthy boys that their schools began to feel compelled to provide safer swimming pools. By 1798 the German teacher Johann GutsMuths advocated bathing pools as 'an indispensable appendage for a public school'.[11] In 1811 the future poet Alexander Pushkin accordingly had mandatory swimming lessons at his imperially sponsored high school near St Petersburg, Russia.[12]

When a fad for rowing started at Eton about this time, the teachers there disapproved, because of the danger from other boats and disease (as the Thames amounted to an open sewer). They refused to recognize the rowing clubs officially, but the fad continued nevertheless. Many of the Eton rowers did not know how to swim, so drownings were not infrequent. One boy drowned while boating in 1820, under the eyes of his friends, who also could not swim. In 1840, when another boy drowned, two teachers pushed for a change in the policy. Now boating was recognized as a legitimate activity for the boys, but no boy was allowed to go boating until he had passed a swimming test. Official bathing-places were laid out, and watermen were hired as swimming teachers and lifeguards.[13]

Similarly, even though a boy drowned in Harrow's swimming pond in 1826, the school's headmaster did not feel that he could shut down swimming there. Instead, the headmaster soon afterwards had the pond lined with brick and supplied with clean water, which was felt to be a great improvement.[14] Attitudes towards swimming had shifted enough to make it seem necessary not only to allow swimming but in some cases to provide lessons.

Young gentlemen continued to swim after leaving school, using risky swimming events to build edgy reputations. When Byron was at Cambridge, he and his friends held diving competitions in the River Cam, 'fourteen feet deep', and in the Greet. Around the same time, he and a friend held a late-night drunken contest to see how many times they could swim back and forth across the Thames without touching the bank. (Byron won.[15]) Like Digby and Locke, Byron associated his swimming with ancient Rome. That's why on 3 May 1810, at the age of 22, he and a friend emulated Leander's fictional swim and became the first people known to have actually swum the 5 kilometres (3 mi.) of ocean across the Hellespont from Europe to Asia. Byron recorded the event in his journal:

> This morning I *swam* from *Sestos* to *Abydos*. The immediate distance is not above a mile [*sic*], but the current renders it hazardous; – so much so that I doubt whether Leander's conjugal affection must not have been a little chilled in his passage to Paradise. I attempted it a week ago, and failed, – owing to the north wind, and the wonderful rapidity of the tide, – though I have been from my childhood a strong swimmer. But, this morning being calmer, I succeeded, and crossed the 'broad Hellespont' in an hour and ten minutes.[16]

A few years later, Pushkin was also an enthusiastic swimmer, whose admiration for Byron led him to sleep with one of Byron's lovers.[17] Young men's fad for swimming claimed many victims: one of Byron's friends drowned in 1811 after getting tangled in the weeds while swimming in the Cam. In 1808 Byron himself had nearly drowned while swimming in the sea at Brighton.[18] But even as he grew older, Byron never lost his enthusiasm for swimming. In 1823, while attending his friend Shelley's cremation at the seashore in Italy, the now 35-year-old Byron swam out to his nearby yacht and then back to shore.

When the graduates of Eton and Harrow were sent out as colonists in India, they took their enthusiasm for swimming with them. Swimming helped them identify with the colonizing Roman Empire. In 1809 the young Englishman John Hearsey reports that he and a companion swam for fun 'across the canal or streamlet to the sandy island'. But other young administrators still struggled to actually swim. On a different occasion, peer pressure led Hearsey's friend to pretend he could swim when he could not: 'I asked him why he had deceived me by telling me he could swim: he replied that, finding the water much deeper than he imagined, he lost confidence and sank.' Hearsey, who was proud of his swimming, reports another incident where two foolish companions rocked their boat dangerously but then 'acknowledged to each other that neither could swim'. On a fourth occasion, Hearsey had to save a young officer who had foolishly ventured into water over his head, though he could not swim.[19] Swimming was so important to these British officers' self-image that they risked their lives rather than admit they could not swim.

Swimming served to prove that Russians, too, belonged to the civilized world. Again some people learned to swim better than others. Russian Cossack soldiers, independent and self-organized, who occupied border zones, refused to pay taxes and 'recognized no state jurisdiction', learned to swim in the early 1700s and kept it up enthusiastically. In 1709 they were described as 'expert swimmers', though actually they 'swam the Dnieper holding on to the tails of their horses'.[20]

Russian swimming was not limited to soldiers. In the 1760s an eleven-year-old Russian girl, whose wealthy mother had progressive ideas, swam every day before breakfast in the summer, and 'could swim across a wide, deep river without any help'.[21] By 1784 Catherine the Great instructed her grandsons' tutors to make sure they learned to swim, too. One future poet's parents taught him to swim about 1800 'by throwing him in the pond one evening'. Similarly, about 1840 a young Leo Tolstoy almost drowned trying to impress girls by diving into a pond fully clothed, and had to be rescued by nearby women raking hay.[22] As adults, the writers Tolstoy, Fyodor Dostoevsky and Anton Chekhov were all enthusiastic swimmers. Apparently Chekhov used to amuse himself during a voyage across the Indian Ocean by 'diving from the bow of the ship while it was sailing at full speed, and catching a rope hanging from the stern'.[23] All across Eurasia, progressive, advanced people wanted to swim.

In the new United States as well swimming was associated with progressive thinking, sophistication and modernity, among both men and women. By 1706 the eccentric William Byrd, the founder of Richmond, Virginia, often swam in the James River after dinner, and encouraged his dinner guests to join him.[24] As in India, so also in America colonists might be pressured into trying to swim when they did not know how: fifty years after Byrd, the Methodist minister John Wesley repeated a friend's terrible story: her husband was talked into going swimming by an evil acquaintance who was a good swimmer. The acquaintance pretended to be standing when he was really treading water, and tricked her husband into getting in over his head, whereupon he drowned.[25]

Benjamin Franklin learned to swim at about the age of ten: 'living near the water, I was much in and about it, learnt early to swim well, and to manage boats.' After reading Locke and Thévenot, he took the art of swimming more seriously: 'I had from a child been ever delighted with this exercise, had studied and practis'd all Thévenot's motions and positions, [and] added some of my own, aiming at the graceful and easy as well as the useful.'[26] A few other revolutionaries, both men and women, could also swim: Alexander Hamilton was a good swimmer, the military messenger Ann Bailey swam well enough to cross rivers, and an American lieutenant escaped the British by swimming across the Hudson river at night, 'with his sword tied around his neck and his watch pinned to his hat'.[27]

AFTER THE REVOLUTION, Americans continued to associate swimming with free spirits and the avant-garde, as well as with the elite. President John Quincy Adams, in the late 1820s, was known for his habit of nude early morning swims in the Potomac River near the White House; he could apparently swim for more than an hour without stopping to rest. The future president Ulysses S. Grant claimed that he too swam as a teenager in the 1840s: 'my parents [had] no objection to rational enjoyments, such as . . . going to the creek a mile away to swim in summer.'[28] The young philosopher Henry Thoreau also swam in Walden Pond, Concord, Massachusetts, in 1845:

> After hoeing, or perhaps reading and writing, in the forenoon,
> I usually bathed again in the pond, swimming across one of its
> coves for a stint, and washed the dust of labor from my person,

or smoothed out the last wrinkle which study had made, and for the afternoon was absolutely free.[29]

Thoreau's younger friend Louisa May Alcott, whose father was particularly devoted to fads and the avant-garde, took swimming lessons as a girl in the 1840s.[30] From Byron to Franklin, Hamilton, Thoreau and Alcott, all the most exciting, forward-thinking people were swimming.

19

THE MIDDLE CLASS

Once these adventurous young people were swimming, more conservative people also began to dip their toes in the water. But was swimming safe? Most northern Eurasians still feared the water. Many people still believed in sea monsters and mermaids; in 1736 Benjamin Franklin (possibly as a prank) printed an article about a merman in the *Pennsylvania Gazette*. Some scholars suggested that water was the natural element of humans; that humans had evolved from water creatures, and mermaids were the missing link. Others doubted the existence of mermaids and sea monsters entirely. These were, they said, simply reflections of people's fear of the water.[1] Swimming was increasingly fashionable, but many people found it terrifying.

Swimming safety

Advocates of swimming tried to allay these fears by emphasizing water safety. Modern precautions, they said, made swimming safe: swimming manuals and lessons, safety belts and life jackets, and trained lifeguards. Learning to swim with these safeguards would, they insisted, do more to prevent drowning than to cause it. In emphasizing water safety, early modern Eurasians reprised northern non-swimming themes that had emerged in the Iron Age, when Zhou Dynasty Chinese proverbs warned swimmers about the dangers of trying to save a drowning friend, and Greek doctors recommended coating your skin with olive oil before going swimming, to protect it from the water. Wynman and Digby, the authors of the first swimming manuals in the 1500s, both emphasized water safety. Wynman promoted swimming to prevent drowning: 'so when you fall into danger you may more easily escape the waves'. He wisely advised students not to swim when they were drunk, and not to be over-confident. They should learn by swimming within their depth, and never swim alone. They should not attempt to save people who were drowning, or at least not without taking careful precautions against being dragged down themselves. Digby probably intended to be provocative by advo-cating swimming, as he was a well-known troublemaker writing just after Cambridge banned it. Nevertheless he had similar concerns about undergraduates drowning. He advised them not to swim on cold or windy days, and again, never alone.[2] Safety concerns led to bans on swimming along some stretches of the Danube in Vienna in the 1780s, 'on account of the supposed offence [of nudity] and the danger of drowning', and in the Seine in revolutionary Paris a few years later. To replace swimming, public baths were created on boats floating in the Danube, where you could hang from a sort of trellis frame and dip your body in 'the natural living current of the Danube'. There were similar public baths in the Seine. Public baths also lined the banks of the Neva River in St Petersburg circa 1835, with a teacher responsible for 'the art of swimming'.[3]

Like the Assyrians and Romans with their inflated goatskins and cork floats, many early modern swimmers also felt safer using artificial flotation devices. Wynman and Digby promoted the use of life jackets. So did the Italian artist and inventor Leonardo da Vinci. Leonardo sketched a variety of devices to help non-swimmers tread water (illus. 84).[4] Wynman's manual describes both cow bladders inflated with air and belts made of cork. Sure enough, the painter Pieter Bruegel depicts a swimming child wearing inflated water wings in the 1560s; these may be the cow bladders Wynman prescribes, or pig bladders (see illus. 78). Shakespeare, in about 1613, similarly mentions 'little wanton boys that swim on bladders' (*Henry VIII*, III.ii.430) who venture dangerously out of their depth. The same bladders were in use in Sweden, along with the older bundles of rushes. In 1624 Francis Bacon equipped his utopian *New Atlantis* with 'swimming-girdles and supporters'.[5] These may have been something like the 'Schwimmgurtels' described by Daniel Schwenter in 1636. These came in two kinds: one that you wrapped around your middle which had tubes for the wearer to blow into to inflate the bal-loons, like today's aeroplane life jackets; the other kind had two little

84 Swimmer wearing a life preserver and diving mask, sketch from
Leonardo da Vinci's notebooks (Paris manuscript в), *c.* 1486–90.

barrels or sets of tubes strapped around the swimmer's waist. In the
American colonies, Benjamin Franklin described 'waistcoats for swimming, which are made of double sailcloth, with small pieces of cork quilted
in between them'.[6] Like the swimming manuals, these flotation devices
reassured nervous swimmers as they got back into the water.

The nineteenth century saw the mass production and marketing of
similar swimming aids. Dozens of companies advertised and sold patented
gadgets that were supposed to make it easier to learn to swim. In the
1840s the discovery that early Assyrian swimmers used flotation devices
further encouraged their use throughout Eurasia, as well as encouraging
Ottoman elites to identify swimming with their powerful forebears (see
illus. 24 and 25). Even in China, where people were still not swimming,
boats carried lifebelts by the late 1800s.[7] One early 1900s British competitive swimmer describes these patent flotation devices contemptuously:

> When the novice is learning he is almost certain to get the idea
> into his head that he will be able to swim so much more easily if
> he has a body-belt of cork round him, or perhaps some air-bladders

tied under his neck; or it may be he will have brought to his notice a wonderful pair of fin-gloves that will enable him to paddle through the water like a duck ...

It is quite true that such contrivances will keep one afloat, but not in a thousand years will they ever teach or enable anyone to swim ... directly his feet left the ground the experimenter ... turned upside down, and in place of his head only his feet could be seen frantically kicking above the water. Of course not a moment was lost in rescuing him from his unenviable position, but that patent was at once relegated to the region where the majority of such 'inventions' and 'aids' ought to be – the dust-bin.[8]

But despite the condemnations of experts, the convergence of the middle class's interest in swimming and the rise of consumer production that dominated the 1800s meant that swimming devices proliferated well into the twentieth century.

Formal swimming lessons also became popular as a scientific and safe way to get back in the water. In ancient Rome, Cato and Augustus had taught their boys to swim. Now when Benjamin Franklin visited England from America in 1724, he tells us,

> I was, to my surprise, sent for by a great man I knew only by name, a Sir William Wyndham, and I waited upon him. He had heard by some means or other of my swimming from Chelsea to Blackfriar's, and of my teaching Wygate and another young man to swim in a few hours. He had two sons, about to set out on their travels; he wish'd to have them first taught swimming, and proposed to gratify me handsomely if I would teach them. They were not yet come to town, and my stay was uncertain, so I could not undertake it; but, from this incident, I thought it likely that, if I were to remain in England and open a swimming-school, I might get a good deal of money; and it struck me so strongly, that, had the overture been sooner made me, probably I should not so soon have returned to America.[9]

Despite Franklin's demurral, swimming lessons took off. A swimming school had opened in Prague by 1810, and there was one in Berlin by 1817.

The essayist Ralph Waldo Emerson, in 1844, mentions the 'swimming-school', and his young protégée Louisa May Alcott, as we have seen, took swimming lessons.[10] In 1906 children were being taught to swim by being floated on fishing poles in the River Thames.[11] By the 1920s middle-class children took swimming lessons at home and at summer camp as a matter of course.

These manuals and lessons served to ease people back into the water. Europeans had spent two hundred years convincing themselves that swimming was a mark of bestiality and barbarism, and that civilized people should not, and indeed could not, learn to swim. Now they were looking for a graceful way to change their minds. Swimming manuals, gadgets and lessons validated their new activity as scientific, so that Europeans conceptualized their own swimming (and Roman swimming) as rational, civilized and not at all like the untrained, natural swimming of people of colour.

Swimming and health

Another aspect of scientific swimming, also copied from Graeco-Roman antiquity, was to approach swimming more as a duty or responsibility than as a good time. Irresponsible Africans and Native Americans might swim for fun, but civilized Eurasians swam for safety, for cleanliness, for their health and for exercise. In 1581 a British schoolmaster was already promoting the health benefits of swimming. Everard Digby asserted that swimming would purge your skin of any external pollutions or uncleanliness. Johann GutsMuths also associated swimming with cleanliness.[12] John Locke, writing in the seventeenth century, presented swimming as a healthy choice: 'But, besides the gaining a skill which may serve him at need, the advantages to health by often bathing in cold water during the heat of summer, are so many, that I think nothing need be said to encourage it.' And yet Locke was also a little nervous about possible ill consequences: 'provided this one caution be us'd, that he never go into the water when exercise has at all warm'd him, or left any emotion in his blood or pulse.' Franklin had similar concerns: 'to throw oneself into cold spring water, when the body has been heated by exercise in the sun, is an imprudence which may prove fatal.' Nevertheless, he tells us that the 'exercise of swimming is one of the most healthy and agreeable in the world'.[13]

This idea that swimming was healthy fitted well with contemporary doctors' advice about bathing. While in the sixteenth century the healing power of water was conceived of in terms of magic or spirits, by the eighteenth century it was the water itself that was healing. Popular spas for 'curative water treatments' opened at Bath and other places in the 1600s, and by the 1700s, as we see in Jane Austen's *Persuasion* and elsewhere, they were centres of elite society. Increasingly doctors prescribed cold-water bathing, even outside of spas, as part of a healthy life.[14]

Swimmers eagerly adopted this idea of swimming for health. Byron loved swimming partly because he had a club foot: 'I can keep myself up for hours in the sea,' wrote Byron. 'I delight in it, and come out with a buoyancy of spirits I never feel on any other occasion.'[15] In 1817 one fourteen-year-old's friends thought of his swimming as a sign of his 'perfect health and vigour'.[16] In the 1870s Tolstoy's family took daily swims together in the pond.[17] Some early adopters extended this idea of healthy swimming to riskier activities like swimming in extremely cold water, as had been recommended by the Roman doctor Galen. William Byrd, in early 1700s Virginia, swam in the winter, 'without being discouraged by frost or Snow'. In the bitter Russian winters of the early 1800s, Pushkin 'would rise early, run down to the river, break the ice with his fist and plunge into the freezing water'. This sort of extremism did not always work out well. One university student went swimming in May 1835, in Maine, when there was still ice 'two feet thick' on the bank. He took cold, and the incident 'terminated in a troublesome cough, so that on my graduation I weighed but ninety-seven pounds'.[18]

Perhaps partly due to this kind of extremism, not everyone was convinced that swimming was healthy. Swimmers encountered considerable resistance from those who felt the water might be dangerous to their health. Catherine the Great, in Russia, struggled to get her grandsons to bathe at least 'every four or five weeks', even in Russian *banias*, oriented around saunas and plunges rather than pools.[19] During the American Revolutionary War, many generals tried to prevent the troops from swimming on the grounds that it was 'dangerous to the health of the troops', or 'on account of the foulness of the water', or because their behaviour was 'utterly inconsistent with decency'. And indeed, the water was often dirty and dangerous. Nevertheless many soldiers did swim whenever they got the chance. Not long after the Revolution, John

Quincy Adams's wife Louisa disapproved of his swimming and convinced the family doctor to warn Adams against it on the grounds that swimming was bad for your liver. But swimmers were quick to dismiss these concerns: Adams says that the doctor 'attempted some demonstration about the absorption of vital air in the water upon the viscera, which I neither understood nor believed'.[20] Early nineteenth-century Russians still feared the *vodianoi*, water devils who caught swimmers and drowned them. In novels, Russian peasants 'did not like the feel of the water, it was unfamiliar and uncanny, and gave them the shivers'.[21] Although swimming is a major plot device in Mark Twain's *Tom Sawyer* (1876), in the late 1800s conservative old women in small American towns like Tom Sawyer's Aunt Polly still might think swimming was dangerously unhealthy. The novel reflects prevailing American attitudes in Aunt Polly's fierce opposition to swimming, and the compulsion the boys in town all seem to feel to go swimming as often as possible. A hint of the close relationship between African American swimming and White American swimming may appear in that, like African swimmers, Tom swims with a charm against cramp, an anklet of rattlesnake rattles.[22] Nevertheless the general idea that swimming was a healthy form of exercise prevailed, enabling Europeans to differentiate their swimming from that of Indigenous and enslaved people.

Manuals, racism and pools

This racist notion of differentiating scientific swimming from Indigenous swimming may underlie the publication of a second rush of swimming manuals in the eighteenth century. Thévenot's *The Art of Swimming* appeared in French in 1696. *The Art of Swimming* appeared in Norwegian in 1788, *Exercise for Young People* in German in 1793, *The Floating Man; or, The Rational Science of Swimming* in Italian in 1794, and four years later GutsMuths's *A Short Course in Teaching Yourself the Art of Swimming*.[23] Swimming 'rationally', as these manuals proposed, separated White swimming from Indigenous and African American swimming. Europeans re-imagined swimming as a science partly in order to market it commercially, so that swimming instructors and writers could profit from it. But the scientific swimming movement also attempted to alleviate the European association of swimming with Indigenous people. Everard Digby's sixteenth-century swimming manual succeeded partly because he presented swimming as a science, reassuring swimmers that they were modern and sophisticated, unlike (in his view) Indigenous and African swimmers.[24] As Digby puts it, 'if we respect throughly the nature of this Art, we may easilie perceaue and see, that it doth not much differ from the rest of the liberall Sciences.'[25]

Several centuries after Digby, Eurasians were still concerned about whether swimming was appropriate for civilized people. In 1820, when a Russian traveller saw factory workers – gunsmiths – swimming in a river just south of Moscow, he worried that this was not the right kind of swimming, without scientific guidance:

> Most of their time they spend in the factory, in the workshop, or in front of the hot forges, and on hot summer days, they spend their off-time swimming. You can't help wondering at their daring when they throw themselves headfirst into the river from a pile, bridge, or lock four or five *sazheni* [about 8–11 m] high. In the water, they are quite confident and use virtually all known swimming styles . . . though they don't learn by rules and don't even know that there are rules and swimming-schools.[26]

Nine years later the French caricaturist J. J. Grandville drew 'The Swimming Lesson', showing men with the heads of frogs, ducks, fish and dogs. Did swimming turn people into animals? In 1834 the *Dublin Penny Journal* was still uncomfortably aware that Indigenous people were better swimmers: 'nor are there any nations so barbarous but that the art of swimming is known among them, and that in greater perfection than among civilized people . . . from imitating the brute animals, most of whom swim naturally.' A few years later, in 1840, an anonymous preface suggested that

> man cannot swim with the same facility as many of the inferior animals, which seem to be led by instinct to use the proper action for their preservation, while rational creatures, being aware of their danger, grow fearful or impatient, and begin to struggle, which has the effect of making them sink in the water.[27]

On the other side of Eurasia, late nineteenth-century North Chinese swimmers also wanted to be reassured that they were not like the darker-skinned, poorer people of southern China, who were traditionally swimmers, or like China's new enemies in Japan.[28] Northern Eurasians, too civilized to learn to swim 'naturally', felt they needed a different approach.

This myth that Europeans were more rational than the people they had colonized and enslaved found an enthusiastic reception. Swimming manuals accordingly tried to explain swimming in terms suitable for rational readers. In addition to the artificial flotation devices and fishing poles we have already seen, experts suggested complicated patterns of motion both in and out of the water to familiarize yourself with the strokes. One 'scientific' method of learning to swim in nineteenth-century Britain, apparently frequently recommended, was 'to place a basin half full of water on the floor, put a frog in it, lie face downwards over a stool, and try to imitate the movements of the frog'.[29]

In the same vein, the *Dublin Penny Journal* article tried to explain swimming in terms of Newton's Laws of Motion: 'The theory of swimming depends upon one very simple principle, namely, that if a force is applied to any body, it will always move towards that side where there is the least resistance.' The article then provides these encouraging and kind (yet hilarious) instructions for learning 'what is called the stroke, or that manner of drawing in and striking out the hands and feet that is necessary to produce progressive motion':

> Choosing a place where the water deepens gradually, walk coolly into it till it is up to your breast, then turn round your face to the shore, and throw an egg into the water, between you and the shore; it will sink to the bottom, and be easily seen there, if the water is clear. It must lie in the water so deep that you cannot reach it to take it but by diving for it . . . In this attempt you will find that the water buoys you up against your inclination; that it is not so easy a thing to sink as you imagined; that you cannot but by active force get down to the egg. Thus you feel the power of the water to support you, and learn to confide in that power; while your endeavours to overcome it, and to reach the egg, teach you the manner of acting on the water with your feet and hands,

which action is afterwards used in swimming to support your head higher above water, or to go forward through it.[30]

As European swimmers showed their eagerness to disassociate themselves from nature and Indigenous people, commercial interests developed new ways to profit from their desires. By 1741 London newspapers were advertising (paid) artificial swimming pools 'convenient for swimming or for gentlemen to learn to swim in', with (paid) instructors available.[31] There was an artificial swimming pool in Liverpool in 1828, and by that time Eton and Harrow were also beginning to construct tiled bathing pools for the boys. In January 1849 London's first public swimming pool opened in Orange Street, near Leicester Square, in the parish of St Martin-in-the-Fields. Three years later, there were seven swimming pools, and all of them were crowded with new swimmers.[32]

Throughout Eurasia, swimmers also declared their civilized status by forming lifesaving clubs and swimming clubs, with formal charters and membership dues, like so many other similar associations at this time. The earliest lifesaving clubs, in China as early as 1708, were not intended to oversee swimmers but to rescue people who accidentally fell off boats. The Chinkiang Association for the Saving of Life, on the lower reaches of the Yangtze River near Nanjing, retrieved the bodies of drowning victims and revived people who were not quite drowned. Lifeboats came into use a generation later further upstream on the same river, in Chongqing, about 1737. By imperial command, the government supplied five lifeboats, though the organization seems to have withered away in later years.[33] But soon these organizations changed their emphasis from drowning to swimming.

Lifesaving clubs oriented towards swimmers formed in Amsterdam around 1767, in Copenhagen in 1772 and in Britain two years later. In Russia, a group of aristocrats established the Neva School of Swimming in 1834. The new middle-class interest in swimming and swimming lessons took hold in Germany as well, with formal nineteenth-century photographs commemorating assemblies of swimming instructors.[34] As the number of people swimming increased, swimming clubs formed as well. Uppsala, Sweden, had a swimming club by 1796, and these clubs quickly spread throughout Europe. During the 1850s and '60s a large number of swimming clubs formed across England. At first the clubs were mostly in London and seaside towns, but they soon spread to almost every larger English town.[35] By 1912 there was an Amateur Swimming Society in Moscow, and that in turn inspired the creation of the Sanitas and Skhodnya swimming clubs and the Society for Mountain Skiing and Aquatic Sports. Plato's old association between reading and swimming also led entrepreneurs to publish, and customers to buy, a multitude of mostly short-lived swimming periodicals: *The Athletic Field and Swimming World*, *Swimming Notes*, *Swimming and Lacrosse* and so on.[36] Enrolment in a formal swimming club, and subscriptions to swimming magazines, signalled that you were not swimming naturally, the way Indigenous and enslaved people did, but rationally, for exercise, for cleanliness and for health.

Bathing machines and bathing costumes

Early swimming advocates focused on preventing drowning, but in order to reach the middle class they had to find ways to assure the public that swimming was morally as well as physically safe. Swimming could not be widely acceptable in Eurasia until advocates addressed the ancient association between swimming and sex, now reinforced by the sexualized representation of Indigenous and African women. The first radical swimmers were not concerned about modesty; they were radicals with regards to sex and nudity as well as swimming. Wynman, writing in the 1500s, advocated letting boys and girls swim together, as he says they did in Switzerland. He cited the Roman girl Cloelia (see Chapter Five) as a model.[37] Byron, Thoreau and Alcott moved in circles where free love was also an important value, and Franklin advocated 'air bathing' as well as sea bathing. But others advised that gentlemen should avoid swimming, because 'to swim you must be naked.'[38] To reach the middle class, swimming advocates had to move away from radicalism and reassure the public that strict decorum would be observed.

Bathing machines were one early way to assure that people could enjoy the water without risking their reputations. The first bathing machines were invented in Britain about 1736; they were small, enclosed wagons drawn by horses. You climbed in on the beach. The horses walked backwards down the beach to push the cabin into the sea, and then you changed into loose flannel robes and stepped directly out of the cabin into the water in relative privacy; in later models, a 'modesty shield' was added on the back of the wagon to prevent anyone from seeing you while you were bathing.[39] After bathing, you stepped back into the cabin to dress as the horses pulled you back up onto the beach.

Bathing machines not only ensured privacy for the swimmer, but fitted in well with the idea that 'rational' Eurasian swimming should involve complicated devices and cost a good deal of money, so as to limit swimming to the wealthier classes and provide a good profit to commercial interests. Using a bathing machine, while it was faintly ridiculous, demonstrated that you were neither a 'natural' swimmer nor a social radical. The machines caught on quickly. By 1768 people were regularly bathing in the sea at Scheveningen in the Netherlands, and around the same time also in Belgium.[40] A German beach resort welcomed visitors to the Baltic coast by 1793. Though in France so-called bathing machines were mostly stationary changing cabins, French holidaymakers were also beginning to go to the beach: as a four-year-old, the future Napoleon III bathed at Dieppe in 1812.[41]

Similar arrangements were also made in Islamic countries. By 1781 enclosed wooden sea *hamams* near Istanbul allowed first men, and later women, to bathe decently. These were bathing huts and wooden fences built to surround a small area of the sea, 'large enough for three or four people to "flap their arms around in"'.[42] In North Africa, both Muslim and Jewish Tunisian women bathed for their health in seaside pavilions or, if they could not afford that, they went down to the beach at night and soaked in the seawater wearing old summer dresses and light veils. As more Europeans visited Islamic countries, they joined local people on the warm sand beaches. Both La Marsa in Tunisia and Tangier in Morocco catered to European visitors as healthy spas.[43]

The new fad for sea bathing received a boost when the Prince of Wales spent his summers at Brighton starting in 1783, and King George III started taking beach holidays in Weymouth soon afterwards, all of which was widely reported in newspapers.[44] Yet we can see from the dark colours and general forlornness of a painting of bathing machines at Brighton in 1790 that sea bathing was still a new fad, and a rather off-beat one (illus. 85). The seaside here is not set up for holidaymakers; there is a windmill and a fishing boat, and even fishermen working. The sea itself is hardly welcoming either, with a heavy surf and lowering

85 Thomas Rowlandson, 'Bathing Machines
(An Excursion to Brighthelmstone)', 1790, etching.

clouds. Europeans were still suspicious of swimming. Most people still associated the coast with smugglers, pirates and fishermen, not with holidays and fun.

Contemporary newspapers also reflected concern about whether sea bathing was respectable. The British caricaturist Thomas Rowlandson published a pair of satirical hand-coloured etchings in 1790 called 'Venus's Bathing (Margate)', including the resort's bathing machines, which illustrate the ambivalence Europeans felt towards the fad (illus. 86). On the one hand, Rowlandson shows that people were eager enough to learn to swim to risk ridicule. Diving from your bathing machine was, in his words, 'fashionable'. But at the same time, Rowlandson's audience saw swimming as potentially ridiculous, and they were ready to see women's swimming in particular as erotic and risqué.

In the other 1790 Rowlandson etching of a woman swimming at Margate, again the woman is completely naked, and furthermore there is no sign of a bathing machine at all – she's swimming in the open sea, all alone and quite far from shore. This cannot have been the usual scenario, but it plays into late eighteenth-century fears of immodest and independent women. A third Rowlandson etching from 1815 subtitled

'A Peep at the Mermaids' shows lustful old men sneaking peeks at women swimming naked, even though women using bathing machines actually made careful use of modesty shields and were chaperoned by attendants. Here again, the scenario is unrealistic, but it reflects the fears that were current as the new fad took hold.

To combat this sort of association, by the late 1700s both men and women started to wear swimming outfits. Despite Rowlandson's caricatures, women using bathing machines usually wore flannel chemises. GutsMuths's swimming manual from 1793 advises even men to wear 'linen drawers, reaching halfway down the thigh'.[45] A French drawing of swimmers from about 1810 shows the men in short skirts and the women in thin shifts.[46] By 1819 an Italian swimming manual follows this French fashion and recommends that men cover the lower body with a fine cloth held up by a belt.[47] By this time, although people still swam naked in some contexts, their nudity had become an expression of privilege and identification with ancient Roman elites, and not the normal situation at the beach.

Eurasians had already been inclined to wear clothing into the water in the late Middle Ages, as we saw at Bath and with Poggio's account of

86 Woman falls comically out of her bathing carriage in Thomas Rowlandson, 'Venus's Bathing (Margate): A Fashionable Dive', c. 1800, etching.

his visit to the spa at Baden. In China, too, men had long worn loincloths into the public baths. Wynman, in 1538, imagined women wearing loose shorts to swim. Now the practice became more widespread, and eventually extended from plain shifts to elaborate bathing costumes.[48] The adoption of bathing costumes is associated with a general tendency for rich people to wear more and more underclothing. Clothing became cheaper with the introduction of commercial cotton in the early 1800s, grown by enslaved labourers in the American South and India, and spun and woven by children working in British mills, so people could afford more of it. But elaborate bathing costumes also suited the desire of Europeans to disassociate themselves from the swimming of Indigenous and African people.

End of the Little Ice Age

If, indeed, the Little Ice Age's cooler summers played a role in discouraging swimming in the late Middle Ages, then the end of the Little Ice Age, about 1850, and the increasingly warmer summers that marked the second half of the nineteenth century, may have encouraged people to get back in the water. The summer of 1868 saw a record temperature of 38.1°C (100°F) at Tonbridge, Kent, on 22 July, and many days over 30°C (86°F). Not all summers were that hot, but the warming trend continued.[49] People had already been experimenting with swimming for cultural reasons before the Little Ice Age ended. But the huge upswell of public interest in swimming in nineteenth-century Europe seems connected to the more attractive swimming conditions of that time.

The Middle Class

All of these devices – bathing costumes, bathing machines, flotation devices and artificial swimming pools – and the presence of lifeguards, together with the increasing popularity of swimming clubs, and warmer summers, combined by the mid-nineteenth century to make swimming seem more attractive to Europe's growing middle class. Slowly an older narrative associating sea bathing with illness gave way to the idea that swimming was for rich, young, good-looking, healthy people.[50] The usual tendency of elite, avant-garde eccentricities to slowly develop into popular pastimes also encouraged middle-class swimming.

As the first novels became popular, their authors often used swimming as a plot device, again connecting swimming with reading. Swimming was important to Robinson Crusoe and Gulliver, but in the nineteenth century it moved from adventurers to the middle class. In 1817 Jane Austen's unfinished novel *Sanditon* was set at the beach. By the time William Makepeace Thackeray published *Vanity Fair*, in 1847–8, his character Becky Sharp claims to 'swim beautifully' and plans to dive under the awning of Miss Crawley's companion, Briggs, when she's bathing and 'insist on a reconciliation in the water'. Again, Becky gets to know Mrs Hook Eagles 'at sea, where they were swimming together'. The authors went swimming as well as their characters. Charles Dickens learned to swim by 1842. In 1844 Dickens took his family on holiday to the beach in Italy (recently freed from Barbary piracy), and his brother 'swam out into the bay', though he nearly drowned doing it and had to be rescued. Then the construction of the first passenger steam railways in England – the line from London to Brighton, for example, opened in 1841 – made it much easier to get to the seaside and encouraged leisure travel. Swimming was the very definition of fashion; the first use in writing of the phrase 'in the swim' dates to 1869.[51]

As with most upper-class fads that are adopted by the middle class, swimmers in the late 1700s and 1800s came in for a good deal of caricature and mockery. At first, cartoons compared elite swimmers to animals.

87 British government officials satirically represented as swimmers – and animals – in J. Barrow, 'The State Spanials after the Duck', 1784, etching.

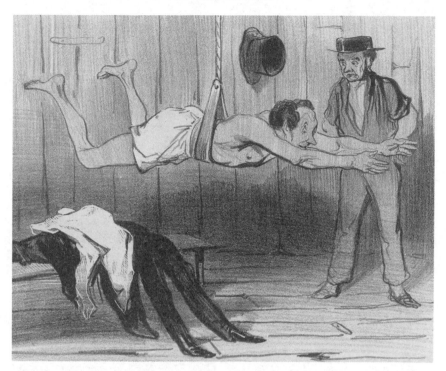

88 Ridiculing middle-class French swimmers: Honoré Daumier, 'La leçon à sec',
Les Baigneurs series, lithograph from *Le Charivari*, 30–31 May 1841.

Then in a political cartoon from 1784, British politicians are represented as naked African swimmers playing the 'Run after Duck' game (illus. 87). In the 1800s satirical cartoonists made good money poking fun at newly inspired middle-class swimmers. In 1828 a British cartoon shows how vanity induced a young swimmer to take off his cork floaters, and now he's holding on to a tree branch in desperation. A French satirical cartoon from 1812 similarly shows a mother delighted because her son has been swimming. The subtext is surely that swimming is dangerous and the current fad for it ill-advised.[52]

Social tension between the upper class and the middle class around swimming found expression in a second series of satirical drawings that appeared in the 1840s and '50s in popular magazines and newspapers. A French cartoon from 1841 shows a foolish-looking young man suspended in mid-air from ropes, learning how to swim breaststroke 'à sec', without even being in the water (illus. 88).[53] Four years later, another cartoon satirizes a woman learning to swim (illus. 89). She is dripping wet, and she has a thick rope tied around her waist; a swimming teacher holds

89 More ridicule: Honoré Daumier, 'Madame Rabourdeau à sa première leçon',
Les Baigneuses series, lithograph from *Le Charivari*, 5 August 1847.

the other end; the inappropriateness of her desire to swim is expressed
by her depiction as both middle-aged and obese. A lithograph published in Belgium in 1856 continues the satirical theme, skewering the
aristocratic pretensions of two nervous swimmers standing in shallow
water. In the caption, the woman says, 'Darn! The marquis of Finoeil,
and I don't have my corset on!' and the man says 'Shoot! The countess
of Crupet, and I don't have my padded suit.'[54] Winslow Homer's similar satirical cartoon shows a crowd of hip American men and women
in complicated, heavy bathing costumes. They are paddling inexpertly
in shallow water just off the coast of the fashionable resort of Newport,
Rhode Island (illus. 90).

By the 1870s even the working class was beginning to take an interest
in swimming, thanks to the popularity of less expensive seaside resorts
such as Atlantic City in New Jersey, Coney Island in New York and
Revere Beach in Massachusetts. A second Winslow Homer cartoon
mocks working-class swimmers at Long Branch, New Jersey. Three women

stand knee-deep in the water in elaborate outfits. One exclaims, 'Oh, ain't it cold!' These women are not hipsters. They may be store clerks, textile workers or servants; what's funny is that the working class is taking up the swimming fad.[55]

These cartoons may also be intended partly to mock the rising women's rights movement, which found expression in swimming as well as bicycle riding. By 1894 popular women's magazines presented the 'new woman' as vigorous and athletic. Her interest in 'aquatic sports' stood in contrast to older images of pale, fragile, invalid Victorian women. The swimming coach Charlotte Epstein promoted long-distance swimming and more practical bathing suits for women. Epstein organized and led the National Women's Lifesaving League, and then used that organization to fight for women's right to vote. In 1915 she challenged gender barriers with a women's swimming contest at New York's Manhattan Beach.[56] Cigarette cards of the 1880s, an earlier version of baseball cards, showed White girls swimming, to encourage them to take up smoking.[57] The bathing suit, like the bloomer suit for riding bicycles (and like smoking), came to represent women's freedom from Victorian strictures.

But none of this means that Europeans or White Americans actually learned to swim. Most of them remained, as northern non-swimmers

90 Ridiculing American swimmers: Winslow Homer (after), 'The Bathe at Newport', engraving from *Harper's Weekly*, 4 September 1858.

always had been, afraid of the water and disinclined to spend much time in it. Or, if they did spend time in the water, they did not swim there. Jane Austen, for example, loved to bathe in the sea, with a bathing machine and a maid to attend her. She and her family, and her fictional characters, frequently visited coastal resorts, which were becoming the fashionable new holiday spots for young people. But neither she nor they seem to have learned to swim.[58] Hans Christian Andersen's 'The Little Mermaid', written in Copenhagen about 1837, reflects the new interest in swimming, but it is still a story mainly about drowning: the handsome prince cannot swim; the swimming mermaid isn't human.[59] Most of the swimming in Dickens's novels, as well, involves drowning. In *The Old Curiosity Shop* (1841) a small boy rescues a drowning dog and Quilp drowns. In *Our Mutual Friend* (1865) the plot turns on boatmen who make a living looting the bodies of drowning victims in the Thames. In *Edwin Drood* (1870) Rosa's mother drowns, and so, apparently, does the title character.[60] Henry James's characters also do not swim, and even his watery metaphors centre on difficulty and drowning.[61]

Everywhere it was the same. In 1801 sports writers were concerned that people were not swimming, and in 1879 safety experts still complained that the 'great majority' of Europeans could not swim, and that, 'strange as it may seem to you, there are many who follow the sea as a profession who cannot swim a stroke.'[62] While historian Kevin Dawson is right to say that 'most white women could not swim,' White men were about equally poor swimmers. In Brazil in 1828 and 1829 White men were 'very rarely seen in the water'. In 1884, similarly, rough Turkoman raiders in Afghanistan considered swimming the Amu Darya to mean 'certain death', and camelmen died because 'like most Pathans' (today's Pashtun) they could not swim. Though they were 'struck at the little the Cossacks seemed to think of swimming a river', English colonial administrators doubted whether they really swam all that well. Even in 1900 the journalist Lillian Griffin marvelled,

> It seems strange, when swimming is the only really comfortable exercise for hot weather, that more [White] people do not master the art. Sea bathing is a more or less popular recreation along the coasts, and some of the bathers are able to keep their noses above water and to propel themselves to a slight extent, but those are

rare who are happily at home in the water, who could keep afloat
for an hour, and, if need be, support another person. A trip to any
of the popular beaches will illustrate this. At high tide thousands
of people swarm the bathing space; they cling to the ropes, churn
up and down, splash each other, and scream hysterically, and that
is their nearest approach to swimming.[63]

Eight years later, Robert Baden-Powell, the founder of the Boy Scouts,
also urged boys to learn to swim: 'What a fool the fellow looks who has
to paddle about in shallow water and can't join his pals in their trips to
sea or down the river.' But Baden-Powell still sounds dubious: he admits
that he himself was afraid of the water at first, and 'couldn't get the hang
of it', but then he 'found the way was to take it slowly and calmly' – that
is, rationally. In 1914 a British competitive swimmer complained about
'the deplorable number of people who are content to paddle in the shallows – afraid to go a foot out of their depth. For one bather who can
swim you will find thirty who cannot.' (He adds that in his experience
women learn to swim faster than men.[64])

Because swimming was fashionable and also a great excuse to paint
nudes, many late nineteenth-century painters eagerly depicted swimming
scenes. But again, very few of these paintings show their models swimming. Frédéric Bazille in France painted men in swimming trunks lazing
on the banks or standing in the water; Thomas Eakins in the United
States painted nude men lounging on a large rock. In Germany, Max
Liebermann painted nude working-class boys diving off a dock. Edgar
Degas in France painted peasant women wading naked. People dress
and undress near water, dry themselves with towels and sun-bathe, but
there is not a single image of anybody actually swimming. Joaquín Sorolla's
children wade, fully dressed, in Valencia. Paul Cézanne and Henri Matisse's
nudes simply stand on the beach. Pablo Picasso painted bathers, but
again either on the beach or wading.[65] There was always considerably
more beach holidaymaking and wading than actual swimming.

As in medieval China, non-swimmers now developed a variety of
ways to indicate their approval and interest in swimming without having
to swim. Many European and European American families took holidays
along the coast, where you could sit on the beach, wade and be fashionable, even if you did not swim.[66] Similar seaside resorts in Turkey added

the opportunity to show how Europeanized you were, wearing *alafranga* bathing suits and goggles (that is, 'à la française', in the French style, illus. 91).[67] In 1890s North Africa, fashionable Tunisians and European colonists both built sophisticated bathing houses:

> The women of La Marsa and Sidi Bou Said take sea baths here far from inquiring eyes. They arrive in carriages with the shades pulled down. In the middle of the building is a swimming pool through which the sea water enters freely. The princesses of the bey's family have a similar bathing house not far away from this one (illus. 92).

Resorts marketed the seaside as a place of freedom and holiday from ordinary obligations, where romance could bloom.[68] They competed to show off better bathing equipment than other resorts had. Elaborate changing cabins, bathing machines, sea baths, water slides and diving boards proliferated all over Europe, North Africa and the United States (illus. 93). All this equipment showed how scientific European-style

91 Bathing structures, Leander's Tower, Strait of Istanbul, 1865–75, photograph by Basile Kargopoulo.

92 Women's bath on La Marsa beach, illustration from
Charles Lallemand, *Tunis et ses environs* (1892).

swimming was. Far from its earlier associations with smugglers and
pirates, the beach now became the summer destination of upper-class
leisure.

Swimming was also presented as a spectator sport. Swimming competitions had a long history in medieval China, in Japan, among Native
American and Australian swimmers and among Africans and enslaved
African Americans, but British promoters now claimed to be inventing
competitive swimming. Europeans loved swimming competitions and
displays like fake mermaid exhibits that allowed you to support swimming without getting wet.[69] Many professional swimmers, like Fred
Beckwith in the mid-1800s, created businesses promoting swimming races,
selling tickets or holding benefits for swimming stunts such as staying
underwater in a glass tank for several minutes or long-distance swims.
Beckwith's daughter Agnes started her professional swimming career at
fourteen, when she completed a heavily promoted 5-mile swim in the
Thames from London Bridge to Greenwich. Soon she was performing
in 'aquatic displays' and teaching swimming lessons.[70] Tolstoy's fictional
Anna Karenina satirizes a similar swimming exhibition in 1878, mocking the performer's 'absurd red "costume de natation"', while at the same
time the real Russian swimmer Leonid Romanchenko set a world record
in marathon swimming.[71] These European swimming races culminated

93 Enjoying the water without swimming: a marine toboggan slide near Bridgeport, Connecticut, from *Scientific American*, LIX/4 (28 July 1888).

in the establishment of the modern Olympic Games in 1896, where the first Games included (as the Greeks had not) four swimming events. Swimmers from four countries participated: Austria, Hungary, Greece and the United States. By 1900 this list had expanded to include twelve European or European-dominated countries.[72]

The rise of international competition also inspired other Eurasian countries to aim for gold: in 1902–3 the writer Liang Qichao in China emphasized the importance of swimming races to build physical strength. Competitive swimming formed part of a nationalist programme to strengthen China's presence on the international scene and resist European colonization – and to distinguish northern Chinese swimming from the 'natural' swimming of southern China. In Russia, sports federations formed to promote competitive swimming, enabling Russia to send three swimmers to the 1912 Olympics. However, when these swimmers failed to bring home medals, Russia did not send any more swimmers to the Olympics until after the Second World War.[73]

BY THE EARLY decades of the twentieth century, some people in Europe and some European-descended people in the United States were very good swimmers, and many others were interested enough to put on suits and dabble a little at the seaside or in the swimming pool. Thousands of people spent their holidays at the beach, or went to see swimming races, even if they never got in the water. Even if relatively few people ever developed sophisticated diving skills or learned to do side breathing, still swimming itself had been effectively normalized.

20

OUT WITH THE OLD, IN WITH THE NEW

As more of the former non-swimmers of Eurasia started taking holidays at the beach, they gradually became more receptive to new ideas about swimming. Slowly they accepted the overhand front crawl stroke as a normal way to swim, though in Europe and Asia the front crawl never became as common or as popular as the breaststroke. Slowly people also accepted that you could not really detect witchcraft by forcibly floating naked women in ponds, no matter how entertaining an afternoon that provided. But even in the first years of the twentieth century, swimming remained enough of a novelty in Asia that it was taken up by young Communist revolutionaries as a symbol of their movement.

From breaststroke to crawl

Well into the nineteenth century most European swimmers were still using the breaststroke and backstroke, and keeping their faces out of the water, even in competition. That is, they swam even less well than the Assyrians, Greeks and Romans had in antiquity, since the ancient swimmers had at least used a crawl stroke. Some Eurasians were aware that Indigenous and African American swimmers used an overhand stroke, which was much faster than the breaststroke. They saw that these 'natural' swimmers used side breathing rather than holding their heads up out of the water. But for decades, swimmers from Britain to China resisted the crawl stroke. They saw the breaststroke as calm and rational, and rejected the crawl as excessively splashy and energetic. As swimming races became more competitive, however, slowly the advantages of the crawl stroke proved irresistible, and more swimmers began to use it.

In the early sixteenth century the illustrations in Digby's early swimming manual show that Europeans swam with their heads out of the water. Even though contemporary European slave traders were already publishing books describing the overhand stroke of African and Native American swimmers, Wynman and Digby only explained four strokes. They knew the breaststroke, backstroke, sidestroke and dog-paddle, and how to tread water and dive underwater, but not the overhand crawl stroke used by Indigenous swimmers.

By the early 1700s American colonists had seen Native Americans swimming overhand strokes and were interested in imitating them.[1] Accordingly, Virginia's William Byrd took lessons from local Native Americans. Byrd wrote in his journal for 1733 that,

> This being Sunday, we were glad to rest from our labors; and, to help restore our vigor, several of us plunged into the river, notwithstanding it was a frosty morning. One of our Indians went in along with us and taught us their way of swimming. They strike not out both hands together, but alternately one after another, whereby they are able to swim both farther and faster than we do.[2]

Byrd's shift to the crawl stroke did not immediately catch on with other American colonists. Probably both John Quincy Adams and Benjamin Franklin still swam the breaststroke. But by the 1830s other swimmers in the United States were emulating Byrd and studying Native American swimming. The American painter George Catlin was inspired to investigate Native American swimming after his brother Julius drowned in a swimming accident. Like other Native Americans, Mandan men and women in what is now North Dakota used the overhand crawl stroke with their faces in the water and side breathing. Catlin was surprised and impressed by it, and thought the crawl was superior to the European breaststroke:

> By this bold and powerful mode of swimming, which may want the grace that many would wish to see, I am quite sure, from the

94 Alfred Jacob Miller, *Indian Women: Swimming*, 1858–60, watercolour on paper.

experience I have had, that much of the fatigue and strain upon
the breast and spine are avoided, and that a man will preserve
his strength and his breath much longer in this alternate and
rolling motion, than he can in the usual mode of swimming, in
the polished world.[3]

Other American painters also painted Native American people swimming, taking care to show how Indigenous swimmers dived head first
into the water, and how they swam with their faces in the water.[4] Catlin's
concern that the overhand stroke was less graceful than the breaststroke,
the 'usual mode of swimming in the polished world', was probably still
the dominant attitude among White Americans in his lifetime. As late
as the 1870s an American traveller mocks the crawl stroke he saw used
in Sudan, where a Nubian swimmer pulling the American's boat 'swims
hand over hand, swinging his arms from the shoulders out of water and
striking them forward splashing along like a side-wheeler'.[5]

However, by 1880 the crawl stroke had apparently become normalized
even among White swimmers in the United States, as an illustration from
Harper's Weekly shows two women using overhand strokes in a river race.
The women have also learned to swim like 'natural' swimmers with their
faces in the water, turning their heads to the side in order to breathe as

they go (illus. 95). The title, 'Swimming à la Mode', highlights that the women are using the latest fashionable stroke.

Difficult as it was for Americans to accept the new overhand swimming stroke, European, Central Asian and Chinese swimmers had much more trouble accepting it. Breaststroke, backstroke and sidestroke remained their only options for longer. In the early 1700s Ottoman artists depicted breaststroke and backstroke. Contemporary Indian paintings also show swimmers holding their arms out stiffly in front of them, as in the breaststroke.[6] By the 1790s avant-garde British swimmers were attempting side strokes and diving, but not the crawl. In Rowlandson's first satirical drawing, the woman is attempting to dive headfirst. In the other she is using a sidestroke, and his caption specifically points it out: 'Side Way or Any Way'.[7] In 1819 a Swiss sports writer describes the sidestroke, or something like it, as the most rapid stroke he knows:

> The body is turned either upon the right or left side, and the feet perform their usual motions. The arm from under the shoulder stretches itself out quickly, at the same time that the feet are striking. The other arm strikes at the same time with the impelling

95 'Swimming à la Mode', engraving from *Harper's Weekly*, 25 September 1880, showing American swimmers finally using the overhand stroke.

of the feet ... As swimming on the side presents to the water a smaller surface than on the [front], where rapidity is required, the former is often preferable to the latter.[8]

Byron described himself as a 'strong swimmer', but he and his friends did not use a crawl stroke, and probably did not swim with their heads underwater unless they were diving.[9] By 1815 magazine illustrations show that some cutting-edge swimmers in France were swimming the crawl stroke, though they were still keeping their heads cautiously out of the water.[10] Corti's 1819 Italian swimming manual also contains an illustration of what Corti calls 'A French and Russian Stroke', which looks like an early form of the crawl. Corti suggests that, when swimming on your front, you use one hand alternating with the other to press the water backwards.[11] He assumes that you will keep your head out of the water. But Corti still considers the overarm stroke to be a novelty, and his go-to stroke remains the breaststroke with a frog kick, 'a guisa di rana'. The breaststroke continued to be the normal Eurasian stroke.

When American swimmers tried to convert Britain to the crawl in the 1840s, they met with considerable resistance. George Catlin was so impressed by Native American swimmers that he brought two Ojibwa men from Lake Superior over to Britain to give swimming demonstrations there. But when these men, going by the stage names Wenishkaweabee and Sahma, accompanied Catlin as part of a swimming demonstration in London, British spectators professed themselves shocked at the crawl stroke's splashing. British swimmers preferred the breaststroke, they said, because it was more decorous and civilized than the crawl. *The Times* described the Ojibwa stroke disgustedly as 'totally un-European': the swimmers 'lashed the water violently with their arms, like the sails of a windmill, and beat downward with their feet, blowing with force and forming grotesque antics'.

Catlin had set up various swimming competitions to please the many spectators who gathered for this event. The two Ojibwa swimmers, who may not have been particularly good swimmers at home, first raced one another several times. Despite its contempt for the crawl stroke, *The Times* reported admiringly that both men swam 'with the rapidity of an arrow, and almost as straight a tension of limb'. In the first race, one of the Ojibwa men swam 130 feet (about 40 metres) in less than half a minute, which was fast for the time. Then, when they were tired, the Ojibwa men raced one of the best swimmers in England, who beat them 'with the greatest ease'. *The Times* reporter chose in the end to disregard the Ojibwas' fine swimming in favour of his desire to support the superiority of British swimmers.[12]

Like that reporter, many British swimmers, alarmed by the new stroke and its associations with Indigenous people, looked for reasons to put down the crawl stroke in favour of the breaststroke with which they were more familiar. They developed the idea that 'graceful and elegant movements, with a minimum of splashing' were the most important aspects of swimming; 'like dancing, the poetry of motion', these were best represented by the breaststroke. The crawl stroke was disparaged as 'ugly gestures' and 'trick' swimming.[13] A struggle developed between competitive swimmers, who wanted to use the new fast stroke to win races, and recreational swimmers, who resented the implication that their swimming owed anything to Indigenous people.

As we have seen, the crawl was probably not entirely unknown in Europe even before the Ojibwa demonstration. After the demonstration, alternating overhand strokes slowly became more popular, aided by increasing British familiarity with Aboriginal Australian swimming as the British Empire colonized Australia. After a British traveller demonstrated Aboriginal Australian swimming strokes in London in 1855, those strokes helped Fred Beckwith win a championship race a few years later.[14] In 1861 a second race between a British swimmer and a Native American man (this time a Seneca man from Lake Erie) was widely promoted, though in the end the race never took place.[15] Publicity from these events caused more Europeans to use the front crawl in the late nineteenth century, calling it 'the Indian stroke'. Catlin's description of the crawl stroke was plagiarized in a swimming manual in 1867.[16] By the 1890s even recreational club swimmers in Britain were beginning to use both the crawl stroke and side breathing.[17] In France, the crawl stroke gained ground after an Aboriginal Australian man called Tartakover gave an impressive demonstration of it in 1906, though apparently French swimmers were still holding their heads out of the water.[18]

Variations on the crawl stroke were promoted by the Cavill brothers, who originated the 'Australian crawl', and by John Trudgen, who promoted a stroke he had learned from Indigenous people in Argentina. The Trudgen stroke was popular because you still kept your head out of the water, and because it used a scissor kick that avoided splashing. Trudgen won a race using this stroke 'peculiar to Indians' in 1873, but despite that, the Trudgen was much slower than the traditional crawl with a flutter kick.[19] The Australian crawl with a flutter kick, on the other hand, turned out to be faster than Native American versions, and soon became popular for competitions. (A younger Cavill brother later invented the butterfly, a faster variation of the breaststroke.)

But crawl strokes still met with suspicious resistance in both Europe and the United States. Even professional swimmers resisted the switch. In 1906 a prominent American swimming coach condemned variations on the Trudgen stroke, 'in vogue among the inhabitants of the Hawaiian Islands, the Indian tribes of South America, and the lifeguards at our summer resorts', as 'very exhausting'. He disapproved of the association with Indigenous people, and with young people. He had to admit that the ordinary crawl stroke with side breathing was 'the fastest of all known swimming strokes'. Nevertheless he opposed it:

> For long distance swimming this stroke is almost useless, as it is very exhausting, owing principally to the fact that the breath must be held, excepting at intervals when the head is raised forward or at one side for breathing purposes. In addition the swimmer finds it difficult to keep a straight course.[20]

By this time many good swimmers in both Europe and the United States were using overhand strokes, but a 1914 book on swimming still contains directions for how to swim the breaststroke – with your head held well above the water.[21] Most American children ended up learning the crawl in the name of speed, but breaststroke is still today by far the most common swimming stroke among Europeans.

The overhand crawl stroke took so long to catch on with Europeans and European-descended people that it could be presented as a novelty by Byrd in the early 1700s, by Catlin in the 1830s, again in *Harper's Weekly* in the 1880s, and still be a novelty in 1906. One British-born swimming coach recalled that in 1906 most instructors still taught the breaststroke first to beginning swimmers. 'At that time,' he says, 'the peculiar crawl style practiced by Pacific islanders had not been refined and was, in fact, barely known in the civilized world.'[22] The coach overlooks that the Pacific islanders themselves had refined their stroke over thousands of years of practice. He may not have known that overarm strokes had been known at least since ancient Egypt, and were common in ancient Greece and Rome.[23] Even modern Europeans had known about the crawl stroke for two hundred years.

But while his casual assertions are not true, they were true for him. Like many people of his time, he still thought of the breaststroke as normal and associated the crawl stroke with foreign danger. And despite the efforts of various early books on swimming, this notion prevailed well into the twentieth century.[24] When Clarabelle Barrett wanted to attempt a swim across the English Channel in 1926, at least one newspaper's photo caption presented her intention to use the crawl stroke as a daring innovation.[25] In 1928 an American swimming coach was still startled to discover that people swam the crawl stroke – the 'modern swimming stroke' – in ancient Greece, and that the Greeks might well have learned it from the Egyptians before them.[26] In the 1960s, when I myself learned to swim, though the 'Australian crawl' was the first stroke taught to American children, it was still regarded as slightly progressive and experimental. And even today, European children learn the breaststroke first. Unless they show promise as swimmers, they do not learn the crawl.[27]

The end of Trial by Water

Astonishingly, while Europeans and European-Americans were relearning how to swim, debating the merits of the crawl and the breaststroke, building swimming pools and inventing bathing suits, their compatriots were still enthusiastically swimming people for witchcraft and ducking women for speaking their minds. People were still floating women as witches in the American colonies in Benjamin Franklin's time. Slowly, however, the tide turned. As more and more people learned to swim, trial by water fell out of fashion.

In the Americas the last accused witches were floated around 1730, when Franklin's newspaper, the *Pennsylvania Gazette*, published a mocking article about the practice on 22 October. The article, very likely written by Franklin himself, gives a good idea of the process:

Burlington, Oct. 12. Saturday last at Mount-Holly, about 8 Miles from this Place, near 300 People were gathered together to see an Experiment or two tried on some Persons accused of Witchcraft . . . the Accusers being very positive that if the Accused . . . were bound and put into the River, they would swim [float]; the said Accused desirous to make their Innocence appear, voluntarily offered to undergo the said Trials, if 2 of the most violent of their Accusers would be tried with them. Accordingly the Time and Place was agreed on, and advertised about the Country; The Accusers were 1 Man and 1 Woman; and the Accused the same . . . the Accusers and the rest of the Mob, not satisfied with this Experiment, would have the Trial by Water; accordingly a most solemn Procession was made to the Mill-pond; where both Accused and Accusers being stripp'd (saving only to the Women their Shifts) were bound Hand and Foot, and severally placed in the Water . . . The more thinking Part of the Spectators were of Opinion, that any Person so bound and plac'd in the Water (unless they were mere Skin and Bones) would swim till their Breath was gone, and their Lungs fill'd with Water. But it being the general Belief of the Populace, that the Womens Shifts, and the Garters with which they were bound help'd to support them; it is said they are to be tried again the next warm Weather, naked.[28]

Ducking stools went out of fashion in the northern colonies about the same time, but women were still being ducked in Virginia in 1767, and further south in Georgia in 1819. Americans could still seriously propose ducking a woman as late as 1824, when judges finally ruled that the punishment was obsolete.[29]

In Britain, where witch persecutions had been more popular, they persisted a little longer, so that people were still swimming women for witchcraft and ducking women as scolds well into the nineteenth century, even as Byron was swimming the Hellespont and British lifesaving clubs were forming. By the mid-eighteenth century, however, trial by water was slowly disappearing due to increased criminal penalties and growing urbanization.[30] Thus in 1751, when a crowd of thousands swam Ruth Osborne in a pond at Tring, Hertfordshire, and she drowned, one of the ringleaders ended up being hanged for murder.[31] A few decades later the crowd's mood had shifted: the crowd that floated a man for witchcraft in July 1776 at Farnham, a small town in Suffolk, ended up 'mortified and disappointed . . . ashamed of themselves and angry at their own weakness and credulity'.[32] In July 1825, several years after Jane Austen wrote *Sanditon*, local officials in Suffolk were still willing to swim one Isaac Stebbings for wizardry, but by 1856, when a man who farmed 40 acres at Hockham, Norfolk, asked a magistrate to swim an old woman for witchcraft, he was laughed out of court. The last gasp of witch swimming in Britain came in 1864, when a crowd at Sible Hedingham, Essex, forcibly swam a deaf and perhaps mentally disabled eighty-year-old fortune teller called 'Dummy', who died as a result. The perpetrators were convicted and served six months hard labour. John Kendrick Bangs's short story 'The Water Ghost of Harrowby Hall', published in 1894, encapsulates the new modernist attitude: a man haunted by a water ghost deals with her by freezing her into ice and storing the ice statue in a refrigerated warehouse.[33]

Ducking remained common in Britain throughout the 1700s, but died out after that. In Yorkshire, there is no evidence of ducking after 1745, but women newly arrived at Bridewell Prison in London were still routinely ducked at least until 1779. Ducking was used at Plymouth in 1808 and at Leominster in 1809. Local officials in Leominster tried to use their ducking-stool on Sarah Leeke as late as 1817, but the water in the pond was too low.[34] After that, nobody in Britain tried half-drowning as a public punishment anymore.

Elsewhere in Europe, where trial by water had started earlier, it also ended earlier. Here trial by water peaked in the 1600s and early 1700s, even as Daniel Schwenter was promoting his flotation devices and the second wave of swimming manuals was being published. The last trials by water were in the late eighteenth century. Trial by water ended earliest in the Netherlands, where Marry Hoernemans was acquitted in 1675, and no more attempts were made.[35] A prominent German legal scholar spoke out against trial by water in 1709, and the practice gradually ceased in Germany in the 1700s, though as in Britain it continued longer in the form of unofficial lynchings.[36] The last official trial for witchcraft in Germany was probably in Swabia, in southwestern Germany, in 1775, falling halfway between the publication of GutsMuths's *Exercise for Young*

People and his *Short Course in Teaching Yourself the Art of Swimming*.[37] As lifesaving clubs formed in Amsterdam about 1767, and in Copenhagen in 1772, the last judicially approved executions for witchcraft in Poland took place in 1776, and the end of trial by water there must have come about the same time.[38]

In Ukraine and the Caucasus, people kept swimming women for witchcraft, but there, too, the practice died out in the late nineteenth century. Ukrainian peasants swam women for witchcraft regularly in the 1700s and well into the 1800s, as Marijke Gijswijt-Hofstra tells us, 'usually . . . in order to establish which of [the female villagers] . . . was responsible for a continuing drought'. These large collective swimmings were still happening as late as 1885 in parts of Ukraine, and further east in Georgia. Sometimes villagers subjected the accused women to the regular floating trial, with their toes tied to their wrists; in other cases they used a simpler model where the women had to carry a pail of water for a certain distance without spilling any of the contents. The close association between witches and water is reflected in the practice of smallholders in some parts of Ukraine in the late 1800s, who to end a drought would dig up the bodies of suspected witches or sorcerers and pour barrels of water into their graves.[39]

As in Western Europe, the Russian government was never very enthusiastic about the practice of swimming accused witches, and eventually put an end to it. By 1811 women who were subjected to this practice wrote letters of complaint to the regional governor: a Ukrainian letter-writer in 1839, for example, complains, 'The drowning of witches during times of drought is not a thing of the past but is, with all its horrible consequences, amazingly enough, still practised in the neighbouring province.' In 1872 both the local priest and the local authorities rejected the tradition of trial by water:

> all of the women from the village of Dzhurkovo . . . were herded together and then taken to the river. Over the objections of the parish priest, they were stripped, bound in the traditional manner, and thrown into the water. One of the victims of the Dzhurkovo swimming suffered permanent loss of hearing while several others fell seriously ill as a result of the ordeal. This prompted the local authorities to launch an investigation. Ultimately the initiators

of the swimming were brought to trial, were convicted, and were punished with imprisonment.[40]

This parallels the American and British position of about a century earlier. Apparently criminal prosecution put a damper on people's enthusiasm for throwing women in the water, because the last known multiple witch swimming in Ukraine was in 1885. After that, as happened slightly earlier in Britain, people forgot the traditional procedures: when farmers suspected Aleksandra Loposhchenkova of being a witch during a drought in 1893, they seized her and dunked her into a pond three times, and then threw her into a hole and poured water over her.[41]

Throughout Europe and the European colonies, the normalization of swimming in the late eighteenth and early nineteenth centuries meant the marginalization of trial by water and ducking. Rather than seeing the water as the realm of demons, Europeans and European settlers throughout the world had now reshaped swimming into a way for colonialists and slave-holders to align themselves with the Roman Empire's assumed scientific rationality and legal acuity. Swimming helped Europeans appropriate Roman prestige to support their imperial ambitions.

Swimming and revolution

By the early twentieth century Asian political leaders built on this European idea of rational swimming to promote swimming as a symbol of progressive, modernist, democratic revolution. Swimming was free, rebellious, independent, and above all it was not Central Asian. As the old Turkic and Manchu powers collapsed, the revolutionaries displacing them used swimming as a way to publicly embody their political leanings. In 1910 Mao Zedong learned to swim as a teenager rebelling against his father, who discouraged exercise as part of a Confucian belief in physical reserve. In Russia the first leader of the Communist Revolution of 1917, Vladimir Lenin, was also an avid (and nudist) swimmer throughout his life. In the 1920s, as the Ottoman Empire collapsed, Kemal Atatürk similarly turned swimming into a symbol of his political intentions. Swimming in public let Atatürk demonstrate that he was modern, not like the ancient Ottoman sultans (though at the same time upper-class and powerful, like the sultans). For the public, Atatürk built a huge swimming complex at

96 Chairman Mao Zedong swimming the Yangtze River in China, 2 September 1967.

Adana, with two outdoor Olympic-size swimming pools, a diving tower and a smaller indoor pool, paralleling Roman imperial baths.[42] In May 1956, when he was 62 years old, Mao swam across the Yangtze River, a distance of about 1.5 kilometres: ten years later Mao showed he was still strong by swimming the same distance again (illus. 96). Both times, as befitted a scientific swimmer, he used the breaststroke.[43] More recently, the Russian president Vladimir Putin has been photographed swimming on several occasions, including doing the butterfly stroke in a cold Siberian lake.

Most Asian politicians never actually learned to swim, but swimming nevertheless became an important political metaphor. Early nationalists in China conceptualized the coming revolution as a tidal wave, a metaphor that became popular and is still frequently seen in China today. As early as 1903 a revolutionary anti-Qing newspaper called itself the *Tide of Zhejiang*, romanticizing 'the unstoppable tide of revolutionary change that was sweeping over China'. A second journal with the same name started publication in 1913. In 1912 Sun Yat-sen prophesied that 'world progress is like a tidal wave. Those who ride it will prosper, and those who fight against it will perish.'[44] In Russia, Leon Trotsky never learned to swim, but in 1939 he too used the tide as a metaphor for the Russian

Revolution: 'He who swims against the current is not connected with the masses.'[45] Again in the 1950s, Mao advised elites to

> join together with the masses. There are some comrades who
> fear the masses as they fear the water . . . To draw an analogy,
> the people are like the water and the leaders at all levels are like
> the swimmers. You mustn't leave the water. You must go with the
> water, you mustn't go against the water.

Earlier Daoist analogies advised people to be like water, flowing around obstacles, but in Mao's new China, people were imagined swimming in the water.[46]

Mao's Communist government strongly encouraged swimming: officials issued a directive calling for widespread 'efforts to enable service-men and civilians, and particularly the youth and children, throughout China to learn to swim'. The People's Liberation Army added swimming as the sixth 'big technique' that soldiers needed to learn. In 1934 a Chinese physical education expert suggested making swimming the Chinese national sport, reasoning that most sports were 'foreign goods', but swim-ming was native to ancient China. Wu doesn't say so, but he must have been hinting that swimming was therefore an act of rejection of Manchu power in China. In the 1940s the Chinese Career Women's Club responded by organizing swimming activities for women.[47] The revolution's ban on footbinding, which had prevented about half of Chinese women from swimming for almost a thousand years, also made it possible for women to swim again. Even today, Chinese writers and businesses still invoke the metaphor of tide play to mean something revolutionary, edgy or avant-garde.[48]

China had not actually ever been comfortable with swimming, how-ever, and as in Europe, most Chinese people never became swimmers. We get a sense of their hesitancy from Mao's essay urging Chinese people to learn to swim. People thought swimming was too hard. Mao urges them to 'just work at it an hour every day, without fail, go today, tomor-row, for a hundred days'. They were inclined, like Europeans, to employ teachers and use a 'rubber life preserver'. They thought swimming was too dangerous, and were reluctant to swim out of their depth. In Russia, even the government soon abandoned swimming with the excuse that the sport was too individualistic and too Western. Joseph Stalin rejected swimming on the grounds that 'mountain people don't swim': he supported Russian folk games and team sports instead. When Stalin died in 1953, not one Moscow school had a swimming pool.[49] In Turkey, a culture of seaside holidays took hold, and today many Turkish families spend their summers at the beach. But the water off Turkish beaches along the Mediterranean and the Black Sea is tricky to swim in, with serious currents and undertows, and there are few public swimming pools. Until 1992 Turkey did not send any swimmers to the Olympic Games, and even then, all three Turkish swimmers had trained in the United States. Although swimming came to symbolize freedom, democracy and modernity throughout Asia, most people remained deeply reluctant to swim.

JUST AS THE great expansion of the Turks and the Mongols put an end to swimming in both Europe and China in the later Middle Ages, the slow disintegration of Central Asian power during the 1700s and 1800s saw people relearning how to swim all across Europe and Asia. As the Ottomans, the Safavids, the Mughals and the Manchu collapsed, Europe gained power. Swimming was one way to express that shift. In the 1700s European and European American swimmers were mainly avant-garde poets and elites, but by the mid-1800s the middle class began to take up swimming. By 1900 even working-class Europeans and European Americans went swimming as a way of demonstrating that they were 'in the swim'. They took beach holidays and visited public swimming pools. They followed competitive swimming in the newspapers and cheered on athletes who tried to swim the English Channel. Soon this new enthusiasm for swimming reached as far as Communist China. And yet most people from the old non-swimming cultures still were not swimming much. They paddled in the shallow end with their heads well clear of the water, or stood in the deep end. They lay on the beach in attractive swimsuits. They paid for their children to have swimming lessons. But neither Eurasians nor their colonial descendants ever approached the level of swimming that had been nearly universal in the Americas and Africa before the colonizers arrived.

21

SWIMMING IS
SO LAST CENTURY

T he swimming fad of the nineteenth century did not, in the end, overcome the northern Eurasian non-swimmers' ancient fear of the water. Not only did northern Eurasians soon lose interest in swimming, but they used their old rationalizations as excuses to force everybody else out of the water too. The old sense that water was sacred combined with the idea that swimming was indecent, and became an excuse to ban nude swimming and segregate beaches. The old fear that swimming was dangerous encouraged colonizers to post 'No Swimming' signs everywhere. Northern Eurasians taught swimming primarily as a way to prevent drowning. Soon the Greek and Roman claim that swimming represented civilization – casting the non-swimming Persians as barbarians and slaves – was extended to bar all people of colour from the pool. Like Plato and Caesar, most people today see swimming as an aristocratic skill primarily intended for a wealthy ruling class.

First the enslaved and colonized

Swimmers at the bottom of social hierarchies were the first to be pushed out of the water, beginning with African women brought to the Americas as slaves. African women were just as good swimmers as the men, but their enslavers' gender prejudices often prevented these women from swimming.[1] By the early nineteenth century enslaved African American men were also kept from learning to swim, because White slaveholders feared they would escape. Indeed, some African Americans did escape by swimming, as we know from the escape narratives of Caribbean and

Brazilian maroons and the accounts of Solomon Northrup and Jacob Green, who both escaped from Southern slavery to the North.[2] In Mark Twain's fictional *Huckleberry Finn*, similarly, the enslaved Jim swims to freedom. Swimming and water symbolized freedom and came to be a marker of African American identity as well.[3] But Northrup reports that enslaved African Americans were 'not allowed to learn the art of swimming' and were 'incapable of crossing the most inconsiderable stream'. Annie Davis was beaten for swimming while she was enslaved. Enslaved African Americans may also have lacked leisure to learn to swim well. Though he had fond memories of splashing in a swimming hole from his enslaved childhood, the abolitionist Frederick Douglass, for example, did not know how to swim. Other African Americans also reported that they themselves could not swim, even as they supposed that most enslaved people could.[4] In addition, African Americans were increasingly influenced by the culture surrounding them. From European-descended slave-holders they learned to fear the water and be ashamed of their naked bodies. By the time Emancipation arrived in 1865, though African Americans retained a sense of themselves as swimmers, many of them already could not swim.

Soon not only the enslaved but all marginalized people were excluded from swimming, as colonizers all over the world took over the good beaches for themselves and relegated local swimmers to inferior swimming holes. Segregated beaches were introduced about 1888, when White South Africans barred first Black Africans and then South Asian immigrants like the nineteen-year-old Mohandas Gandhi. From South Africa, segregation spread to neighbouring Southern Rhodesia (now Zimbabwe), and by 1894 to Singapore. Racial segregation of beaches reached North Africa in 1901, and Mozambique about 1920, even though legally everyone in Mozambique was equally a Portuguese citizen.[5] White Americans pushed Black citizens out of public pools starting in 1913, and by the 1920s, as refugees from the Russian Revolution poured into Western Europe, first Roma and then Jewish swimmers were barred from European public baths, pools, beaches and spas.[6] Japanese rule did nothing to restore local access to beaches or pools in Singapore, and only 8 per cent of Singaporeans swim regularly today.[7] Traditional swimming contests fell by the wayside as drowning rates soared in Vietnam and Bangladesh. The eighteenth-century Vietnamese folk hero Quận He is remembered as an excellent swimmer, and a village saying from the mid-1800s still refers to swimming contests.[8] Today, however, most adults in Vietnam, Cambodia and Bangladesh do not know how to swim.[9]

In India, many people wanted to believe they could swim. Thus in a Rohinton Mistry short story the Indian narrator claims that 'most Indians swim like fish. I'm an exception to the rule,' even faced with a Canadian who has noticed that many Indians do not know how to swim.[10] But as Mistry was surely aware, many Indians were already non-swimmers even before colonization, and today even fewer know how to swim. (It's a colonialist joke in Rudyard Kipling's 1901 novel *Kim* that the lama is seeking a holy river, but then when he finds it he almost drowns in it; he doesn't know how to swim.) Similarly, most North Africans had already lost their ability to swim under Islamic rule in the Middle Ages, and did not regain it under British and French colonization in the nineteenth century. All along the coast of North Africa, most people did not swim beyond their depth. European colonists were surprised to see an Algerian woman swimming.[11] And in South Africa, where Indigenous people had been good swimmers, today only about one in twenty people can swim, most of them White.[12] Throughout colonized countries, most Indigenous people no longer know how to swim.

Some more rural and isolated people managed to keep control of nearby riverbanks and ponds into the early twentieth century. For a while, rural Vietnamese peasants might still 'take their sons out to the river to teach them to swim and dive'. Native Americans were swimming in the 1830s, when George Catlin painted the Mandan along the Missouri River, and Sauk families in Wisconsin swam away from United States Army attacks on them.[13] They were still swimming in the 1880s, when the Hidatsa tribe member Lean Wolf drew himself drowning a bison in the Missouri River with his bare hands. Cheyenne children in Wyoming swam in the river and did somersault dives in 1904 (illus. 97). And in 1918 a Native American soldier fighting in the First World War swam a river without difficulty, even carrying a heavy cable. Similarly in Australia, Aboriginal people were 'efficient swimmers' in the late 1800s. In 1911 an Aboriginal Australian boy, Mallyalega, swam well enough even in handcuffs to save a White policeman from drowning.[14] Where they had the opportunity, Indigenous people were still enthusiastic and skilled swimmers at the beginning of the twentieth century.

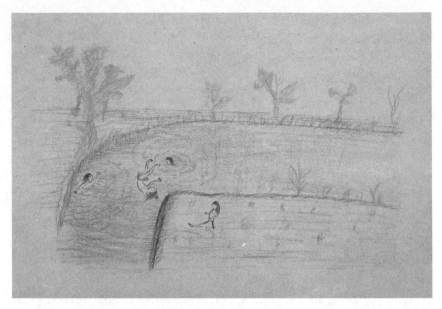

97 Children of the Cheyenne Nation swimming in a river, *c.* 1904–6, ledger drawing
by Cheyenne artist Nakoimens, also called Charles Murphy.

But Indigenous swimmers worldwide were rapidly losing access to
the water. By 1914 White Australians were surprised to see even a Hawaiian
swimming well.[15] Native Americans and South Americans had lost control of most of their swimming spots. Today less than one-third of Native
American, Asian American and African American children in the United
States think they could swim the length of a standard swimming pool.
Fourteen per cent of African American children cannot swim at all.[16]
Fewer than half of Latinx children can swim a length. Drowning rates
have skyrocketed correspondingly: people of colour, especially African
Americans and Native Americans, have much higher drowning rates
than White people in the United States, especially if they are living in
poverty. Most people in South America today cannot swim very far.[17]
Though Malian people from West Africa were good swimmers in the
1700s, when a boat overturned on the Niger River in 2013 most of the
people aboard drowned because they did not know how to swim. When
South African military consultants were recently training special Ugandan
army forces, they had to teach the Ugandan soldiers to swim.[18]

In the early 1900s White people segregated swimming pools and
beaches, and refused to allow people of colour to swim in them. Even
Asians who were themselves part of the northern non-swimming

community lost access to the water. Despite efforts to find substitute swimming holes, most people of colour, especially if they were poor, lost the ability to swim.

Then the colonizers themselves

But only a few decades later most Eurasians also lost interest in swimming. In China, Mao Zedong's example did not even extend to other early revolutionary leaders.[19] Few Central Asians can swim, though the Mandan were enthusiastic and skilled swimmers in the equally landlocked and chilly Dakotas. (The Lonely Planet's website page titled 'Swimming in Mongolia' is entirely and amusingly blank.[20]) Official Russian policy has been to promote swimming: around 1960 the Russian leader Nikita Krushchev announced an effort 'to teach all children to swim in the next 3–5 years', and the USSR did build some public pools in the late 1960s and early '70s. Under Leonid Brezhnev an amateur police force for teenagers, called the Cheka, required swimming, as the Cossacks had long ago. But there were never enough pools, and they were always 'reserved for the sporting or political elite'. Some Russians did get to swim on holiday on the beaches of the Black Sea, or at family dachas alongside rivers or ponds, but 'few learned the breaststroke or crawl' and probably they swam mainly performatively, rather than regularly.[21] Today, posting a scenic image of yourself swimming on social media is an easy way to collect 'likes'; liking other people's swimming posts is an even easier way to show your followers who you think you are.[22]

Europeans today associate swimming with school, safety and exercise, rather than with fun. Most European schools require swimming lessons, but in Germany fewer than half the children can swim by the time they are ten years old, although in 'the past, almost all of the children could swim when they got to school', and 'the number of drowned children is increasing dramatically.' In the United Kingdom, things are a little better, but still only about 60 per cent of children can swim the length of a pool.[23] In southern Europe, despite the heat and the beautiful beaches, almost no one will swim beyond their depth. In the United States, only a little more than half of White children (58 per cent) think they could swim a length of a standard pool. Where many colleges and universities once had swimming requirements, today only a few still insist that students learn to swim, and the number grows smaller every year.[24] After investing a lot of effort installing private pools in back gardens all across the country, Americans are losing interest in them. Backyard swimming pools have come to seem both too dangerous and too boring. Wealthy Brazilians spend a lot of time on the beach, but they swim even less than Americans, 'even on a sunny day when the water is calm and the waves weak'.[25] Britain today is the same way: 'for more moderate swimmers, a brief autumnal dip in the sea offers an opportunity for a social gathering, with a slice of cake or a nip of whiskey afterward.' The artist Banksy's 2015 project *Dismaland*, 'a gloomy anti-Disneyland', was a sad commentary on 'the distinctive melancholy of Britain's run-down seaside resorts'.[26]

Nobody really knows accurately how many people can't swim, or how many people drown globally; the World Health Organization warns that there is 'a wide range of uncertainty around the estimate of global drowning deaths'. But even without good statistics we can see a precipitous decline in swimming ability around the world. Health organizations report that China and Russia have very high drowning rates, and say the same thing about Bangladesh and Cambodia.[27] The WHO estimates that more than half of all drowning deaths occur in the western Pacific and Southeast Asia, while drowning rates are highest in Africa.[28] Today, only a few Eurasians still swim, while most of the swimmers from other parts of the world have forgotten how.

The usual explanations

Historians have generally been content to see racism as the main reason that people of colour stopped swimming. But then to explain why Europeans and European-descended people also do not swim well, they suggest practical factors. Maybe bridges and boats mean that they don't need to swim for practical reasons like crossing rivers anymore? Maybe it's increased urbanization, or the high cost of building and maintaining swimming pools? Certainly many swimming pools have been closing, and yes, bridges help us cross rivers.[29] But these are unlikely to have been the motivating factors. People have always swum at least as much for social as for practical reasons. In Old Kingdom Egypt, the king's children had swimming lessons. Two thousand years later, an enslaved Egyptian girl swam in the Nile with her friends, and boys raced each other in the bay of Hippo. Women played in the water in medieval India, and Cambodian families shared a pool. Boys and girls played together in the surf in eighteenth-century Ghana. They surfed in Hawaii and dived into the Missouri river in the Dakotas. When Europeans learned to swim again in the 1800s, they too formed swimming clubs and socialized in the surf. Swimming has never been primarily a practical skill, and the decreasing need to swim across rivers is not the reason that people swim less today.

Nor is the decline in swimming due to urbanization. Egyptian, East African and Indonesian cities did not prevent swimming. Increased urbanization in the Roman Empire coincides with an increased interest in swimming, not with the end of it. Conversely in the High Middle Ages, the last time Europeans gave up swimming, nearly everybody lived in a rural area. Even towns were small enough that a short walk would have taken you to a swimming hole; Paris and Genoa had only about 100,000 people each, Marseilles about 25,000.[30] And yet people stopped swimming anyway.

The late nineteenth century, when urbanization took off, also saw the high point of the next Eurasian craze for swimming. Enthusiastic swimmers were not deterred by city living: they built thousands of swimming pools, one for each neighbourhood, or even one for each backyard. In just the one medium-sized town of Birmingham, for example, thirteen new public pools were built between 1852 and 1937.[31] Not satisfied with these pools, the newly urbanized working classes throughout Europe also organized cheap weekend excursions to the beach by bus or train. They insisted on longer, week-long or month-long, holidays so they could go to the beach in the summer. They sent mothers and children to the lakeside so they could swim while men worked in the city. Or they sent the children to lakeside summer camps, while both the men and the women worked in the city. All of these options are still open now, but we no longer care to use them.

And it is hard to blame the demise of a pastime so inexpensive that Neanderthals could indulge in it on the outrageous expense. This is surely the most prosperous situation the world has been in since the Stone Age. There is fast-growing interest in cycling and cross-country skiing, and yet we cannot afford to indulge in a sport that requires no equipment?[32] Other explanations, such as the First World War and the 1918 flu epidemic, are no better. Post-war austerity in Britain did not affect the United States, and yet there, too, public swimming-pool construction ground to a halt. In Birmingham, where so many pools were built in the early 1900s, no new pools have opened since the Second World War. Several old pools there have closed and have not been replaced.[33] It is true that other sports requiring expensive equipment and accompanied by strict rules, like roller-skating and ice-skating rinks, have also come to seem old-fashioned. The artificiality of swimming pools, which seemed advanced and civilized a hundred years ago, now seems preposterously disconnected from nature; the chlorine seems poisonous. The many small rules of swimming pools, which seemed appropriate in the more rule-bound society of the 1940s and '50s, now seem chafing and absurd. But there has not been a concomitant move to swimming in open water, on beaches, in lakes and streams, which cost little to maintain and could be available to everyone with fewer rules.[34] Issues of cost and convenience apply to nearly any activity, but they beg the question of why swimming has seemed to be an appropriate place to make budget cuts.

Ancient rationalizations

Better explanations of the decline of swimming reflect the old excuses Eurasian non-swimmers have been making since the Bronze Age. First, northern Eurasian non-swimmers have always felt that water is sacred, and entering it, or putting anything in it, makes it unclean. Second, they have always associated water with indecency, and been reluctant to show their bodies. Third, northern non-swimmers think of water as dangerous. And fourth, they think of the ability to swim as a racial distinction demonstrating cultural or even biological differences that divide two groups. These same rationalizations were revived in the late nineteenth and early twentieth centuries to push not only Eurasians themselves but many Indigenous swimmers out of the water.

Water is sacred

As far back as Hesiod and the Zoroastrian hymns, northern non-swimmers had a religious sense of the sacredness of water. In modern times, swimmers can still seem 'somehow more than human', as if only gods could swim.[35] That sense underlies a variety of visceral, even violent, reactions to people getting into the water. Like Hesiod and the Zoroastrians, many Eurasians are deeply disgusted by the idea of people urinating in the water. Many people do not even like to swim in the ocean for fear of coming into contact with other people's urine.[36] The new understanding of bacteria and viruses, combined with the cholera epidemic that terrorized the nineteenth century, medicalized this fear of the water and made it seem reasonable and even scientific. Early soap advertisers seized on this fear to sell soap by associating it with cleanliness, whiteness and race (illus. 98). Similarly, Eurasians do not like to put their faces in the water. Northern non-swimmers prefer the breaststroke, which, though much slower than the front crawl, lets you hold your head up out of the water. The breaststroke also reduces splashing; it is calmer and seems more respectful of the water. Even radical 'wild swimmers' in Britain, who prefer ponds to swimming pools, repeatedly mention the desirability of swimming 'without kicking or thrashing around', being 'considerate of your effect on others', and the 'meditative' aspect of swimming. They prefer to enter the water 'gradually while keeping your head above the surface'. British swimmers bemoan the 'recklessly vigorous breaststroke' and prefer 'slipping' into the water.[37] This aversion to disturbing the water is surely derived from Bronze Age religious strictures.

If urine and germs could make the water unclean, Eurasian non-swimmers also worried that any peculiarities in human bodies might corrupt the water.[38] People were forced out of the water on the grounds that they smelled bad (medieval Muslims and modern Turks), or were dirty (European missionaries), carried disease (Americans), were unhygenic (Aboriginal Australians) or polluted the water (Italian Jews).[39] In Eastern Europe and Russia, pools demanded doctors' certificates of good health.[40] Swimmers reimagined Blackness as dirt that might come off in the water. Even in 2009 White women in Philadelphia pulled their children out of the water rather than let them swim with Black children.[41] The Iron Age sense that Persians and Scythian 'barbarians' did not belong in the water was extended in the twentieth century to include anyone perceived as racially different.

Alongside the issue of race, Eurasian non-swimmers' concerns grew to include physical and mental disabilities. They mocked people at the pool for having cerebral palsy or polio or amputations; people said

WHETHER you bathe in stream or in tub, in cold water or in warm, morning or evening, the way to benefit most from the bath is to use Ivory Soap.

The water is carried into the pores by the mild, copious, bubbling Ivory lather instead of merely touching the surface. The excretions of the skin combine with the lather instead of remaining in the pores. The skin is cleansed thoroughly so that it enjoys to the fullest degree whatever exhilarating or soothing properties the water may have.

And the delightful effects are not lessened by any irritation from the soap because Ivory is as pure and gentle as the water itself.

IVORY SOAP .. .. 99$\frac{44}{100}$% PURE

IT FLOATS

98 Swimming, cleanliness and Whiteness: Ivory Soap advertisement by Procter & Gamble in *National Geographic*, August 1915.

swimming amputees were 'scaring the children'. In the 1960s many experts believed that people with intellectual disabilities could not swim; people said they had 'misshapen bodies' and would sink to the bottom. People looked askance at swimmers who were even slightly overweight, or old. Travel posters showed swimmers as tall, blond, White, thin, young and healthy, while cartoons mocked overweight, middle-aged swimmers (see illus. 79 and 89). Magazine articles asked whether your body was ready for the beach.[42] Moral disqualifications were added to physical and mental ones: Indians, Hawaiians and African Americans were said to be too lazy to go swimming; learning to swim would only discourage them from working.[43] Pools even barred swimmers for having the wrong lotion, the wrong haircut or the wrong type of swimsuit.

But Eurasian fears of polluting the water sat awkwardly next to an equally ancient belief in the healing powers of bathing shared by both swimmers and non-swimmers. From the Iron Age onwards, healers all over the world prescribed bathing (in hot or cold water) for a wide variety of illnesses: arthritis, asthma, psoriasis, psychosis, tuberculosis, paralysis. Throughout the twentieth century, people's faith in water cures continued unabated. These two ideas merged in the disability rights movement, which fought for equal access to swimming pools and beaches. The Deaflympics (starting in 1924), the Paralympics (1948) and the Special Olympics (1968) all held swimming races. In the 1990s the Americans with Disabilities Act forced swimming pools to install chair lifts or sloped entries to help wheelchair users get into the pool, and some European pools have also added accessibility options. Obese people also challenged their exclusion with 'big-only' swimming clubs.

Public pools now often have hours set aside for rehabilitation and physical therapy sessions, and for 'fat-only swim nights', but many swimming pools are still inaccessible to people with disabilities, or keep their special nights and therapy hours separate from the regular swimming sessions. A typical public pool schedule today reserves about half the hours for swimming (including lessons and team practices) and the other half for water aerobics and similar activities.[44] Modern swimming enthusiasts tell us that people swim first 'for survival' and then for 'healing, and health'. British 'wild swimmers' swim to 'boost the immune system' and strengthen their moral character, regarding hot showers after a cold plunge as 'a decadence'. Similarly, American winter surfers describe the water as 'brutal', demanding 'mental fortitude'.[45] Many people seem to have no idea that swimming is fun.

Water and sexuality

Another way to shame swimmers out of the water was to invoke the ancient association between water and sexuality, making it seem indecent to take off your clothes to go swimming. Following the example of earlier travellers, European slave traders and travellers in Africa and the Americas claimed to be shocked by Indigenous swimmers' nudity.[46] Swimming also impeded male control of Indigenous women's bodies, as women used swimming to escape European men's sexual assaults.[47] As Christian missionaries banned swimming and surfing in Hawaii, Hawaiians came to believe that swimming was an inherently un-Christian activity, and soon many Hawaiians no longer knew how to swim. The Spanish colonial government similarly forced Indigenous swimmers out of the Amazon and its tributaries on the grounds of immodesty.[48] Then, although Japanese artists had similarly eroticized the Ama, or Ainu pearl divers, starting in the 1700s, they found this idea turned against them in the late 1800s, when Europeans used charges of immodesty against the Japanese in order to position them as uncivilized.[49] Europeans claimed to be shaming Indigenous swimmers only for their nudity, but they did not offer any practical alternative to naked swimming. They intended Indigenous swimmers to leave the water, not to put up screens or start wearing swimsuits.

On the other hand, Europeans also knew that the ancient Greeks and Romans swam in the nude, and wanted to emulate them. Even as they were complaining about Indigenous swimmers' immodesty, White travellers were themselves swimming naked in the Amazon, and all around the globe, 'in free, white, nakedness, like happy mermaids'.[50] In Islamic countries where nineteenth-century women swam in old dresses, or even in a dress covered by a long veil, European colonists' nudity or near-nudity consciously emulated Greek and Roman nudity.[51] Just as ancient Greeks had mocked Scythians' and Persians' long stockings and sleeves, metaphorically contrasting Persian slavery with Greek freedom and nudity, now European colonists mocked Islamic modesty as the mark of the slave. When violent attacks on swimsuited foreigners, and widespread harassment of bikini-wearing women, did not succeed in stopping European beach holidays, many North Africans and Indonesians stopped swimming.[52] In the same way, while ethnically Japanese people experienced communal nude bathing as community-building, Japanese Koreans have had different experiences. For them, as for African Americans, the sea represents the home they cannot go back to, and communal bathing often excludes them.[53] Shikitei Sanba's popular early nineteenth-century novel *Ukiyoburo*, set in a bathhouse, reinforced the centrality of bathing to Japanese identity. Over time, however, American expressions of shock at Japanese mixed communal bathing led to its decline.[54] Colonialists wielded attitudes towards nudity to force both clothed and unclothed swimmers out of the water.

This same sexualization of swimming led northern non-swimming cultures to segregate swimming pools by gender. Early swimming pools in the United States and Britain separated men and women. (Despite widespread references to the idea that nineteenth-century European and American women swam less than men, there is little to suggest that was the case.[55]) Though most European, Asian and American pools now allow mixed bathing, in modern Afghanistan and Iran women still swim mainly on women-only beaches or in special, very limited and expensive women's hours in swimming pools. As a result, women in these places are less likely to learn to swim, or to be able to enjoy swimming once they have learned.[56] And even in today's Europe, many British 'wild swimmers' prefer the 'Ladies' Pond'.[57] Sexualized mermaids from Disney's Little Mermaid to the Starbucks logo feed this association between swimming, sex and gender, and their images are exported around the world.[58] Immodesty is the age-old excuse, going back to the Bronze Age, but it is swimming that Eurasians fear.

The sexualization of swimming met up with the idealization of Greek culture to produce a nineteenth-century association between homosexuality and swimming, which may also have discouraged some twentieth-century swimmers. Byron swam with his male lovers, and Pushkin's admiration for Byron led him to swim enthusiastically.[59] In America, Thomas Eakins painted naked men diving from stone ruins to evoke the connection of both swimming and nudity to classical antiquity.[60] Gay men in London met each other at swimming pools, or just watched each other swim.[61] But in modern Australia, homophobic surfers scorn swimmers as queer, and in America straight men may fear exposing their bodies in swimsuits.[62] This homophobia has discouraged many men from swimming.

In places where Europeans and European-descended people embraced sexualized swimming, and came to think of pools as a dating scene, they then rejected the idea that White women might share the water, or the beach, with men whose skin was darker. The popularity of mixed-gender bathing led to the segregation of beaches according to late nineteenth-century ideas about race in South Africa.[63] In North Africa, segregation by race was supplanting segregation by gender by 1901.[64] The opening of the first mixed-gender pool in St Louis in 1913 precipitated racial segregation in the United States.[65] Around the world, beach segregation and segregated swimming clubs were justified as absolutely necessary 'in the interest of public decency and morality'.[66] Sadly, White feminists, pushing for access to pools for themselves, were eager to push both Black men and Black women out of the water, with racist references to 'dark-faced mobs'. Even today, White Australians still use the association of sex and swimming to force immigrants off their beaches. In December 2005 about 5,000 White Australians attacked people of 'Middle Eastern appearance' on a beach near Sydney, on the grounds that the immigrants were 'affronting "our women"'.[67] These ancient associations between swimming, sexuality and race still prevent many people from swimming.

Water and danger

Swimming also continued to seem dangerous, as it had since the Bronze Age. The ancient sense that water and swimming were inherently dangerous allowed many administrators from non-swimming cultures to deal with the real dangers of drowning and pollution by ruling ponds and rivers off-limits, rather than by cleaning them up. British swimmers, for example, complain about the 'privatization of once public waters'. As racist legislation forced Indigenous swimmers off the good beaches and out of public swimming pools, they found that previously available rivers had been blocked by hydroelectric dams, flood controls or pollution. In Buenos Aires, the banks of the Río de la Plata, where people had used to swim and sunbathe on the beaches, were formalized into reinforced concrete quays, off-limits to swimmers. The banks of the Columbia and

Willamette Rivers around Portland, Oregon, were similarly consolidated starting in the 1860s. 'When I was young, we often swam in the Tamsui,' recalled an elderly Taipei resident thirty years ago. 'It was very clean, especially during high tide, and when you dove into the water you could see brilliantly colored fish.' But today swimming is 'totally out of the question' due to pollution. The same is true for many other spots favoured by Indigenous swimmers.[68]

Swimmers turned to less desirable swimming holes like abandoned quarries, local creeks and ponds, or less-used beaches.[69] Some of these were dangerous because of hidden hazards, stinging jellyfish or under-tows; others were again badly polluted. Phyllis Arnold recalls how in early twentieth-century Birmingham, England, 'many of the local youths used to go swimming in the canals on a Sunday. She frequently heard the screams of mothers who had just been informed that [their sons] had just been drowned.' In 1980 the United Kingdom had no inland waters that were acceptable to swim in by the standards of the European Union, though some have been cleaned up since then. All over the world, non-tourist beaches are often covered with sewage and factory effluents, or used as informal garbage dumps.[70] As Mistry's Indian narrator explains,

> My house was five minutes walking distance from Chaupatty beach in Bombay. It's one of the most beautiful beaches in Bombay, or was, before the filth took over ... The devil was money, always scarce, and kept the private swimming clubs out of reach; the deep blue sea of Chaupatty beach was gray and murky with garbage, too filthy to swim in. Every so often we would muster our courage and Mummy would take me there to try and teach me. But a few minutes of paddling was all we could endure. Sooner or later something would float up against our legs or thighs or waists, depending on how deep we'd gone in, and we'd be revulsed and stride out to the sand.[71]

Authorities from non-swimming cultures often banned swimming at these places. 'No Swimming' signs like the one Norman Rockwell famously painted in 1921 proliferated.[72] These swimming holes were dangerous: 'nearly every summer' several African American children drowned at Horse Hole in Charleston, South Carolina. This danger was mocked by racist cartoons like the appalling 'alligator bait' theme, which showed young African American children being attacked by alligators while swimming in creeks or ponds. 'Alligator bait' china figurines, pencil holders, T-shirts and bottle openers have been widely sold since the late 1800s, and are still sold today. The combined danger of children drowning or being arrested for swimming illegally, and of their parents being charged with neglect for letting them swim, forced African American parents to tell their own children not to swim.[73]

People also continued, as they had in antiquity and the Middle Ages, to see dangers where there were none, or where the dangers were far outweighed by the pleasure of swimming. By the late nineteenth century swimmers had ceased to fear mermaids or sea monsters, but now they worried about cramp, sharks and rip tides. Even swimming advocates now refer to 'the paradox of water as a source of life and death'. Swedish swimmers think of swimming as 'a form of life insurance', mainly for safety rather than pleasure. German newspapers warn that it is dangerous to jump into cold water on a hot day, or to swim alone, or to be inattentive, while popular American articles retell the story of a man who had a heart attack from swimming in cold water. Japanese swimmers again warn of the danger of swimming in cold water.[74] Light-skinned people from Japan to Scotland, and their descendants throughout the world, grew reluctant to expose skin at the beach or the pool for fear of tanning, whether they attribute that to a fear of skin cancer or to social pressure to seem as pale as possible. For safety's sake, many modern pools are also too shallow for real swimming, or real fun: Japanese school pools, most swimming pools in China and many urban American public pools are only about a metre deep. Children learn that when you are tired of swimming, all you have to do is stand up. Adults stand in the water and cool off, but they don't swim (see illus. 81).

Teaching children swimming mainly as insurance against drowning made swimming seem like a chore, rather than a fun social game. Swimming texts from the 1930s emphasize how the 'growth of professional courses in the pedagogy of swimming and in methods of teaching swimming has created a demand for scientific teaching material in the field', which would include 'mechanical, physiological, psychological, [and] sociological' sophistication.[75] Policies intended to prevent drowning by making sure everyone learns how to swim scientifically have given people the impression that swimming is something you have to do when you are a child, and give up as soon as you can when you are grown. Well-meaning European authorities encouraged immigrant children from non-swimming Pakistan and India to learn to swim in order to assimilate. When one child who had emigrated from Pakistan to a town near Manchester 'managed to learn to swim a length', his teacher and classmates cheered him on, 'since I hated the cold water and swimming'. Further south in Birmingham, a local primary school in another immigrant neighbourhood took the children swimming at the local public pool every week, where they, too, hated the cold water.[76] Similarly in French colonies in Senegal, and in British ones in Sudan and India, colonial schools taught local children how to swim.[77] These children resented the ordeal and naturally did not swim as adults, when they would in any case not have been welcome on the good beaches.

Even for relatively well-off White children, rules that required swimming children to be closely supervised by parents saved lives but eliminated playing from swimming. Today, Houston pool rules in Texas require all children under ten to have an adult within arm's reach at all times. They also forbid riding your children on your back, doing handstands in the water or 'any kind of horseplay'. Diving boards, especially high boards, have also been removed from most pools. In the name of safety, local governments made swimming supervised, rule-driven and boring. A far higher level of risk is tolerated in other sports, even for children: football, downhill skiing, horseback riding, rock climbing. But popular swimming books remind us that swimming is dangerous even before listing reasons for swimming.[78] Both for Indigenous people and for non-swimming colonialists, swimming grew so hedged about with fear and regulations that it lost any sense of adventure or fun.

Swimming and race

The idea that swimming divided people from each other, that it was a marker of cultural or racial difference, also dates back to the Bronze Age. In the Bronze Age, swimming was something Africans and Southeast Asians did, but not northerners. During the early modern period, colonizers used this same racialization of swimming to justify colonizing and enslaving Indigenous people all over the global South and throughout

North America. Well into the twentieth century, colonizers continued to force Indigenous swimmers into pearl diving, sponge diving, ferrying and other dangerous and underpaid work. The term 'blackbirding', meaning the forced recruitment of Aboriginal Australians for diving work, gives an idea of the nature of the industry.[79] Similarly, Sudanese and Egyptian boatmen worked to pull American travellers' boats up the Nile, and were paid partly by Americans tossing coins into the water for the Africans to dive for. In Indonesia, local children dived in the harbour for coins. Indonesian parents kept lighter-skinned children out of the water, hoping to establish their racial privilege.[80]

But this early modern rejection of swimming as a slave's activity ran smack into the Greek and Roman revival, which taught European aristocrats that swimming was the hallmark of the civilized upper class. Caesar was a good swimmer, they learned. The free Greeks swam, while the Persians did not. Plato associated swimming with reading, after all. While traces of the early modern view still surface from time to time, the nineteenth-century appropriation of swimming as a signifier of power has for the most part emerged victorious. By the late 1860s and '70s, British swimmers claimed that there was 'no instance of any foreigner, civilised or uncivilised, whose achievements in the water surpass those of the British', and that none 'of the black people that I have ever known approach a first-class English swimmer'.[81] Since the year 2000 one swimming writer has insisted that nineteenth-century England was 'the world's leading swimming country', and another has claimed that 'England introduced competitive swimming as a sport.'[82]

Once Europeans and colonialists attached swimming to civilization, literacy, colonialism and power, they felt it was impossible to swim with the people they had colonized and enslaved. They created a tourism industry centred on the Whiteness of beaches and swimming. Posters promoting seaside resorts showed only White people, most of them blond. Seaside resort towns became highly racialized places where White people could 'escape' the complicated multiculturalism of their daily lives in cities.[83] From the Caribbean to Southeast Asia, White holidaymakers demanded resorts that played to their fantasies of life in a White paradise, where all the White people were rich and all the Black people were 'friendly, efficient and unobtrusive' servants who would behave like the enslaved characters in *Gone with the Wind*. If people of colour living near these resorts wanted to swim, they had to hide at out-of-the-way, less pleasant and often more dangerous beaches.[84] Thus Hawaiian surfers lost their beach after the Second World War when developers bought it and built a tourist hotel on it. By the time Hawaii became a state in 1959, Hawaiians had been almost completely pushed out of the water. Even at less attractive beaches like those of Namibia, where the beaches are too cold for comfort and so is the water, German colonists promoted them to White holidaymakers, depicting White people as 'the only legitimate beneficiaries of comfort, enjoying the luxury of leisure time'.[85] Today, White swimmers and dark-skinned service people still predominate at holiday resorts, while descriptions of 'mostly middle-aged or older' British swimmers simply assume their Whiteness.[86]

North Africans tried to break into this privileged group of swimmers. After all, they had given up swimming around the time they converted to Islam, in the early Middle Ages, so they identified with the northern non-swimmers. Nevertheless, European colonists marginalized North Africans (including Egyptians) as dark-skinned and refused to allow them on to their beaches. In 1940s Algeria, French and Algerian beaches were completely separate. On the beach outside Algiers 'everyone knew' where French people sat and where Algerian people sat. King Mohamed v of Morocco tried to secure access to European privilege by raising his daughter and her associates with European skills – including swimming – but to no avail.[87] In Tunisia, European sex tourism forced the government to separate Tunisian swimmers from tourists, giving the revenue-bringing tourists all the best beaches. From Brazil to North Africa and the South Pacific, the only dark-skinned people on the best beaches today are vendors selling soft drinks and sunscreen.[88]

THE MOST STRIKING aspect of this recent process of losing interest in swimming is how traditional it is. The same old themes come up that non-swimmers have been using since the Ice Age to explain their reluctance to get in the water. Once again, swimming is portrayed as dangerous, even if now we cast danger in terms of unattended children, horseplay and diving boards. Once again, swimming is sexualized, though now homophobia and transphobia are bigger issues than they were in the past, and sexism has become more closely connected to racism. Racism, in turn, now emerges more clearly with claims to biological and genetic roots, though it is really just as much a social fiction, a cultural construct, as the earlier sense that swimming was for foreigners. And although we are less open about our fear that swimming angers the gods, we are still trying to keep each other from splashing or peeing in the pool.

22

EVERYONE OUT OF THE WATER

Even as Europeans and European-descended people have become increasingly dubious, reluctant swimmers, they have maintained a close relationship between beach houses, pool memberships and power. In advertisements, television shows and films, swimming still represents success. As a result, the people they have marginalized have fought to get access to these bastions of wealth and privilege. Some have tried to become effectively White enough to be admitted to Whites-only spaces. Others have used legal cases to desegregate pools and beaches. Those who could afford it have established their own pools or beach resorts, and some of those have then in turn begun to discriminate against the less fortunate. Although few people are actually jumping in, access to swimming pools remains a powerful way to establish cultural identity.

Asian swimming

In the nineteenth century Europeans sought to monopolize swimming for themselves. They marginalized East Asians along with Indigenous swimmers. Some East Asians, however, were able to fight their way back into the pool. In Japan, people had been enthusiastic swimmers for five centuries (see illus. 80). After the Mongol and then Manchu conquests of China and Korea, swimming became a way for Japan to proudly assert their independence from Central Asian dominance.[1] In the 1700s they were still swimming, using at least five different named strokes. In 1810 Japan's shogun held a three-day swimming competition involving fifty swimmers. Ota Sutezo wrote a manual formalizing Japanese swimming strokes. By the late nineteenth century swimming was being taught in Japanese schools and, starting in 1903, all Tokyo schoolteachers had to be able to swim.[2] As in Britain, much emphasis was laid on moving gracefully and serenely through the water.[3] In Japan, as much as in Europe, people were swimming scientifically.

But the first modern European visitors to Japan in the late nineteenth century saw only more Indigenous swimmers. They mocked Japanese swimming as 'like a big, brown frog kicking about in the water', and tossed pennies for Japanese swimmers to collect. From California to Canada, Japanese immigrants to North America found themselves barred from swimming pools and beaches: 'no coloreds allowed.'[4] To reposition themselves as civilized rather than colonized, Japanese swimmers imitated upper-class Eurasian swimming. They wore the latest European swimsuits and segregated men's and women's beaches. Japanese women, who had not traditionally been swimmers, began to learn to swim (illus. 99).[5] By the early 1900s Japanese swimming clubs were building public pools like those in Europe and the United States, and, as in Britain, they were emphasizing how they had been swimming 'from ancient times'. Swimming, they said, is 'as natural to the Japanese as walking, because Japan is surrounded by sea'.[6]

At first the idea that Japanese swimmers were exceptionally skilled was convincing. Traditional overhand Japanese swimming strokes like the *Chimba-Nuki* and the *Nukite* were faster than the strokes being used in Europe. This became clear when Japanese swimmers won the first international swimming meet in 1898 in Yokohama and continued to win throughout the early 1900s. Swimming became more popular than ever in Japan as a way of demonstrating that Japanese athletes could beat Europeans.[7] But the Hawaiian Duke Kahanamoku's modern crawl stroke dominated the 1920 Olympic Games, and as a result Japan won no swimming medals that year. During the 1920s, therefore, like competition swimmers around the world, Japanese swimmers adopted the front crawl with side breathing. They successfully used elements of their own strokes to improve the adopted version, and were competitive again in both front crawl and breaststroke in the 1930s, but then they were no longer swimming primarily in their own tradition.[8]

Today, most Japanese schools have (shallow) swimming pools, and most children are taught to swim. In theory, you have to know how to

99 A Japanese woman wears a version of a European-style swimsuit
in a triptych of woodblock prints by Utagawa Kokunimasa, 'Swimming at Ōiso',
from the series *Distant Views of Mount Fuji*, 1893.

swim before you can graduate from high school. And yet the skilled swimming that was once taught in Japan is now almost gone.[9] Japanese parents now give their children swimming lessons because 'it is a skill that can save your life' or because it might help their asthma. Most Japanese swimmers no longer venture out of their depth. The desire for paler skin encourages adults to avoid the sun, and drowning rates are high.[10] While Japanese people are now more accepted in American swimming pools, they no longer swim as well as they did three centuries ago.

Still not swimming

The situation of Korean and Indian swimming illustrates the complicated swimming attitudes of the late nineteenth century. Both Koreans and Indians had been part of the larger Eurasian non-swimming culture for at least 3,000 years. Few Korean or Indian people knew how to swim. Nevertheless when Europeans drew up racialized distinctions, Korean and Indian people found themselves stranded among the colonized, being treated as if they had been Indigenous swimmers. In Japan, where there were many Korean immigrants and workers, Japanese swimmers looked down on Koreans for not knowing how to swim. When Japan opened swimming pools and formalized swimming, these pools often excluded

Korean immigrants.[11] Swimming helped Japanese people to present themselves as civilized, powerful and White, in opposition to their oppressed, non-swimming Chinese and Korean neighbours.[12] Even in the 1980s ethnic Koreans raised in Japan did not swim much.[13]

Similarly in India, where most people had not been swimmers at least since the Yamnaya settlement of India around 1500 BCE, Indians did not now learn how to swim. British colonists excluded Indian people from swimming pools and beaches, and then mocked them as lazy and ignorant for not knowing how to swim: again, the Tibetan lama in Kipling's *Kim* falls into the sacred river he has been seeking and nearly drowns. Today, even Indians themselves often believe that there are biological reasons why they cannot swim well. Very few people in India know how to swim.[14] Thus Korean and Indian people, who were very much part of the Eurasian non-swimming culture, have remained non-swimmers even as Europeans learned to swim. More powerful people kept them out of the pool.

Forced out of the water

In North America, as well, racism kept many people of colour from learning to swim. Beach resorts and swimming pools were rigidly segregated. When well-off African American people organized their own beach resorts, their efforts met with violent resistance from White Americans who saw Black people on beaches as interlopers. Black beach clubs were burned down. Black resorts saw the state of California seize their land by eminent domain. White developers described African Americans as a 'menace to the bay district', and White real estate agents refused to sell beach houses to Black families.[15]

As a justification for this racism, White Americans portrayed their own swimming as both proof of and justified by their moral superiority to people of colour. As the British did in India, many White Americans insisted that African Americans were poor because they were lazy and idle. When African Americans tried to get access to beaches or swimming holes, White people countered with patronizing remarks about how Black people could not expect to get ahead if they would not work.[16]

By the mid-1900s White Americans and Europeans were even claiming – wrongly – that it was physically, genetically impossible for African Americans to swim. This claim reversed earlier accounts suggesting that genetic adaptations helped African and Hawaiian people to swim. According to nineteenth-century American travellers, Sudanese men and women swam under conditions that would be 'certain death to anybody not made of cork'. The Hawaiian Olympic swimmer Duke Kahanamoku was said to swim 'naturally', to be 'bred from generations of swimming ancestors' and therefore to have feet 'shaped like paddles'. Newspapers wrote that 'no white man has a chance against this human fish, who was reared in the sea.' As late as 1927 one American traveller thought the people of Sierra Leone swam in ways that White people could never hope to emulate, 'not being born that way'.[17]

But new scientific studies (the authors were zoologists) in the 1950s and '60s reversed this idea to claim that African Americans could not swim well. They asserted that, since the average Black athlete has lower body fat than White athletes, Black swimmers would be less buoyant and would not be able to swim competitively. Though this theory was completely wrong, many White people found it attractive. White 'experts' repeated the buoyancy theory everywhere: on television, in academic journals and in sports books as recently as 2012.[18] Other reasons were also proposed: scientific experts suggested that Black people were not good swimmers because 'the water closes their pores so that they cannot get rid of carbon dioxide and they tire quickly,' or because Black people have higher bone density than White people.[19] None of this is true. For most of human history, Africans have been much better swimmers than Europeans, and in the last century African Americans have won at least five Olympic swimming medals.[20] The larger number of White medallists has nothing to do with genetics and a great deal to do with racism.

Ancient fears centred on swimming led White Americans to fight the integration of swimming pools with a vehemence they did not bring to any other form of racial segregation. When the courts forced them to desegregate the pools, American cities 'employed every tool imaginable' to avoid integrated swimming. They sold pools and beaches to private (White) organizations, or closed them entirely, sometimes filling them with concrete.[21] White mobs numbering in the thousands beat up Black people trying to swim in nominally public pools. In the 1950s,

> if Negroes ventured onto the beach [in Biloxi, Mississippi] to
> enjoy it for themselves, they generally got cursed, harassed, spat

upon, kicked, hit, or run off by White ruffians or property owners from across the highway. Law enforcement officers routinely stood back and watched this harassment and did nothing. More often than not, lawmen themselves acted to remove blacks from the beach. In 1959, when a White nun teaching at a black Catholic school took her students to the beach in Gulfport for a class project, the Gulfport police summarily removed the teacher and her students from the beach.[22]

This was a much stronger feeling than the segregation that affected lunch counters and trains. In 1962 a White American complained that 'he could tolerate integration anywhere but in swimming pools.' White Americans used swimming pools specifically to establish and maintain racial distinctions. In 1964, when African Americans tried to desegregate a Florida motel pool by jumping in, the motel manager poured muriatic acid (a form of hydrochloric acid) into the pool to burn them. In August 1977 White beachgoers – with the help of the Federal Bureau of Investigation and local police mounted on horses – fought with Black teenagers to force them off Carson Beach in Boston.[23] In Australia as well, when Aboriginal Australians tried to desegregate mineral springs in 1965, a White crowd 'threw eggs and tomatoes, and some of the students were punched, one to the ground'. Even in the last few years, people of colour in Europe, Australia and the United States still report that White men and women call them racial epithets or even attack them when they go to the pool or the beach.[24]

Not only did White people refuse to swim with people of colour; they felt strongly that people of colour must not swim at all. Swimming could only be for one race, and it was now going to be for White people. When forced to provide beaches or pools for African Americans, cities arranged for them to be as unpleasant as possible. In Chicago in 1925, for example, African American swimmers complained that their designated beach 'had no bathhouse or shower' and was overrun by rats. As White people moved to the suburbs, American city pools declined and city high schools did not get swimming pools. The few new urban public pools built in the 1960s were cramped, concrete prison-like structures. Many of these pools were only just over 90 centimetres (3 ft) deep, and they were so crowded that swimming was impossible; there was never room to do more than stand and splash. Similarly, the Australian government also often neglects to build swimming pools near where Aboriginal Australians live.[25] Today, the few free hours at public pools are often so crowded as to effectively prevent swimming. In the last century, swimming has become a relatively expensive, and therefore upper-class, form of entertainment or exercise.

Swimming and power

With all of their fears, it is noticeably the most powerful, wealthiest people everywhere who have kept swimming. Swimming was used as a class marker perhaps as early as the Old Kingdom in Egypt; it was certainly a class marker by the Iron Age, when it drew a line between the poor and those who had grown up with the leisure to learn how to swim. Like reading, as Plato pointed out, swimming takes a long time to learn and cannot be faked. Naked, you can show that you are truly a member of the upper class through your accent, your literacy and your swimming. This association of reading and swimming appears in Virginia Woolf's metaphors in the 1920s, and it survived into the late 1900s to show up in a Russian professor's 1970s argument that Lenin's support of communist public libraries also applied to swimming pools. Even contemporary writers such as Jenny Landreth still associate swimming with reading: 'I can't remember not being able to read … but I *can* remember not being able to swim.'[26]

Wealthy Eurasians' desire to use swimming to draw a line between rich and poor could even, under some circumstances, trump race in segregating pools. In Singapore, when European colonists limited access to the beach in 1894, they excluded not only native Singaporeans and all women but poor White men. In 1920s Serbia, Roma people were generally banned from public swimming pools, but richer Roma who 'had a respected occupation and led a regular lifestyle' were grudgingly allowed in.[27] The first Indian member of the exclusive Calcutta Swimming Club, in 1964, was the wealthy maharaja of Koch Bihar. The Bronze Age view that associated swimming with race generally aligned with the Iron Age view of swimming as a class marker, but where the two conflicted, awkward compromises emerged.

The nineteenth-century revival of this connection between swimming and social class dovetailed neatly with the search for ways to monetize swimming. Liverpool, for example, had first-, second- and third-class swimming pools, and charged accordingly. The cheap pools were hard to swim in because they were often too crowded. Complicated arrangements of hallways and changing rooms physically separated rich swimmers from poor. Swimming teachers thought it was 'more important for aristocrats to learn to swim than the lower classes', claiming that the rich would travel more and so ran more risk of drowning; the ability to pay well for lessons probably figures into this opinion.[28] Americans arranged for richer YMCAs and community centres to have swimming pools, while the ones in poorer neighbourhoods did not. When richer YMCAs let swimmers from other neighbourhoods come in for a few hours a week, they marked them as second-class swimmers by making them use the side entrance.[29]

Beaches also separated rich from poor. In 1920s Britain the 'low sands' consisted of a dirty beach, ragged children and 'bus-loads of rowdy trippers in hot, dusty, best-suited clumps drinking jugs of ale'. The 'big sands', which were more expensive, boasted a 'promenade, hot water for tea, bathing-tents and clean sand'. France gestured towards equality by sending poor city children to summer camps at the seashore, but nevertheless most beaches served a more exclusive, bourgeois class.[30]

The association of swimming with wealth found reinforcement in commercial advertising. Talcum powder was sold to treat sunburn from a day at the beach. Soap ads optimistically showed girls washing at the beach. Chrysler photographed their cars against the backdrop of a swimming pool, and Pepsi ads showed a man drinking soda by the side of a pool.[31] The swimmer Annette Kellerman promoted swimming 'for the woman who swelters in her kitchen or lolls in a drawing room, for the man who sits half his life in an office chair', but not for nannies or subway conductors.[32] Magazines presented swimming as the activity of a wealthy minority, the sort of people who could afford a membership in a country club or a backyard pool, and who might also buy new cars. To reinforce class distinctions, beginning about 1910, at the height of the swimming craze, many American colleges required undergraduates to know how to swim in order to graduate. Even more colleges added the requirement in the 1940s. Nominally these tests were part of a national goal of military preparedness, but the U.S. Army has never included a swimming requirement in basic training, and until the Second World War neither did the U.S. Navy. Few college students were going to fight on the front lines, while women as well as men were subject to college swimming tests. Evidently these tests were more about social class than about war.[33]

Minority swimming clubs

Wealthier groups of immigrants who found themselves excluded from pools on racial grounds built their own pools or beach resorts and excluded whomever they could. Despite frequent opposition, African Americans bought beachfront property and established their own swimming clubs. In 1893 Charles and Laura Douglass, the son and daughter-in-law of the abolitionist Frederick Douglass, founded a Black beach resort at Highland Beach in Maryland. Many well-known and well-off Black people of the time came to stay there: the activists Harriet Tubman and Paul Robeson, W.E.B. Du Bois and the poets Langston Hughes and Paul Dunbar, as well as Frederick Douglass himself. The resort was successful, and remains largely African American today.[34] At the historically Black Howard University, founded in 1867 (only a couple of years after Emancipation), swimming was again among the first athletic activities.

Jewish Europeans and Jewish Americans were banned from many pools through most of the twentieth century, but they were often able to build their own swimming pools. In the 1910s and '20s Jewish people were shut out of Polish swimming clubs and Prague swimming pools. Jewish people lost access to both pools and beaches in Germany in 1933, and by 1941 this ban extended across Eastern Europe. Even wealthy Jews were banned from American country club pools. But many Jewish people who could not swim in the Christian YMCA and YWCA pools had the resources and social power to build their own pools. New York Jews started the Young Women's Hebrew Association (YWHA), which built its first swimming pool in 1916. Jewish summer camps sprang up all over upstate New York, and Jewish country clubs with pools opened in many wealthy suburbs.[35] Similarly, wealthy Chinese merchants in Singapore started their own beach club in 1909. In America, Chinese immigrants barred from White pools built their own YMCA swimming pool in San Francisco.[36] Thus despite racist exclusions, many well-off people of all racial and ethnic backgrounds still found ways to gain access to the water and the high social status of swimming.

Each of these groups also inflicted their own exclusions on others. Korean immigrants in Japan enforced internal class and gender distinctions. In Kenya and Uganda, Indian immigrants demonstrated their affinity with Europeans by taking beach holidays and morning dips, but excluding Indigenous Africans.[37] American Jewish country-club membership was almost entirely made up of German Jews, excluding both Eastern European Jews and Sephardic Jews from the Mediterranean.[38] The Singapore Chinese swimming club did not admit Chinese women or local Singaporeans. Chinese girls and women were barred from the Chinese American YMCA pool, too. They had to make do with occasional side-door access to the main San Francisco YWCA pool.[39] Many Jewish country clubs did not allow women to swim. The wealthy African American beach property owners at Highland Beach and other Black resorts wrote regulations designed to keep out poorer Black swimmers.[40] Everywhere people used swimming to reinforce their own power and exclude others.

Poverty prevented many excluded people around the world from opening their own pools. Afro-Brazilians could not afford to build swimming pools until the 1960s, even when they built their own private athletic clubs.[41] Since Latinos were locked out of taxpayer-funded pools all over California and Texas, they, too, lacked money, or access to bank loans, to build their own swimming pools. Swimming pools and beaches pile on rules to exclude people living in poverty: Atlanta public pools do not accept cash payments; Los Angeles public pools require an adult for every child under seven and an approved swimsuit; many Rhode Island beaches charge for access. In Europe, the admission price for public pools is often too high for low-income families. As a result, higher-income people worldwide are much more likely to know how to swim.[42]

The image of swimming

When people swim today, it is often to claim upper-class status. At its most ambitious, that means swimming lessons for children and lap swimming for adults. Competitive swimming is still supported, especially in the United States, Australia and the United Kingdom, in order to win prestigious Olympic swimming medals.[43] But many people's swimming urges can be satisfied with much less. Although most Americans say they have 'been swimming' in the last year, most of them have stayed well within their depth. They are wading, not swimming. Similarly, British 'wild swimmers' admit that many of them do not really like the swimming so much as the scenery. Many enthusiastic participants in 'wild swimming' really 'just get in and bob about for a bit'.[44] But even these dilettantes still enthusiastically buy bikinis, swim rings, bathing caps and beach houses. They take beach holidays. Even if they do not swim at all, they buy books about swimming: London bookshops devote whole shelves to swimming books. Many more people simply watch Olympic swimming competitions every four years.

Enthusiasm for swimming remains, as it has been for centuries, tied to nostalgia for a glorious past. Virtually all swimming books remind us that Julius Caesar was an excellent swimmer and that Lord Byron swam the Hellespont. Some British swimmers still prefer to swim naked, the way these heroes did. Even where we misunderstand it, the past holds power: French physical education specialists still claim, against the evidence, that the breaststroke is the canonical Western stroke, going back to antiquity. In swimming breaststroke, they too feel connected to the Greeks and Romans.[45] No avant-garde artist or writer today would use swimming as a metaphor for radicalism; it is too closely tied to the British Empire. Swimming appears in articles and art as a romantic memory, amid nostalgia for lost empires, lost colonies and White supremacy.

Trying to be White

In pursuit of upper-class status, many Indigenous swimmers have abandoned their own traditions to imitate the swimming of the European upper class. Indigenous swimming, for many people, is now too closely associated with exploitation, enslavement and misery. Indigenous swimmers themselves, not liking to have their swimming compared to the swimming of dogs, frogs and ducks, chose to emulate these powerful colonizers. As early as the 1840s Aboriginal Australian swimmers apparently started to imitate the British breaststroke: 'The Aborigines, both young and old, at first swam in their own style, which we called dog-paddling, but some of them soon got into our way of breast-stroke swimming.'[46] In Ghana, too, Asante people seem to have started to use the breaststroke alongside their traditional overhand stroke.[47] In Thailand, Indigenous swimming lasted into the early 1900s, with Thai children swimming 'like fishes' in the water around their houses.[48] But as Thailand's upper class adopted European clothing and habits, they took over the good beaches for themselves. Today most Thai children cannot swim, and river drowning is now the leading cause of death for Thai children after infancy.[49]

Colonizing governments also encouraged Indigenous swimmers to adopt more European bathing habits, including the use of swimsuits, swimming pools and the breaststroke. The British in India tried to teach local boys to swim as part of raising them to be colonial bureaucrats. The Vichy French even recommended building a high-school swimming pool in Senegal as part of France's *mission civilatrice*. Sudan's Christian mission schools in the 1970s had girls' swimming teams.[50] In the late 1930s the Girl Scouts ran camps for Native American girls in the Great Plains and in the Southwest, and the American YMCA opened summer camps for both African American and Asian American boys.[51] Today, United Nations programmes in Bangladesh teach children how to swim using European-style lessons.[52]

Where wealthier or more powerful Indigenous people have regained access to the water, they now often swim like northern Eurasians, haltingly and fearfully, and with much use of flotation devices and artificial pools. They keep their heads out of the water, stay generally within their depth and swim mainly in the context of supervising children. They buy beach houses and sit by the pool in deckchairs drinking cocktails. They have done a great deal of work to sustain swimming, but most of it has gone to the promotion of European-style swimming as a way to regain lost power. They have built swimming pools for African American children to use: generations of local Black children learned to swim in the Howard University pool. By the mid-1950s Black Africans in South Africa and Zimbabwe were organizing regional swimming competitions.[53] In 1966 these regional organizations representing Black swimming joined together to form the South African Amateur Swimming Federation. Activists have fought for the right to access public pools as well. In Singapore local residents finally got their first public swimming pool in 1931. Throughout the 1930s and '40s the NAACP and other organizations sued municipalities for the right to swim in public pools. In 1969 Navajo activists demanded their own swimming pools.[54] Brazilian protesters saved the Julio Delamare Aquatic Park. Recent public works projects in Lima, Peru, have brought some public swimming pools to poorer neighbourhoods.[55] Indigenous swimmers have even, in imitation of Chinese Communists, adopted the use of swimming as a metaphor for revolution. In Vietnam revolutionaries 'as terrifying as crocodiles' would 'swim freely in the boundless ocean'.[56] In Algeria nationalist 'fish' swam in the 'water' of the general population. In Sierra Leone the biography of an activist can be titled *Swimming Against the Tide*.[57]

But in Brazil, Peru, the United States and elsewhere, these public pools are mostly dingy and sad, and there are not enough of them. And even equal access to swimming pools and beaches (a dream that has not yet been achieved) would not mean that Indigenous swimmers swam the way they did in the 1700s. Instead, they have learned to swim like non-swimmers – mostly metaphorically.

Indigenous swimming

There are still a few parts of the world that are sufficiently independent and isolated to have preserved the old way of swimming. Across the middle of Africa, on Navajo land, in rural South India, Indonesia and Hawaii, there are people whose swimming is just what it always was.[58] Their swimming is integrated into their everyday lives. In remote South India, 'women and children bathe and do laundry while boys swim' in the river. In Benin, in the 1940s, young children swam as part of fetching water from the river. Today's Bajau sea nomads, in Indonesia, learn to swim before they can walk. Two- and three-year-olds 'can dive with ease'.[59] Among Ibo people in Nigeria, swimming (using an overarm crawl stroke) is an 'ordinary accomplishment', and swimmers are 'as happy in the water as out of it', 'perfectly fearless' even when there is a flood. Swimming, often combined with canoeing or surfing, is intensely social.[60] It may be included in traditional festivals, as in Nigeria and Kenya, or have spiritual significance, as in Hawaii.[61] In parts of Central Africa boys and girls swim together; they play hide and seek in the water; they challenge each other to get to a target first, dive from heights or swim underwater the furthest (see illus. 82). They are 'perfectly at home in the water, and swim about for hours without any signs of tiring'. They compete to gather empty bottles and cans dropped from passing boats. Adult men swim to catch fish to sell.[62] Indigenous swimmers routinely dive to the bottom, as local children did in rural Morocco for the fun of helping a visiting research team collect mussels.[63] Swimming is an ordinary social activity. Where British swimmers see swimming as 'a way of transporting you out of your normal world', for old-style Indigenous swimmers water activities are their normal, everyday life, from socializing to playing, cultural festivals and working.[64]

But even these remaining outposts of Indigenous swimming will probably be lost to development and colonization over the next century. Tourism is spreading to previously neglected African beaches. Resort hotels and beach houses are taking over Lake Langano in Ethiopia. As peace returns after Somalia's civil war, local entrepreneurs are beginning to make plans for luxury beach hotels catering to Americans and Europeans. In Eretria, most beaches that are not polluted are now mainly for European tourists, with local people relegated to selling shell necklaces on the beach as in North Africa and Brazil.[65] Under pressure from the International Monetary Fund, West African countries like Guinea are also working to develop their beaches for European tourism.[66]

THE YEAR 2000 marked the end of the eleventh millennium since northern Eurasians emerged from the last Ice Age having forgotten how to swim. Over the years they have learned how to swim a little, and then forgotten again, and learned again, and now they are well on their way to forgetting again. In all that time they have not become comfortable with the water. Not only that, northern Eurasian non-swimmers have now exported their fear of the water all around the world, so that today Africans, Southeast Asians and Native Americans are even less likely to know how to swim than Europeans. All over the world, swimming pools are closing. Beaches are full of sunbathers and waders, but the ocean is empty. Though parents still dutifully bring their children to a few token swimming lessons, lap swimming remains a popular form of elite exercise and lake houses remain an important way to display wealth, the nineteenth-century fad for swimming is essentially over. The descendants of the old northern non-swimmers are settling back into not swimming, satisfied with having converted nearly everyone else in the world to their way of thinking.

EPILOGUE

We know very little about the past, and much of what we think we know is wrong. We assume that people have been gradually getting better at things in general, and at swimming in particular, from antiquity to the present day, with a slight crisis in the Middle Ages that was quickly made up for in the Renaissance. That assumption is unwarranted. Change is not always for the better, and the fall of Rome was not the time when people forgot how to swim. Instead, from the Neanderthals on, people on all the continents were good swimmers, using an overhand alternating stroke, diving and enjoying the water. Their happy splashing was first interrupted by the last Ice Age, when northerners forgot how to swim. When the Ice Age ended and these northerners realized that other people could swim, they rationalized and ratified the cultural difference by associating swimming with danger and evil. Yet starting in the late Bronze Age, and continuing through the fall of Rome, these northern non-swimmers slowly began to learn to swim again. It was not the fall of Rome but the rise of the Turks and Mongols that stopped them from swimming in the late Middle Ages. Europeans did not start to swim again in the Renaissance: that is when they started to float women for witchcraft. Instead, it took until the late 1700s before they relearned how to swim, and then they soon lost interest again.

Nor is it justified to assume that Central Asia has always been a cultural backwater: a place that receives new ideas rather than spawning them. It was probably the vast expansion of Central Asian power in the beginning of the second millennium CE – the conquests of the Turks and the Mongols – that convinced people on the periphery of Central Asia to stop swimming. Central Asians like Saladin, Alp Arslan and Genghis Khan were winners. Central Asians dominated the new technology of the time: knotted carpets, bowed musical instruments, yoghurt, steel, cotton, sugar. Central Asians used composite bows, they wrestled, they lifted heavy weights, but they did not swim. By 1400 neither did the Chinese and West Asian people they had conquered. Even in Europe, where the Turks were turned back, swimming seemed weird, suspicious, possibly super-natural. Europeans adopted the Central Asian use of swimming as a test for witchcraft. The few remaining swimmers in Europe could only dog-paddle or swim breaststroke. Thanks to Central Asian influence, crawl strokes and diving disappeared.

Many swimming books also assume that women historically swam less than men, but women have always been swimmers. In addition to the images of women swimming from every country and every age, literary references often describe women swimming as well. Under some limited circumstances, it is true, women have been blocked from swimming. In India under the Raj, for example, women were not allowed into British swimming clubs. In modern East Africa, West Asia and Europe, Islamic ideas about female modesty sometimes have the effect of blocking women from swimming. In the United States, strongly held beliefs about African American women's hair have recently kept many women of colour out of swimming pools. But in general, women have been enthusiastic swimmers around the world. Women swam in the Bronze Age and in classical antiq-uity. They continued to swim through the Victorian revival of swimming in Europe. Even today, more women swim than men in most countries.

On the other hand, we tend to gloss over the close relationship between swimming and power. Swimming lends itself to the creation and maintenance of hierarchy, because some beaches and riverbanks are nat-urally nicer than others, and people with more access to power will find they can seize these good beaches for themselves and force others to swim at the bad beaches, or not to swim at all. Eurasians, who came late to swimming, adopted it as a sign of upper-class status, and today swimming is, for the most part, limited to the upper class: an emblem of slave-holders, settlers and White supremacy. Though swimming demonstrates, like reading obscure literature, riding horses, sailing or skiing, that you grew up with money, it has never been as important to swim well as it has been to swim at the right beaches.

Then also, and most perniciously, people tend to assume that White Europeans brought skills to the areas they colonized but learned nothing from the Indigenous people they met there. Europeans brought with them new navigational techniques and guns, but everywhere the people they met were much better swimmers. In West Africa in the late 1400s, Europeans reported with awe the swimming skills of the Senegalese people they met, and in the early 1500s they were enchanted by the swimming abilities of the Cherokee and the Panamanians. In the 1800s Europeans learned the crawl stroke from the Mandan, the Aboriginal Australians and the Argentinians. Modern competitive swimming strokes are the strokes of Indigenous swimmers.

And finally, there is the idea that people are rational, that they make decisions based on facts, that they draw conclusions based on what they know. It is far more likely that people will bend the facts to suit their opinions. Europeans, when they found that people of colour could swim better than most White people, at first pretended that Indigenous swimmers were like animals because they could swim, as animals did. They used this idea to justify enslaving Africans and Native Americans. Then, when the Europeans wanted to learn to swim themselves, they pushed Black and Indigenous people out of the water rather than swim with people racialized as inferior. White people soon decided that they themselves were civilized because they could swim, and concluded that Black people could not swim because their bodies were not sufficiently buoyant – which many people still believe. Our ideas are too often only rationalizations of what we wish to confirm, or of what we assume to be normal.

In that spirit, I must acknowledge that many of the ideas presented in this book will probably turn out the same way, and a hundred years from now they, too, will be superseded. I have done my best to show northern Eurasians not as the default normal but as the deviants who have imposed their deviance on swimmers everywhere. Decolonization, in the context of swimming, would mean abandoning the cultural association between swimming and power. It would mean that the remaining Indigenous swimmers could keep on swimming, or go back to swimming. They would be free to swim at the good beaches. Even timorous northern Eurasian non-swimmers might eventually follow their example. Swimming could once again hold the place it has held for most people throughout history as a fun social activity open to everyone.

CHRONOLOGY

c. 140,000 BCE	Fishing at Blombos Cave in South Africa
c. 100,000 BCE	Neanderthals in Europe dive for shellfish
c. 2900 BCE	Hieroglyphs show the front crawl stroke in Egypt
c. 2000 BCE	Yamnaya spread fear of the water south to India
1274 BCE	Hittites begin to learn how to swim
860s BCE	Assyrians swim using inflated goatskins
c. 700 BCE	Odysseus swims in Homer's epic
500s BCE	South Chinese images of underwater swimming
c. 400s BCE	Maya frieze depicts divers in Central America
c. 300s BCE	South African carving of front crawl stroke
c. 500 CE	Front crawl in a mural from Teotihuacan, Mexico
1000s CE	Song Dynasty diving performances in China
1153	Women tied and floated for witchcraft in Kyiv
1250s	Body-surfing competitions in southern China
1260s	First evidence of the breaststroke in European art
1300s	First evidence of the backstroke appears in Iran
1375	Last use of the front crawl in Europe
1400s	Underwater divers on earspool from Ecuador
1415	First frog kick and backstroke in European art
c. 1500	Leonardo da Vinci designs flotation devices
1538	First written swimming manual published in Latin

1571	Swimming banned at the University of Cambridge
1584	Trial by water for witchcraft in Germany
1590	Breaststroke appears in Indian miniatures
1603	Swimming competitions in Japan
1695	Tibetan swimming competition
1700s	Europeans see surfing in West Africa and in Hawaii
1733	Native Americans teach colonists overhand stroke
c. 1736	First bathing machines in use in Britain
1800s	First written swimming manual in Japanese
1810	Lord Byron swims the Hellespont
1825	Last official trial by water for witchcraft in Britain
1849	First public swimming pool opens in London
c. 1888	First racially segregated beaches in South Africa
1896	First modern Olympic Games in Athens
1933	Butterfly stroke introduced in competition
1948	Paralympics welcomes swimmers with disabilities

REFERENCES

1 ONCE EVERYONE COULD SWIM

1 Astrida Neimanis points out that although mammals aren't swimmers, we are, in some sense, oceans, and trillions of one-celled bacteria spend their lives swimming inside us: Steve Mentz, *Ocean* (New York, 2020), p. 108; Bonnie Tsui, *Why We Swim* (Chapel Hill, NC, 2020), pp. 82ff.

2 Pliny, *Natural Histories* 8.10.2 (8.11); Strabo, *Geography* 15.1.43.

3 Max Westenhöfer, *Der Eigenweg des Menschen* (Berlin, 1942), then Elaine Morgan, *The Scars of Evolution: What Our Body Tells about Human Origins* (London, 1990), but, refuting them, see Holger Preuschoft and Signe Preuschoft, 'The Aquatic Ape Theory, Seen from Epistemological and Palaeoanthropological Viewpoints', in *The Aquatic Ape: Fact or Fiction? The First Scientific Evaluation of a Controversial Theory of Human Evolution*, ed. Machteld Roede et al. (London, 1991), pp. 142–73, and, more recently, David Cameron and Colin Groves, *Bones, Stones and Molecules* (London, 2004). For the more moderate swimming hypothesis favoured here, see Carsten Niemitz, 'The Evolution of the Upright Posture and Gait: A Review and a New Synthesis', *Naturwissenschaften*, 97 (2010), pp. 241–63; Howard Means, *Splash! 10,000 Years of Swimming* (London, 2020), pp. 17–18. For the evolution of cetaceans, see Felix Marx et al., *Cetacean Paleobiology* (Chichester, 2016).

4 Yes, many newborns will hold their breath and make swimming motions: Myrtle McGraw, 'Swimming Behavior of the Human Infant', *Journal of Pediatrics*, XV (1939), pp. 485–90. But human infants do not learn to keep themselves safe in the water: Committee on Sports Medicine and Fitness, 'Swimming Programs for Infants and Toddlers', *Pediatrics*, CV (2000), pp. 868–70.

5 Christopher Henshilwood and Judith Sealy, 'Bone Artefacts from the Middle Stone Age at Blombos Cave, Southern Cape, South Africa', *Current Anthropology*, XXXVIII (1997), pp. 890–95 (p. 895). Nearby archaeological sites also yield extensive mussel-shell middens: Antonieta Jerardino, 'Excavations at Pancho's Kitchen Midden, Western Cape Coast, South Africa: Further Observations into the Megamidden Period', *South*

African Archaeological Bulletin, LIII (1998), pp. 16–25 (p. 20). For more accounts of early fishing (without direct evidence of swimming), see Sue O'Connor et al., 'Pelagic Fishing at 42,000 Years Before the Present and the Maritime Skills of Modern Humans', *Science*, CCCXXXIV (2011), pp. 1117–21; Yaowu Hu et al., 'Stable Isotope Dietary Analysis of the Tianyuan 1 Early Modern Human', *Proceedings of the National Academy of Sciences*, CVI/27 (2009), pp. 10971–4; Michael Richards and Erik Trinkaus, 'Isotopic Evidence for the Diets of European Neanderthals and Early Modern Humans', *Proceedings of the National Academy of Sciences*, CVI (2009), pp. 16034–9; Abdeljalil Bouzouggar et al., 'Reevaluating the Age of the Iberomaurusian in Morocco', *African Archaeological Review*, XXV (2008), pp. 3–19.

6 Paola Villa et al., 'Neandertals on the Beach: Use of Marine Resources at Grotta dei Moscerini (Latium, Italy)', PLOS ONE, XV (2020), pp. 1–35; João Zilhão et al., 'Last Interglacial Iberian Neandertals as Fisher-Hunter-Gatherers', *Science*, CCCLXVII (2020), pp. 1–13.

7 Ulrich Hallier and Brigitte Hallier, 'Nageurs dans les montagnes de la Tassili n'Ajjer??', *Stonewatch*, XXXVIII (2010), pp. 1–29.

8 Jean-Loïc Le Quellec, Pauline de Flers and Philippe de Flers, 'Prehistoric Swimmers in the Sahara', *Arts et Cultures, Revue des Musées Barbier-Müller* (2007), pp. 46–61.

9 Toby Wilkinson, *Early Dynastic Egypt* (London, 1999), p. 104, citing a 1st Dynasty inscription (*c.* 2900 BCE) in William Flinders Petrie, *Royal Tombs of the Earliest Dynasties*, vol. II (London, 1901), pl. XIX, pp. 146–50.

10 'The Inscription of Kheti II', in James Breasted, *Ancient Records of Egypt*, I (Chicago, IL, 1906), p. 190, § 413. For more ancient sources on swimming, see Erwin Mehl, *Antike Schwimmkunst* (Munich, 1927).

11 Tomb of D2rj: Herbert Winlock, 'The Museum's Excavations at Thebes', *Metropolitan Museum of Art Bulletin*, XXVII (1932), pp. 1, 4–37 (p. 29, fig. 30); Wolfgang Decker, *Bildatlas zum Sport im alten Ägypten* (Leiden, 1994), fig. 2.4; for more examples and discussion, see Ashraf Abdel-Raouf Ragheb, 'Notes on Diving in Ancient Egypt', *International Journal of Nautical Archaeology*, XL (2011), pp. 424–7, figs 1–3.

12 'The Instructions of Tuauf to his son Pepi'; Papyrus Sallier II, British Museum EA10182,II, trans. Ernest Wallis Budge, *The Literature of the Ancient Egyptians* (London, 1914), pp. 251–2.

13 Papyrus Chester Beatty I: Abdel-Raouf Ragheb, 'Notes on Diving in Ancient Egypt', p. 424, citing Alan Gardiner, *Late Egyptian Stories* (Brussels, 1932), p. 48; *Ancient Egyptian Literature: A Book of Readings*, vol. II: *The New Kingdom*, trans. Miriam Lichtheim (Berkeley, CA, 1976), p. 218.

14 The Cairo Vase 1266 + 25218, in *Ancient Egyptian Literature*, vol. II, trans. Lichtheim, p. 193.

15 Plutarch, *Antony* 29.3.

16 Adolf Erman, *The Literature of the Ancient Egyptians*, trans. Aylward Blackman (London, 1927), p. 243.

17 Dorothy Phillips, 'Cosmetic Spoons in the Form of Swimming Girls',
    Metropolitan Museum of Art Bulletin, xxxvi (1941), pp. 173–5; Jean Capart,
    Documents pour servir à l'étude de l'art égyptien, vol. 1 (Paris, 1927), pl. 73a;
    Decker, *Bildatlas*, pl. 2.5.
18 Near Oxyrhynchus: Adam Lusher, 'Ancient Egypt: Citizen Scientists
    Reveal Tales of Tragedy Unearthed from Centuries-Old Rubbish Dump',
    The Independent, 1 March 2016. The association with the disgraced Dirk
    Obbink, however, may now cast doubt on this papyrus's authenticity. For
    another passing mention of Egyptian swimming in the Roman period,
    see Strabo, *Geography* 17.1.44 on the people of Tentyra, who swam with
    crocodiles and served as keepers for crocodiles displayed at Rome.
19 Pliny the Elder, *Natural Histories* 9.9 (9.8.26); Pliny the Younger, *Letters*
    9.33.
20 Sarah Bond, 'Why We Need to Start Seeing the Classical World in
    Color', *Hyperallergic*, 7 June 2017; Jeremy Tanner, 'Introduction to the New
    Edition: Race and Representation in Ancient Art: *Black Athena* and After',
    in *The Image of the Black in Western Art: From the Pharaohs to the Fall of
    the Roman Empire*, vol. 1, ed. David Bindman, Henry Louis Gates Jr and
    Karen Dalton (Cambridge, MA, 2010), pp. 1–39.
21 Roger Ling, *The Insula of the Menander at Pompeii*, vol. 1: *The Structures*
    (New York, 1997), pp. 140–42.
22 Roger Hornback, *Racism and Early Blackface Comic Traditions: From
    the Old World to the New* (Cham, Switzerland, 2018), p. 43; John Clarke,
    *Looking at Lovemaking: Constructions of Sexuality in Roman Art, 100 BC–AD
    250* (Berkeley, CA, 1998), pp. 122–3.
23 From the House of the Doctor (VII 5.24), Pompeii: Caitlín Eilís Barrett,
    Domesticating Empire: Egyptian Landscapes in Pompeian Gardens (Oxford,
    2019), fig. 2.4.
24 Pliny, *Natural Histories* 8.38, 9.12.
25 Philostratus, *Imagines* 1.5, quoted in Molly Swetnam-Burland, *Egypt in
    Italy* (Cambridge, 2015), pp. 157–8.
26 Ointment spoon from Abusir, Egypt. Dynasty XVIII, between 1410 and
    1372 BC, now in the Brooklyn Museum: Jean Vercoutter and William Ryan,
    'The Iconography of the Black in Ancient Egypt: From the Beginnings to
    the Twenty-Fifth Dynasty', in *The Image of the Black in Western Art*,
    ed. Bindman, Gates and Dalton, pp. 33–89 (fig. 52).
27 These stories were collected between 1997 and 2001 by Elizabeth Laird
    under the auspices of the Ministry of Education and the British Council,
    and can be found at https://ethiopianfolktales.com, accessed 9 August 2021.
28 Djanka Tassey Condé, *Sunjata: A West African Epic of the Mande Peoples*,
    ed. and trans. David Conrad (Indianapolis, IN, 2004), pp. 191–5; Charles
    Verlinden, *L'Esclavage dans l'Europe médiévale* (Ghent, 1955–77), pp. 494–5.
29 Wande Abimbola, 'The Locust-Bean Seller', 'The Headstrong Bride',
    and 'The Hunter's Best Friend' (all Yoruba stories); Lantei Lawson,
    'The Yam Farm and the Problem Tongue' (a Ga story from Ghana),
    T. Y. Enin, 'The River's Judgment' and 'Asiedo and the Fish Child'

(both Sefwi stories; see other river judge stories in pp. 19, 47, 9); and the anonymous Ashanti story 'The Tail of the Elephant Queen', all in *West African Folk Tales*, trans. Jack Berry, ed. Richard Spears (Evanston, IL, 1991), pp. 35, 49, 59, 60–62, 115, 161, 174; Condé, *Sunjata*, p. 89.

30 T. Y. Enin, 'What Spider Knows' (a Sefwi story), *West African Folk Tales*, p. 84; Condé, *Sunjata*, p. 135.

31 Ibn Battuta, *Travels in Asia and Africa, 1325–1354*, trans. and ed. Hamilton Gibb, Hakluyt Society, 2nd ser., vols CX, CXVII, CXLI, CLXXVIII, CXC (1929) (London, 1994), p. 967.

32 Dietrich Sahrhage and Johannes Lundbeck, *A History of Fishing* (1992) (Berlin, 2012), pp. 16–17 and fig. 7c, from Harald Pager, *Stone Age Myth and Magic as Documented in the Rock Paintings of South Africa* (Graz, 1975), p. 20. With a photo in Ronald Singer and John Wymer, *The Middle Stone Age at Klasies River Mouth in South Africa* (Chicago, IL, 1982), pl. 48, though see the arguments against this figure being a swimmer proposed by David Pearce, 'Later Stone Age Burial Practice in the Eastern Cape Province, South Africa', PhD thesis, University of the Witwatersrand, Johannesburg (2008), pp. 167–84.

2 LEAVING AFRICA

1 Harriet Crawford, *Dilmun and Its Gulf Neighbors* (Cambridge, 1998), p. 29; Allison Karmel Thomason, *Luxury and Legitimation: Royal Collecting in Ancient Mesopotamia* (London, 2005), p. 80; Robert Hoyland, *Arabia and the Arabs: From the Bronze Age to the Coming of Islam* (London, 2001), p. 34; A. Leo Oppenheim, 'The Seafaring Merchants of Ur', *Journal of the American Oriental Society*, LXXIV (1954), pp. 6–17 (pp. 7, 15).

2 Pliny, *Natural Histories* 6.32 (28); Athenaeus, *Deipnosophistae* 3.46.

3 Al-Idrisi, *Edrisi-Géographie*, trans. Pierre Amédée Jaubert (Paris, 1836), pp. 373–7.

4 Edward Alpers, *The Indian Ocean in World History* (Oxford, 2014), p. 9.

5 Adapted from *Jaina Sutras*, trans. Hermann Jacobi (Delhi, 1895), vol. II, pp. 141–2.

6 Patrick Olivelle and Suman Olivelle, *Manu's Code of Law: A Critical Edition and Translation of the Mānava-Dharmásāstra* (Oxford, 2005), p. 128 (ch. 4.77).

7 *Tamil Love Poetry: The Five Hundred Short Poems of the Ainkurunuru, an Early Third-Century Anthology*, ed. Martha Ann Shelby (New York, 2011), pp. 44–5.

8 Indira Viswanathan Peterson, *Poems to Śiva: The Hymns of the Tamil Saints* (Princeton, NJ, 1989), p. 256.

9 Ibn Battuta, *Travels in Asia and Africa, 1325–1354*, trans. and ed. Hamilton Gibb, Hakluyt Society, 2nd ser., vols CX, CXVII, CXLI, CLXXVIII, CXC (1929) (London, 1994), p. 857. See also references to swimming in Zacharias Thundy, *South Indian Folktales of Kadar* (Meerut, 1983).

10 *Mahavamsa: Great Chronicle of Ceylon*, trans. and ed. Wilhelm Geiger (Oxford, 1912), pp. 61 and 78.

11 Megasthenes' *Indica* has been lost; his record of pearl-diving in Sri Lanka is paraphrased by Arrian (*Indica* 8.1). Notice the claim that Sri Lankans 'hunt shellfish with nets'.

12 Pliny, *Natural Histories* 6.22 (24); his 'Taprobane' is modern Sri Lanka.

13 *The Mahavansi, the Raja-Ratnacari, and the Raja-vali*, ed. and trans. Edward Upham (London, 1833), vol. II, p. 191.

14 Al-Idrisi, *Edrisi-Géographie*, p. 75.

15 William Wood, *A History of Siam* (London, 1924), p. 101.

16 From the epic poem *Khun Chang Khun Paen*, in David Streckfuss, *Truth on Trial in Thailand: Defamation, Treason, and Lèse-Majesté* (Abingdon, 2010), p. 66.

17 Zhou Daguan, *The Customs of Cambodia*, 23a–b, paraphrased by Edward Schafer, 'The Development of Bathing Customs in Ancient and Medieval China and the History of the Floriate Clear Palace', *Journal of the American Oriental Society*, LXXVI (1956), pp. 57–82 (p. 62).

18 Hữu Ngọc, *Viet Nam: Tradition and Change* (Athens, OH, 2016), p. 218; Tri C. Tran and Tram Le, *Vietnamese Stories for Language Learners: Traditional Folktales in Vietnamese and English* (North Clarendon, VT, 2017), pp. 48, 58, 150.

19 Ooi Keat Gin, *Southeast Asia: A Historical Encyclopedia, from Angkor Wat to East Timor* (Santa Barbara, CA, 2004), vol. I, p. 1000; Cynthia Chou, *The Orang Suku Laut of Riau, Indonesia: The Inalienable Gift of Territory* (Abingdon, 2010), pp. 8, 42.

20 W. Ramsay Smith, *Myths and Legends of the Australian Aboriginals* (1932) (Mineola, NY, 2003), p. 304.

21 Te Rangi Hīroa, *The Coming of the Maori* (Nelson, New Zealand, 1929), p. 240; the earliest good written version is George Grey's *Polynesian Mythology* (London, 1855).

22 Eric Knudsen, *Teller of Tales: Stories from Kauai* (Honolulu, HI, 1945).

23 David Branner, 'Phonology in the Chinese Script and Its Relationship to Early Chinese Literacy', in *Writing and Literacy in Early China*, ed. Li Feng and David Branner (Seattle, WA, 2011), pp. 85–137 (p. 111); Andrew Morris, '"To Make the Four Hundred Million Move": The Late Qing Dynasty Origins of Modern Chinese Sport and Physical Culture', *Comparative Studies in Society and History*, XLII (2000), pp. 876–906 (p. 876).

24 Eleanor von Erdberg-Consten, 'A Hu with Pictorial Decoration: Werner Jannings Collection, Palace Museum, Peking', *Archives of the Chinese Art Society of America*, VI (1952), pp. 18–32 (p. 24, fig. 6). Another example is illustrated in Alfred Schinz, *The Magic Square: Cities in Ancient China* (Stuttgart, 1996), p. 96, fig. 2.3.6.16, but Schinz has taken elements of his drawing from Erdberg's piece.

25 Liu An, *The Huainanzi* 1.8, ed. and trans. John Major et al. (New York, 2010), p. 57.

26 Fan Chengda, 'Well-Balance Records of Guihai: Records of Savage: Tanka', and Zhou Qufei: 'The Tanka Savage', *Representative Answers from*

the Region Beyond Mountains, 3, both cited in Zhu Ruixin et al., *A Social History of Middle-Period China: The Song, Liao, Western Xia and Jin Dynasties* (Cambridge, 2016), pp. 282, 480.

27 Gang Deng, *Maritime Sector, Institutions, and Sea Power of Premodern China* (Westport, CT, 1999), p. 109; Klaas Ruitenbeek, 'Mazu, the Patroness of Sailors', in Chinese Pictorial Art', *Artibus Asiae*, LVIII (1999), pp. 281–329; Mike Speak, 'Recreation and Sport in Ancient China: Primitive Society to AD 960', in *Sport and Physical Education in China*, ed. James Riordan and Robin Jones [1999] (New York, 2002), pp. 20–44 (p. 42).

28 Joseph Needham and Colin Ronan, *The Shorter Science and Civilisation in China* (Cambridge, 1978), vol. III, p. 253; the shark story is from Lu Dian's *Piya*, a Song Dynasty Chinese dictionary (*c.* 1096 CE).

29 Needham and Ronan, *Science and Civilisation in China*, vol. III, pp. 246–53; for the mermaids in the *Sou Shén Ji*, see Vaughn Scribner, *Merpeople: A Human History* (London, 2020), p. 222.

30 Naian Shi, *The Water Margin: Outlaws of the Marsh*, trans. J. H. Jackson (Clarendon, VT, 2010), pp. 450–51, 496, 730, 741; see also Chapter Fifteen.

31 Zhou Mi, 'Observing the Tidal Bore', *Recollections of Wulin*, in *Inscribed Landscapes: Travel Writing from Imperial China*, ed. and trans. Richard Strassberg (Berkeley, CA, 1994), pp. 253–6 (pp. 254–5); Geremie Barmé, 'The Tide of Revolution', *China Heritage Quarterly*, XXVIII (2011), n.p.

32 María Theresa Uriarte, 'The Teotihuacan Ballgame and the Beginning of Time', *Ancient Mesoamerica*, XVII (2006), pp. 17–38.

33 Miwok: as recorded by Stephen Powell, *The Tribes of California*, Contributions to North American Ethnology, III (Washington, DC, 1877), p. 366; Wasco: Ella Clark, *Indian Legends of the Pacific Northwest* (Berkeley, CA, 1953), p. 102; Haida: John Bierhorst, *The Mythology of North America* (Oxford, 2002), p. 48; Squamish: Ella Clark, *Indian Legends of Canada* [1960] (Toronto, 2011), p. 30; there are more swimming stories in *Tales of the North American Indians* [1929], ed. Stith Thompson (Cambridge, MA, 1966).

34 Knud Rasmussen and W. Alexander Worster, 'Âtârssuaq', in *Eskimo Folk Tales* (London, 1921), pp. 142–6.

35 George Grinnell, *Blackfoot Lodge Tales: The Story of a Prairie People* (New York, 1907), p. 121.

36 Charles Leland, *The Algonquin Legends of New England* (Boston, MA, 1884), p. 230; Philip Barbour, ed., *The Jamestown Voyages under the First Charter, 1606–1609* (Cambridge, 1969), vol. I, p. 92, cited in Gregory Waselkov, 'Shellfish Gathering and Shell Midden Archaeology', *Advances in Archaeological Method and Theory*, X (1987), pp. 93–210 (p. 97).

37 Tom Mould, *Choctaw Tales* (Jackson, MS, 2004), p. 80. Against this, however, we must set John Rogers's story that 'The Choctaws laboured under a disadvantage which lost them many men, which was the want of the art of swimming' [1792], cited in Harold Gill Jr, 'Colonial Americans in the Swim', *Journal of the Colonial Williamsburg Foundation*, XXII–XXIV (2001–2), p. 27.

38 William Keegan and Lisabeth Carlson, *Talking Taíno: Essays on Caribbean Natural History from a Native Perspective* (Tuscaloosa, AL, 2008), pp. 57–8.

39 We know the story from the Maya text Popol Vuh. For the text of the
    Popol Vuh, see *Popol Vuh: The Definitive Edition of the Maya Book of the
    Dawn of Life and the Glories of Gods and Kings,* trans. Dennis Tedlock
    (New York, 1985); for a retelling of this story, see Karl Taube, *Aztec and
    Maya Myths* (Austin, TX, 1997). But see James Doyle and Stephen Houston,
    'A Watery Tableau at El Mirador, Guatemala', 12 April 2012, at https://
    mayadecipherment.com, accessed 13 December 2021, which suggests an
    alternative identification for the swimming figure. Note also an image
    of a merman, or a man emerging from a fish, in the Dresden Codex,
    c. 1200–1250 CE.
40 Heather McKillop, 'Prehistoric Maya Reliance on Marine Resources:
    Analysis of a Midden from Moho Cay, Belize', *Journal of Field Archaeology,*
    XI (1984), pp. 25–35 (p. 30); Karl Ruppert et al., *Bonampak, Chiapas, Mexico*
    (Washington, DC, 1955), p. 50, cited in Frederick Lange, 'Marine Resources:
    A Viable Subsistence Alternative for the Prehistoric Lowland Maya',
    American Anthropologist, LXXIII (1971), pp. 619–39 (p. 632).
41 Mary Helms, *Ancient Panama* (Austin, TX, 1979), p. 182.
42 Anna Roosevelt et al., 'Eighth Millennium Pottery from a Prehistoric Shell
    Midden in the Brazilian Amazon', *Science,* CCLIV (1991), pp. 1621–4 (p. 1624).
43 Robert A. Benfer Jr, 'The Preceramic Period Site of Paloma, Peru:
    Bioindications of Improving Adaptation to Sedentism', *Latin American
    Antiquity,* I (1990), pp. 284–318.
44 Joanne Pillsbury, 'The Thorny Oyster and the Origins of Empire:
    Implications of Recently Uncovered Spondylus Imagery from Chan
    Chan, Peru', *Latin American Antiquity,* VII (1996), pp. 313–40.

3 A NORTHERN SWIMMING HOLE

1 Tom Higham et al., 'The Earliest Evidence for Anatomically Modern
   Humans in Northwestern Europe', *Nature,* CDLXXIX (2011), pp. 521–4;
   Saioa López et al., 'Human Dispersal Out of Africa: A Lasting Debate',
   Evolutionary Bioinformatics Online, XI, suppl. 2 (2015), pp. 57–68.
2 John Inge Svendsen et al., 'Geo-Archaeological Investigations of
   Palaeolithic Sites along the Ural Mountains: On the Northern Presence
   of Humans during the Last Ice Age', *Quaternary Science Reviews,* XXIX
   (2010), pp. 3138–56; Alexander Gavashelishvili and David Tarkhnishvili,
   'Biomes and Human Distribution during the Last Ice Age', *Global Ecology
   and Biogeography,* XXV (2016), pp. 563–74.
3 Stefano Benazzi et al., 'Early Dispersal of Modern Humans in Europe and
   Implications for Neanderthal Behaviour', *Nature,* CDLXXIX (2011), pp. 525–8;
   Odile Peyron et al., 'Climatic Reconstruction in Europe for 18,000 YR B.P.
   from Pollen Data', *Quaternary Research,* XLIX (1998), pp. 183–96; Patrick
   Bartlein et al., 'Pollen-Based Continental Climate Reconstructions at 6 and
   21 ka: A Global Synthesis', *Climate Dynamics,* XXXVII (2011), pp. 775–802, fig. 7;
   Jeremiah Marsicek et al., 'Reconciling Divergent Trends and Millennial

Variations in Holocene Temperatures', *Nature*, DLIV (2018), pp. 92–6, and Patrick Bartlein, personal communication.

4 Norbert Aujoulat, *Lascaux: Movement, Space and Time* (New York, 2005), pp. 177–8, 182.

5 Iain Mathieson et al., 'Genome-Wide Patterns of Selection in 230 Ancient Eurasians', *Nature*, DXXVIII (2015), pp. 499–503.

6 Sébastien Villotte, Sofija Stefanovic and Christopher Knüsel, 'External Auditory Exostoses and Aquatic Activities during the Mesolithic and the Neolithic in Europe: Results from a Large Prehistoric Sample', *Anthropologie* (Czech Republic), LII (2014), pp. 73–89.

7 *Lament for Sumer and Urim* c.2.2.3, *The Epic of Gilgamesh: The Babylonian Epic Poem and Other Texts in Akkadian and Sumerian*, trans. Andrew George (Harmondsworth, 1999), pp. 92, 162; *Epic of Gilgamesh* Tablets IX and XI, *The Epic of Gilgamesh*, trans. Maureen Kovacs (Stanford, CA, 1985), pp. 100–101.

8 Gina Konstantopoulos, 'The Bitter Sea and the Waters of Death: The Sea as a Conceptual Border in Mesopotamia', *Journal of Ancient Civilizations*, XXXV (2020), pp. 171–97 (pp. 171, 175, 177); Lorenzo Verderame, 'The Sea in Sumerian Literature', *Water History*, XII (2020), pp. 75–91 (p. 77). Margaret Cool Root (personal communication) confirms that she knows of no Mesopotamian seals with images of swimming.

9 Sargon and Ur-Zababa c.2.1.4, *Lament for Sumer and Urim* c.2.2.3, c.2.5.3.4, Proverbs 5.42, 3.88, *Electronic Text Corpus of Sumerian Literature*, https://etcsl.orinst.ox.ac.uk, accessed 3 May 2021; Jerrold Cooper, review of Hermann Behrens, *Enlil und Ninlil: Ein sumerischer Mythos aus Nippur*, *Journal of Cuneiform Studies*, XXXII (1980), pp. 175–88 (p. 180). An inscription of Iahdun-Līm (*c.* 1800 BCE) does mention that his conquering troops 'bathed themselves in the sea', however: Konstantopoulos, 'The Bitter Sea', p. 183.

10 Sharukkin I: Benjamin Foster, 'Another Sargonic Water Ordeal?', *Nouvelles assyriologiques brèves et utilitaires*, III (1989), pp. 56–91 (pp. 56, 90–91, no. 115); David Owen, 'A Unique Late Sargonic River Ordeal in the John Frederick Lewis Collection', in *A Scientific Humanist: Studies in Memory of Abraham Sachs*, ed. E. Leichty et al. (Philadelphia, PA, 1988), pp. 305–11; Egbert Von Weiher, 'Bemerkungen zu § 2 KH und zur Andwendung des Flussordals', *Zeitschrift für Assyriologie*, LXXI (1981), pp. 95–102. Third Dynasty of Ur: J. Nicholas Postgate, *Early Mesopotamia: Society and Economy at the Dawn of History* (London, 1992), p. 26; Guillaume Cardascia, 'L'ordalie fluviale dans la Mésopotamie ancienne', *Revue historique de droit français et étranger*, LXXI (1993), pp. 169–84; Sophie Lafont and Bertrand Lafont, 'Un récit d'ordalie', *Nouvelles assyriologiques brèves et utilitaires*, III (1989), p. 28, no. 43, and especially Jean Bottéro, 'L'ordalie en Mésopotamie ancienne', *Annali della Scuola Normale Superiore di Pisa*, XI (1981), pp. 1005–67.

11 *Code of Hammurabi* 2, 133a; Niek Veldhuis, *Elementary Education at Nippur: The Lists of Trees and Wooden Objects* (Groningen, 1997), pp. 127–8 (ll. 19–24);

see also Bendt Alster, *Proverbs of Ancient Sumer: The World's Earliest Proverb Collections* (Bethesda, MD, 1997), p. 12, sec. D4: 'Even a millstone will float in the river for a righteous man.' The establishment of the Akkadian Empire may have turned Mesopotamians more away from the Persian Gulf and the swimmers there: Verderame, 'The Sea in Sumerian Literature', pp. 86–7.

12 Péter Tóth, 'River Ordeal – Trial by Water – Swimming of Witches: Procedures of Ordeal in Witch Trials', in *Demons, Spirits, Witches*, ed. Gábor Klaniczay and Éva Pócs (Budapest, 2008), vol. III, pp. 129–63 (p. 131); Charles Horne, 'Introduction', *The Code of Hammurabi*, trans. L.W. King (1915), https://sourcebooks.fordham.edu/ancient/hamcode.asp, accessed 5 August 2021.

13 See Isaiah 25:11; Ezekiel 47:5; Exodus 2 and 14:13–30; translations adapted from the New King James Version. The story probably draws from a well-known Egyptian story, already a thousand years old in the time of Moses, in which a magician parts the waters of a pool to retrieve an entertainer's lost jewel. Like that story (known to us from the Westcar Papyrus), the Exodus story employs a 'speech within a speech' structure.

14 Carlo Peretto et al., 'Living-Floors and Structures from the Lower Paleolithic to the Bronze Age in Italy', *Collegium antropologicum*, XXVIII (2004), pp. 63–88 (p. 76); Antonio Tagliacozzo, 'Animal Exploitation in the Early Neolithic in Central-Southern Italy', *Munibe (Antropologia-Arkeologia) 57: Homenaje a Jesús Altuna* (2005), pp. 429–39.

15 Sarah Parcak, *Archaeology from Space: How the Future Shapes Our Past* (New York, 2019), pp. 137–42.

16 'Swim', 'Mere' and 'Natant', *Oxford English Dictionary Online*; Anatoly Liberman, 'Watered Down Etymologies (*Ocean* and *Sea*)', *Oxford Etymologist*, 7 October 2009, https://blog.oup.com, accessed 3 May 2021; Robert Beekes, *Pre-Greek: Phonology, Morphology, Lexicon* (Leiden, 2014), p. 14; see also Adam Hyllested, *Word Exchange at the Gates of Europe: Five Millennia of Language Contact* (Copenhagen, 2014), p. 59.

17 Peter Warren, 'The Miniature Fresco from the West House at Akrotiri, Thera, and Its Aegean Setting', *Journal of Hellenic Studies*, XCIX (1979), pp. 115–29. The exact date of the eruption is disputed.

18 Ibid., p. 126; Sinclair Hood, *The Arts in Prehistoric Greece* [1978] (New Haven, CT, 1994), p. 161; Agnès Sakellariou, 'La Scène du "Siège" sur le rhyton d'argent de Mycènes d'après une nouvelle reconstitution', *Revue archéologique*, n.s., II (1975), pp. 195–208.

19 Arthur Evans, *The Palace of Minos at Knossos* (London, 1921), vol. I, figs 228–30; Hood, *Arts in Prehistoric Greece*, p. 132; Warren, 'The Miniature Fresco', p. 126; Spyridon Marinatos, 'The "Swimmers' Dagger" from the Tholos Tomb at Vaphio', in *Essays in Aegean Archaeology Presented to Sir Arthur Evans*, ed. Stanley Casson (Oxford, 1927), pp. 63–71; Arthur Evans, *The Palace of Minos* (London, 1930), vol. III, p. 127.

20 Abdul Jamil Khan, *Urdu/Hindi: An Artificial Divide: African Heritage, Mesopotamian Roots, Indian Culture and British Colonialism* (New York, 2006), p. 93.

21 *Hymns of the Rig Veda*, Hymns 98, 71, 10.71, 15, trans. Ralph Griffith [1889] (Kotagiri, 1896).

22 Or, perhaps, that the women were tied up. In the Han Dynasty *Shiji*. See Wei Wang and Lachun Wang, 'The Influence of Witchcraft Culture on Ancient Chinese Water Relations: A Case Study of the Yellow River Basin', *European Journal of Remote Sensing*, LIII (2020), pp. 93–103.

23 Poem 35, 'Valley Wind'; translation adapted for the rhyme; see also Poem 9, 'The Han is Broad'; Shijing, *The Book of Songs*, ed. Joseph Allen, trans. Arthur Waley [1937] (London, 2005), pp. 82, 101.

24 *Zhuangzi* 19; adapted from Burton Watson, *The Complete Works of Zhuangzi* (New York, 2013), p. 298, and other similar translations.

25 *Yellow Emperor's Classic of Internal Medicine*, quoted in Don Wyatt, 'A Certain Whiteness of Being: Chinese Perceptions of Self by the Beginning of European Contact', in *Race and Racism in Modern East Asia: Western and Eastern Constructions*, ed. Rotem Kowner and Walter Demel (Leiden, 2013), pp. 307–26 (pp. 320–21).

26 Menglong Feng, *Stories to Caution the World: A Ming Dynasty Collection*, trans. Shuhui Yang and Yunquin Yang (Seattle, WA, 2005), pp. 366–7.

27 The recent excavation of the skeleton of a man who appears to have died in a shark attack does not necessarily indicate that he was swimming; he might just as well have fallen out of a boat (J. Alyssa White et al., '3000-Year-Old Shark Attack Victim from Tsukumo Shell-Mound, Okayama, Japan', *Journal of Archaeological Science: Reports*, XXXVIII (2021), 103065).

28 *From the Morning of the World: Poems from the Manyoshu: The First Anthology of Japanese Poetry*, trans. Graeme Wilson (London, 1991), p. 46.

29 Sei Shōnagon, *The Pillow Book*, trans. Meredith McKinney (London, 2006), p. 243.

30 Susan Hanley, *Everyday Things in Premodern Japan: The Hidden Legacy of Material Culture* (Berkeley, CA, 1999), p. 99; Scott Clark, *Japan: A View from the Bath* (Honolulu, HI, 1994), pp. 22–7.

4 DANGER, SEX, GODS AND STRANGERS

1 Hesiod, *Works and Days*, ll. 737–41, 758–9.

2 Herodotus, *Histories* 1.138.2, 4.75.

3 *The Sacred Books of the East: Pahlavi Texts*, I, ed. F. Max Müller (Oxford, 1880), pp. 84–7; Ezekiel 32:2–14.

4 *Book of Arda Viraf* 20.4–5, 41.5–8, 58, 72 (*The Sacred Books and Early Literature of the East*, vol. VII: *Ancient Persia*, ed. Charles Horne, trans. Martin Haug (New York, 1917)); Jason BeDuhn, *The Manichaean Body: In Discipline and Ritual* (Baltimore, MD, 2000), p. 48. Dating of the *Book of Arda Viraf* is uncertain; it could be as late as the 900s CE. But Hesiod, too, warns against bathing in water where a woman has bathed.

5 Edward Schafer, 'The Development of Bathing Customs in Ancient and Medieval China and the History of the Floriate Clear Palace', *Journal of*

the American Oriental Society, LXXVI (1956), pp. 57–82 (pp. 57–80). Schafer suggests that Native American traditions of sweat lodges may have come with them from East Asia. See also Lee Butler, '"Washing Off the Dust": Baths and Bathing in Late Medieval Japan', *Monumenta Nipponica*, LX (2005), pp. 1–41 (p. 6).

6 *Epic of Gilgamesh*, Tablet 1, pp. 8–9; Homer, *Odyssey*, book 12. See H. N. Couch, 'Swimming among the Greeks and Barbarians', *Classical Journal*, XXIX (1934), pp. 609–12 (p. 611), though Couch mistakenly imagines that the Greeks were great swimmers.

7 Bathsheba: 2 Samuel 11:2; Susanna: Daniel 13; *The Jataka Tales*, trans. Henry Francis and Edward Thomas (Cambridge, 1916), pp. 259–60. For more references to bathing, see *The Jātaka; or, Stories of the Buddha's Former Births*, VI, trans. Edward Cowell and William Rouse (Cambridge, 1907), pp. 21, 43, 92 and *passim*. More bathing tanks appear on pp. 159, 161–3 and 205.

8 Howard Giskin, *Chinese Folktales* (Lincolnwood, IL, 1997), p. 58; Schafer, 'Bathing Customs', pp. 59–62.

9 The William Davidson Talmud (https://sefaria.org, accessed 9 August 2021): *Pesachim* 51a. The Talmud is a Jewish commentary on the Torah (the Bible) written in Babylon in the 500s CE.

10 Cicero, *Pro Caelio* 36; *De moralia* 1.35; Plutarch, *Cato the Elder* 20.5; Fikret Yegül, *Bathing in the Roman World* (Cambridge, 2010), pp. 29–30, with other examples.

11 Ovid, *Ars amatoria* 3.9; *Metamorphoses* 5.572 ff, 3.138; see also the terrible story of Scylla's transformation into a monster while she's wading (*Metamorphoses* 14.1–74); the transformation of the Lycians into frogs (*Metamorphoses* 6.313–81); and so on. For a more complete list, see Robert Schmiel, 'The Story of Aura (Nonnos, 'Dionysiaca' 48.238–978)', *Hermes*, CXXI (1993), pp. 470–83.

12 From the tenth canto of the *Bhagavad Purana* (800–1000 CE). The story reflects a new South Indian interpretation of Krishna as playful lover that appears around this time: Sugata Ray, *Climate Change and the Art of Devotion: Geoaesthetics in the Land of Krishna, 1550–1850* (Seattle, WA, 2019), p. 10.

13 Schafer, 'Bathing Customs', pp. 64–5; Talmud: *Gittin* 67.

14 Piers Mitchell, 'Human Parasites in the Roman World: Health Consequences of Conquering an Empire', *Parasitology*, CXLIV (2016), pp. 48–58.

15 Homer, *The Odyssey*, trans. Emily Wilson (New York, 2017), ll. 89–108; Vaughn Scribner, *Merpeople: A Human History* (London, 2020), pp. 9–10; Manal Shalaby, 'The Middle Eastern Mermaid: Between Myth and Religion', in *Scaled for Success: The Internationalisation of the Mermaid*, ed. Philip Hayward (Bloomington, IN, 2018), pp. 7–20 (pp. 9–11); Genesis 7:19–22.

16 Job 41:1–34; John Day, *God's Conflict with the Dragon and the Sea: Echoes of a Canaanite Myth in the Old Testament* (Cambridge, 1985), pp. 2, 11, 43 and *passim*.

17 Leonidas, *Anthologia Palatina* 7.604, 7.506; Pliny, *Natural Histories* 9.4.4–5; S. Rhie Quintanilla, *History of Early Stone Sculpture at Mathura, ca. 150 BCE–100 CE* (Leiden, 2007), pp. 21 and 74; Ray, *Climate Change*, p. 41, fig. 1.12; Pausanias 1.44.8; Oppian, *Halieutica* 5.21–2, c. 170 CE; Emily Kneebone, *Oppian's Halieutica: Charting a Didactic Epic* (Cambridge, 2020), pp. 339, 353. All the monsters of the sea, Oppian says, are worse than their counterparts on land.

18 Zhong Guan, *Guanzi: Political, Economic, and Philosophical Essays from Early China: A Study and Translation*, trans. W. Allyn Rickett (Princeton, NJ, 1998), vol. I, p. 64 (I, 2), and vol. II, pp. 105–6 (XIV, 39); Gan Bao, 'Sou Shen Ji' 搜神记: *Collection of Folk Legends on Ghosts, Immortals and Spirits in Ancient China* (London, 2018), p. 158 (12.7); Jan Groot, *The Religious System of China*, vol. II: *On the Soul and Ancestral Worship* (Leiden, 1892), p. 522; Michael Foster, *The Book of Yokai: Mysterious Creatures of Japanese Folklore* (Berkeley, CA, 2015), p. 159. The sixth-century CE pilgrim Xuanzang used scripture to ward off demons when he crossed rivers: *Journey to the West*, trans. and ed. Anthony Yu, revd edn (Chicago, IL, 2012), vol. I, p. 65.

19 Pliny, *Natural Histories* 8.81; Augustine, *City of God* 18.17; Isidore, *Etymologies* 11.4.1.

20 Fredegar, *Chronicles* 3.9, from Burgundy in France; he calls the monster a *quinotaur*. Duane Roller has collected other examples of Greek and Roman fear of the ocean: *Through the Pillars of Herakles: Greco-Roman Exploration of the Atlantic* (Abingdon, 2006), pp. 2, 11 and *passim*.

21 Rodney Needham, 'Jātaka, Pañcatantra, and Kodi Fables', *Journal of the Humanities and Social Sciences of Southeast Asia*, CXVI (1960), pp. 232–62 (pp. 250–51). A similar story appears in Praphulladatta Goswami, *Essays on the Folklore and Culture of North-Eastern India* (Guwahati, 1982), p. 32.

22 No early version of this story survives; the oldest complete literary version is in Ovid's *Heroides* 18–19, and shortly afterwards it is illustrated on several wall frescoes at Pompeii.

23 Abolqasem Firdawsi, *Shahnameh: The Persian Book of Kings*, trans. Dick Davis [1997] (New York, 2006), pp. 70–101; Dick Davis, 'Women in the Shahnameh: Exotics and Natives, Rebellious Legends, and Dutiful Histories', in *Women and the Medieval Epic: Gender, Genre, and the Limits of Epic Masculinity*, ed. Sara Poor and Jana Schulman (New York, 2007), pp. 67–90 (p. 70).

24 For a long list of Greek and Roman drownings, see John McManamon, *Caligula's Barges and the Renaissance Origins of Nautical Archaeology under Water* (College Station, TX, 2016), p. 153, and his 'Neither Letters nor Swimming', pp. 257–8.

25 This story was recorded by Pliny (*Natural Histories* 9.8.3–6), Aelian (*On Animals* 6.15), Aulus Gellius (*Attic Nights* 6.8) and Apion (*Aegyptiaca* 5), who claimed to have seen it himself.

26 Isidore, *Etymologies* 5.27.35; Quran 11.50 (trans. Arthur Arberry, *The Koran Interpreted* (New York, 1955)).

27 Liu An, *The Huainanzi*, trans. John Major et al. (New York, 2010), p. 57, Proverb 1.8; Schafer, 'Bathing Customs', pp. 61–2.

28 Pliny, *Natural Histories* 7.2, based on the account of Phylarchus from the 200s BCE; there may be some relationship here to Arrian's repeated description of the water currents around the Black Sea being lighter (warmer) so they flow on top of heavier (colder) water in his *Periplus of the Euxine Sea*. Plutarch (*Symposium* 5.7) also quotes Phylarchus to the effect that they were magicians who could sicken people with a look (as Pliny says) or with their breath, but without mentioning floating.

29 *Zhuangzi* 18, from *The Complete Works of Zhuangzi*, trans. Watson, p. 143 and *passim*; Aristotle, *History of Animals* 8.2; see Jessica Gelber, 'Aristotle on Essence and Habitat', *Oxford Studies in Ancient Philosophy*, XLVIII (2015), pp. 267–93; Philo, *On the Creation*, XX–XXI, Loeb Classical Library 226, pp. 49–51; and see also the apochryphal *Wisdom of Solomon* 19, probably also written in Alexandria around the time of Philo; Edward West, *The Sacred Books of the East: Pahlavi Texts* (Oxford, 1880), vol. I, p. 179. A century after Philo, Oppian expands on this idea in his *Halieutica*; it appears again in the late medieval tales of Sindbad the Sailor (*Sindbad the Sailor and Other Stories from the Arabian Nights*, trans. Laurence Housman (London, 1911), p. 38).

5 LEARNING TO SWIM

1 Iamblichus, *Life of Pythagoras*; Herodotus, *Histories* 1.30.1. Martin Bernal's *Black Athena: The Afroasiatic Roots of Classical Civilization* (Ithaca, NY, 1987), vol. I, was the first serious look at the enormous influence Africans had on the Greeks, but now see, for example, Caitlín Eilís Barrett, 'Egypt in Roman Visual and Material Culture', Oxford Handbooks Online, May 2017, www.oxfordhandbooks.com, and Roger Matthews and Cornelia Roemer, ed., *Ancient Perspectives on Egypt* [2003] (London, 2016).

2 Leviticus 19:19; Deuteronomy 22:11; Aeschylus, *Suppliants*, ll. 234–45; Molly Swetnam-Burland, *Egypt in Italy* (Cambridge, 2015), p. 20; Margarita Gleba, 'Linen Production in Pre-Roman and Roman Italy', in *Purpureae Vestes: Actas del I Symposium Internacional sobre Textiles y Tintes del Mediterráneo en época romana 2002*, ed. Carmen Alfaro Giner, John Wild and Benjamí Costa Ribas (Ibiza, 2004), pp. 29–38.

3 Herodotus, *Histories* 1.1.1: they brought Egyptian trade goods; 2.36–7: Egyptian customs; 2.43: Herakles comes from Egypt.

4 Amelia Blanford Edwards, *Pharaohs, Fellahs and Explorers* (New York, 1891), p. 209; James Breasted, *The Battle of Kadesh: A Study in the Earliest Known Military Strategy* (Chicago, IL, 1903), pl. III.

5 For example, OI A22289A, on exhibit; Harold Liebowitz, 'Late Bronze II Ivory Work in Palestine: Evidence of a Cultural Highpoint', *Bulletin of the American Schools of Oriental Research*, CCLXV (1987), pp. 3–24 (pp. 12–14). The Oriental Institute calls these spoons 'Palestinian', but

that seems anachronistic. For another ivory example from Cyprus, see British Museum 1897, 0401.1125.

6 Ralph Thomas, *Swimming* (London, 1904), pp. 78–9.

7 For a different opinion, see Eric Chaline, *Strokes of Genius: A History of Swimming* (London, 2017), p. 91.

8 II Kings 5:8–13; see also Leviticus 15:1–13; see Esti Dvorjetski, *Leisure, Pleasure and Healing: Spa Culture and Medicine in Ancient Eastern Mediterranean* (Leiden, 2007), p. 72.

9 Leviticus 11:9–12.

10 Zhong Guan, *Guanzi: Political, Economic, and Philosophical Essays from Early China: A Study and Translation*, trans. W. Allyn Rickett, vol. II (Princeton, NJ, 1998), pp. 454–5. The word 'swimmers' in the context of the battle is, however, an emendation where the text is faulty.

11 Proverbs 17.5, 11.5; 11.21; 14.10; 14.14, in Liu An, *The Huainanzi*, ed. and trans. John Major et al. (New York, 2010), pp. 404, 428, 541, 542, 666.

12 Shiju 49, 0166d; Edward Schafer, 'The Development of Bathing Customs in Ancient and Medieval China and the History of the Floriate Clear Palace', *Journal of the American Oriental Society*, LXXVI (1956), pp. 57–82 (p. 60).

13 David Knechtges, 'Southern Metal and Feather Fan: The "Southern Consciousness" of Lu Ji', and Xiaofei Tian, 'Fan Writing: Lu Ji, Lu Yun and the Cultural Transactions between North and South', both in *Southern Identity and Southern Estrangement in Medieval Chinese Poetry*, ed. Ping Wang and Nicholas Williams (Hong Kong, 2015), pp. 19–42 (p. 39) and pp. 43–78 (p. 43); Karen Carr, 'A Short History of Feather Fans' Spread and Cultural Connotations, from Bronze Age Africa East to China and West to Europe', *Journal of World History*, XXXIII (2022), pp. 1–36.

14 Schafer, 'Bathing Customs', p. 71. The Bronze Age Egyptian *Story of the Green Jewel*, in which King Snefru rides in a boat rowed by pretty girls wearing bead-net dresses (Aylward Blackman, 'Philological Notes', *Journal of Egyptian Archaeology*, II (1925), pp. 210–15) provides an older parallel, but the Egyptian version omits the shipwreck.

15 Li Daoyuan, *Annotated Classic of Water (Shui jingzhu)*, cited in Fan Ka-wai, 'The Period of Division and the Tang Period', in *Chinese Medicine and Healing: An Illustrated History*, ed. T. J. Hinrichs and Linda Barnes (Cambridge, MA, 2013), pp. 65–96 (p. 80).

16 Soldiers: Dunhuang (Mogao) Cave 12 South Wall, lower right of main panels (www.e-dunhuang.com); on the lower left of the scene, one swimmer may be using a breaststroke; swimmers, Cave 212 (Cave of the Seafarers), Kizil, Kucha, about 500 CE. Now in Museum für Indische Kunst, Berlin, III 8398. Marylin Rhie, *Early Buddhist Art of China and Central Asia* (Leiden, 2010), fig. 5.50, after *Along the Ancient Silk Routes: Central Asian Art from the West Berlin State Museums*, ed. Herbert Härtel and Marianne Yaldiz, exh. cat., Metropolitan Museum of Art, New York, 1982, no. 15.

17 Lotus ponds and apsaras: Ceiling of Cave 257, Dunhuang (439–534 CE): Ning Qiang, *Art, Religion, and Politics in Medieval China: The Dunhuang Cave of the Zhai Family* (Honolulu, HI, 2004), p. 33, fig. 1.20; Naomi

McPherson, ed., *Frescoes and Fables: Mural Stories from the Mogao Grottoes in Dunhuang* (Beijing, 1998), p. 145; more swimming apsaras: The Maitrakanyaka Legend: Cave 212 (Cave of the Seafarers), *Along the Ancient Silk Routes*, pp. 218–19. See also Caves 217 and 420 at Dunhuang, and a stone stele from Sichuan: Dorothy Wong, 'Four Sichuan Buddhist Steles and the Beginnings of Pure Land Imagery in China', *Archives of Asian Art*, LI (1998/9), pp. 56–79 (fig. 1A).

18 Xu Jing (or Hsü Ching) (1093–1155), Chinese emissary to Korea, paraphrased by Schafer, 'Bathing Customs', p. 62.

19 In the *Nihon Shoki* and the *Kojiki*; Scott Clark, *Japan: A View from the Bath* (Honolulu, HI, 1994), pp. 21–2; Lesley Wynn, 'Self-Reflection in the Tub: Japanese Bathing Culture, Identity, and Cultural Nationalism', *Asia Pacific Perspectives*, XII (2014), pp. 61–78 (pp. 61, 67–8).

20 Stephen Turnbull, *The Samurai: A Military History* [1977] (New York, 1996), p. 53; a variant of this story forms part of the third act of Namiki Senryū and Miyoshi Shōraku's play *Gempei Nunobiki no Taki* (Osaka, 1749). Note the similarity to (and differences from) an earlier story told by both Suetonius and Tacitus about the Roman empress Agrippina the Younger and her enslaved attendant (see Chapter Six).

21 *Odyssey* 5.334–457, trans. Emily Wilson (New York, 2017). I have mangled the poetry to shorten this important passage.

22 Jeffrey Hurwit, 'The Shipwreck of Odysseus: Strong and Weak Imagery in Late Geometric Art', *American Journal of Archaeology*, CXV (2011), pp. 1–18 (p. 7).

23 Boris Mijat, 'Schwimmer und Ertrinkende, Gefallene und Wasserleichen: Betrachtungen zu Seekrieg und Seenot in der geometrischen Vasenmalerei des 8. Jh.s. v. Chr.', *Skyllis: Zeitschrift für Unterwasserarchäologie*, I (2012), pp. 22–30.

24 Ibid., p. 27.

25 *Odyssey* 4.84, 4.226–32, 4.351; Middle Kingdom story adapted from Ernest Wallis Budge, *The Literature of the Ancient Egyptians* (London, 1914), p. 210; Tim Whitmarsh, *Narrative and Identity in the Ancient Greek Novel: Returning Romance* (Cambridge, 2011), p. 14; James Morrison, *Shipwrecked: Disaster and Transformation in Homer, Shakespeare, Defoe, and the Modern World* (Ann Arbor, MI, 2014), pp. 30–33.

26 Silius Italicus 1.261–4: *ignotique amnis tranare sonantia saxa atque e diversa socios accersere ripa*; Appian, *Punica*, 20, about the Roman general Scipio's siege of Carthage during the Second Punic War; Livy, *History of Rome* 28.36.12–13, telling the story of the Carthaginian general Mago's attack on the Romans in Spain during the same war; see John McManamon, 'Neither Letters nor Swimming': The Rebirth of Swimming and Free-Diving (Leiden, 2021), p. 140. Despite McManamon's suggestion (p. 137) that Hannibal prized swimming because his father had drowned, Hamilcar is said to have drowned not swimming but riding a horse across a river (Diodorus Siculus 25.10.4).

27 Jean Turfa, 'International Contacts: Commerce, Trade, and Foreign Affairs', in *Etruscan Life and Afterlife: A Handbook of Etruscan Studies*,

ed. Larissa Bonfante (Detroit, MI, 1986), pp. 66–91 (p. 67); Jean Gran-Aymerich and Jean Turfa, 'Economy and Commerce through Material Evidence: Etruscan Goods in the Mediterranean World and Beyond', in *The Etruscan World*, ed. Jean Turfa (New York, 2013), pp. 373–425.

28 Emmanuel Voutyras, 'The Introduction of the Alphabet', in *A History of Ancient Greek: From the Beginnings to Late Antiquity*, ed. Anastasios-Phoivos Christidis (Cambridge, 2007), pp. 266–76 (p. 273).

29 Robert Palmer, *Rome and Carthage at Peace* (Stuttgart, 1997), pp. 55, 61 and *passim*.

30 Annette Rathje, 'Silver Relief Bowls from Italy', *Analecta Romana Instituti Danici*, IX (1980), pp. 7–47 (esp. pp. 11, 14); Bruno d'Agostino and Giovanni Garbini, 'La patera orientalizzante da Pontecagnano riesaminata', *Studi Etruschi*, XLV (1977), pp. 51–62 (p. 53).

31 Livy, *History of Rome* 2.10; 2.12.5; 2.13.6–9.

32 Diodorus Siculus, *Library of History* 14.114.6–7 (Battle of the Allia).

33 From Vulci, by the Micali painter, now Vatican Museum cat. 34604 (520–510 BCE), among many examples.

34 R. Ross Holloway, 'The Tomb of the Diver', *American Journal of Archaeology*, CX (2006), pp. 365–88.

35 For example, British Museum 1909.0617.2, Hermitage Museum KO.–II; for a Greek version, see Metropolitan Museum of Art 31.11.13; Herodotus, *Histories* 4.23.2.

36 Thucydides, *History of the Peloponnesian War* 7.30.

37 Plutarch, *Life of Alexander* 58; Arrian, *The Campaigns of Alexander* 2.4.7–8; McManamon, *Neither Letters nor Swimming*, pp. 132–3.

38 Related to the Thracians: Herodotus, *Histories* 7.75; Xenophon and Strabo agree. Driven into the water: Appian, *Mithridates* 7.50.

39 Ammianus Marcellinus, *Res Gestae* 30.1.8. They eventually cross by swimming their horses.

40 For example, British Museum GR 1837.6–9.59 (Cat. Vases E 135); Istanbul Archaeology Museum, frieze of women on horseback from Dascylenium, 5th century BCE, https://flickr.com/photos/carolemage/5690685241.

41 Herodotus, *Histories* 1.8–10.

42 Johannes Haubold, 'The Achaemenid Empire and the Sea', *Mediterranean Historical Review*, XXVII (2012), pp. 5–24.

43 Vālmīki, *The Ramayana*, trans. Manmatha Dutt (Calcutta, 1893), pp. 1519, 1542, 1677, 1931 and *passim*.

44 *The Jataka Tales*, trans. Henry Francis and Edward Thomas, pp. 111, 405, 126; Uma Chakravarti, *The Social Dimensions of Early Buddhism* [1987] (Delhi, 1996), p. 137; *The India Travel Planner* (New Delhi, 1995), p. 359.

45 Buddha walks on water: Great Stupa in Sanchi, 3rd century BCE; river monsters: Government Museum, Mathura, 17.1344, both illustrated in Sugata Ray, *Climate Change and the Art of Devotion: Geoaesthetics in the Land of Krishna, 1550–1850* (Seattle, WA, 2019), p. 41, figs 1.11, 1.12.

46 *The Jātaka*, vol. VI, p. 23.

6 ANCIENT GREECE AND ROME

1 Herodotus, *Histories* 1.10.3, 1.131–40.
2 On shifting distinctions among race, ethnicity and identity, see Edith Hall, *Inventing the Barbarian* (Oxford, 1989); Denise McCoskey, *Race: Antiquity and Its Legacy* (Oxford, 2012); and Rebecca Futo Kennedy, 'Why I Teach About Race and Ethnicity in the Classical World', *Eidolon*, 11 September 2017, https://eidolon.pub, accessed 4 May 2021. On Greek identity following the Peloponnesian War, see *Ethnicity and Identity in Herodotus*, ed. Thomas Figueira and Carmen Soares (Abingdon, 2020).
3 Herodotus, *Histories* 6.44.3; Pausanias, *Description of Greece* 1.32.7.
4 Apollonides, in *Anthologia Palatina* 9.29; Herodotus, *Histories* 8.8; Frank Frost, 'Scyllias: Diving in Antiquity', *Greece and Rome*, xv (1968), pp. 180–85.
5 Herodotus, *Histories* 1.138, 8.89.
6 *Pace* Barry Strauss, who thinks that the Persian allies 'would surely have mastered the skill of swimming': *The Battle of Salamis: The Naval Encounter that Saved Greece – and Western Civilization* (New York, 2004), p. 204.
7 Eleni Manolaraki, '*Aqua Trajana*: Pliny and the Column of Trajan', paper presented at the 103rd Meeting of the Classical Association of the Middle West and South, Cincinnati, OH, 2007; John McManamon, *Caligula's Barges and the Renaissance Origins of Nautical Archaeology Under Water* (College Station, TX, 2016), p. 168.
8 *Iliad* 21.136–99, 16.745–50. See John McManamon, '*Neither Letters nor Swimming': The Rebirth of Swimming and Free-Diving* (Leiden, 2021), pp. 63, 149.
9 Herodotus, *Histories* 1.136.2.
10 μήτε γράμματα μήτε νεῖν ἐπίστωνται: Plato, *Laws*, Book III, 689d: 'in the words of the proverb, they know neither their letters nor how to swim.' An earlier hint of the same attitude may appear in Homer, whose Sirens tempt Odysseus to drown himself by promising him 'greater knowledge, since . . . we know/ whatever happens anywhere on earth'. *Odyssey* 12.188–91, trans. Emily Wilson (New York, 2018). For other ancient uses of this proverb, see McManamon, '*Neither Letters nor Swimming*', pp. 5–6.
11 Cicero, *Letters to His Friends* 7.10; Ovid, *Ex Ponto* 1.8.38; Seneca, *Epistles* 83; Horace, *Odes* 3.7.
12 Swimming races: Pausanias 2.35, about 150 CE; see also Lucian, *Toxaris* 20, cited in Lionel Casson, *Ships and Seamanship in the Ancient World* (Baltimore, MD, 1995), p. 181 n. 66; the late antique poet Nonnus also writes about (fictional) swimming races: *Dionysiaca* 11.7–55, 11.404–31; see McManamon, '*Neither Letters nor Swimming*', pp. 164–5.
13 Strabo, *Geography* 6.2.9.
14 William Harris, *Ancient Literacy* (Cambridge, MA, 1989) estimates that about 20–30 per cent of the residents of Hellenistic cities could read. Ralph Thomas doubted long ago that most Greeks could either read or swim (*History and Bibliography of Swimming* (London, 1904), p. 88). This undermines Fabio Maniscalco's argument that not knowing how to swim

was as anomalous as not knowing how to read ('Il Nuoto nel Mondo Antico', *Mélanges de l'école française de Rome*, III (1999), pp. 145–56).

15 Suetonius, *Julius Caesar* 57.1 (the scouts) and 64 (the papers); Plutarch, *Caesar* 49; Appian, *Civil Wars* 2.13 (90). Caesar is not swimming underwater in Appian, as McManamon would have it, but only out of his depth: 'fleeing by leaping into the sea and swimming across the very deep water': φεύγων ἐς τὴν θάλατταν ἐξήλατο καὶ ἐς πολὺ ἐν τῷ βυθῷ διενήξατο (McManamon, *'Neither Letters nor Swimming'*, p. 337). For a more positive view of Roman (but not Greek) swimming, see Janick Auberger, 'Quand la nage devint natation . . .', *Latomus*, 55 (1996), pp. 48–62.

16 Andocides, Louvre F197 (cp 3481) and Priam Painter, (Athens, 520–510 BCE, now Museo Nazionale Etrusco 106463, Villa Giulia, Rome); Janet Grossman, 'Six's Technique at the Getty', *Greek Vases in the J. Paul Getty Museum*, V (1991), pp. 12–16 (p. 12, no. XXXII bis).

17 Robert Sutton thinks the swimmers may simply be ordinary women: 'Female Bathers and the Emergence of the Female Nude in Greek Art', in *The Nature and Function of Water, Baths, Bathing and Hygiene from Antiquity through the Renaissance*, ed. Anne Scott and Cynthia Kosso (Leiden, 2009), pp. 61–86 (p. 69).

18 Christopher Love disagrees: 'An Overview of the Development of Swimming in England, c. 1750–1918', *International Journal of the History of Sport*, XXIV (2007), pp. 568–85 (p. 569).

19 Bruce Winter, *Roman Wives, Roman Widows: The Appearance of New Women and the Pauline Communities* (Grand Rapids, MI, 2003), p. 3; Elaine Fantham, 'The "New Woman": Representation and Reality', in *Women in the Classical World: Image and Text*, ed. Fantham et al. (Oxford, 1995), pp. 280–93.

20 Agrippina: Tacitus, *Annals* 14.5; Suetonius, *Nero* 34.3. Nero's envoys stabbed Agrippina to death later that night.

21 Ovid, *Ars amatoria* 3.385–6: *Nec vos Campus habet, nec vos gelidissima Virgo,/ Nec Tuscus placida devehit amnis aqua*; Cynthia: Propertius, *Elegies* 1.11; Pausanias, *Description of Greece* 10.19.1. For the complete list of references to Hydna, see Dunstan Lowe, 'Scylla, the Diver's Daughter: Aeschrion, Hedyle, and Ovid', *Classical Philology*, CVI (2011), pp. 260–64.

22 Suetonius, *Tiberius* 44, *Domitian* 22; Alan Cameron, 'Sex in the Swimming Pool', *Bulletin of the Institute of Classical Studies*, XX (1973), pp. 149–50; Michael Charles and Eva Anagnostou-Laoutides, 'The Sexual Hypocrisy of Domitian: Suet, Dom. 8, 3', *L'Antiquité classique*, LXXIX (2010), pp. 173–87 (p. 175 n.11).

23 Susan Walker, 'Carry-On at Canopus: The Nilotic Mosaic from Palestrina and Roman Attitudes to Egypt', in *Ancient Perspectives on Egypt*, ed. Roger Matthews and Cornelia Roemer [2003] (London, 2016), pp. 263–78 (esp. p. 266).

24 Auberger, 'Quand la nage', pp. 49–50. Eric Chaline, *Strokes of Genius: A History of Swimming* (London, 2017), p. 91; McManamon, *Caligula's Barges*, p. 168; and now McManamon, *'Neither Letters nor Swimming'*, p. 151.

25 Euripides, *Hippolytus*, ll. 469–70.

26 For the complicated sources on Menander's drowning in 291 BCE, see
    Menander, *Samia (The Woman from Samos)*, ed. Alan Sommerstein
    (Cambridge, 2013), p. 4. Life-saving techniques: Ovid, *Ex Ponto* 2.2.126,
    To Messalinus; metaphor: *Ex Ponto* 2.3.1–48: *To Cotta Maximus*; for the
    shipwreck: *Elegy* 10: *To Graecinus*, ll. 33–4.

27 John 6:19, Matthew 14:25, Mark 6:48–9. Tacitus, *Annals* 2.24: *monstros maris*.

28 Oppian, *Halieutica* 3.36–7; Emily Kneebone, *Oppian's Halieutica: Charting
    a Didactic Epic* (Cambridge, 2020).

29 Soranus of Ephesus, quoted in Caelius Aurelianus, *De acutis morbis* 2.44–8,
    and cited by Esti Dvorjetski in *Leisure, Pleasure and Healing: Spa Culture
    and Medicine in Ancient Eastern Mediterranean* (Leiden, 2007), p. 86; trans.
    Ralph Jackson, 'Waters and Spas in the Classical World', *Medical History*,
    suppl. 10 (1990), pp. 1–13 (p. 11).

30 Celsus, *De medicina* 4.12, 5.27.2; Dvorjetski, *Leisure, Pleasure and Healing*,
    p. 86; Brian Campbell, *Rivers and the Power of Ancient Rome* (Chapel Hill,
    NC, 2012), p. 338.

31 Aelius Aristides, *Orations* 48.20 K; *Hieroi Logoi* 2.78–80. For other
    examples, see Ido Israelowich, *Society, Medicine, and Religion in the Sacred
    Tales of Aelius Aristides* (Leiden, 2012), p. 90 and *passim*.

32 *Historia Augusta*, Hadrian 22.7–8. For more sources see Erwin Mehl,
    Antike Schwimmkunst (Munich, 1927), pp. 114–15.

33 Hippocrates, *Ancient Medicine* 21; *On Regimen in Acute Diseases* 18; Celsus,
    De medicina 3.21; Horace, *Satires* 2.1 (This may indeed be satire, because
    swimming three times across would leave you on the wrong side to retrieve
    your clothes!); greasing up: Oribasius 6.27. I used to take my children
    swimming just before bedtime for this reason, and can report that it is very
    effective. Horace may also be riffing on his own name, the same as that
    Horatius who swam across the Tiber. See Alex Nice, 'C. Trebatius Testa
    and the British Charioteers: The Relationship of Cic. Ad. Fam. 7.10.2 to
    Caes. BG 4.25 and 33', *Acta Classica*, XLVI (2003), pp. 71–96.

34 Herodotus, *Histories* 7.176.3; Strabo, *Geography* 9.4.13; Galen, *On Medical
    Material* 10.10: 'for we too become cooled and braced, just as the iron does
    when, having become red hot, it is dipped into cold water'; The William
    Davidson Talmud: *Berakhot* 22a: 'If it is because it is difficult for you
    to immerse in the cold waters of the ritual bath, it is possible to purify
    oneself by immersing oneself in the heated bathhouses . . . Is there ritual
    immersion in hot water? Rav Huna said to him: Indeed, doubts with regard
    to the fitness of baths have been raised.'

35 Plato, *Republic* 5.453d.

36 Kurt Schütze, 'Warum kannten die Griechen keine Schwimmwett-
    kämpfe?', *Hermes*, 73 (1938), pp. 355–7, rejecting the older view represented
    by Mehl, *Antike Schwimmkunst*, pp. 61–2; Judith Swaddling, *The Ancient
    Olympic Games* [1980] (Austin, TX, 1999), p. 34; Donald Kyle, 'Greek
    Athletic Competitions: The Ancient Olympics and More', in *A Companion
    to Sport and Spectacle in Greek and Roman Antiquity*, ed. Paul Christesen and
    Donald Kyle (Hoboken, NJ, 2014), pp. 21–35 (p. 31).

37 Campbell, *Rivers*, p. 335.

38 Josephus, *Antiquities of the Jews*, 15.3.3; Suetonius, *Tiberius* 44; Pliny the Younger, *Letters* 5.6.25–6.

39 The distinction between *frigidarium* and *natatio* is not easy to make: *frigidaria* are supposed to be indoor pools while *natationes* are outdoors, but historians of architecture do not even agree on whether the Baths of Caracalla were roofed or not.

40 Fikret Yegül, *Bathing in the Roman World* (Cambridge, 2010), p. 16.

41 For example, Chaline, *Strokes of Genius*, p. 13; Aelius Aristides, *Orations* 48.20; Israelowich, *Society, Medicine, and Religion*, p. 90 and *passim*.

42 Vegetius, *De re militari* 1.10. Vegetius convinced Mehl (*Antike Schwimmkunst*, 69) that Romans swam for military reasons, but they probably did not.

43 Caterina Cicirelli, 'Comune di Ottaviano – Località Bosco di Siervo', *Rivisti di Studi Pompeiani*, VII (1985–6), pp. 185–8 (p. 188); Ovid, *Metamorphoses* 4.353: *alternaque bracchia ducens* and Manilius, *Astronomica* 5.422ff.: *alterna ferens in lentos bracchia tractus*; also Statius, *Thebaid* 6.544; backstroke: Plato, *Phaedrus* 264a; Caitlín Eilís Barrett, *Domesticating Empire: Egyptian Landscapes in Pompeian Gardens* (Oxford, 2019), fig. 2.4; Manilius 5.428: *immota ferens in tergus membra*. The swimming figures in the mosaic from the third- to fourth-century CE Villa de la Vega Baja in Toledo, Spain, are just entering the water, and their outstretched arms probably indicate diving more than breaststroke. As Guadalupe López Monteagudo suggests, the context implies that the swimmers are sponge- or oyster-divers (López Monteagudo, 'Nets and Fishing Gear in Roman Mosaics from Spain', in *Ancient Nets and Fishing-Gear: Proceedings of the International Workshop on 'Nets and Fishing Gear in Classical Antiquity: A New Approach'*, ed. Tønnes Bekker-Nielsen and Dario Bernal Casasola (Cádiz, 2007), pp. 161–85 (pp. 167, 174–5)). For other examples, supporting the view that the crawl stroke predominated, see H. A. Sanders, 'Swimming among the Greeks and Romans', *CJ*, XX (1924–5), pp. 566–8. For the contrasting opinion that 'the [crawl] stroke rarely appeared in ancient sources' and 'they generally used the breaststroke', see McManamon, '*Neither Letters nor Swimming*', pp. 288–9, 337.

44 Pompeii house 1.12.11; house VI.15.1; House of the Vettii, see Richard Engelmann, *Pompeii*, trans. Talfourd Ely (London, 1904), p. 87, fig. 122.

45 Ovid, *Heroides* 18.35–6, in the voice of Leander writing to Hero: *Obstitit inceptis tumidum iuvenalibus aequor,/ Mersit et adversis ora natantis aquis.*

46 Statius, *Thebaid* 6.544.

47 Nonnus, *Dionysiaca* 7.184–9 (*c.* 425 CE): καὶ Σεμέλην ὁρόωσα παρ' Ἀσωποῖο ῥεέθροις/ λουομένην ἐγέλασσεν ἐν ἠέρι φοιτὰς Ἐρινὺς/ μνησαμένη Κρονίωνος, ὅτι ξυνήονι πότμῳ/ ἀμφοτέρους ἤμελλε βαλεῖν φλογόεντι κεραυνῷ./ κεῖθι δέμας φαίδρυνε, σὺν ἀμφιπόλοισι δὲ γυμνὴ/ χεῖρας ἐρετμώσασα δι' ὕδατος ἔτρεχε κούρη:/ καὶ κεφαλὴν ἀδίαντον ἐκούφισεν ἴδμονι τέχνῃ/ ὕψι τιταινομένην ὑπὲρ οἴδματος, ἄχρι κομάων/ ὑγροβαφής, καὶ στέρνον ἐπιστορέσασα ῥεέθρῳ/ ποσσὶν ἀμοιβαίοισιν ὀπίστερον ὤθεεν ὕδωρ.

In the same poem, a young man drowns when a wave forces water into his open mouth. For more discussion, see McManamon, 'Neither Letters nor Swimming', pp. 163–4.

48 Ovid, *Tristia* 2.485: *hic artem nandi praecipit*; Plutarch, *Cato the Elder* 20.4; Suetonius, *Augustus* 62. When Suetonius declares that Caligula did not know how to swim, it is meant to show the emperor's poor character (*Caligula*, 54); Janick Auberger, 'Quand la nage devint natation ...,' *Latomus*, 55 (1996), pp. 48–62.

49 Horace, *Satire* 1.4 120; Talmud: *Beitzah* 36b; Plautus, *Aulularia*, 595 ff.: *quasi pueri qui nare discunt scirpea induitur ratis./ qui laborent minus, facilius ut nent et moveant manus*; Columella, *De re rustica*, 10.383.

7 SOLDIERS AND DIVERS

1 Xenophon, *Anabasis* 4.3.12; see also 1.5.10, where they use straw and skins to make flotation devices (thanks Stephen DeCasien). Arrian, *Anabasis* 2.23; *Indica* 8.24, in what is now Hingol National Park, Pakistan; John McManamon's description of these villagers as 'survivors of the Stone Age' is outdated ('*Neither Letters nor Swimming': The Rebirth of Swimming and Free-Diving* (Leiden, 2021), p. 125).

2 For Diodorus Siculus' version, see Chapter Five. Livy, *History of Rome* 5.38.8, (*hausere gurgites*), 23.1.8–9, 27.47.8–9; McManamon, '*Neither Letters nor Swimming*', pp. 136, 140. The Roman general Scipio, however, is said to have been a strong swimmer.

3 Livy, *History of Rome* 21.27–8; Caesar, *Civil Wars* 1.48.

4 Polybius, *Histories* 3.84: συνωθούμενοι [μὲν] γὰρ εἰς τὴν λίμνην οἱ μὲν διὰ τὴν παράστασιν τῆς διανοίας ὁρμῶντες ἐπὶ τὸ νήχεσθαι σὺν τοῖς ὅπλοις ἀπεπνίγοντο: 'forced into the lake, trying the idea to swim they were drowned by their armour'; Livy, *History of Rome* 22.6.5–7: *pars magna, ubi locus fugae deest, per prima vada paludis in aquam progressi, quoad capitibus umerisque extare possunt, sese inmergunt. fuere quos inconsultus pavor nando etiam capessere fugam inpulerit, quae ubi inmensa ac sine spe erat, aut deficientibus animis hauriebantur gurgitibus aut nequiquam fessi vada retro aegerrime repetebant atque ibi ab ingressis aquam hostium equitibus passim trucidabantur*: 'A large part, having nowhere to flee to, first waded out into the shallow water, as far as they could go with their heads and shoulders out. An unreasoning terror drove some to try to escape by swimming; but in that vastness it was hopeless. So either their spirits failed them and they sank in the abyss, or else, having tired themselves out for nothing, they turned back with the greatest difficulty to the shallow water, and there they were butchered all over the place by the enemy cavalry, who rode into the water.' Interestingly, Sertorius is said to have swum across the Rhône with his breastplate and shield in the second century BCE, and a second-century CE tombstone (Corpus Inscriptionum Latinarum (CIL) 3.3676) records one of Emperor Hadrian's horse guards having swum

across the Danube in full armour: Plutarch, *Sertorius* 3.1, see McManamon, *'Neither Letters nor Swimming'*, pp. 139–41; Michael Speidel, 'Swimming the Danube under Hadrian's Eyes: A Feat of the Emperor's Batavi Horse Guard', *Ancient Society*, xx (1991), pp. 277–82; Mary Boatwright, 'Hadrian', *Lives of the Caesars*, ed. Anthony Barrett (Oxford, 2009), pp. 155–80 (p. 164). But even in the fourth century, Roman soldiers still struggled to cross rivers: Ammianus Marcellinus 24.2, 24.6.

5 Livy 42.61.6–8, cited by McManamon, *'Neither Letters nor Swimming'*, pp. 140–41. Chaline, *Strokes of Genius*, p. 98; Appian, *Civil Wars* 5.11.104; Caesar (attrib.), *Spanish Wars*, 1.40; Plutarch, *Caesar* 16; Caesar, *Gallic Wars* 4.25: *maxime propter altitudinem maris*; Caesar, *Gallic Wars* 4.25, Cicero, *Letters to His Friends* 7.10.2, Vegetius, *De re militari* 1.10: *Natandi usum aestiuis mensibus omnis aequaliter debet tiro condiscere*; McManamon, *Neither Letters nor Swimming*, pp. 153–5; Alex Nice, 'C. Trebatius Testa and the British Charioteers: The Relationship of Cic. Ad. Fam. 7.10.2 to Caes. BG 4.25 and 33', *Acta Classica*, xlvi (2003), pp. 71–96, H. A. Sanders, 'Swimming among the Greeks and Romans', *Classical Journal*, xx (1924–5), pp. 566–8 (p. 567). See for the chronology of the texts T. P. Wiseman, 'The Publication of De Bello Gallico', in *Julius Caesar as Artful Reporter*, ed. K. Welch and A. Powell (London, 1998), pp. 1–9.

6 Nicholas Wynman, in the 1500s, nationalistically promoted the idea that Germans had always been good swimmers, and the Third Reich's desire to promote German identity and athleticism underlies a new Nazi edition of Wynman's *Colymbetes* in 1937; see McManamon, *'Neither Letters nor Swimming'*, p. 263.

7 Chaline, *Strokes of Genius*, p. 98; Caesar, *Gallic Wars* 1.53, 4.15. Pliny suggests in rhetoric that Germans are good swimmers but gives no examples (*Panegyricus* 82.6). By the second century CE Tacitus does mention Germans (in 69 CE) swimming successfully to an island in the Po (*nando*; *Histories* 2.35), and in the third century Cassius Dio has the Britons swimming rivers naked, in contrast to the Romans who must use boats (Epitome 62.5.6, see Eric Adler, 'Boudica's Speeches in Tacitus and Dio', *Classical World*, ci (2008), pp. 173–95 (p. 189)), while Herodianus also says the Germans are good swimmers (7.2.6). Yet the Germans still drown when forced into rivers in the fourth century as well (Ammianus Marcellinus 16.11.8–9, 16.12.55–57; Libanius 18.60).

8 Tacitus, *Annals* 14.29.

9 Tacitus, *Agricola* 18: *ita repente inmisit, ut obstupefacti hostes, qui classem, qui navis, qui mare expectabant, nihil arduum aut invictum crediderint sic ad bellum venientibus*: 'he sent over an attack so unexpected that the incredulous enemy, who were on the lookout for a fleet, ships, and a sea attack, thought that for those coming to war this way nothing would be hard or invincible.'

10 Tacitus, *Agricola* 18: *depositis omnibus sarcinis lectissimos auxiliarium, quibus nota vada et patrius nandi usus, quo simul seque et arma et equos regunt*: 'leaving behind all their packs, the best of the auxiliaries, who knew the fords and

had that ancestral experience in swimming, which enables them
simultaneously to take care themselves, and their weapons, and their
horses'; also *Histories* 4.12; Cassius Dio, *Roman History* 60.20.2: οἷς ἔθος ἦν
καὶ διὰ τῶν ῥοωδεστάτων ῥᾳδίως αὐτοῖς: 'the Celts ... habit (*ethos*) being
to easily plunge even into the roughest water, even wearing their armour'.

11 Tacitus, *Histories* 5.14: 'The place was like that, tricky from the uncertain
fords, and no good for us. For the Roman soldier is heavily equipped
and afraid to swim, while the German, who is used to rivers, prevails
by the lightness of his equipment and the height of his body.' See
McManamon, '*Neither Letters nor Swimming*', pp. 145–6; Cassius Dio,
60.20.5-6: καὶ ῥᾳδίως αὐτὸν διαβάντων ἅτε καὶ τὰ στέριφα τά τε εὔπορα
τοῦ χωρίου ἀκριβῶς εἰδότων, οἱ Ῥωμαῖοι ἐπακολουθήσαντές σφισι ταύτῃ
μὲν ἐσφάλησαν, διανηξαμένων δ᾽ αὖθις τῶν Κελτῶν: 'themselves easily
walking across, knowing precisely the solid and easy [fords] of that
place. When the Romans pursuing them were balked, the Celts swam
across again.'

12 Thucydides, *History of the Peloponnesian War* 4.26.8 (the text says only
'divers', though it's telling that Thomas Hobbes's 1843 translation renders
it 'such as could dive'), 7.25.5–7; Arrian, *Anabasis* 2.21.

13 Oppian, *Halieutica* 4.593–615; CIL, XIV, suppl. 4620 and note to l. 9, cited in
Lionel Casson, *Ships and Seamanship in the Ancient World* (Baltimore, MD,
1995), p. 370 n. 45.

14 CIL, VI, 1872; Aristotle (or somebody claiming to be Aristotle), *Problems* 32;
both cited by Frank Frost, 'Scyllias: Diving in Antiquity', *Greece and Rome*,
XV (1968), pp. 182, 184; McManamon, '*Neither Letters nor Swimming*',
pp. 2, 226.

15 Oppian, *Halieutica* 5.612–74, see Emily Kneebone, *Oppian's Halieutica:
Charting a Didactic Epic* (Cambridge, 2020).

16 Arrian, *Anabasis* 2.22.5: φόνος δὲ τῶν ἐπιβατῶν οὐ πολὺς ἐγένετο. ὡς γὰρ
ᾔσθοντο ἐχομένας τὰς ναῦς ἀπενήξαντο οὐ χαλεπῶς ἐς τὸν λιμένα.

17 1 Maccabees 9:48, *c.* 150 BCE; *Acts* 27:42–4.

18 Josephus, *Antiquities of the Jews* 15.3.3; the young man is Aristobulus III.

19 Matthew 14:22–33.

20 Josephus, *Jewish Wars* 3.522 (3.10.9).

21 Manal Shalaby, 'The Middle Eastern Mermaid: Between Myth and
Religion', in *Scaled for Success: The Internationalisation of the Mermaid*,
ed. Philip Hayward (Bloomington, IN, 2018), pp. 7–20 (fig. 1); Stefanie
Hoss, *Baths and Bathing: The Culture of Bathing and the Baths and
Thermae in Palestine from the Hasmoneans to the Moslem Conquest*, British
Archaeological Reports International Series 1346 (Oxford, 2005), p. 90.

22 *The Selections of Zadspram*, trans. Edward West [1880], ed. Joseph Peterson
(Kasson, MN, 1995), pp. 32–3.

23 Ausonius, *Mosella* 270–82; Strabo, *Geography* 17.1.44; Pliny, *Natural History*
8.38.

24 Philo, *Concerning Noah's Work as a Planter* XXXV (trans. adapted from
Francis Colson and George Whitaker, Loeb Classical Library 247, p. 287);

Philo, *On the Creation* LI (trans. Colson and Whitaker, Loeb Classical Library 226, p. 117). See also Philo, *The Confusion of Tongues* XV.

25 Philo, *On the Creation* XX–XXI (Loeb Classical Library 226, pp. 49–51). For other examples, see Chapter Four.

26 Philo, *On the Confusion of Tongues* 3.1.3, 15.66, 27.100.

8 MEDIEVAL ASIA

1 Xue Juzheng, *Jiu Wudai Shi* (*Old History of the Five Dynasties, c.* 970 CE), in *Twenty-Four Histories*, ed. Sun Xingwu (Beijing, 2012).

2 Sima Guang et al., *Zizhi Tongjian* (1084) 16.352–3, cited in Johannes Kurz, *China's Southern Tang Dynasty, 937–976* (Abingdon, 2011), p. 80.

3 Tang Dynasty lexicographer Hui-lin, quoted in Edward Schafer, *The Golden Peaches of Samarkand: A Study of T'ang Exotics* [1963] (Berkeley, CA, 2016), p. 125; Zhu Yuchen and Hu Renfen, 'A Brief Analysis of Semantic Interactions between Loanwords and Native Words in the Tang Dynasty', in *Chinese Lexical Semantics: 20th Workshop*, ed. Zhang Yangsen and Hong Jia-Fei (Berlin 2020), pp. 123–9 (p. 124).

4 Edward Schafer, 'The Development of Bathing Customs in Ancient and Medieval China and the History of the Floriate Clear Palace', *Journal of the American Oriental Society*, LXXVI (1956), pp. 57–82 (pp. 60–61, 65); Tansen Sen, *Buddhism, Diplomacy, and Trade: The Realignment of Sino-Indian Relations, 600–1400* (Honolulu, HI, 2003), p. 46; Fan Ka-wai, 'The Period of Division and the Tang Period', in *Chinese Medicine and Healing: An Illustrated History*, ed. T. J. Hinrichs and Linda Barnes (Cambridge, MA, 2013), pp. 65–96 (p. 80).

5 Men Yuanlao, *Dongjing Meng Hua Lu* (1187); *Sports and Games in Ancient China* (Beijing, 1986), p. 66; Chongbang Cai et al., *A Social History of Middle-Period China: The Song, Liao, Western Xia and Jin Dynasties* (Cambridge, 2016), pp. 479–80.

6 Ching-hsiung Wu, untitled, in *T'ien Hsia Monthly*, 2 (1936), p. 106; Zhiling Huang, 'Dragon Boat Races Popular on Holiday', *China Daily*, 13 June 2013.

7 Men Yuanlao, *Dongjing Meng Hua Lu* (1187); Victor Mair et al., *Hawai'i Reader in Traditional Chinese Culture* (Honolulu, HI, 2005), p. 416; Cai, *Social History of Middle-Period China*, p. 480; L. Han, 'Racing for the Target: The Imperial Symbolism of Boat Racing in Song China, 960–1279 CE', *Chinese Semiotic Studies*, 11 (2015), pp. 135–57.

8 Paolo Squatriti, *Water and Society in Early Medieval Italy, AD 400–1000* (Cambridge, 1998), p. 58; John Chrysostom, *Homily 7 on Matthew 7*; see Ze'ev Weiss, *Public Spectacles in Roman and Late Antique Palestine* (Cambridge, MA, 2014), p. 139. John McManamon suggests, as seems likely, that the women swam in the nude (McManamon, *'Neither Letters nor Swimming': The Rebirth of Swimming and Free-Diving* (Leiden, 2021), pp. 166–7.

9 Jalal al-Din al-Suyuti, *History of the Caliphs*, trans. Henry Jarrett (Calcutta, 1881), p. 417.

10 Hazrat ibn Umar reports the hadith, 'Teach your children swimming, archery and horse riding.' Another hadith tells Muslims that, 'Any action without the remembrance of Allah is either a diversion or heedlessness except four acts: walking from target to target (during archery practice), training a horse, amusing oneself with one's wife, and learning to swim' (*Targheeb Wa Tarheeb* 2, p. 389; Al-Tabarani, *Dar Ihya al-Turaath*). Al-Mubarrad, in Baghdad in the ninth century CE, reports that the second caliph, Mohammed's successor Omar ibn Al-Khattab, also thought people should teach their children swimming, archery and horse-riding; see al-Mubarrad, *The Kamil of el-Mubarrad*, ed. William Wright (Leipzig 1874–92), vol. I, p. 185, cited in Khahil Totah, *The Contribution of the Arabs to Education* [1926] (New York, 2002), p. 50.

11 The William Davidson Talmud: *Kiddushin* 29a.

12 Talmud: *Niddah* 51b; Quran 5:96. Ibn Tulun in sixteenth-century Damascus rejects shellfish as food (*al-Dhakhā'ir al-Qaṣr*, biography of Muḥammad b. ʿAbd al-Qādir b. ʿAlī al-ʿŪshī al-Shāfiʿī). See Torsten Wollina, 'Biography of a Crustacean', in *Damascus Anecdotes*, 4 April 2018, and 'The Crustacean Returns: A Possible Context for Ibn Tulun's Observations', in *Damascus Anecdotes*, 25 August 2019, https://thecamel. hypotheses.org.

13 Talmud: *Pesachim* 16a, *Leviticus* (*Kohanim*) 15:16–17 and so on.

14 Talmud: *Shabbat* 40b, 41a, *Beitzah*, *Baba Bathra* 74b. See Stefanie Hoss, *Baths and Bathing: The Culture of Bathing and the Baths and Thermae in Palestine from the Hasmoneans to the Moslem Conquest*, British Archaeological Reports International Series 1346 (Oxford, 2005), pp. 67–70.

15 Talmud: *Niddah* 51b, *Berakhot* 16, *Taanit* 13a, *Moed Katan* 3; Maimonides, *Mishneh Torah* 7.

16 *Justinian Code* 23.3.16; Fikret Yegül, *Bathing in the Roman World* (Cambridge, 2010), pp. 182–3; also Hoss, *Baths and Bathing*, p. 94; Talmud *Shabbat* 41a (though this example does envision bathing in a river).

17 John Moschus, *Pratum spirituale*, retold in Garrett Fagan, *Bathing in Public in the Roman World* (Ann Arbor, MI, 1999), p. 27. The story is in Elpidio Mioni, 'Il Pratum Spirituale di Giovanni Mosco: Gli episodi inediti del Cod. Marciano greco II, 21', *Orientalia Christiana Periodica*, XVII (1951), pp. 61–94 (pp. 92–3, no. 11).

18 Stephanus Byzantinus, *Εθνικων Quae Supersunt*, ed. Anton Westermann (Leipzig, 1839), p. 138.

19 Al-Yaʿqūbī, 'The History (Taʾrīkh): The Rise of Islam to the Reign of al-Muʿtamid', in *The Works of Ibn Wāḍiḥ al-Yaʿqūbī*, ed. and trans. Matthew Gordon et al. (Leiden, 2018), vol. III, pp. 595–1294 (pp. 977, 1059, 1069, 1154).

20 Ahmad Ibn Yahya al-Baladhuri, *Kitab Futuh al-Buldan*, trans. Philip Khurri Hitti (New York, 1916), pp. 356, 385.

21 *The Confessions of al-Ghazali*, trans. Claud Field (London, 1909), pp. 39–40.

22 Talmud: *Gittin* 67b, *Avodah Zarah* 28b.

23 Ibn Sina, *Canon of Medicine*, in *Avicenna's Medicine: A New Translation*, trans. Mones Abu-Asab, Hakima Amri and Mark Micozzi (Toronto, 2013), 3.16.3; 2.9.19; 3.13.2; 3.13.5.

24 Nicholas McLeod, 'Race, Rebellion, and Arab Muslim Slavery: The Zanj Rebellion in Iraq, 869–883 c', MA thesis, University of Louisville, 2016, pp. 89ff.; al-Tabari, *The History of al-Tabarī*, vol. XXXVI: *The Revolt of the Zanj*, trans. David Waines (Albany, NY, 1991), pp. 44, 138.

25 Jeffrey Fynn-Paul, 'Empire, Monotheism and Slavery in the Greater Mediterranean Region from Antiquity to the Early Modern Era', *Past and Present*, CCV (2009), pp. 3–40 (p. 22).

26 *Akhbār majmūʿa fī fath al-Andalus* (Collected Reports on the Conquest of al-Andalus), cited in Janina Safran, *The Second Umayyad Caliphate: The Articulation of Caliphal Legitimacy in Al-Andalus* (Cambridge, MA, 2000), pp. 127–8.

27 Qasim al-Samarrai, 'Abbasid Gardens in Baghdad and Samarra', *The Authentic Garden: A Symposium on Gardens*, ed. Leslie Tjon Sie Fat and Erik de Jong (Leiden, 1991), pp. 115–22.

28 Adapted from Mansur al-Hallaj, *'I am the Truth' (Anal Haq): Diwan of al-Hallaj*, trans. Paul Smith, revd edn (Campbells Creek, Vic., 2016), pp. 123, 365; and Mansur al-Hallaj, *Hallaj: Poems of a Sufi Martyr*, trans. Carl Ernst (Evanston, IL, 2018), p. 76; there are many more examples.

29 'The Story of the Fisherman and the Demon', in *The Arabian Nights*, trans. Husain Hadawy, ed. Muhsin Mahdi (New York, 1990), p. 32; see Manal Shalaby, 'The Middle Eastern Mermaid: Between Myth and Religion', in *Scaled for Success: The Internationalisation of the Mermaid*, ed. Philip Hayward (Bloomington, IN, 2018), pp. 7–20 (pp. 13–15).

30 Abul-Qâsem Firdawsi, *Shahnameh: The Persian Book of Kings*, trans. Dick Davis [1997] (New York, 2006), pp. 302, 383.

31 Ananias of Sirak, *Geography*, ed. and trans. Robert Hewsen (Wiesbaden, 1992). The sixth-century Roman historian Procopius mentions the Slavs' reverence for rivers, as well: Procopius, *De bellis* 7.14.24: σέβουσι μέντοι καὶ ποταμούς τε καὶ νύμφας καὶ ἄλλα ἄττα δαιμόνια.

32 *The Song of Igor's Campaign: An Epic of the 12th Century*, trans. Vladimir Nabokov (New York, 1960), p. 18; see the list of other translations and discussion in Henry Cooper, *The Igor Tale: An Annotated Bibliography of 20th Century Non-Soviet Scholarship on the Slovo O Polku Igoreve* (White Plains, NY, 1978).

33 John Windhausen claims that 'universal sports like bonfire jumping, wrestling, fist-fighting, spear hurling, and swimming were frequently encountered in literature describing the lifestyles of the early nobles, the druzhiny and boyars,' but the general history of sport he cites, published in 1962, does not inspire confidence: Windhausen and Irina Tsypkina, 'National Identity and the Emergence of the Sports Movement in Imperial Russia', in *International Journal of the History of Sport*, vol. XII: *Tribal Identities: Nationalism, Europe, Sport*, ed. James Mangan (London, 1996), pp. 164–82 (p. 165), citing Vitally Stolbov and Ivan Chudinov, *Istoriia fizicheskoi kultury*

(Moscow, 1962), pp. 79–84. Edward Keenan thinks the *Song of Igor's Campaign* may date to the eighteenth century rather than the twelfth (*Josef Dobrovský and the Origins of the Igor' Tale*, Cambridge, 2003), but see Robert Mann's review and rebuttal in *Slavic and East European Journal*, XLVIII (2004), pp. 299–302.

34 *The Russian Primary Chronicle* (also called the *Chronicle of 1113*), ed. and trans. Samuel Cross and Olgerd Sherbowitz-Wetzor (Cambridge, MA, 1953), p. 85, for the year 968 CE.

35 Basil Dmytryshyn, *Medieval Russia: A Source Book, 850–1700*, 3rd edn (Boston, MA, 1991), pp. 59, 60–61, 89 (*Tale of Igor*), 130 and 236 (both *Chronicle of Novgorod*).

36 *Russian Primary Chronicle*, pp. 54, 74, 79, 170.

37 Ibn Battuta, *Travels in Asia and Africa, 1325–1354*, trans. and ed. Hamilton Gibb, Hakluyt Society, 2nd ser., vols 110, 117, 141, 178, 190 [1929] (London, 1994), p. 481.

38 *Ibi magnam Sclavorum multitudinem reperit, eiusdem fluminis alveo . . . lavandis corporibus se immersisse. Quorum nuda corpora animal, cui praesidebat, pertimescens, tremere coepit, et ipse vir Dei eorum fetorem exhorruit* (Eigil Fuldensis, *Vita S. Sturmii*, Patrologia Latina CV, 7. For the (mis)translation, which describes the Slavs as swimming, see Eigil, Bishop of Fulda, 'The Life of St Sturm', in *The Anglo-Saxon Missionaries in Germany, Being the Lives of SS. Willibrord, Boniface, Leoba and Lebuin together with the Hodoepericon of St Willibald and a selection from the correspondence of St Boniface*, ed. and trans. Charles Talbot (London, 1954), p. 186.

39 Most recently Michael McCormick, 'Slavery from Rome to Medieval Europe and Beyond: Words, Things, and Genomes', in *On Human Bondage: After Slavery and Social Death*, ed. John Bodel and Walter Scheidel (Chichester, 2016), pp. 249–64 (pp. 250–51; Fynn-Paul, 'Empire, Monotheism and Slavery', pp. 4–5: 'the rise of Christian and Islamic monotheism created a hyper-exploitation of African and Russian populations for slaving purposes'; Nell Painter, *The History of White People* (New York, 2010), pp. 32–5; also by McCormick, 'New Light on the "Dark Ages": How the Slave Trade Fuelled the Carolingian Economy', *Past and Present*, CLXXVII (2002), pp. 17–54, and *Origins of the European Economy: Communications and Commerce, AD 300–900* (Cambridge, 2001); Charles Verlinden, *L'Esclavage dans l'Europe médiévale* (Ghent, 1955–77).

40 Martin Ježek, 'A Mass for the Slaves: from Early Medieval Prague', *Frühgeschichtliche Zentralorte in Mitteleuropa*, ed. Jiří Macháček and Šimon Ungerman (Bonn, 2011), pp. 623–42; Joachim Henning, 'Slavery or Freedom? The Causes of Early Medieval Europe's Economic Advancement', *Early Medieval Europe*, XII (2003), pp. 269–77.

9 MEDIEVAL EUROPE

1 Tertullian, *De spectaculis* 8.9–10; Clement of Alexandria, *Paidagogus* 3.31–2, 46–8; Palladius 1.39: *quae res et voluptati plurimum conferat et saluti,* Augustine, *Confessions* 9.12.32, Isidore, *Etymologies* 15.2.40; John McManamon, *'Neither Letters nor Swimming': The Rebirth of Swimming and Free-Diving* (Leiden 2021), p. 183; Elizabeth Archibald, 'Bathing, Beauty and Christianity in the Middle Ages', *Durham University Insights,* v (2012), pp. 2–13; Garrett Fagan, *Bathing in Public in the Roman World* (Ann Arbor, MI, 1999), p. 88; Fikret Yegül, *Baths and Bathing in Classical Antiquity,* revd edn (Cambridge, MA, 1995), pp. 315–17.

2 *Beowulf,* ll. 508–16; for other examples of early medieval British swimming, see Nicolas Orme, *Early British Swimming, 55 BC–AD 1719* (Exeter, 1983), pp. 12–13.

3 *The Life and Death of Cormac the Skald,* trans. William Collingwood and Jón Stefansson (Ulverston, 1901), p. 36.

4 Ammianus Marcellinus, *Histories* 31.4.5.

5 Gregory of Tours, *History of the Franks,* 3.15, 5.49, 6.26; McManamon, *'Neither Letters nor Swimming',* pp. 177–8.

6 Gregory of Tours, *Glory of the Martyrs* 68, in Raymond Van Dam, *Gregory of Tours: Glory of the Martyrs* (Liverpool, 1988), pp. 92–3, or ibid. 69 (*statum super aquas ferri coepit*). In the following story (69/70) God puts a pillar under the water for the innocent woman to stand on.

7 References to the saints' story first appear in the eighth century CE. On the probable fictionality of these two saints, made famous by Shakespeare's St Crispin's Day speech in *Henry v,* see A.H.M. Jones, John Martindale and John Morris, *The Prosopography of the Later Roman Empire,* vol. I: AD 260–395 (Cambridge, 1971), p. 766. For the drowning story, see Paul the Deacon, *History of the Lombards* 6.35; McManamon, *'Neither Letters nor Swimming',* pp. 180–81.

8 Paul the Deacon, *History of the Lombards* 1.15; Einhard, *Life of Charlemagne* 22. I wrote a paper about Suetonius' influence on Einhard for an undergraduate seminar, but as that remains unpublished, I'll cite instead Matthew Innes, 'The Classical Tradition in the Carolingian Renaissance: Ninth-Century Encounters with Suetonius', *International Journal of the Classical Tradition,* III (1997), pp. 265–82. McManamon is sceptical of Charlemagne's swimming, but Einhard is explicit: *natatu* (McManamon, *'Neither Letters Nor Swimming',* pp. 179–80); we agree, in any case, that medieval swimming was seen as appropriate 'only for a select group' (p. 184).

9 Ambrose of Milan, *Exposition of the Christian Faith* 5.16.194; Jerome, *Apology against Rufinus* (Book II); Paulinus' letter to Augustine (Letter 25) in 394 CE; John Cassian, 'The Discourse of the Old Man on the State of the Soul and its Excellence', *Conferences,* chap. 4.

10 Cyprian, *On the Dress of Virgins* (*De habitu virginum*) 19, see David Brakke, *Athanasius and the Politics of Asceticism* (Oxford, 1995), pp. 42–3, Athanasius,

Second Letter to Virgins, in Brakke, *Athanasius*, p. 297, chap. 15–17. Jerome, Letter 22: *Ad Eustochium*, Patrologia Latina xx, 12; Archibald, 'Bathing, Beauty and Christianity', pp. 4–5; Elizabeth Archibald, 'Did Knights Have Baths? The Absence of Bathing in Middle English Romance', in *Cultural Encounters in the Romance of Medieval England*, ed. Corinne Saunders (Cambridge, 2005), pp. 101–15.

11 Vaughn Scribner, *Merpeople: A Human History* (London, 2020), pp. 39–40; there is an earlier example of a mermaid spreading her tail from the 1100s in the Museo Civico, Pavia.

12 Jamil Abun-Nasr, *A History of the Maghrib in the Islamic Period* (Cambridge, 1987), p. 95.

13 Peter Alphonsi, *The Disciplina Clericalis of Petrus Alfonsi*, ed. and trans. Eberhard Hermes (London, 1977), pp. 113–15, cited in Orme, *Early British Swimming*, p. 28.

14 Jeffrey Fynn-Paul, 'Empire, Monotheism and Slavery in the Greater Mediterranean Region from Antiquity to the Early Modern Era', *Past and Present*, ccv (2009), pp. 3–40 (p. 31).

15 Suger, *The Deeds of Louis the Fat* 11, trans. Richard Cusimano and John Moorhead (Washington, DC, 1992), p. 56. For an opposing view that medieval people did not exercise, or value swimming, see John McClelland, *Body and Mind: Sport in Europe from the Roman Empire to the Renaissance* (London, 2007), pp. 4, 36–50, and now McManamon, '*Neither Letters nor Swimming*', pp. 175–81.

16 Modernized slightly from 'The Song of Roland' 201, in *Epic and Saga: Beowulf; The Song of Roland; The Destruction of Dá Derga's Hostel; The Story of the Volsungs and Niblungs*, trans. John O'Hagan, ed. Charles Eliot (New York, 1909), p. 176. There is a similar episode in the related twelfth-century Spanish *Chronicle of the Cid*, where the Islamic Almoravid army is frightened away from relieving the siege of Valencia because of high water and floods: *Chronicle of the Cid* 6.14, trans. Robert Southey (London, 1808).

17 Marina Montesano, *Classical Culture and Witchcraft in Medieval and Renaissance Italy* (London, 2018), p. 40.

18 Ibn Sina, *Canon of Medicine*, in *Avicenna's Medicine: A New Translation*, trans. Mones Abu-Asab, Hakima Amri and Mark Micozzi (Toronto, 2013), 2.9.19.

19 Translation mine, but see Lambert of Ardres, *The History of the Counts of Guines and Lords of Ardres*, trans. Leah Shopkow (Philadelphia, PA, 2011), p. 169. She was the wife of Arnoul d'Ardres. Orme, *Early British Swimming*, p. 37, sees this as a negative assessment of women swimming, but the context is more approving than he makes it out to be.

10 CENTRAL ASIAN POWER

1 *Formulae Liturgicae Slavicae*, in *Select Historical Documents of the Middle Ages*, trans. Ernest Henderson (London, 1910), pp. 314–17.

2 Russell Zguta, 'The Ordeal by Water (Swimming of Witches) in the East
Slavic World', *Slavic Review*, XXXVI (1977), pp. 220–30 (p. 225). For more
on witch swimming, see Chapters Sixteen and Nineteen.

3 *Gesta Principum Polonorum: The Deeds of the Princes of the Poles*, ed. and
trans. Schaer Frank Gallus and Paul Knoll (Budapest, 2003), p. 189. The
Vistula's water level varies; it is often very low from late summer well into
spring, and then floods in the spring.

4 Ibid., pp. 53 (probably the Bug River, which can often be waded in
summer), 155, 285.

5 Henry Cooper, *The Igor Tale: An Annotated Bibliography of 20th Century Non-
Soviet Scholarship on the Slovo O Polku Igoreve* (White Plains, NY, 1978), p. 16.

6 Stanford Shaw, *History of the Ottoman Empire and Modern Turkey*
(Cambridge, 1976), vol. I, p. 19.

7 Stephen Chrisomalis, *Numerical Notation: A Comparative History*
(Cambridge, 2010), p. 275.

8 Hélèna Bellosta, 'Burning Instruments: From Diocles to Ibn Sahl',
Arabic Sciences and Philosophy, XII/2 (2002), pp. 285–303; Jim Al-Khalili,
*The House of Wisdom: How Arabic Science Saved Ancient Knowledge and
Gave Us the Renaissance* (London, 2011), pp. 152–71; David Lindberg, *Roger
Bacon: Perspectiva* (Oxford, 1996), introduction and p. 345; Vincent Ilardi,
Renaissance Vision from Spectacles to Telescopes (Philadelphia, PA, 2007),
p. 4; Shen Kuo (or Gua), *Brush Talks from Dream Brook*, trans. Wang Hong
and Zhao Zheng (Reading, 2011), pp. 31–2; Ya Zuo, *Shen Gua's Empiricism*
(Cambridge, MA, 2018), p. 185; Oliver Moore, 'Zou Boqi on Vision and
Photography in Nineteenth-Century China', in *The Human Tradition in
Modern China*, ed. Kenneth Hammond and Kristin Stapleton (Plymouth,
2008), pp. 33–54 (p. 42).

9 Pliny, *Natural Histories* 34.41; Alan Williams, *The Sword and the Crucible:
A History of the Metallurgy of European Swords up to the 16th Century*
(Leiden, 2012), p. 26.

10 Ibid., pp. 35 and 39.

11 Ibid., pp. 35ff; Ann Feuerbach, 'The Glitter of the Sword: The Fabrication
of the Legendary Damascus Steel Blades', *Minerva*, XIII (2002), pp. 45–8
(p. 45).

12 Alan Williams, 'Crucible Steel in Medieval Swords', in *Metals and Mines:
Studies in Archaeometallurgy*, ed. Susan La Niece, Duncan Hook and Paul
Craddock (London, 2007), pp. 233–41; Anna Fedrigo et al., 'Extraction of
Archaeological Information from Metallic Artefacts: A Neutron Diffraction
Study on Viking Swords', *Journal of Archaeological Science: Reports*, XII (2017),
pp. 425–36 (p. 426); Jeffrey Fynn-Paul, 'Empire, Monotheism and Slavery
in the Greater Mediterranean Region from Antiquity to the Early Modern
Era', *Past and Present*, CCV (2009), pp. 3–40 (p. 23): 'our model suggests that
the Caliphate's effective demand for slaves was one of the major causes of
Viking and other pagan raids on Europe during the Dark Ages.'

13 Anne Wardwell, 'Flight of the Phoenix: Crosscurrents in Late
Thirteenth- to Fourteenth-Century Silk Patterns and Motifs', *Bulletin of*

the Cleveland Museum of Art, LXXIV (1987), pp. 2–35; Sophie Desrosiers, 'Sur
l'origine d'un tissu qui a participé à la fortune de Venise: le velours de soie',
in *La seta in Italia dal Medioevo al Seicento*, ed. Luca Molà et al. (Venice,
2000), pp. 35–61 (p. 44); Lisa Monnas, 'The Impact of Oriental Silks on
Italian Silk Weaving in the Fourteenth Century', in *The Power of Things
and the Flow of Cultural Transformations*, ed. Lieselotte E. Saurma-Jeltsch
and Anja Eisenbeiß (Berlin, 2010), pp. 65–89 (p. 71); BuYun Chen, *Silk and
Fashion in Tang China* (Seattle, WA, 2019), p. 133.

14 Maureen Mazzaoui, *The Italian Cotton Industry in the Later Middle Ages,
1100–1600* (Cambridge, 1981), p. 12.

15 Lynn White, *Medieval Religion and Technology: Collected Essays*
(Berkeley, CA, 1978), p. 275.

16 Katherine Burke, 'A Note on Archaeological Evidence for Sugar
Production in the Middle Islamic Periods in Bilād al-Shām', *Mamlūk
Studies Review*, VIII (2004), pp. 109–18 (p. 109); Sucheta Mazumdar,
Sugar and Society in China: Peasants, Technology, and the World Market
(Cambridge, MA, 1998), p. 1.

17 See one attributed to Zhou Fang, 'Court Lady with Servants', now in the
Palace Museum in Beijing.

18 The earliest known example appears in Simone Martini's *St Louis of
Toulouse* altarpiece, in which the saint is seen crowning his brother,
Robert of Anjou, king of Naples.

19 Lisa Jardine and Jerry Brotton, *Global Interests: Renaissance Art between
East and West* (Ithaca, NY, 2000), pp. 72–3.

20 As seen on a Byzantine ivory casket now in the Museo Nazionale del
Bargello, Florence (Coll. Carrand, No. 26).

21 Fred Rosner, *The Medical Legacy of Moses Maimonides* (Brooklyn, NY,
1998), p. 253.

22 *Mystical Poems of Rūmī*, vol. I: *First Selection, Poems 1–200*, trans. Arthur
Arberry (New York, 1968), pp. 39, 86; revd as *Mystical Poems of Rūmī*
(Chicago, IL, 2009).

23 *Secret History of the Mongols*, trans. Paul Kahn [1984] (Boston, MA, 1998),
p. 173.

24 Ibn Battuta, *Travels in Asia and Africa, 1325–1354*, trans. and ed. Hamilton
Gibb, Hakluyt Society, 2nd ser., vols 110, 117, 141, 178, 190 [1929] (London,
1994), p. 454; see Ross Dunn, *The Adventures of Ibn Battuta, a Muslim
Traveler of the Fourteenth Century* (Berkeley, CA, 1986), p. 154.

25 Ibn Battuta, *Travels in Asia and Africa*, pp. 728, 727, 261–2. Other instances
of people swimming to save themselves: pp. 393 (Yemen), 552 (the Indus
River). Some Yemeni men cross a river by swimming: p. 395. Other
instances of people drowning: pp. 393, 413, 717, 725.

26 Ibid., p. 466.

27 Ibid., p. 147.

28 Salma Jayyusi, *Classical Arabic Stories: An Anthology* (New York, 2012),
p. 197; Ibn Battuta, *Travels in Asia and Africa*, p. 395, where the traveller
was nearly drowned by a treacherous guide.

29 'The Tale of the First Lady, the Mistress of the House', in *The Arabian Nights*, trans. Husain Hadawy, ed. Muhsin Mahdi (New York, 1990), p. 140.

30 'The Third Dervish's Tale', ibid., p. 123.

31 'The Second Old Man's Tale', ibid., p. 28.

32 Ibn-Khaldun, *Histoire des Berbères et des dynasties musulmanes*, trans. Baron de Slane, 3 vols (Algiers, 1852–6), vol. I, pp. 407 and 413.

33 Alvar Nuñez Cabeza de Vaca, *The Narrative of Cabeza de Vaca*, trans. Rolena Adorno and Patrick Charles Pautz (Lincoln, NB, 2003), p. 101.

34 'Abd al-Ḥaiy ibn Aḥmad ibn al-'Imād, *Shadharāt al-dhahab fī akhbār man dhahab*, 8 vols (Cairo, 1931–2, repr. Beirut, 1982), vol. VIII, pp. 259–60; Sharaf al-Dīn Mūsā ibn Ayyūb, *Kitāb al-rawḍ al-'āṭir fīmā tayassiru min akhbār ahl al-qarn al-sābi' ilā khitām al-qarn al-'āshir*, Staatsbibliothek Berlin, MS Wetzstein II 289. I am grateful to Torsten Wollina for the references and translations.

35 Ottaviano Bon, *The Sultan's Seraglio*, trans. Samuel Purchas and slightly updated (Glasgow, 1905), p. 328 (2.9.1583); Eremya Çelebi Kömürcüyan, *Istanbu Tarihi*, trans. and ed. Hrand Andreasyan (Istanbul, 1952), pp. 34–5, quoted in Ebru Boyar and Kate Fleet, *A Social History of Ottoman Istanbul* (Cambridge, 2010), p. 210.

36 Jennifer Howes, *Courts of Pre-Colonial South India* [2002] (London, 2012), p. 130.

37 *The Lalitavistara; or, Memoirs of the Early Life of Śākya Siñha*, trans. Rajendralala Mitra (Calcutta, 1881), p. 204 (chap. 12); Benjamín Preciado-Solís, *The Kṛṣṇa Cycle in the Purāṇas: Themes and Motifs in a Heroic Saga* (Delhi, 1984), p. 55; *contra* Kishin Wadhwaney, *The Story of Swimming* [1924] (New Delhi, 2002), p. 4.

38 Ibn Battuta, *Travels in Asia and Africa*, p. 616.

39 Also in Abu'l-Fazl's *Akbarnama*, folio 73r shows Nizam the watercarrier using a wooden barrel to help Humayun across the Ganges, and other images show men using inflated sacks to cross rivers. See also a painted illustration of the *Hamzanāma*, from 1562 to 1577, showing the prophet Elias trying (and failing) to rescue Hamza's nephew, Prince Nur ad-Dahr, in water full of monsters. Illustrated in Sugata Ray, *Climate Change and the Art of Devotion: Geoaesthetics in the Land of Krishna, 1550–1850* (Seattle, WA, 2019), p. 44, fig. 1.14.

40 British Museum 1974.0617.0.10.45; Brooklyn Museum 77.208.2, 'Sohni Swims to Meet Her Lover Mahinwal', and so on.

41 Lang Ye et al., *China: Five Thousand Years of History and Civilization* (Hong Kong, 2007), p. 91; Alan Sanders, *Historical Dictionary of Mongolia* [1996] (Lanham, MD, 2010), p. 520.

42 Timothy Brook, *The Troubled Empire: China in the Yuan and Ming Dynasties* (Cambridge, MA, 2010), p. 155.

43 'The Daoist Immortal Lü Dongbin Crossing Lake Dongting', Boston Museum of Fine Arts 17.185.

44 Naian Shi, *The Water Margin: Outlaws of the Marsh*, trans. J. H. Jackson [1963] (Clarendon, VT, 2010), pp. 225, 702.

45 Ibid., p. 504. See Vietnamese stories of Quận He in Chapter Nine.

46 Zhe School, 'Daoist Immortals Walking on Water', late fifteenth century (Washington, DC, Freer Gallery F1916.588); 'Eight Immortals Crossing the Sea', 1465–1505 (on exhibit in Sichuan Provincial Museum).

47 Jonathan Chaves, ed., *The Columbia Book of Later Chinese Poetry: Yüan, Ming, and Ch'ing Dynasties (1279–1911)* (New York, 1986), p. 79.

48 *The Journey to the West*, trans. and ed. Anthony Yu, revd edn (Chicago, IL, 2012), vol. IV, pp. 364, 441; vol. II, p. 358; Menglong Feng, *Stories to Caution the World: A Ming Dynasty Collection* [1624], trans. Shuhui Yang and Yunquin Yang (Seattle, WA, 2005), p. 74.

49 'Yang Sichang ji' (seventeenth century), in Patricia Ebrey, *Chinese Civilization: A Sourcebook*, 2nd edn (New York, 2009), p. 209; Feng, *Stories to Caution the World*, p. 195.

50 Jacques Gernet, *A History of Chinese Civilization*, trans. J. R. Foster (Cambridge, 1982), pp. 502–5, quoted by Mike Speak, 'The Emergence of Modern Sport: 960–1840', in *Sport and Physical Education in China*, ed. Robin Jones and James Riordan (London, 2002), p. 58.

51 Speak, 'The Emergence of Modern Sport', pp. 59–60.

52 Chiu Tsz-yung, 'A Lament for Fortune's Frailty', in *The Shorter Columbia Anthology of Traditional Chinese Literature*, ed. Victor Mair (New York, 2000), p. 288 n. 4.

53 I am indebted to Dan Martin for the transcriptions.

54 Könchog Jigmé Wangpo, *Dkon-mchog-'jigs-med-dbang-po, Chos kyi rnam grangs (=Mdo rgyud bstan bcos du ma nas 'byung ba'i chos kyi rnam grangs shes ldan yid kyi dga' ston)* (Xining, 1992), p. 121, trans. Dan Martin, 'The Tibetan Olympics of 1695. The Nine Men's Sporting Events', *Tibeto-logic*, 3 May 2008.

55 Stephen Turnbull, *The Samurai: A Military History* (New York, 1977), p. 86.

56 Lesley Wynn, 'Self-Reflection in the Tub: Japanese Bathing Culture, Identity, and Cultural Nationalism', *Asia Pacific Perspectives*, XII (2014), pp. 61–78 (p. 67); Scott Clark, *Japan: A View from the Bath* (Honolulu, HI, 1994), p. 25; Lee Butler, '"Washing Off the Dust": Baths and Bathing in Late Medieval Japan', *Monumenta Nipponica*, LX (2005), pp. 1–41 (pp. 2–4 and figs 1, 8, 20, 32); Michael Seth, *A Concise History of Korea: From Antiquity to the Present* [2006] (London, 2020), p. 208.

57 Turnbull, *Samurai*, p. 208.

58 Karl Friday and Fumitake Seki, *Legacies of the Sword: The Kashima-Shinryū and Samurai Martial Culture* (Honolulu, HI, 1997), p. 199 n.5, citing Sasama Yoshihiko, *Zusetsu Nihon budō jiten* (Tokyo, 1982), pp. 605–6.

59 William Deal, *Handbook to Life in Medieval and Early Modern Japan* (New York, 2005), p. 156.

60 Turnbull, *Samurai*, p. 147.

61 Koichi Kiku, 'The Development of Sport in Japan: Martial Arts and Baseball', in Eric Dunning et al., *Sport Histories: Figurational Studies*

in the Development of Modern Sports (London, 2004), pp. 153–71 (p. 159); François Oppenheim, *The History of Swimming* (North Hollywood, CA, 1970), p. 241.

11 A FAMOUS DROWNING

1 Ansbert, *Historia de expeditione Frederici imperatoris*, trans. Graham Loud, *The Crusade of Frederick Barbarossa: The History of the Expedition of the Emperor Frederick and Related Texts* (Farnham, 2010), p. 88. Loud's introduction elucidates the sources of this chronicle.

2 The actual role of Barbarossa's death in the failure of the Third Crusade is more complex and less direct, but some contemporary chronicles present this account.

3 *Epistola de morte Friderici imperatoris*, trans. Loud, ibid., p. 172.

4 *Chronicle of Ibn al-Athir for the Crusading Period*, from al-Kamil fi'l-ta'rikh, Part 2, *The Years 541–589/1146–1193: The Age of Nur al-Din and Saladin*, trans. Donald Richards (Aldershot, 2007), pp. 374–5.

5 *Saxon Chronicle*, trans. Hans Helmolt, in *The World's History: Central and Northern Europe* [1901] (London, 1907), p. 396.

6 Jacques de Vitry, 'Sermo [primus] ad coniugatos', Paris, Bibliothèque Nationale de France, MS. Lat. 3284, fol. 177v. For a published translation, see Thomas Crane, *The Exempla or Illustrative Stories from the Sermones vulgares of Jacques de Vitry* (London, 1890), pp. 94–5.

7 *Niebelungenlied*, trans. Cyril Edwards (Oxford, 2010), ll. 1575–9, p. 144.

8 De Joinville, in *Parthians, Sassanids, and Arabs: The Crusades and the Papacy*, ed. Henry Williams [1904] (London, 1907), p. 437.

9 Gui, a household knight of the Viscount of Melun, in *The Seventh Crusade, 1244–1254: Sources and Documents*, ed. Peter Jackson [2007] (Aldershot, 2020), p. 88.

10 *Bedfordshire Historical Records Society*, XLI (1961), Entry 23, ed. and trans. Roy Hunnisett.

11 Nicolas Orme, *Early British Swimming: 55 BC–AD 1719* (Exeter, 1983), p. 34.

12 Jacobus de Voragine, *Legenda Sanctorum*, trans. as *The Golden Legend: Readings on the Saints* by William Ryan, ed. Eamon Duffy (Princeton, NJ, 2012), p. 410.

13 George Ferzoco, 'Preaching by Thirteenth-Century Italian Hermits', in *Medieval Monastic Preaching*, ed. Carolyn Muessig (Leiden, 1998), pp. 145–59 (pp. 147–8), with Latin text in the notes.

14 Jan Lustig, *Knight Prisoner: Thomas Malory Then and Now* (Brighton, 2013), p. 66.

15 Jacobus, *Legenda Sanctorum*, pp. 50–51, 238–9, 335, 382, 410, 474, 701. Some of these stories are not in Duffy's collection but can be found in *The Golden Legend or Lives of the Saints*, trans. William Caxton, ed. Frederick Ellis (London, 1931), vol. III, p. 246, and vol. VII, pp. 25–6. There are many more examples.

16 John Lydgate's *Lives of Saints Edmund and Fremund* (1461–*c.* 1475), Yates
    Thompson 47 (British Library), f. 94v. Coroners' reports from 1485 to 1688
    cite drowning as the cause of over half of all accidental deaths of children
    under fourteen: John McManamon, *'Neither Letters nor Swimming':*
    The Rebirth of Swimming and Free-Diving (Leiden, 2021), p. 273.

17 Giovanni Boccaccio, *The Decameron*, trans. Walter Kelly (London, 1855),
    p. 66 (Second Day: The Fourth Story).

18 Ibid., p. 277 (Fifth Day: The Sixth Story).

19 Jeffrey Fynn-Paul, 'Empire, Monotheism and Slavery in the Greater
    Mediterranean Region from Antiquity to the Early Modern Era',
    Past and Present, ccv (2009), pp. 3–40 (pp. 33–4).

20 *Orkneyinga Saga*, trans. Jon Hjaltalin and Gilbert Goudie, ed. Joseph
    Anderson (Edinburgh, 1873), pp. 77, 123; *Njal's Saga* (*The Story of Burnt
    Njal*), trans. George Dasent, ed. Rasmus Anderson and J. W. Buel (London,
    1911), p. 30; *Egil's Saga*, trans. Bernard Scudder, ed. Svanhildur Óskarsdóttir
    (London, 2002), pp. 69, 76, 88.

21 *Saga of Grettir the Strong*, trans. Bernard Scudder, ed. Örnólfur Thorsson
    (London, 2005), pp. 129, 133, 137, 153, 169, 200; John McManamon agrees
    that in these sagas, 'commoners likewise distinguished themselves for their
    capacity to swim': McManamon, *'Neither Letters nor Swimming'*, p. 185.

22 Seneca, *Epistle* 56.2; Ibn Sina, *Canon of Medicine*, in *Avicenna's Medicine:*
    A New Translation, trans. Mones Abu-Asab, Hakima Amri and Mark
    Micozzi (Toronto, 2013), 2.9.19; Michael Bohn, *Heroes and Ballyhoo: How the
    Golden Age of the 1920s Transformed American Sports* (Lincoln, NE, 2009), p. 113;
    Eric Chaline, *Strokes of Genius: A History of Swimming* (London, 2017), p. 106;
    Fikret Yegül, *Bathing in the Roman World* (Cambridge, 2010), p. 21; Glenn
    Stout, *Young Woman and the Sea: How Trudy Ederle Conquered the English
    Channel and Inspired the World* (Boston, MA, and New York, 2009), p. 13.

23 Unless there is an example from tenth-century western China, in Mogao
    Cave 12, South Wall, lower right of main panels (www.e-dunhuang.com);
    on the lower left of the scene. McManamon suggests that Scandinavian
    sagas comparing swimming to rowing are describing the breaststroke:
    'Neither Letters nor Swimming', p. 187.

24 Takuya Soma, 'Ethnoarchaeology of Horse-Riding Falconry', in *The Asian
    Conference on the Social Sciences* (Osaka, 2013), pp. 82–95; Tomoko Masuya,
    'Ilkhanid Courtly Life', in *The Legacy of Genghis Khan: Courtly Art and
    Culture in Western Asia, 1256–1353*, ed. Linda Komaroff and Stefano Carboni
    (New York, 2002), p. 83. For an even more pessimistic take on Frederick's
    falconer, see McManamon, *'Neither Letters nor Swimming'*, pp. 181–2.

25 Sadaqa b. Abu'l-Qasim Shirazi, *Kitab-i Samak 'Ayyar*, Oxford, Bodleian
    Library, MS. Ouseley 381, 166b). The Bodleian Library, which houses this
    manuscript, seems to think there are two men; the illustration, from a
    Persian romance, is poorly understood.

26 Suetonius, *Julius Caesar* 64. The Boucicaut Master is illustrating a French
    translation of Boccaccio's retelling in *Concerning the Fates of Illustrious Men
    and Women*.

27 Brian Campbell, *Rivers and the Power of Ancient Rome* (Chapel Hill, NC, 2012), p. 335. The fourteenth-century swimmer from a manuscript of Vegetius now in Paris (https://gallica.bnf.fr/ark:/12148/btv1b100855893/f11. item; note not folio 5 as in McManamon *'Neither Letters nor Swimming'*, p. 183 n. 19) may be intended to represent side breathing as McManamon suggests, but in the absence of any other evidence, the awkwardness of the stroke here does not support any firm conclusion.

28 'Siege of Baghdad', from Sharaf al-din 'Ali Yazdi's *Zafarnama* (*Book of Victories*), Shiraz, 1435–6, now New York, Metropolitan Museum of Art 67.266.1. For another example of the *gopis* swimming breaststroke from 1560–70, see San Diego Museum of Art 1990.586, illustrated in Sugata Ray, *Climate Change and the Art of Devotion: Geoaesthetics in the Land of Krishna, 1550–1850* (Seattle, WA, 2019), p. 26, fig. 1.1.

29 Shigeo Sagita, 'History of Swimming', in *Swimming in Japan*, ed. Shigeo Sagita and Ken Uyeno (Tokyo, 1935), pp. 1–40 (p. 5); Masaji Kiyokawa, 'Back Stroke', ibid., pp. 162–73 (p. 165).

12 THE LITTLE ICE AGE

1 Paraphrased by Edward Schafer in 'Fusang and Beyond: The Haunted Seas to Japan', *Journal of the American Oriental Society*, CIX (1989), pp. 379–99.

2 See Chet van Duzer, *Sea Monsters on Medieval and Renaissance Maps* (London, 2013); Vaughn Scribner, *Merpeople: A Human History* (London, 2020), p. 59.

3 Hugh of Fouilloy, *Aviarium*, from northern France, now British Library, Sloane 278, fol. 47; Psalter, Assisi, Biblioteca, Fondo Antico Cod. VIII (1300s), fol. 144v; Philip J. Pirages Catalog 70.365 (France, *c.* 1270). For more examples, see Scribner, *Merpeople*.

4 'The Story of the Fisherman and the Demon', in *The Arabian Nights*, trans. Husain Hadawy, ed. Muhsin Mahdi (New York, 1990), p. 33.

5 'The Third Dervish's Tale', ibid., p. 117.

6 Catherine of Siena, 'Of the perversities, miseries, and labors of the disobedient man; and of the miserable fruits which proceed from disobedience', in *Dialogue of St Catherine of Siena*, trans. Algar Thorold [1907] (New York, 2007), p. 316. On a lighter note, see *Latin Sermon Collections from Later Medieval England: Orthodox Preaching in the Age of Wyclif*, ed. and trans. Siegfried Wensel (Cambridge, 2005), p. 302, where a monk tries (and fails) to learn to swim.

7 'The Story of Jullanar of the Sea', *Arabian Nights*, p. 413.

8 'The Third Dervish's Tale', ibid., p. 115.

9 *Little Flowers of Saint Francis of Assisi*, trans. Thomas Arnold (London, 1907), p. 304; both Noah's Flood images: Chartres window 47 (1205–35); Holkham Bible, early 1300s, London, British Library, Add MS 47682 fols 7v–8.

10 'The Washerman and His Son Who Were Drowned in the Nile', in the *Book of Sindbad* [*c.* 1200], ed. William Clouston, trans. Forbes Falconer (London, 1841), p. 15. Most of the Egyptian stories were probably added in the 1200s. In another version of this story, the boy can swim but is seized with a cramp in his arms (Richard Burton, *Arabian Nights*, 1885), though all the stories reported by Burton must be taken with several grains of salt.

11 For example Museo Nazionale di Spina 5029; British Museum E135; see Barry Cunliffe, *The Scythians: Nomad Warriors of the Steppe* (Oxford, 2019), p. 207.

12 Quran 24.30–31; 33.59.

13 'The Story of the Porter and the Three Ladies', *Arabian Nights*, pp. 73–4; see also Joseph Sadan, 'Maidens' Hair and Starry Skies', *Israel Oriental Studies*, vol. XI: *Studies in Medieval Arabic and Hebrew Poetics*, ed. Sasson Somekh (Leiden, 1991), pp. 57–90 (p. 81).

14 *The Journey to the West*, trans. and ed. Anthony Yu, revd edn, vol. III (Chicago, IL, 2012), pp. 328–9, 336.

15 Scribner, *Merpeople*, p. 220 and illus. 105; Douglas Fraser, 'The Fish-Legged Figure in Benin and Yoruba Art', in *African Art and Leadership*, ed. Fraser and Herbert Cole (Madison, WI, 1972), pp. 261–94 (p. 287); Ibn Battuta, *Travels in Asia and Africa, 1325–1354*, trans. and ed. Hamilton Gibb, Hakluyt Society, 2nd ser., vols CX, CXVII, CXLI, CLXXVIII, CXC [1929] (London, 1994), p. 965.

16 Giovanni Boccaccio, *The Decameron*, trans. Walter Kelly (London, 1855), p. 212 (Fourth Day: The Second Story); Paolo Squatriti, *Water and Society in Early Medieval Italy, AD 400–1000* (Cambridge, 1998), p. 58 n. 64.

17 John Lydgate, *The Pilgrimage of the Lyfe of Man*, cited in Elizabeth Archibald, 'Bathing, Beauty and Christianity in the Middle Ages', *Durham University Insights*, V (2012), pp. 2–13 (p. 9); Jill Caskey, 'Steam and "Sanitas" in the Domestic Realm: Baths and Bathing in Southern Italy in the Middle Ages', *Journal of the Society of Architectural Historians*, LVIII (1999), pp. 170–95 (p. 170); Scribner, *Merpeople*, p. 61; Squatriti, *Water and Society*, p. 59.

18 Stefanie Hoss, *Baths and Bathing: The Culture of Bathing and the Baths and Thermae in Palestine from the Hasmoneans to the Moslem Conquest*, British Archaeological Reports International Series 1346 (Oxford, 2005), p. 90.

19 Ibn Sina, *Canon of Medicine*, in *Avicenna's Medicine: A New Translation*, trans. Mones Abu-Asab, Hakima Amri and Mark Micozzi (Toronto, 2013), 2.9.19, 3.13.5: 'if they use the bathtub, they should only stay until their skin becomes red and puffy, and leave at the start of the dispersion of their bodily waste . . . then they should rinse quickly and get out'; Maimonides, *Human Temperaments* 16, in Fred Rosner, *The Medical Legacy of Moses Maimonides* (Brooklyn, NY, 1998), pp. 223–4.

20 Edward Schafer, 'The Development of Bathing Customs in Ancient and Medieval China and the History of the Floriate Clear Palace', *Journal of the American Oriental Society*, LXXVI (1956), pp. 57–82 (p. 61).

21 Ibn Sina, *Canon of Medicine*, 2.9.19; Ibn Battuta, *Travels in Asia and Africa*, p. 329.

22 Guy Geltner, 'The Path to Pistoia: Urban Hygiene before the Black Death', *Past and Present*, CCXLVI (2020), pp. 3–33 (p. 15); Caskey, 'Steam and "Sanitas"', pp. 170–95.

23 Elizabeth Archibald, 'Did Knights Have Baths? The Absence of Bathing in Middle English Romance', in *Cultural Encounters in the Romance of Medieval England*, ed. Corinne Saunders (Cambridge, 2005), pp. 101–15; see also Richard Raiswell and Peter Dendle, 'Demon Possession in Anglo-Saxon and Early Modern England: Continuity and Evolution in Social Context', *Journal of British Studies*, XLVII (2008), pp. 738–67 (pp. 738, 749, 751).

24 Caskey, 'Steam and "Sanitas"', p. 188.

25 Schafer, 'Bathing Customs', p. 71.

26 Ibid., p. 59.

27 Ibn Battuta, *Travels in Asia and Africa*, p. 329.

28 Poggio Bracciolini, letter to Niccolo Niccoli, in *The Life of Poggio Bracciolini*, trans. William Shepherd (Liverpool, 1802), pp. 70–71. See Stephen Greenblatt, *The Swerve: How the World Became Modern* (New York, 2011); Georges Vigarello, *Concepts of Cleanliness: Changing Attitudes in France since the Middle Ages* (Cambridge, 1988); McManamon, *'Neither Letters nor Swimming': The Rebirth of Swimming and Free-Diving* (Leiden, 2021), p. 187.

29 Nicolas Orme, *Early British Swimming, 55 BC–AD 1719* (Exeter, 1983), pp. 37–8.

30 Archibald, 'Bathing, Beauty and Christianity', pp. 9–10; Philippe Braunstein, 'Toward Intimacy: The Fourteenth and Fifteenth Centuries', in *A History of Private Life*, vol. II: *Revelations of the Medieval World*, trans. A. Goldhammer, ed. Philippe Ariès and Georges Duby (Cambridge, MA, 1988), pp. 535–630; Squatriti, *Water and Society*, p. 57.

31 Caskey, 'Steam and "Sanitas"', pp. 172, 184.

32 Karen Liebreich, *Fallen Order: Intrigue, Heresy, and Scandal in the Rome of Galileo and Caravaggio* (London, 2004), p. 65.

33 Caskey, 'Steam and "Sanitas"', p. 170; McManamon also attributes the decline in swimming to increasing Christianization (*'Neither Letters nor Swimming'*, p. 181).

34 Jean Charles Poncelin, 'Dissertation sur les Bains', introducing the 4th edn of Melchisédech Thévenot, *L'Art de Nager* (Paris, 1781), pp. 14–16. See Rebekka v. Mallinckrodt, 'French Enlightenment Swimming', in *Sports and Physical Exercise in Early Modern Culture*, ed. Mallinckrodt and Angela Schattner (London, 2016), pp. 231–51.

35 Michael Bohn, *Heroes and Ballyhoo: How the Golden Age of the 1920s Transformed American Sports* (Lincoln, NE, 2009), p. 113; Cecil Colwin, *Breakthrough Swimming* (Champaign, IL, 2002), p. 5; Kevin Dawson, 'Swimming, Surfing and Underwater Diving in Early Modern Atlantic Africa and the African Diaspora', in *Navigating African Maritime History*, ed. Carina Ray and Jeremy Rich (Oxford, 2009), pp. 81–116 (p. 88); Liz Sharp, *Reconnecting People and Water: Public Engagement and Sustainable Urban Water Management* (London, 2017), p. 71.

36 Geltner, 'The Path to Pistoia', pp. 3–4.

37 John McManamon, *Caligula's Barges and the Renaissance Origins of Nautical Archaeology Under Water* (College Station, TX, 2016), p. 168.

38 Michael McCormick, *Origins of the European Economy: Communications and Commerce, AD 300–900* (Cambridge, 2001); McManamon, *'Neither Letters nor Swimming'*, p. 181.

39 Franck Lavigne and Sébastien Guillet, 'The Unknown AD 1275 Stratospheric Eruption: Climatic Impacts in Europe and Tentative Volcanic Source', in *Past Vulnerability: Vulcanic Eruptions and Human Vulnerability in Traditional Societies Past and Present*, ed. Felix Riede (Aarhus, 2015), pp. 63–74 (p. 64).

40 Philipp Blom, *Nature's Mutiny: How the Little Ice Age of the Long Seventeenth Century Transformed the West and Shaped the Present* (New York, 2017), pp. 10, 17.

41 Brian Fagan, *The Little Ice Age: How Climate Made History, 1300–1850* (New York, 2000), p. 159. In Johanna Spyri's *Heidi* [1881], for example, the very poorest people in the most isolated hamlet in the Alps are still mournfully eating black bread.

42 Lavigne and Guillet, 'The Unknown AD 1275 Stratospheric Eruption', p. 69; Timothy Shanahan et al., 'Atlantic Forcing of Persistent Drought in West Africa', *Science*, CCCXXIV (2009), pp. 377–80 (p. 378); David Anderson et al., 'Increase in the Asian Southwest Monsoon during the Past Four Centuries', *Science*, CCXCVII (2002), pp. 596–9: 'the cooling during the Little Ice Age may have weakened the southwest monsoon [that brings rain to India] several hundred years ago'; Anil Gupta et al., 'Abrupt Changes in the Asian Southwest Monsoon during the Holocene and their Links to the North Atlantic Ocean', *Nature*, CDXXI (2003), pp. 354–7.

43 Anil Gupta et al., 'Abrupt Changes in Indian Summer Monsoon Strength during the Last ~900 years and Their Linkages to Socio-Economic Conditions in the Indian Subcontinent', *Palaeogeography, Palaeoclimatology, Palaeoecology*, DXXXVI (2019), pp. 354–7.

44 Sugata Ray, *Climate Change and the Art of Devotion: Geoaesthetics in the Land of Krishna, 1550–1850* (Seattle, WA, 2019), pp. 22, 27, 38, 45.

45 Ibid., pp. 37, 58.

13 AFRICAN SWIMMERS

1 John McManamon, *Caligula's Barges and the Renaissance Origins of Nautical Archaeology Under Water* (College Station, TX, 2016), p. 151; Thomas Earle, *Black Africans in Renaissance Europe* (Cambridge, 2005), p. 34; Kevin Dawson, *Undercurrents of Power: Aquatic Culture in the African Diaspora* (Philadelphia, PA, 2018), p. 1.

2 Philipp Blom, *Nature's Mutiny: How the Little Ice Age of the Long Seventeenth Century Transformed the West and Shaped the Present* (New York, 2017), p. 24; Anthony Pagden, *European Encounters with the New World: From Renaissance to Romanticism* (New Haven, CT, 1993), p. 6.

3 Herodotus describes the Niger River: *Histories* 2.32 and India: *Histories* 3.94–106; al-Idrisi's map, the *Tabula Rogeriana*, was drawn in Palermo, Sicily, in 1154; his *Geography*, *Nuzhat al-Mushtaq* mentions the Atlantic seaweed patch (the Sargasso Sea), as does Avienus' much earlier *Ora Maritima* (fourth century CE). See also Maximus Planudes's map, drawn at Constantinople *c.* 1300, or Genoese mapmaker Pietro Vesconte's map from 1321, British Library Add. MS 27376.

4 Cathie Carmichael, *A Concise History of Bosnia* (Cambridge, 2015), pp. 22–3; Molly Greene, 'The Ottomans in the Mediterranean', in *The Early Modern Ottomans: Remapping the Empire*, ed. Daniel Goffman and Virginia Aksan (Cambridge, 2007), pp. 104–11 (pp. 105–6, 111); Michael McCormick, *Origins of the European Economy: Communications and Commerce, AD 300–900* (Cambridge, 2001), pp. 761–74; Jeffrey Fynn-Paul, 'Empire, Monotheism and Slavery in the Greater Mediterranean Region from Antiquity to the Early Modern Era', *Past and Present*, CCV (2009), pp. 3–40 (pp. 36–7).

5 Olivia Remie Constable, 'Muslim Spain and Mediterranean Slavery: The Medieval Slave Trade as an Aspect of Muslim-Christian Relations', in *Christendom and Its Discontents: Exclusion, Persecution, and Rebellion, 1000–1500*, ed. Scott Waugh and Peter Diehl (Cambridge, 1996), pp. 264–84 (p. 265).

6 John Wright, *The Trans-Saharan Slave Trade* (Abingdon, 2007), pp. 18–28.

7 Gomes Eanes de Zurara, *Crónica de Guiné* [*c.* 1453], in *The Portuguese in West Africa, 1415–1670: A Documentary History*, ed. Malyn Newitt (Cambridge, 2010), pp. 44–6 (p. 46). Jacques Le Maire reports that in the 1680s, when their ship was about to be burnt, 'some Moors and Dutch . . . swam for it': Le Maire, *The Voyages of the Sieur Le Maire to the Canary Islands, Cape-Verde, Senegal, and Gambia*, in *A Collection of Voyages and Travels*, trans. E. G., ed. Thomas Osborne (London, 1745), vol. II, pp. 596–620 (pp. 603, 607).

8 Zamba, *The Life and Adventures of Zamba, an African Negro King; and His Experience of Slavery in South Carolina* (London, 1847), pp. 1, 168–70. The authenticity of this slave narrative is admittedly uncertain, but Duarte Lopez affirms that the people of Congo often swim across a channel to nearby islands: *Relatione del reame del Congo*, trans. Filippo Pigafetta (Rome, 1591); as *History of the Kingdom of Congo*, trans. Margarite Hutchinson (London, 1881), p. 20.

9 Benjamin Prentiss, *The Blind African Slave, or Memoirs of Boyrereay Brinch, Nick-Named Jeffrey Brace* (St Albans, 1810), pp. 68–9, 70, 96, 124; Dawson, *Undercurrents of Power*, p. 23; Jean Baptiste Labat, *Nouvelle relation de l'Afrique occidentale* (Paris, 1728), vol. I, p. 158: along the Atlantic coast of Senegal, two 'Moors' swam up to the canoe to exchange news, but didn't want to climb in.

10 Dawson, *Undercurrents of Power*, p. 25, quoting Robert Rattray, *Ashanti* (Oxford, 1923), pp. 61–5. See also Le Maire, *Voyages*, p. 617: West Africans 'are good swimmers' who don't mind if their canoes overturn; for a longer

description of the same, see Labat, *Nouvelle relation*, vol. ii, pp. 128–9; on p. 130 they are excellent swimmers, used to swimming.

11 Richard Burton, *Wanderings in West Africa from Liverpool to Fernando Po* (London, 1863), vol. i, p. 195; Lopez, *History*, pp. 18–19; Jean Barbot, *Barbot on Guinea: The Writings of Jean Barbot on West Africa, 1678–1712*, ed. Paul Hair et al. (London, 1992), vol. ii, p. 489; Dawson, *Undercurrents of Power*, p. 58.

12 Jan Hogendorn, 'A "Supply-Side" Aspect of the African Slave Trade: The Cowrie Production and Exports of the Maldives', *Slavery and Abolition*, ii (1981), pp. 31–52.

13 Pieter de Marees, *Description and Historical Account of the Gold Kingdom of Guinea* [1602], ed. and trans. Albert van Dantzig and Adam Jones (Oxford, 1987), p. 186.

14 Barbot, *Barbot on Guinea*, p. 532; see Isak Lidström and Ingvar Svanberg, 'Ancient Buoyancy Devices in Sweden: Floats Made of Reed, Club-Rush, Inflated Skins and Animal Bladders', *Folk Life: Journal of Ethnological Studies*, lvii (2019), pp. 85–94; Dawson, *Undercurrents of Power*, pp. 29–31.

15 Alfred Drayson, *Sporting Scenes amongst the Kaffirs of South Africa* (London, 1858), chap. ii.

16 Alvaro Velho and João de Sá, *A Journal of the First Voyage of Vasco Da Gama, 1497–1499*, ed. and trans. Ernst Ravenstein (London, 1898), pp. 37, 39; see also Afonso de Albuquerque, *Commentaries*, trans. Walter de Gray Birch (London, 1884), vol. iv, p. 28.

17 Hiob Ludolf, *A New History of Ethiopia*, trans. J. P. Gent (London, 1682), pp. 290–91. Ludolf wrote this history in cooperation with Aba Gorgorios; he says explicitly that he heard this swimming anecdote 'from Gregorie's own Lips' in the 1650s.

18 Labat, *Nouvelle relation*, vol. ii, p. 350, translation mine. (Not Jacques Le Maire, though the attribution is unclear in *A New General Collection of Voyages and Travels*, ed. John Green and Thomas Astley (London, 1745), vol. ii, p. 362. But see Le Maire, *Voyages*, p. 611: swimmers attacked by sharks and crocodiles.)

19 Samuel Baker, *The Nile Tributaries of Abyssinia and the Sword Hunters of the Hamran Arabs*, 3rd edn (London, 1868), p. 376.

20 C. Herbert Gilliland, *Voyage to a Thousand Cares: Master's Mate Lawrence with the African Squadron, 1844–1846* (Annapolis, MD, 2004), p. 64: 'three of [the West African Kroomen] divested themselves of their clothing in a twinkling and were in the Ocean in chase of him.'

21 Labat, *Nouvelle relation*, vol. ii, p. 347; Dawson, *Undercurrents of Power*, p. 41.

22 John Weeks, *Among Congo Cannibals* (Philadelphia, PA, 1913), pp. 332–3; Dawson, *Undercurrents of Power*, pp. 41–5, 49, 59.

23 Olaudah Equiano, *The Interesting Narrative of the Life of Olaudah Equiano or Gustavus Vassa the African* (London, 1789), esp. pp. 54, 79; de Marees, *Description and Historical Account*, p. 186.

24 Vaughn Scribner, *Merpeople: A Human History* (London, 2020), p. 220 and illus. 105, though Douglas Fraser suggests that merpeople images reached

Africa through the Byzantine Empire (Fraser, 'The Fish-Legged Figure in Benin and Yoruba Art', in *African Art and Leadership*, ed. Fraser and Herbert Cole (Madison, WI, 1972), pp. 261–94).

25   Alvise Cà da Mosto, *Relation des voyages à la côte occidentale d'Afrique, 1455–1457* (Paris, 1895), p. 85; see Newitt, *The Portuguese in West Africa*, p. 76.

26   Jean Barbot, in *Barbot on Guinea*, vol. II, p. 545 n. 50; cited in Kevin Dawson, 'Swimming, Surfing, and Underwater Diving in Early Modern Atlantic Africa and the African Diaspora', in *Navigating African Maritime History*, ed. Carina Ray and Jeremy Rich (Oxford, 2009), pp. 81–116.

27   De Marees, *Description and Historical Account*, p. 187; Dawson, *Undercurrents of Power*, p. 15.

28   Newitt, *The Portuguese in West Africa*, p. 69.

29   Johann von Lübelfing, in *German Sources for West African History, 1599–1669*, ed. Adam Jones (Wiesbaden, 1983), p. 12.

30   Jan van Riebeeck, *Journal*, trans. J. Smuts (Cape Town, 1897), entry for 4 February 1656.

31   Mungo Park, *Travels in the Interior Districts of Africa: Performed under the Direct Patronage of the African Association, in the Years 1795, 1796, and 1797* (London, 1799), pp. 71–2, esp. 72, 210–11, esp. 210; Mungo Park, *Travels of Mungo Park containing Book One, The First Journey: Travels in the Interior Districts of Africa and Book Two, The Second Journey: The Journal of a Mission to the Interior of Africa in the Year 1805* (London, 1815), pp. 53–4, 161.

32   And because he was under attack from local people who did not want him to pass: Mark Duffill, *Mungo Park* (Edinburgh, 1999), p. 133.

33   Kevin Dawson, 'Enslaved Swimmers and Divers in the Atlantic World', *Journal of American History*, 92 (2006), pp. 1327–55 (p. 1332).

34   *Sindbad the Sailor and Other Stories from the Arabian Nights*, trans. Laurence Housman (London, 1914), pp. 9, 22, 25, 29, 42, 48–9, 57, 188.

35   Pagden, *European Encounters with the New World*, p. 6; Josiah Blackmore, *Moorings: Portuguese Expansion and the Writing of Africa* (Minneapolis, MN, 2008), pp. 22–4.

36   Anthony Pagden, *Peoples and Empires: A Short History of European Migration, Exploration, and Conquest, from Greece to the Present* (New York, 2001), p. 108; see David Davis, *In the Image of God: Religion, Moral Values, and Our Heritage of Slavery* (New Haven, CT, 2001), p. 126.

37   De Marees, *Description and Historical Account*, p. 26; see Dawson, *Undercurrents of Power*, p. 23.

38   Willem Bosman, *New and Accurate Description of the Coast of Guinea* (London, 1704), pp. 121–2.

39   Barbot, *Barbot on Guinea*, pp. 501 n. 16, 532, 639–40.

40   Cecil Colwin, *Breakthrough Swimming* (Champaign, IL, 2002), p. 4. Equally, nobody's lives are unchanged through 'time immemorial'.

41   William Percey, *The Compleat Swimmer* (1658); quoted in Dawson, 'Enslaved Swimmers and Divers', p. 1332.

42   Preface by the editor, in Benjamin Franklin's *Art of Swimming Rendered Easy*, p. 3, quoted in Dawson, 'Enslaved Swimmers', p. 1332.

43 For modern instances of this same belief, see Adam Waytz, Kelly Hoffman and Sophie Trawalter, 'A Superhumanization Bias in Whites' Perceptions of Blacks', *Social Psychological and Personality Science*, VI (2014), pp. 352–9.

44 Wilma King, '"Prematurely Knowing of Evil Things": The Sexual Abuse of African American Girls and Young Women in Slavery and Freedom', *Journal of African American History*, XCIX (2014), pp. 173–96.

45 Bosman, *New and Accurate Description*, pp. 121–2; Dawson, *Undercurrents of Power*, p. 58.

46 Charles Stewart, *Diary of Chas. J. Stewart: New York to Monrovia, West Coast Africa* (St Thomas Public Library, Manuscript Microfilm No. 382, 1861), p. 52, cited in Dawson, *Undercurrents of Power*, p. 58.

47 Equiano, *The Interesting Narrative*, p. 47; see Roxanne Wheeler, *The Complexion of Race: Categories of Difference in Eighteenth-Century British Culture* (Philadelphia, PA, 2000), p. 272.

48 *The World Displayed; or, A Curious Collection of Voyages and Travels*, ed. Samuel Johnson et al. (London, 1767), vol. XVII, p. 103.

49 Mia Bay, *The White Image in the Black Mind: African-American Ideas about White People, 1830–1925* (Oxford, 2000), pp. 3–4; Wheeler, *The Complexion of Race*, p. 272.

50 Dawson, *Undercurrents of Power*, p. 16.

51 Walter Scheidel, *Escape from Rome: The Failure of Empire and the Road to Prosperity* (Princeton, NJ, 2019), p. 457; Matthew Cobb, *Rome and the Indian Ocean Trade from Augustus to the Early Third Century CE* (Leiden, 2018); Edward Alpers, *The Indian Ocean in World History* (Oxford, 2013).

52 Pacifico Sella, *Il Vangelo in Oriente: Giovanni da Montecorvino, frate minore e primo Vescovo in terra di Cina, 1307–1328* (Assisi, 2008), p. 132 and *passim*.

53 Timothy Insoll, *The Land of Enki in the Islamic Era: Pearls, Palms, and Religious Identity in Bahrain* (London, 2005), p. 319.

54 Sanjay Subrahmanyam, *The Portuguese Empire in Asia, 1500–1700: A Political and Economic History* (New York, 2012), p. 99.

55 Mahmood Kooria, '"Killed the Pilgrims and Persecuted Them": Portuguese Estado da India's Encounters with the Hajj in the Sixteenth Century', in *The Hajj and Europe in the Age of Empire*, ed. Umar Ryad (Leiden, 2017), pp. 14–46 (p. 24).

56 Gaspar Correa, *The Three Voyages of Vasco da Gama, and His Viceroyalty*, trans. Henry Stanley (London, 1869), p. 252.

57 Ibid., p. 333.

14 IN THE AMERICAS

1 George Tinker and Mark Freeland, 'Thief, Slave Trader, Murderer: Christopher Columbus and Caribbean Population Decline', *Wičazo Ša Review*, XXIII (2008), pp. 25–50 (p. 26).

2 Entry for Thursday, 11 October 1492, translation slightly adapted from Edward Bourne, 'Original Narratives of the Voyages of Columbus', in

The Northmen, Columbus, and Cabot, 985–1503, ed. Julius Olson and Edward Bourne (New York, 1906), pp. 77ff.

3   Amerigo Vespucci, letter to Pier Soderini in Florence [1497], in *American Historical Documents, 1000–1904*, ed. Charles Eliot, Harvard Classics XLIII (Cambridge, MA, 1910), p. 33.

4   Bernal Diaz del Castillo, *The Memoirs of the Conquistador Bernal Diaz del Castillo*, ed. and trans. John Lockhart (London, 1844), vol. I, p. 11.

5   Alvar Nuñez Cabeza de Vaca, *The Narrative of Cabeza de Vaca*, trans. Rolena Adorno and Patrick Pautz (Lincoln, NE, 2003), pp. 97, 98, 101.

6   Tomas de la Torre, 'The Journey Across the Atlantic', in *Colonial Travelers in Latin America*, ed. William Bryant and Irving Leonard (New York, 1972), p. 38 (20 August).

7   Francisco Lopez de Mendoza Grajales, 'The Founding of St Augustine', in *The Library of Original Sources*, vol. V: *9th to 16th Centuries*, ed. Oliver Thatcher (New York, 1907), pp. 327–41. See also Bartolomé de las Casas, *Historia de las Indias*, ed. André Saint- Lu (Caracas, 1986), vol. III, pp. 120, 180–81, 277, 296, all referring to 'those who could not swim'.

8   Fernand Braudel, 'History and the Social Sciences: The Longue Durée', trans. Immanuel Wallerstein, *Review (Fernand Braudel Center)*, XXXII/2 (2009), pp. 171–203 (p. 195); Josiah Blackmore, *Manifest Perdition: Shipwreck Narrative and the Disruption of Empire* (Minneapolis, MN, 2002), pp. 28, 91; Jonathan Schorsch, *Swimming the Christian Atlantic: Judeoconversos, Afroiberians and Amerindians in the Seventeenth Century* (Leiden, 2009), p. 9.

9   Vaughn Scribner, *Merpeople: A Human History* (London, 2020), p. 63.

10 John Major, *In secundum librum Sententiarum*, 2nd edn (Paris, 1519), quoted by Anthony Pagden, 'The Peopling of the New World: Ethnos, Race and Empire in the Early-Modern World', in *The Origins of Racism in the West*, ed. Miriam Eliav-Feldon and Benjamin Isaac (Cambridge, 2009), pp. 292–312 (p. 301), now also in Pagden, *The Burdens of Empire: 1539 to the Present* (Cambridge, 2015), pp. 97–119.

11 Jean de Léry, *History of a Voyage to the Land of Brazil, otherwise Called America*, trans. Janet Whatley (Berkeley, CA, 1992), pp. 96–7.

12 John McManamon, *Caligula's Barges and the Renaissance Origins of Nautical Archaeology Under Water* (College Station, TX, 2016), p. 151; Kevin Dawson, *Undercurrents of Power: Aquatic Culture in the African Diaspora* (Philadelphia, PA, 2018), p. 64.

13 Pietro Martire d'Anghiera, *De orbe novo: The Eight Decades of Peter Martyr d'Anghera* [*sic*], trans. Francis MacNutt (New York, 1912), p. 191.

14 The French friar Anastasius Douay, in *The Journeys of Rene Robert Cavelier Sieur de La Salle*, ed. Isaac Cox (New York, 1922), vol. I, p. 266.

15 Junius Bird, 'The Alacaluf', in *Handbook of South American Indians*, ed. Julian Steward, Smithsonian Institution, Bureau of American Ethnology, 143 (1946), pp. 55–80 (p. 60); cited in Gregory Waselkov, 'Shellfish Gathering and Shell Midden Archaeology', *Advances in Archaeological Method and Theory*, X (1987), pp. 93–210 (p. 97).

16 Martire d'Anghiera, *De orbe novo*, p. 192.

17 Bartoleme de las Casas, *A Short Account of the Destruction of the Indies*, ed. and trans. Nigel Griffin (London, 1992), pp. 93–4.

18 De Marees, *Description and Historical Account*, p. 186.

19 *Contra* Dawson, *Undercurrents of Power*, p. 61, but see p. 80; Molly Warsh, 'Enslaved Pearl Divers in the Sixteenth Century Caribbean', *Slavery and Abolition*, XXXI (2010), pp. 345–62 (p. 348).

20 Dawson, 'Enslaved Swimmers and Divers in the Atlantic World', *Journal of American History*, 92 (2006), pp. 1327–55 (pp. 1346, 1350); Dawson, *Undercurrents of Power*, p. 65; McManamon, *Caligula's Barges*, pp. 150–51, though Peter Mancall (*Nature and Culture in the Early Modern Atlantic*, Philadelphia, PA, 2017, p. 160) warns us not to take assertions of breath-holding too literally.

21 Dawson, *Undercurrents of Power*, p. 18.

22 Jean Charles Poncelin, 'Dissertation sur les Bains', introducing the 4th edn of Melchisédech Thévenot, *L'Art de Nager* (Paris, 1781), pp. 16–18; McManamon, 'Neither Letters nor Swimming', pp. 326–7, 370–71.

23 Dawson, *Undercurrents of Power*, pp. 22, 84; Judith Carney, *Black Rice: The African Origins of Rice Cultivation in the Americas* (Cambridge, MA, 2001), pp. 65–8; Dawson, 'Enslaved Swimmers and Divers', pp. 1351–2.

24 Harriet Beecher Stowe, *Uncle Tom's Cabin* [1852] (New York, 1981), p. 233; Dawson, *Undercurrents of Power*, pp. 57–63.

25 Lee Pitts, *Black Splash: The History of African American Swimmers* (Fort Lauderdale, FL, 2007), p. 2; Solomon Northrup, *Twelve Years a Slave: Narrative of Solomon Northrup, a Citizen of New-York, Kidnapped in Washington City in 1841, and Rescued in 1853* (Auburn, NY, 1853), p. 137; more examples in Dawson, *Undercurrents of Power*, p. 40.

26 George Pinckard, *Notes on the West Indies* (London, 1806), vol. II, p. 321.

27 James Johnston, *From Slave Ship to Harvard: Yarrow Mamout and the History of an African American Family* (New York, 2012), p. 79; Slave Narrative of Bill Crump, Federal Writers' Project, *North Carolina Slave Narratives*, XIV (Washington, DC, 1938), p. 208; Dawson, *Undercurrents of Power*, pp. 81–3.

28 Dawson, *Undercurrents of Power*, pp. 27, 33–4.

29 Andrew Kahrl, 'On the Beach: Race and Leisure in the Jim Crow South', PhD thesis, Indiana University, 2008, p. 20. See Dawson, 'Enslaved Swimmers and Divers', pp. 1327–55; Dawson, *Undercurrents of Power*, pp. 19–20.

30 John Lawson, *New Voyage to Carolina*, ed. Hugh Lefler (Chapel Hill, NC, 1967), p. 158; Dawson, *Undercurrents of Power*, pp. 41–53.

31 Dawson, 'Enslaved Swimmers', p. 1333; Dawson, *Undercurrents of Power*, pp. 45–50; Jane Carson, *Colonial Virginians at Play* (Charlottesville, VA, 1958), p. 67.

32 Dawson, *Undercurrents of Power*, pp. 47–8, 53–4.

33 English Combatant, *Battlefields of the South from Bull Run to Fredericksburgh; with Sketches of Confederate Commanders, and Gossip of the Camps* (London, 1863), p. 273; for more examples see Dawson, *Undercurrents of Power*, pp. 17–18, 53.

34 Edward Long, *The History of Jamaica: or, General Survey of the Antient and Modern State of that Island: With Reflections on its Situation, Settlements, Inhabitants, Climate, Products, Commerce, Laws and Government* (London, 1774), vol. II, pp. 353–6.

35 Pinckard, *West Indies*, pp. 148–9, 150, cited by Dawson, 'Enslaved Swimmers', n. 33.

36 See Dawson, *Undercurrents of Power*, pp. 15–19.

37 *Journeys of Rene Robert Cavelier Sieur de La Salle*, pp. 229–30.

38 Richard Mandell, *Sport: A Cultural History* (New York, 1984), pp. 179–80; cited in Dawson, 'Enslaved Swimmers', p. 1329.

39 *Journeys of Rene Robert Cavelier Sieur de La Salle*, p. 296; William Kip, *The Early Jesuit Missions in North America* (Albany, NY, 1846), pp. 71, 216–18.

40 Meriwether Lewis and William Clark, *Original Journals of the Lewis and Clark Expedition, 1804–1806*, ed. Reuben Thwaites (New York, 1904), vol. II, p. 37. Lewis also describes the incident, but does not mention swimming: 'the Indian woman to whom I ascribe equal fortitude and resolution, with any person onboard at the time of the accedent, caught and preserved most of the light articles which were washed overboard' (p. 39).

41 Lewis and Clark, *Original Journals* (New York, 1904), vol. I, p. 40.

42 Al-Idrisi, *Geography (Nuzhat al-Mushtaq)*, in *Medieval West Africa: Views from Arab Scholars and Merchants*, ed. Nehemia Levtzion and Jay Spaulding (Princeton, NJ, 2003), p. 31; Ibn Battuta, *Travels in Asia and Africa, 1325–1354*, trans. and ed. Hamilton Gibb, Hakluyt Society, 2nd ser., vols 110, 117, 141, 178, 190 [1929] (London, 1994), p. 965; Ibn Khaldun, *Muqaddima* 1.169–70, cited in John Hunwick, 'A Region of the Mind: Medieval Arab Views of African Geography and Ethnography and Their Legacy', *Sudanic Africa*, XVI (2005), pp. 103–36 (p. 131).

43 Leo Africanus, *The History and Description of Africa and of the Notable Things Therein Contained*, trans. John Pory, ed. Robert Brown (New York, 1896), pp. 186–7.

44 Juan López Palacios Rubios, 'Insularum mari Oceani tractatus', in *De las islas del mar Océano*, ed. Augustin Millares Carlo (Mexico City, 1954), p. 24; quoted by Pagden, 'The Peopling of the New World', p. 303.

45 De Marees, *Description and Historical Account*, p. 186.

46 Richard Ligon, *A True and Exact History of the Island of Barbadoes* [1673] (Portland, OR, 1998), p. 51; Keith Sandiford, *Theorizing a Colonial Caribbean-Atlantic Imaginary: Sugar and Obeah* (New York, 2010), p. 89.

47 John Stedman, *Narrative of Five Year's Expedition Against the Revolted Negroes of Surinam, in Guiana, on the Wild Coast of South America; from the Year 1772, to 1777* (London, 1813), vol. II, pp. 375–6; Dawson, *Undercurrents of Power*, pp. 40, 49, 52.

48 Stedman, *Narrative*, pp. 7, 295.

49 John Warren, *Para: or, Scenes and Adventures on the Banks of the Amazon* (New York, 1851), p. 9; the reference to mermaids is probably taken from Herman Melville's 1846 novel *Typee*, as quoted below.

50 Charles Charlton, 'Margarite Campos, 14 years old Cuna, Albino from Yantuppu Island, Swimming in Water' (Panama, 1924), now in the Smithsonian Institution, National Anthropological Archives Inv. 04276800, Washington, DC.

15 CHINA AND THE PACIFIC OCEAN

1 'Navigation and Voyage which Fernando Magalhaes made from Seville to Maluco in the year 1519 (by a Genoese Pilot)', *The Library of Original Sources*, vol. v: *9th to 16th Centuries*, ed. Oliver Thatcher (Milwaukee, WI, 1907), pp. 41–57; Diogo Lopez de Sequeira, in Afonso de Albuquerque, *Commentaries*, trans. Walter de Gray Birch (London, 1880), p. 151.

2 Pedro Chirino, *Relación de las Islas Filipinas I de lo que en ellas an trabaiado los padres dae la Compañia de Iesus* (Rome, 1604), pp. 21–2; cited by Stefan Smith, *Creolization and Diaspora in the Portuguese Indies: The Social World of Ayutthaya, 1640–1720* (Leiden, 2011), p. 106.

3 Captain King, 'Journal of the Transactions on Returning to the Sandwich Islands', in James Cook et al., *The Voyages of Captain James Cook* (London, 1846), vol. II, p. 425 (March 1779).

4 Amasa Delano, *Narrative of Voyages and Travels in the Northern and Southern Hemispheres* (Boston, MA, 1817), p. 191.

5 Kevin Dawson, *Undercurrents of Power: Aquatic Culture in the African Diaspora* (Philadelphia, PA, 2018), p. 1.

6 Thomas Trecher, in John Rickman, *Journal of Captain Cook's Last Voyage to the Pacific Ocean* (London, 1781), p. 213; James Cook, *Voyages Round the World* (London, 1896), p. 234.

7 François Peron, *A Collection of Modern and Contemporary Voyages and Travels* (London, 1809), Atlas Plate IV.

8 Joseph Banks, John Hawkesworth and James Cook, *The Three Voyages of Captain Cook Round the World* (London, 1821), vol. I, p. 98; Dawson, *Undercurrents of Power*, p. 31.

9 *Contra* Nicholas Orme, *Early British Swimming, 55 BC–AD 1719* (Exeter, 1983), p. 101.

10 Daniel Defoe, *The Adventures of Robinson Crusoe* [1719] (London, 1872), pp. 19–20, 46, 190–91; Jonathan Swift, *Gulliver's Travels* [1726], ed. Claude Rawson (Oxford, 2005), pp. 16, 67, 97, 248–9.

11 William Byrd, *The Writings of 'Colonel William Byrd, of Westover in Virginia, Esqr.'*, ed. John Bassett (New York, 1901), p. 305.

12 Pieter de Marees, *Description and Historical Account of the Gold Kingdom of Guinea* [1602], ed. and trans. Albert van Dantzig and Adam Jones (Oxford, 1987), pp. 186–7.

13 Richard Ligon, *A True and Exact History of the Island of Barbadoes* [1673] (Portland, OR, 1998), p. 51; Dawson, *Undercurrents of Power*, p. 50.

14 Aboriginal Australians: William Wilson, *The Swimming Instructor: A Treatise on the Arts of Swimming and Diving* (London, 1883), p. 127;

Hawaiians: Richard Nelligan, *The Art of Swimming: A Practical Working Manual* (Boston, MA, 1906), pp. 27–9; Cecil Colwin, *Breakthrough Swimming* (Champaign, IL, 2002), p. 4.

15 Willem Bosman mentions swimming the backstroke, 'as our Boys commonly do', in 1721: *A New and Accurate Description of the Coast of Guinea* (London, 1705), p. 266.

16 *The Life and Letters of St Francis Xavier*, ed. Henry Coleridge, vol. II, 2nd edn (London, 1890), pp. 331–50; reprinted in *Modern Asia and Africa, Readings in World History*, ed. William McNeil and Mitsuko Iriye, vol. IX (Oxford, 1971), pp. 20–30.

17 Alessandro Valignano, *Historia del principio y progreso de la Compañía de Jesús en las Indias Orientales (1542–64)*, ed. Josef Wicki (Rome, 1944), pp. 127–54, trans. Donald Lach, *Asia in the Making of Europe* (Chicago, IL, 2010), vol. I, book 2, pp. 684–5.

18 Edward Schafer, 'The Development of Bathing Customs in Ancient and Medieval China and the History of the Floriate Clear Palace', *Journal of the American Oriental Society*, LXXVI (1956), pp. 57–82 (p. 71).

19 Timothy Brook, *The Troubled Empire: China in the Yuan and Ming Dynasties* (Cambridge, MA, 2010), p. 51.

20 Dawson, *Undercurrents of Power*, pp. 73–4; Song Yingxing, *Tiangong Kaiwu* [1637], cited in Joseph Needham and Colin Ronan, *The Shorter Science and Civilisation in China* (Cambridge, 1978), vol. III, pp. 246–53; fig. 243.

21 Michael Cooper, *Rodrigues the Interpreter: An Early Jesuit in Japan and China* (New York, 1974), p. 64.

16 FLOATING FOR WITCHCRAFT

1 Marina Montesano, *Classical Culture and Witchcraft in Medieval and Renaissance Italy* (London, 2018), pp. 48–54, 84–9, 174–86.

2 *Formulae Liturgicae Slavicae*, trans. Ernest Henderson, in *Select Historical Documents of the Middle Ages* (London, 1910), pp. 314–17.

3 Soissons: Guibert of Nogent, *De vita sua* 3.17, ed. René Labande (Paris, 1982), pp. 428–34: they 'proceeded to the water . . . Clement being then thrown into the tun floated on top like a stick'; the case of Ailward, falsely accused by Fulk the Reeve, cited in James Whitman, *The Origins of Reasonable Doubt: Theological Roots of the Criminal Trial* (New Haven, CT, 2008), p. 86; the Cathars at Vezelay, described by Hugh of Poitiers, *Historia Viziliacensis monasterii* 4, Patrologia Latina CXCIV, cols 1681–2; Péter Tóth, 'River Ordeal – Trial by Water – Swimming of Witches: Procedures of Ordeal in Witch Trials', in *Demons, Spirits, Witches*, vol. III: *Witchcraft Mythologies and Persecutions*, ed. Gábor Klaniczay and Éva Pócs (Budapest, 2008), pp. 129–63 (pp. 135–6).

4 Fourth Lateran Council, under Pope Innocent III: Finbarr McAuley, 'Canon Law and the End of the Ordeal', *Oxford Journal of Legal Studies*, XXVI (2006), pp. 473–513; Thomas Aquinas, *Summa Theologica* 650.

5 Peter Maxwell-Stuart, *Witch Beliefs and Witch Trials in the Middle Ages: Documents and Readings* (London, 2011), pp. 42–3, 182–7.

6 Russell Zguta, 'The Ordeal by Water (Swimming of Witches) in the East Slavic World', *Slavic Review*, XXXVI (1977), pp. 220–30 (p. 225); also Tóth, 'River Ordeal', p. 132.

7 Abu Hāmid al-Gharnātī, in François-Bernard Charmoy, *Relation de Mas'oudy et d'autres musulmans sur les anciens Slaves* (St Petersburg, 1834), pp. 342–3; the river is probably the Dnieper.

8 *The Russian Primary Chronicle*, ed. and trans. Samuel Cross and Olgerd Sherbowitz-Wetzor (Cambridge, MA, 1953), pp. 134, 150–51 (also known as the *Chronicle of 1113*, from Kyiv).

9 Evgeny Petukhov, 'Serapion Vladimirskii, russkii propovednik XIII veka', *Zapiski istoriko-filologicheskago fakul'teta Imperatorskago S.- Peterburgskago universiteta*, 17 (1888), pp. 11–12 (Appendix, text of sermon), pp. 63–8 (commentary), translated in Zguta, 'Ordeal by Water', p. 223.

10 Osama Ibn Munqidh, *Kitab al-I'tibar*, trans. Philip Hitti (New York, 1929), p. 168, cited in Avner Falk, *Franks and Saracens: Reality and Fantasy in the Crusades* (London, 2010), p. 141.

11 Willem Bosman, *A New and Accurate Description of the Coast of Guinea* (London, 1704), p. 359; Bosman goes on to complain that because West Africans were good swimmers, 'I never heard that this River ever yet convicted any Person; for they all come out.' Keith Dawson, 'Swimming, Surfing, and Underwater Diving in Early Modern Atlantic Africa and the African Diaspora', in *Navigating African Maritime History*, ed. Carina Ray and Jeremy Rich (Oxford, 2009), pp. 81–116 (p. 98).

12 Pausanias, *Description of Greece* 3.23.8; 5.7.5.

13 Stephanus Byzantinus, Εθνικων *quae supersunt*, ed. Anton Westermann (Leipzig, 1839), p. 138 (see Chapter Four); Hincmar von Reims, *De divortio Lotharii regis et Theutbergae reginae*, Paris, Bibliothèque National de France, lat. 2866, ed. Letha Böhringer (Hanover, 1992), pp. 156–8: *non potest mergi, quia pura natura aque . . . mendacio infectam non recognoscit puram et ideo eam non recipit . . . non mirabitur in iudicio aquae frigide innocentes ab aqua recipi, nocentes autem non recipi*; Zguta, 'Ordeal by Water', p. 221.

14 Zguta, 'Witchcraft Trials in Seventeenth-Century Russia', *American Historical Review*, LXXXII (1977), pp. 1187–207 (p. 1192).

15 Martin Luther, *Colloquia Mensalia*, trans. Henry Bell (London, 1652), p. 315; see M. Miles, 'Martin Luther and Childhood Disability in 16th Century Germany: What Did He Write? What Did He Say?', *Journal of Religion, Disability and Health*, IV (2001), pp. 5–36.

16 Mandate of the Zurich council against the Anabaptists (7 March 1526), quoted in Hans-Jürgen Goertz, *The Anabaptists*, trans. Trevor Johnson [1980] (London, 1996), p. 158, but see also pp. 12, 19, 120–21.

17 Christopher Marlowe, *The Massacre at Paris* (London, 1593), p. 7.

18 Eamon Darcy, *The Irish Rebellion of 1641 and the Wars of the Three Kingdoms* (Woodbridge, 2013), p. 114.

19 *The Journey to the West*, trans. and ed. Anthony Yu, revd edn (Chicago,
    IL, 2012), vol. II, pp. 256–7.

20 Luo Guanzhong, *The Three Sui Quash the Demons' Revolt*, trans.
    Patrick Hanan (New York, 2017, under the title *Quelling the Demons'
    Revolt: A Novel from Ming China*), p. 64.

21 Philip Kuhn, *Soulstealers: The Chinese Sorcery Scare of 1768* (Cambridge,
    MA, 1990), pp. 11, 19.

22 Glenn Stout, *Young Woman and the Sea: How Trudy Ederle Conquered
    the English Channel and Inspired the World* (Boston, MA, and New York,
    2009), p. 12.

23 Keith Thomas, *Religion and the Decline of Magic: Studies in Popular
    Beliefs in Sixteenth and Seventeenth Century England* (Oxford, 1971),
    pp. 491–501; for a similar phenomenon in Italy, see Montesano,
    Classical Culture and Witchcraft, pp. 187–8.

24 Zguta, 'The Ordeal by Water', p. 225 and 'Witchcraft Trials', p. 1189.

25 Wolfgang Behringer, *Witches and Witch-Hunts: A Global History*
    (Cambridge, 2004), p. 153.

26 Ildikó Kristóf, 'Witch-Hunting in Early Modern Hungary', in
    *The Oxford Handbook of Witchcraft in Early Modern Europe and
    Colonial America*, ed. Brian Levack (Oxford, 2013), pp. 334–54
    (p. 346).

27 Tóth, 'River Ordeal', pp. 130, 140.

28 Ibid., pp. 145–6.

29 Philipp Blom, *Nature's Mutiny: How the Little Ice Age of the Long
    Seventeenth Century Transformed the West and Shaped the Present*
    (New York, 2017), p. 58, has some evidence linking witch trials to
    weather concerns.

30 Behringer, *Witches and Witch-Hunts*, p. 112; Johan Wier,
    De praestigiis daemonum [1563] (Basel, 1568), pp. 588–9: *Caeterum
    quod manibus pedibusque colligatis, uel pollice manus dextrae, magno
    digito sinistri pedis, et uitissim pollice sinistrae, digito magno magno
    dextri pedis transuerse uinculo astrictis, Lamias* [witches] *maleficii reas,
    aquae iniectas nunquam submergi, at supernatare . . .* ; Henry Lea,
    Materials Toward a History of Witchcraft (Philadelphia, PA, 1939),
    pp. 892–3, also describes a decision in 1581 by Wier's employer,
    Duke Wilhelm of Jülich, that 'the proof of whether she is guilty
    of sorcery is to be determined by the water ordeal'.

31 Scribonius, *De examine et purgatione sagarum per aquam frigidam
    epistola* [1583], in Gerhild Williams, 'Demonologies', in *The Oxford
    Handbook of Witchcraft*, pp. 69–83 (p. 77); Tóth, 'River Ordeal', p. 139.

32 Hermann Neuwalt, *Exegesis purgationis sive examinis sagarum super
    aquam frigidam* [1584], in Williams, 'Demonologies', p. 77.

33 Ibid.; Antonius Praetorius, *Gründlicher Bericht über die Zauberey*
    [1598], in Gerhild Williams, *Ways of Knowing in Early Modern
    Germany: Johannes Praetorius as a Witness to His Time* (Aldershot,
    2006), p. 93.

34 Johann Goedelmann, *De Magis, Veneficis et Lamiis* (Frankfurt, 1592), vol. I chap. 5, pp. 21–30, cited in Brian Levack, *The Witch-Hunt in Early Modern Europe* [1987] (New York, 2006), p. 260.

35 Williams, *Ways of Knowing*, p. 93.

36 Orna Darr, *Marks of an Absolute Witch: Evidentiary Dilemmas in Early Modern England* (London, 2011), p. 162.

37 H. C. Erik Midelfort, *Witch Hunting in Southwestern Germany, 1562–1684: The Social and Intellectual Foundations* (Stanford, CA, 1972), pp. 76–7. We may wonder whether Löb had much choice in the matter.

38 In Herford: Oskar Wächter, *Vehmgerichte u. Hexenprozesse in Deutchland* (Stuttgart, 1882), pp. 137–8, who gives no source, but is perhaps reading local transcripts of trials.

39 In the Champagne-Ardennes region: Brian Levack, 'State-Building and Witch Hunting in Early Modern Europe', in *The Witchcraft Reader*, ed. Darren Oldridge (Abingdon, 2008), pp. 200–213 (p. 221), reprinted from *Witchcraft in Early Modern Europe: Studies in Culture and Belief*, ed. Jonathan Barry et al. (Cambridge, 1996), pp. 96–116; Alfred Soman, 'Decriminalizing Witchcraft: Does the French Experience Furnish a European Model?', *Criminal Justice History*, X (1989), pp. 1–22 (p. 6).

40 Kuhn, *Soulstealers*, pp. 7, 19, 30, 232 and *passim*.

41 With the exception of the northern Netherlands, where in 1594 the courts forbade the use of the swimming test in witchcraft cases: Levack, *The Witch-Hunt in Early Modern Europe*, p. 215; Claudia Swan, *Art, Science, and Witchcraft in Early Modern Holland: Jacques de Gheyn II (1565–1629)* (Cambridge, 2005), p. 165.

42 Tóth, 'River Ordeal', p. 139.

43 James VI and I, *Daemonologie: A Critical Edition*, ed. Brett Warren (London, 2016), p. 94.

44 Lynda Boose, 'Scolding Brides and Bridling Scolds: Taming the Woman's Unruly Member', in *Materialist Shakespeare: A History*, ed. Ivo Kamps (London, 1995), pp. 239–79 (p. 244), also in *Shakespeare Quarterly*, XLII (1991), pp. 179–213; Erika Gasser, *Vexed with Devils: Manhood and Witchcraft in Old and New England* (New York, 2017), pp. 26–7.

45 Owen Davies, *Witchcraft, Magic and Culture, 1736–1951* (Manchester, 1999), p. 87.

46 *Witches Apprehended, Examined and Executed, for notable villanies by them committed both by Land and Water. With a strange and most true trial how to know, whether a woman be a Witch or not* (London, 1613), n.p., reproduced in Katharine Briggs, *Pale Hecate's Team* (London, 1962), pp. 56ff.

47 Davies, *Witchcraft, Magic and Culture*, pp. 86–8. Davies adds that he has 'come across no evidence that corroborates Keith Thomas's statement that swimming "was being used in witch cases in England by 1590"', and I have not either (Thomas, *Religion and the Decline of Magic*, p. 551), although see now Gregory Durston, *Crimen Exceptum: The English Witch Prosecution in Context* (Eastbourne, 2019), p. 147.

48 John Cotta, *The Triall of Witch-Craft* [1616], in Brian Levack, 'The Decline and End of Witchcraft Prosecutions', *Witchcraft and Magic in Europe*, vol. v: *The Eighteenth and Nineteenth Centuries*, ed. Bengt Ankarloo and Stuart Clark (Philadelphia, PA, 1999), pp. 1–94 (p. 24); Sir Robert Filmer, *An Advertisement to the Jurymen of England Touching Witches, together with a Difference between a Hebrew and an English Witch*, ed. Richard Royston (London, 1653), n.p. and p. 11. Digby, in 1587, had already been aware of people's natural tendency to float.

49 *Great News from the West of England* (London, 1689), p. 1; Durston, *Crimen Exceptum*, p. 151.

50 Deposition before the Grand Jury at the Assizes at Leicester (London, British Library, Hardwicke Papers, Add. MS 35838, fol. 404), cited in Cecil Ewen, *Witch Hunting and Witch Trials (RLE Witchcraft): The Indictments for Witchcraft from the Records of the 1373 Assizes Held from the Home Court 1559–1736 AD* [1929] (Abingdon, 2013), p. 314.

51 Francis Hutchinson, *An Historical Essay Concerning Witchcraft, with Observations of Matters of Fact*, 2nd edn (London, 1720), p. 175; Davies, *Witchcraft, Magic and Culture*, pp. 89, 93.

52 Alison Games, *Witchcraft in Early North America* (Plymouth, 2012), p. 16.

53 *Wyllys Papers*, W-2 in *Witch-Hunting in Seventeenth-Century New England: A Documentary History, 1638–1693*, ed. David Hall, 2nd edn (Durham, NC, 1999), p. 159; Walter Woodward, *Prospero's America: John Winthrop, Jr, Alchemy, and the Creation of New England Culture, 1606–1676* (Chapel Hill, NC, 2010), p. 235.

54 Increase Mather, *An Essay for the Recording of Illustrious Providences* (Boston, MA, 1684), p. 139. See *Witch-Hunting in Seventeenth-Century New England*, p. 151; the man and woman are probably William and Judith Ayres.

55 Richard Godbeer, *Escaping Salem: The Other Witch Hunt of 1692* (Oxford, 2004), pp. 120, 125.

56 Games, *Witchcraft in Early North America*, pp. 141–2, citing Edward James, 'Grace Sherwood, the Virginia Witch', *William and Mary Quarterly*, III/3 (1894), pp. 99–100, III/4 (1895), pp. 191–2, IV (1895), pp. 242–5, IV/1 (1895), pp. 18–19.

57 Jean Baptiste du Tertre, *Histoire générale des Antilles habitées par les Francois* (Paris, 1667), vol. II, p. 448, in *Chronological History of the West Indies*, trans. Thomas Southey (London, 1827), vol. II, p. 22.

17 DUCKING STOOLS

1 For more on cucking-stools, see John Spargo, *Juridical Folklore in England, Illustrated by the Cucking-Stool* (Durham, NC, 1944); Lynda Boose, 'Scolding Brides and Bridling Scolds: Taming the Woman's Unruly Member', in *Materialist Shakespeare: A History*, ed. Ivo Kamps (London, 1995), pp. 239–79 (p. 245); Carl Lounsbury, *The Courthouses of Early Virginia: An Architectural History* (Charlottesville, VA, 2005), pp. 182, 224.

2 Spargo, *Juridical Folklore*, pp. 85, 95, 98.
3 From the marginalia of the Rutland Psalter, London, British Library, Add. MS. 62925, fol. 86r. A note of scepticism is rightly sounded by Sandy Bardsley, *Venomous Tongues: Speech and Gender in Late Medieval England* (Philadelphia, PA, 2006), p. 188 n. 4.
4 Thomas Brushfield, 'On Obsolete Punishments, with Particular Reference to those of Cheshire: Part II: The Cucking-Stool and Allied Punishments', *Journal of the Architectural, Archaeological and Historic Society, for the County, City, and Neighbourhood of Chester*, ser. 1, II (1861), pp. 200–234 (pp. 204, 215); Spargo, *Juridical Folklore*, p. 30; *Satire on the People of Kildare* [1308], in Judith Bennett, *Ale, Beer, and Brewsters in England: Women's Work in a Changing World, 1300–1600* (Oxford, 1996), p. 105; I have slightly modified Bennett's modernization of the language.
5 Leet Book of Coventry, in Bennett, *Ale, Beer, and Brewsters*, pp. 104–5; Brushfield, 'On Obsolete Punishments', p. 215.
6 Thieves and whores: Spargo, *Juridical Folklore*, p. 3; Harlots: David Underdown, 'The Taming of the Scold: the Enforcement of Patriarchal Authority in Early Modern England', in *Order and Disorder in Early Modern England*, ed. Anthony Fletcher and John Stevenson (Cambridge, 1985), pp. 116–36 (p. 124).
7 Spargo, *Juridical Folklore*, pp. 86–7, 94–5.
8 Brushfield, 'On Obsolete Punishments', pp. 218–20. For Norwich, see also Helen Kavanaugh, 'The Topography of Illicit Sex in Later Medieval English Provincial Towns', MPhil thesis, Royal Holloway, University of London, 2020, p. 101.
9 At Wakefield Sessions and Whitby: Ernest Pettifer, *Punishments of Former Days* (Bradford, 1939), p. 106; other seventeenth-century examples abound in Brushfield, 'On Obsolete Punishments', pp. 223–4. The stated offence was usually arguing or nagging, but that is not the point: nothing can justify torture.
10 Underdown, 'The Taming of the Scold', pp. 125–6.
11 Randle Holme, *The Academy of Armory*, vol. III, ch. 126 (Chester, 1688), p. 351, quoted in Brushfield, 'On Obsolete Punishments', p. 227 and available at https://quod.lib.umich.edu/e/eebogroup.
12 At Grimsby: George Oliver, 'Beating of Bounds: The Ducking Stool', *Gentleman's Magazine*, CCI/2 (December 1831), pp. 504–5 (p. 505), with another similar example, quoted in Brushfield, 'On Obsolete Punishments', pp. 225–6.
13 Julia Spruill, *Women's Life and Work in the Southern Colonies* [1938] (New York, 1972), p. 332.
14 Brushfield, 'On Obsolete Punishments', pp. 218–31; Dorothy Mays, *Women in Early America: Struggle, Survival, and Freedom in a New World* (Santa Barbara, CA, 2004), p. 366. Mays doubts whether ducking stools were actually much used.
15 Lounsbury, *The Courthouses of Early Virginia*, p. 224.
16 Spruill, *Women's Life and Work*, p. 331.

17 Elizabeth City, Frederick and King George: Lounsbury, *The Courthouses of Early Virginia*, pp. 182, 224; Augusta: *The Virginia Historical Register, and Literary Note Book* 3, ed. William Maxwell (Richmond, VA, 1850), p. 76.

18 Giuseppe Baretti, *A Journey from London to Genoa: Through England, Portugal, Spain, and France* (London, 1770), vol. I, p. 9 (16 August 1760), quoted in Brushfield, 'On Obsolete Punishments', p. 231.

19 A sex worker: James Orange, *History and Antiquities of Nottingham* (London, 1840), vol. II, p. 864.

20 Gerhild Williams, *Ways of Knowing in Early Modern Germany: Johannes Praetorius as a Witness to His Time* (Aldershot, 2006), p. 93.

21 Richard Raiswell and Peter Dendle, 'Demon Possession in Anglo-Saxon and Early Modern England: Continuity and Evolution in Social Context', *Journal of British Studies*, XLVII (2008), pp. 738–67 (pp. 738, 749, 751).

22 Liz Sharp, *Reconnecting People and Water: Public Engagement and Sustainable Urban Water Management* (London, 2017), p. 71; Tracy Borman, *The Private Lives of the Tudors: Uncovering the Secrets of Britain's Greatest Dynasty* (New York, 2016), pp. 333–4.

23 Anthony Wood, in Keith Thomas, *Religion and the Decline of Magic: Studies in Popular Beliefs in Sixteenth and Seventeenth Century England* (Oxford, 1971), p. 491; see Matthew 8:28–34, where the demons enter the pigs and the pigs run into the water and drown.

24 Raiswell and Dendle, 'Demon Possession', p. 759.

25 Michael Foster, *The Book of Yokai: Mysterious Creatures of Japanese Folklore* (Berkeley, CA, 2015), p. 159; Imron Harits and Stefan Chudy, 'The Legend of *Vodnik* (Water Goblin): Slavic Tradition and Cultural Adaptation', *Proceedings of the 5th ELTLT International Conference* (Semarang, Indonesia, 2016), pp. 307–11 (p. 308); see also Monika Kropej, *Supernatural Beings from Slovenian Myth and Folktales* (Ljubljana, 2012), pp. 99–100, 155–66; 'Kelpie', *Oxford English Dictionary*; see Aude Marie Le Borgne, 'Clootie Wells and Water-Kelpies: An Ethnological Approach to the Fresh Water Traditions of Sacred Wells and Supernatural Horses in Scotland', PhD thesis, University of Edinburgh (2002), pp. 120ff.

26 Alexander Murray, *Suicide in the Middle Ages: The Violent against Themselves* (Oxford, 1998), vol. I, p. 151.

27 Michael Zell, 'Suicide in Pre-Industrial England', *Social History*, XI (1986), pp. 303–17 (p. 311); Jeffrey Watt, *From Sin to Insanity: Suicide in Early Modern and Modern Europe* (Ithaca, NY, 2004), p. 32.

28 Riikka Miettinen, 'Gendered Suicide in Early Modern Sweden and Finland', in *Gender in Late Medieval and Early Modern Europe*, ed. Marianna Muravyeva and Raisa Toivo (Abingdon, 2012), pp. 173–90 (p. 176).

29 Murray, *Suicide in the Middle Ages*, p. 404.

30 Judith Graham, *Puritan Family Life: The Diary of Samuel Sewall* (Boston, MA, 2000), pp. 95–7, 126.

31 Nicholas Wynman, *Colymbetes sive De arte natandi* (Augsburg, 1538), who speaks out against the ban; Eric Chaline, *Strokes of Genius: A History of*

Swimming (London, 2017), p. 104. Contemporary bans on washing clothes in the rivers may also be related to a reluctance to disturb the water, or to related concerns about decency.

32 The son of Walter Haddon: Frank Reeve, *The Cambridge Nobody Knows* (Cambridge, 1977), pp. 42–3; Nicolas Orme, *Early British Swimming, 55 BC–AD 1719* (Exeter, 1983), p. 64; Chris Ayriss, *Hung Out to Dry: Swimming and British Culture* (Morrisville, NC, 2009), p. 17; Chaline, *Strokes of Genius*, p. 103. The vice-chancellor was John Whitgift.

33 William Shakespeare, *Julius Caesar*, Act I, 2; *Two Gentlemen of Verona*, Act I, I; *As You Like It*, Act IV, I. For other swimming references in Shakespeare, see *Henry VI, Part III*, Act V, 4; *Macbeth*, Act I, 2; *Rape of Lucrece*; Marlowe, *Hero and Leander* (1598), ll. 153–78; Rubens, *Hero and Leander, c.* 1605 (Dresden, Gemäldegalerie). See Barbara A. Mowat, "'Knowing I loved my books': Reading *The Tempest* Intertextually', in *The Tempest and Its Travels*, ed. Peter Hulme and William H. Sherman (London, 2000), pp. 27–36 (pp. 29–32).

18 THE AVANT-GARDE

1 Niccolò Machiavelli, *The Art of War*, trans. Henry Neville [1674] (Mineola, NY, 2012), pp. 43–4. Earlier though less illustrious Italian examples from the 1400s also cite Roman sources to emphasize military uses and water safety: Vergerio, Alberti, Piccolomini. The Dutch scholar Erasmus, too, included Roman comments on swimming in his 1508 *Adages*; see John McManamon, *'Neither Letters nor Swimming': The Rebirth of Swimming and Free-Diving* (Leiden, 2021), pp. 238–43.

2 Nicholas Wynman, *Colymbetes sive De arte natandi* (Augsburg 1538), F7–F8, Franz Friedlieb, *Exegesis Germaniae* 2.23 (Hagenau, 1518), fols 36v–37; Olaus Magnus, *Historia de gentibus septentrionalibus* (Rome, 1555), 10.23; Everard Digby, *De arte natandi* [1587], trans. Melchisedech Thévenot as *L'Art de Nager* (Paris, 1696). For summaries and commentary on these manuals, see Nicolas Orme, *Early British Swimming, 55 BC–AD 1719* (Exeter, 1983); John McManamon, *Caligula's Barges and the Renaissance Origins of Nautical Archaeology Under Water* (College Station, TX, 2016), pp. 151–4; McManamon, *'Neither Letters nor Swimming'*, pp. 203–8, 270–71; and Alexandra Heminsley, *Leap in: A Woman, Some Waves, and the Will to Swim* (New York, 2017), p. 154.

3 *Rymes of Robin Hood: An Introduction to the English Outlaw*, ed. Richard Dobson and John Taylor (London, 1976), p. 163, cited in Orme, *Early British Swimming*, p. 44.

4 Thomas Elyot, *The Book of the Governor*, ed. Henry Croft (London, 1883), pp. 173–8; Roger Ascham, *The Schoolmaster* (London, 1570), p. 217. Rosso Fiorentino fresco, Galerie François I, Château de Fontainebleau (1535–7); see McManamon, *'Neither Letters nor Swimming'*, pp. 288–9, who thinks Chiron may be teaching Achilles an overhand stroke, perhaps in imitation of the ancients; Karen Syse, 'Ideas of Leisure, Pleasure and the River in

Early Modern England', *Perceptions of Water in Britain from Early Modern Times to the Present: An Introduction*, ed. Karen Syse and Terje Oestigaard (Bergen, 2010), pp. 35–57.

5 John Windhausen and Irina Tsypkina, 'National Identity and the Emergence of the Sports Movement in Late Imperial Russia', in *International Journal of the History of Sport*, vol. XII: *Tribal Identities: Nationalism, Europe, Sport*, ed. James Mangan (London, 1996), pp. 164–82 (p. 166).

6 John Locke, *Some Thoughts Concerning Education and Of the Conduct of the Understanding*, ed. Ruth Grant and Nathan Tarcov (Indianapolis, IN, 1996), p. 14.

7 Robert Massie, *Peter the Great: His Life and World* (New York, 1980), p. 824.

8 Ibid., p. 315.

9 Samuel Chandler, *Journal* [1773], quoted in *The Harvard Book: Selections from Three Centuries*, ed. William Bentinck-Smith [1953] (Cambridge, MA, 1982), pp. 116–17. Slavery was legal in Massachusetts until 1783.

10 Lord Waldegrave: Henry Lyte, *A History of Eton College, 1440–1875* (London, 1875), pp. 353–4.

11 Johann GutsMuths, *Kleines Lehrbuch der Schwimmskunst zum Selbtsunerricht* (Weimar, 1798), trans. in Eric Chaline, *Strokes of Genius: A History of Swimming* (London, 2017), p. 110.

12 Charles Sprawson, *Haunts of the Black Masseur: The Swimmer as Hero* (Minneapolis, MN, 1992), pp. 118–19 (the title is from a racist story by Tennessee Williams).

13 Lyte, *A History of Eton College*, pp. 442–3.

14 'Harrow School', *Blackwood's Magazine*, XCIV (1863), pp. 457–81 (p. 481); Christopher Love, 'An Overview of the Development of Swimming in England, *c.* 1750–1918', *International Journal of the History of Sport*, XXIV (2007), pp. 568–85 (p. 570).

15 Byron also swam across the Tagus River in Lisbon in 1809, which took almost two hours. Thomas Moore, *Life of Lord Byron* (London, 1835), vol. I, pp. 95, 133, 277 and n. 138.

16 With William Ekenhead: *Letters and Journals of Lord Byron*, Letter 413 (21 February 1821); Moore, *Life of Lord Byron*, p. 316; John Galt, *Life of Lord Byron* (London, 1830), pp. 141–2. The latter also mentions that people in the area remembered other crossings of the Hellespont by 'a Jew' and someone from Naples, and that other members of the crew of Byron's ship had swum longer distances, though not at that location.

17 Sprawson, *Haunts of the Black Masseur*, pp. 118–19.

18 Moore, *Life of Lord Byron*, p. 186 and n. 137.

19 Hugh Pearse, *The Hearseys: Five Generations of an Anglo-Indian Family* (Edinburgh, 1905), pp. 141–4, 166, 229–30.

20 Serhii Plokhy, *The Cossack Myth: History And Nationhood in the Age of Empires* (Cambridge, 2012), pp. 9–10, 33.

21 Anna Labzina, *Days of a Russian Noblewoman: The Memories of Anna Labzina, 1758–1821* (DeKalb, IL, 2001), p. 21, quoted in Priscilla Roosevelt,

Life on the Russian Country Estate: A Social and Cultural History (New Haven, CT, 1995), p. 181.

22 Robert Massie, *Catherine the Great: Portrait of a Woman* (New York, 2011), p. 564; Peter Vyazemsky, in Roosevelt, *Life on the Russian Country Estate*, p. 301; Rosamund Bartlett, *Tolstoy: A Russian Life* (New York, 2011), p. 78.

23 Peter Sekirin, ed., *The Dostoevsky Archive: Firsthand Accounts of the Novelist from Contemporaries' Memoirs and Rare Periodicals* (Jefferson, NC, 1997), p. 293; Alexander Chudakov, 'Dr Chekhov: A Biographical Essay (29 January 1860–15 July 1904)', in *The Cambridge Companion to Chekhov*, ed. Vera Gottlieb and Paul Allain (Cambridge, 2000), pp. 3–16 (p. 4); Bartlett, *Tolstoy*, pp. 95, 203, 207.

24 Edwards Park, 'To Bathe or Not to Bathe: Coming Clean in Colonial America', *Colonial Williamsburg Journal*, XXII (2000), pp. 12–16.

25 John Wesley, *The Journal of John Wesley: Founder of the Methodist Movement* (North Charleston, SC, 2013), p. 198 (28 July 1756), see also pp. 35, 110, 240.

26 Benjamin Franklin, *The Autobiography of Benjamin Franklin* [1791] (Boston, MA, 1906), pp. 10, 50. See also Scott Cleary, 'The Ethos Aquatic: Benjamin Franklin and the Art of Swimming', *Early American Literature*, 46 (2011), pp. 51–67; Sarah Pomeroy, *Benjamin Franklin, Swimmer: An Illustrated History*, Transactions of the American Philosophical Society (Philadelphia, PA, 2021).

27 Philip Tucker, *Alexander Hamilton's Revolution: His Vital Role as Washington's Chief of Staff* (New York, 2017), p. 119; Anne Royall, *Royall's Sketches of History, Life, and Manners in the United States* [1826] (Carlisle, MA, 2007), p. 49; Howard Zinn, *A People's History of the United States* (New York, 1980), p. 78.

28 Ulysses S. Grant, *Personal Memoirs of U. S. Grant* (New York, 1885), p. 3.

29 Henry Thoreau, *Walden or Life in the Woods* [1854] (New York, 1910), p. 221.

30 Louisa May Alcott, *Hospital Sketches: And, Camp and Fireside Stories* [1863] (Boston, MA, 1922), p. 18.

19 THE MIDDLE CLASS

1 Vaughn Scribner, *Merpeople: A Human History* (London, 2020), pp. 101, 116.

2 Nicolas Wynman, *Colymbetes sive De arte natandi* (Augsburg, 1538), pp. A5, C7–C8, E5–E6; John McManamon, 'Neither Letters nor Swimming': *The Rebirth of Swimming and Free-diving* (Leiden, 2021), pp. 254–61, 269.

3 Johann Pezzl, 'Bäder', *Skizze von Wien* (Vienna, 1787), vol. IV, pp. 599–601, trans. William Meredith (https://beethovens-vienna.sjsu.edu); Elaine Sciolino, *The Seine: The River that Made Paris* (New York, 2019), p. 100; John Stephens, *Incidents of Travels in Egypt, Arabia Petraea and the Holy Land* (London, 1836), p. 97.

4 Now Bibliothèque de Institut de France MS 2173 B folio 81v, Paris, perhaps based on Francesco di Giorgio's slightly earlier sketch of a similar device.

5 William Shakespeare, *Henry VIII*, Act III, 2; Isak Lidström and Ingvar Svanberg, 'Ancient Buoyancy Devices in Sweden: Floats Made of Reed, Club-Rush, Inflated Skins and Animal Bladders', *Folk Life: Journal of Ethnological Studies*, LVII (2019), pp. 85–94; Francis Bacon, *The Works of Francis Bacon*, ed. Basil Montagu (New York, 1884), vol. I, p. 269. For other examples of early flotation devices starting in the 1400s, see McManamon, *'Neither Letters nor Swimming'*, pp. 295–300.

6 Daniel Schwenter, *Deliciae Physico–Mathematicae* (Nuremberg, 1636), title page (no. 13) and p. 467; Benjamin Franklin, *The Works of the Late Benjamin Franklin*, ed. Benjamin Vaughan (New York, 1794), vol. II, p. 57 ('On the Art of Swimming').

7 'Birth of the Republic', *Free China Review*, XXIII/1 (1973), https://taiwantoday.tw/tr.php?post=442, accessed 19 November 2021.

8 Montague Holbein, *Swimming* (London, 1904), p. 17; 'On Swimming', *Dublin Penny Journal*, 3 May 1834, pp. 346–7.

9 Franklin, *Works*, vol. I, p. 78; Alexandra Heminsley, *Leap In: A Woman, Some Waves, and the Will to Swim* (New York, 2017), p. 154.

10 Klemens Wildt, *Daten zur Sportgeschichte: Europa von 1750 bis 1894* (Stuttgart, 1972), vol. I, p. 154; Ralph Waldo Emerson, *Selected Essays, Lectures and Poems*, ed. Robert Richardson Jr [1965] (New York, 2007), pp. 99, 276; Louisa May Alcott, *Hospital Sketches: And, Camp and Fireside Stories* [1863] (Boston, MA, 1922), p. 18.

11 Ropes were also used to teach children to swim in Istanbul, as Claire Messud's father remembered: Claire Messud, *Kant's Little Prussian Head and Other Reasons Why I Write: An Autobiography in Essays* (New York, 2020); Ekrem Buğra Ekinci, 'Sea Bathing, the Good Old Fashion Way', *Daily Sabah*, 10 September 2014.

12 Richard Mulcaster, *Positions* (London, 1888), and Johann GutsMuths, *Kleines Lehrbuch der Schwimmskunst zum Selbtsunerricht* (Weimar, 1798), both cited in Eric Chaline, *Strokes of Genius: A History of Swimming* (London, 2017), pp. 102–3, 110; Everard Digby, *De arte natandi* (Cambridge, 1587), n.p.

13 John Locke, *Some Thoughts Concerning Education and Of the Conduct of the Understanding*, ed. Ruth Grant and Nathan Tarcov (Indianapolis, IN, 1996), p. 14; Franklin, *Works*, vol. II, p. 57 ('On the Art of Swimming').

14 Liz Sharp, *Reconnecting People and Water: Public Engagement and Sustainable Urban Water Management* (London, 2017), pp. 71–3.

15 *Journal of the Conversations of Lord Byron*, ed. Thomas Medwin (London, 1824), p. 117, cited in Lynn Sherr, *Swim: Why We Love the Water* (New York, 2012), p. 48.

16 Clement Shorter, *George Borrow and His Circle* (New York, 1913), p. 419 n. 1.

17 Rosamund Bartlett, *Tolstoy: A Russian Life* (Boston, MA, 2011), pp. 95, 203, 207; Henri Troyat, *Tolstoy*, trans. Nancy Amphoux [1965] (Paris, 2001), pp. 142, 433.

18 William Byrd, 1706 letter, quoted in Richmond Beatty, *William Byrd of Westover* (New York, 1932), p. 55; Henri Troyat, *Pushkin: A Biography*, trans.

Randolph Weaver (New York, 1950), p. 216; Benjamin Butler, *Butler's Book: Autobiography and Personal Reminiscences of Major-General Benjamin Butler* (Boston, MA, 1892), p. 69.

19 Virginia Rounding, *Catherine the Great: Love, Sex, and Power* (New York, 2006), p. 399; like Roman baths, these were in fact major causes of dysentery: Konstantin Kashin and Ethan Pollock, 'Public Health and Bathing in Late Imperial Russia: A Statistical Approach', *Russian Review*, LXXII (2013), pp. 66–93.

20 Harry Ward, *George Washington's Enforcers: Policing the Continental Army* (Carbondale, IL, 2006), p. 95; John Quincy Adams, diary entry for 18 November 1826; see Paul Nagel, *John Quincy Adams: A Public Life, A Private Life* (New York, 1997), Book 4.

21 Linda Ivanits, *Russian Folk Belief* (London, 1989), pp. 70–74; Fred Whishaw, *The Romance of the Woods* (London, 1895), p. 277, though Whishaw's colonialist novels cannot be trusted as fact.

22 Mark Twain, *The Adventures of Tom Sawyer* (Toronto, 1876), p. 159.

23 Johan Bachstrøm, *Den Kunst at svømme* (Copenhagen, 1778); Johann GutsMuths, *Gymnastik für die Jugend* (Schnepfenthal, 1793) (first translated into English probably by Mary Wollstonecraft before her death in childbirth in 1797); Oronzio de Bernardi, *L'uomo galleggiante, ossia l'arte ragionata del nuoto* (Naples, 1794); GutsMuths, *Kleines Lehrbuch* (Weimar, 1798); in 1864 it was William Woodbridge's *The Swimmers Practical Manual of Plain Facts and Useful Hints*.

24 Chaline, *Strokes of Genius*, p. 105; Arnd Krüger, 'Swimming and the Emergence of the Modern Spirit', in *Sport and Culture in Early Modern Europe*, ed. John McClelland and Brian Merrilees (Toronto, 2009), pp. 409–29 (p. 409).

25 Everard Digby, *A Short Introduction for to Learne to Swimme*, trans. Christofer Middleton (London, 1595), n.p.

26 Andrei Glagolev, *Notes of the Russian Traveller* (St Petersburg, 1837), Tula, March 10; James Riordan mistakenly cites this passage as I. S. Glagolev, *Razvlechiniya zhitelei Tuly* (Moscow, 1734), p. 78, in his *Sport in Soviet Society* (Cambridge, 1977), p. 29.

27 'On Swimming', *Dublin Penny Journal*, pp. 346–7; Franklin, *The Art of Swimming Rendered Easy*, ed. anon. (Glasgow, c. 1840), p. 3.

28 Don Wyatt, 'A Certain Whiteness of Being: Chinese Perceptions of Self by the Beginning of European Contact', in *Race and Racism in Modern East Asia: Western and Eastern Constructions*, ed. Rotem Kowner and Walter Demel (Leiden, 2013), pp. 307–26 (pp. 316, 319–22); also Sufen Sophia Lai, 'Racial Discourse and Utopian Visions in Nineteenth-century China', ibid., pp. 327–49.

29 John Wood, quoted by Archibald Sinclair and William Henry, *Swimming* (London, 1893), p. 65. Perhaps first mentioned in the *Encyclopaedia Britannica* of 1797.

30 'On Swimming', *Dublin Penny Journal*, pp. 346–7; the same egg method had been proposed by Digby in the late 1500s, and by Franklin and

Jean-Charles Poncelin de La Roche-Tilhac (in an expanded version of Thévenot's manual) in the 1700s. Notice again the assumption that you will want your face out of the water even after you learn to swim.

31 Harold Gill, 'Colonial Americans in the Swim', *Colonial Williamsburg Journal*, XXII–XXIV (2001–2), p. 26; Christopher Love, 'An Overview of the Development of Swimming in England, *c.* 1750–1918', *International Journal of the History of Sport*, XXIV (2007), pp. 568–85 (p. 569).

32 For details, see Chris Ayriss, *Hung Out to Dry: Swimming and British Culture* (Morrisville, NC, 2009), p. 22.

33 Clayton Evans, *Rescue at Sea: An International History of Lifesaving, Coastal Rescue Craft and Organisations* (Annapolis, MD, 2003), p. 15; George Worcester (with Doris Worcester), *The Junks and Sampans of the Yangtze: A Study in Chinese Nautical Research* (Shanghai, 1947), p. 305.

34 John Stephens, *Incidents of Travels in Egypt, Arabia Petraea and the Holy Land* (London, 1837), p. 97; David Day and Margaret Roberts, *Swimming Communities in Victorian England* (Manchester, 2019), p. 8 and *passim*; Love, 'An Overview', pp. 571–3; Julius Kricheldorff, 'Schwimmlehrer-Personal des 4. Garde-Regts' [1877], now in the Museum Europäischer Kulturen der Staatlichen Museen in Berlin D (33 Y 55) 1175/1981.

35 Love, 'An Overview', pp. 568–85, gives details of the nineteenth-century clubs.

36 Riordan, *Sport in Soviet Society*, p. 11; Love, 'An Overview', p. 577, has more examples.

37 Wynman, *Colymbetes*, B8v; McManamon, *Caligula's Barges*, p. 152.

38 George Borrow, quoted in Charles Sprawson, *Haunts of the Black Masseur: The Swimmer as Hero* (Minneapolis, MN, 1992), p. 2.

39 Probably invented by John Setterington. The earliest 'modesty shields' appear in Rupert Green's 'The Bathing Place, Ramsgate', hand-coloured etching and aquatint, 1782, now British Museum 2010, 7081.2574.

40 Alain Corbin, *The Lure of the Sea: The Discovery of the Seaside in the Western World, 1750–1840* (Berkeley, CA, 1994), p. 37; Henri Noppe, *Guide des baigneurs* (Ostend, 1853), p. 84.

41 Jean-Didier Urbain, *At the Beach*, trans. Catherine Porter (Minneapolis, MN, 2002), p. 32; Gerd-Helge Vogel, *Die Entstehung des ersten deutschen Seebades Doberan-Heiligendamm: unter dem Baumeister Carl Theodor Severin (1763–1836)* (Niederjahna, Germany, 2018), pp. 14–15.

42 Burkay Pasin, 'Bathing in the Bosporus', *Ottoman History Podcast*, CXLV (Izmir, 2014); Ebru Boyar and Kate Fleet, *A Social History of Ottoman Istanbul* (Cambridge, 2010), p. 283.

43 Julia Clancy-Smith, 'Where Elites Meet: Harem Visits, Sea Bathing, and Sociabilities in Precolonial Tunisia, *c.* 1800–1881', in *Harem Histories: Envisioning Places and Living Spaces*, ed. Marilyn Booth (Durham, NC, 2010), pp. 177–210 (pp. 183, 198); Richard Pennell, *Morocco since 1830: A History* (New York, 2000), p. 120.

44 Jeremy Black, *George III: America's Last King* (New Haven, CT, 2006), pp. 120, 283 and *passim*.

45 Rachel Johnson, 'The Venus of Margate: Fashion and Disease at the Seaside', *Journal for Eighteenth-Century Studies*, XL (2017), pp. 587–602 (p. 587); Chaline, *Strokes of Genius*, p. 110.

46 'Les Nageurs', from the series *Le Supreme Bon Ton*, No. 15 (Paris, *c.* 1810–15).

47 Adolfo Corti, *L'arte del Nuoto teorico-pratica dimostrata secondo i principii della fisica, con relative figure* (Venice, 1819).

48 These were not necessarily safe; Dickens tells the story of a girl at Lausanne who died after tangling her feet in the skirts of her bathing-costume: John Forster, *The Life of Charles Dickens*, vol. 1 (Boston, MA, 1875), p. 233. Wynman, *Colymbetes*, CI: *interulis utuntur in hoc commode factis*; see McManamon, *'Neither Letters nor Swimming'*, p. 245.

49 Brian Fagan, *The Little Ice Age: How Climate Made History, 1300–1850* (New York, 2000), p. 196.

50 Johnson, 'The Venus of Margate', pp. 587–602.

51 On Dickens's swimming abilities, see John Mullan, *The Artful Dickens: The Tricks and Ploys of the Great Novelist* (London, 2021), pp. 309–11; Mamie Dickens, *My Father as I Recall Him* (London, 1897), p. 75; *Oxford English Dictionary*, citing *Macmillan's Magazine*, LXX/2 (1869).

52 After William Harvey, 'Penalty of Conceit, Boy and Corks', wood-engraving, British Museum 1900,0613.315, from James Northcote, *Fables* (London, 1828); 'Le ravissement maternel', hand-coloured etching, published by Pierre La Mésangère (Paris, 1812), now British Museum 1866,0407.898.

53 Honoré Daumier, 'La Leçon à sec', *Le Charivari* (Paris, 30–31 May 1841).

54 Félicien Rops, 'Déballages I', lithograph, from *Uylenspiegel*, XXVIII, 10 April 1856, now Los Angeles County Museum of Art M.84.243.19.

55 Winslow Homer, 'Bathing at Long Branch, – "Oh, Ain't It Cold!"', wood-engraving from *Every Saturday*, 26 August 1871, now Smithsonian American Art Museum 37123.

56 Sidney Bland, 'Shaping the Life of the New Woman: The Crusading Years of the Delineator', *American Periodicals*, XIX (2009), pp. 165–88 (p. 170); Gerald Gems, Linda Borish and Gertrud Pfister, *Sports in American History: From Colonization to Globalization* (Champaign, IL, 2008), p. 251; Heminsley, *Leap In*, p. 161.

57 'Swimming', from the Games and Sports series (C165) for Old Judge Cigarettes (Goodwin & Company 1889), now Metropolitan Museum of Art 63.350.214.165.46.

58 Claire Tomalin, *Jane Austen: A Life* (New York, 1997), pp. 177, 187.

59 Steve Mentz, *Ocean* (New York, 2020), p. 85.

60 Charles Dickens, *The Mystery of Edwin Drood* (London, 1870), chapter 21. See Mullan, *The Artful Dickens*, pp. 309 ff.

61 For example, Henry James, *The Portrait of a Lady* [1881] (New York, 1917), pp. 90, 127, 182, 514, 581; *The Ambassadors* [1903] (London, 1923), p. 152; see also Emily Dickinson, 'I started Early – Took my Dog –' (*c.* 1862).

62 Joseph Strutt, *Glig-Gamena Angel Ðeod; or, The Sports and Pastimes of the People of England* (London, 1801); Love, 'An Overview', p. 569;

Theodorus Mason, *The Preservation of Life at Sea* (New York, 1879), pp. 2–3.

63 Dawson, *Undercurrents of Power*, pp. 17, 37; Robert Walsh, *Notice of Brazil in 1828 and 1829* (Boston, MA, 1831), vol. I, p. 281; Charles Yate, *Northern Afghanistan, or Letters from the Afghan Boundary Commission* [1888] (Edinburgh, 2003), pp. 245, 303–5; Lillian Griffin, 'How to Swim', *The Puritan*, VIII (1900), pp. 389–95 (p. 389).

64 Robert Baden-Powell, *Scouting for Boys* (London, 1908), Yarns 6 and 9, cited by Ayriss, *Hung Out to Dry*, p. 28; Holbein, *Swimming*, pp. 12, 17–18.

65 Love, 'An Overview', p. 572.

66 Ibid., p. 571.

67 Boyar and Fleet, *A Social History*, p. 285.

68 Clancy-Smith, 'Where Elites Meet', p. 183; Johnson, 'The Venus of Margate', pp. 599–600.

69 Dawson, *Undercurrents of Power*, pp. 53–4; Strutt, *Glig-Gamena Angel Đeod*; Love, 'An Overview', pp. 568–85; Scribner, *Merpeople*, p. 146.

70 David Day, 'Kinship and Community in Victorian London: the "Beckwith Frogs"', *History Workshop Journal*, LXXI (2011), pp. 184–218 (pp. 204–5); Day and Roberts, *Swimming Communities*, p. 8 and *passim*; Love, 'An Overview', p. 578, though 'female swimming' was certainly not new.

71 Tolstoy, *Anna Karenina* (New York, 1899), p. 302; John Windhausen and Irina Tsypkina, 'National Identity and the Emergence of the Sports Movement in Imperial Russia', in *International Journal of the History of Sport*, vol. XII: *Tribal Identities: Nationalism, Europe, Sport*, ed. James Mangan (London, 1996), pp. 164–82 (p. 173).

72 Love, 'An Overview', p. 580; by 1900 crowds of people watched women's water polo competitions in Swansea: 'Women as Players of Water Polo', *The Sphere*, 13 October 1900, p. 53, www.waterpololegends.com (thanks to Bruce Wigo and Alex Nice).

73 Andrew Morris, '"To Make the Four Hundred Million Move": The Late Qing Dynasty Origins of Modern Chinese Sport and Physical Culture', *Comparative Studies in Society and History*, XLII (2000), pp. 876–906; Windhausen and Tsypkina, 'National Identity', pp. 165, 170.

20 OUT WITH THE OLD, IN WITH THE NEW

1 Jane Carson, *Colonial Virginians at Play* (Charlottesville, VA, 1958), pp. 86, 192.

2 William Byrd, 30 September 1733, cited in Carson and in Harold Gill, 'Colonial Americans in the Swim', *Colonial Williamsburg Journal*, XXII–XXIV (2001–2), p. 26.

3 George Catlin, *Letters and Notes on the Manners, Customs, and Conditions of North American Indians* (London, 1844), Letter 13, apparently plagiarized by Charles Steedman in his *Manual of Swimming* (London, 1867); see also

Glenn Stout, *Young Women and the Sea: How Trudy Ederle Conquered the English Channel and Inspired the World* (Boston, MA, and New York, 2008), p. 28.

4 Alfred Miller, *Indian Women: Swimming*, watercolour on paper (sketched 1837, finished 1858), now Baltimore, MD, Walters Art Museum 37.1940.194.

5 Charles Warner, *My Winter on the Nile* (Boston, MA, 1981), vol. I, p. 242.

6 'Lord Krishna and Radha Talk while her Friends Swim', opaque watercolour and gold on paper, folio from a Satsaiya series (Mewar, India, 1700s), Harvard Art Museums 1973.153.

7 Rachel Johnson, 'The Venus of Margate: Fashion and Disease at the Seaside', *Journal for Eighteenth-Century Studies*, XL (2017), pp. 587–602.

8 Peter Clias, *Gymnastique élémentaire* (Paris, 1819), trans. in *Swimming*, ed. Archibald Sinclair and William Henry (London, 1893), p. 78; Ralph Thomas, *Swimming* (London, 1904), p. 237; see Eric Chaline, *Strokes of Genius: A History of Swimming* (London, 2017), p. 109.

9 *Letters and Journals of Lord Byron with Notices of His Life*, ed. George Byron (London, 1833), pp. 263–6, Letter 413 (21 February 1821); Alexandra Heminsley, *Leap In: A Woman, Some Waves, and the Will to Swim* (New York, 2017), p. 152.

10 Anonymous, 'Les Nageurs' (The Swimmers), from the series *Le Supreme Bon Ton*, 15 (Paris, *c.* 1810–15).

11 Adolfo Corti, *L'arte del Nuoto teorico-pratica dimostrata secondo i principii della fisica, con relative* (Venice, 1819).

12 Harold Kenworthy: *The Times* [London], 22 April 1844; Cecil Colwin, *Breakthrough Swimming* (Champaign, IL, 2002), p. 3.

13 Ibid., p. 3; Charles Sprawson, *Haunts of the Black Masseur: The Swimmer as Hero* (Minneapolis, MN, 1992), p. 22.

14 Charles Wallis: William Wilson, *The Swimming Instructor: A Treatise on the Arts of Swimming and Diving* (London, 1883), p. 127.

15 Day, 'Kinship and Community', p. 200; 'Deerfoot and Beckwith', *The Times* [London], 21 October 1861, p. 7; Rose Posse, 'An Indian Athlete', *Posse Gymnasium Journal*, VIII (1900), pp. 6–7 (which leaves out the swimming).

16 Charles Steedman, *Manual of Swimming* (London, 1867).

17 1893: Stephen Dadd, 'Serpentine Club – Christmas Morning', in Sinclair and Henry, *Swimming*, frontispiece; 1896: Henri Fantin-Latour, 'Naiad', oil on canvas, St Petersburg, Hermitage Museum ГЭ-8906; 1897: William Small, 'A Water Polo Match at a London Swimming Club', *The Graphic* (7 August 1897); 1919: Charles Shannon, 'The Pursuit', in *Modern Woodcuts and Lithographs by British and French Artists*, ed. Geoffrey Holme (London, 1919).

18 In Paris: 'Origines des techniques de nage', *Service interuniversitaire des activités physiques et sportives* (Université de Rennes, n.d.).

19 Robert Watson, *Swimming Record and Chronicle of Sporting Events*, I/15 (1873), p. 3.

20 Richard Nelligan, *The Art of Swimming: A Practical Working Manual* (Boston, MA, 1906), pp. 27–9.

21 Montague Holbein, *Swimming* (London, 1904), pp. 12, 17–18; see Harold
   Ulen and Guy Larcom, *The Complete Swimmer* (New York, 1945), p. 98, which
   praises the breaststroke's 'grace and ease', and Pat Besford's *Encyclopedia of
   Swimming* (New York, 1971), p. 37, where breaststroke is 'so much beloved by
   traditionalists'.
22 Matt Mann, 'The Breaststroke', *Sports Illustrated* (July 1960), pp. 48–50.
23 Louis Handley, writing in 1929, is unaware that the crawl was the Greek
   stroke; Handley and William Howcroft, *Crawl-Stroke Swimming*
   (London, 1929), pp. 9–11.
24 For example, Sinclair and Henry, *Swimming*, p. 3.
25 Catalogue card, photograph RSN 18435 (Box 3.1.71), in the Smithsonian
   Institution, National Museum of American History, Washington, DC,
   Barrett, the swimming teacher at James Monroe High School in Brooklyn,
   did not make it, but Gertrude Ederle did in the same year.
26 Jane Stafford, 'Greeks Used Modern Swimming Stroke', *Science News-
   Letter*, XIV (1928), pp. 285–6.
27 Even in 2007 Christopher Love thought it seemed likely that
   'breaststroke, the oldest of the "classical" strokes now used in competitive
   swimming, was the stroke of choice for early swimmers': Christopher
   Love, 'An Overview of the Development of Swimming in England,
   c. 1750–1918', *International Journal of the History of Sport*, XXIV (2007),
   pp. 568–85 (p. 568).
28 Full report available at 'A Witch Trial at Mount Holly, 22 October 1730',
   Founders Online, National Archives, https://founders.archives.gov, accessed
   5 June 2021.
29 Dorothy Mays, *Women in Early America: Struggle, Survival, and Freedom
   in a New World* (Santa Barbara, CA, 2004), p. 366; Alice Earle, *Colonial
   Dames and Good Wives* (Boston, MA, 1895), p. 95.
30 Owen Davies, 'Urbanization and the Decline of Witchcraft: An
   Examination of London', in *The Witchcraft Reader*, ed. Darren Oldridge
   (Abingdon, 2008), p. 354.
31 Orna Darr, *Marks of an Absolute Witch: Evidentiary Dilemmas in Early
   Modern England* (Burlington, VT, 2011), p. 44; William Burns, *Witch Hunts
   in Europe and America: An Encyclopedia* (Westport, CT, 2003), p. 95.
32 *Ipswich Journal*, 20 July 1776.
33 *The Times* [London], 19 July 1825; *Bury and Norwich Post*, 21 April 1857;
   Bury and Norwich Post, 15 March 1864 (repr. in *The Times*, 24 September
   1865), available at 'The Hedingham Witchcraft Case' and 'The Swimming
   of Witches: Indicium aquae', Foxearth and District Local History Society,
   www.foxearth.org.uk, accessed 5 June 2021; John Kendrick Bangs, *The Water
   Ghost, and Others* (New York, 1894), pp. 1–19.
34 Ernest Pettifer, *Punishments of Former Days* (Bradford, 1939), p. 106;
   Thomas Brushfield, 'On Obsolete Punishments, with Particular Reference
   to those of Cheshire: Part II: The Cucking-Stool and Allied Punishments',
   *Journal of the Architectural, Archaeological and Historic Society, for the County,
   City, and Neighbourhood of Chester*, ser. I, II (1861), pp. 200–234 (pp. 232–3).

35 *Repertorium der verhandelingen en bijdragen betreffende de geschiedenis des vaderlands, in mengelwerken en tijdschriften tot op 1860 verschenen,* ed. Robert Fruin (Charleston, SC, 2012). For French arguments against the efficacy of trial by water, see Hubert-Pascal Ameilhon, 'Sur l'épreuve judiciaire appelé vulgairement l'épreuve de l'eau froide', in *Collection des Meilleurs Dissertations, Notices, et Traités Particuliers,* ed. Constant Leber (Paris, 1838), vol. VI, pp. 420–42.

36 Felix Brähm, *De fallacibus indiciis magiae* (Magdeburg, 1709), p. 47.

37 Erik Midelfort, *Exorcism and Enlightenment: Johann Joseph Gassner and the Demons of Eighteenth-Century Germany* (New Haven, CT, 2005), p. 11.

38 Marijke Gijswijt-Hofstra, 'Witchcraft after the Witch Trials', *Witchcraft and Magic in Europe,* vol. V: *The Eighteenth and Nineteenth Centuries,* ed. Bengt Ankarloo and Stuart Clark (Philadelphia, PA, 1999), p. 159.

39 Ibid., p. 159; Russell Zguta, 'The Ordeal by Water (Swimming of Witches) in the East Slavic World', *Slavic Review,* XXXVI (1977), pp. 220–30 (pp. 224–5); Christine Worobec, 'Witchcraft Beliefs and Practices in Prerevolutionary Russian and Ukrainian Villages', in *Witchcraft in the Modern World,* ed. Brian Levack (New York, 2002), pp. 47–69 (p. 59 n. 44).

40 Zguta, 'The Ordeal by Water', pp. 225, 228–9.

41 Worobec, 'Witchcraft Beliefs', p. 59 n. 44.

42 Roland Boer, *Lenin, Religion and Theology* (New York, 2013), p. 264 n. 18; Andrew Mango, *Ataturk: The Biography of the Founder of Modern Turkey* (New York, 1963), p. 36; 'Adana International Swimming Complex', ntvmsnbc.com, 2 December 2009. Since 1988, an annual 'Victory Day swim' across the Hellespont honours Ataturk (Douglas Booth, 'Swimming, Open Water', Berkshire Publishing Group, 2013).

43 At Wuhan in central China.

44 Geremie Barmé, 'The Tide of Revolution', *China Heritage Quarterly,* XXVIII (2011), n.p.; Barmé, 'Tides Chao', *China Heritage Quarterly,* XXIX (2012), n.p.

45 Bertram Wolfe, *Three Who Made a Revolution: A Biographical History of Lenin, Trotsky, and Stalin* [1948] (New York, 2001), p. 188; Leon Trotsky, 'Fighting Against the Stream', *Fourth International,* II/4 (May 1941), pp. 125–37.

46 Mao Zedong, *The Writings of Mao Zedong, 1949–1976: January 1956– December 1957,* trans. Mao's Writings Project (Armonk, NY, 1992), pp. 629–30.

47 Jonathan Kolatch, *Sports, Politics and Ideology in China* (Middle Village, NY, 1972), pp. 160, 162; Wu Cheng, in Andrew Morris, *Marrow of the Nation: A History of Sport and Physical Culture in Modern China* (Berkeley, CA, 2004), p. 119; Ling-ling Lien, 'Leisure, Patriotism, and Identity: Chinese Career Women's Club in Wartime Shanghai', in *Creating Chinese Modernity: Knowledge and Everyday Life, 1900–1940,* ed. Peter Zarrow (New York, 2006), pp. 213–40 (p. 224).

48 'Birth of the Republic', *Free China Review*; Barmé, 'Tides Chao'.

49 James Riordan, *Sport in Soviet Society: Development of Sport and Physical Education in Russia and the* USSR (Cambridge, 1977), pp. 44, 179, 377; Simon Montefiore, *Stalin: The Court of the Red Tsar* (New York, 2003), p. 80.

21 SWIMMING IS SO LAST CENTURY

1 Kevin Dawson, *Undercurrents of Power* (Philadelphia, PA, 2018), p. 61.

2 Bernarda Bryson, 'Escape, possibly Harriet Tubman', ink and watercolour on paper, 1934/5, Washington, DC, Library of Congress 2004678973; Solomon Northrup, *Twelve Years a Slave: Narrative of Solomon Northup, a Citizen of New-York, Kidnapped in Washington City in 1841, and Rescued in 1853* (Auburn, NY, 1853), p. 137; Jacob Green, *Narrative of the Life of J. D. Green, a Runaway Slave, from Kentucky* (Huddersfield, 1864), pp. 24, 31; Sylviane Diouf, *Slavery's Exiles: The Story of the American Maroons* (New York, 2014), pp. 70, 95, 168–9; Franklin Wright, *General History of the Caribbean* UNESCO, vol. III: *The Slave Societies of the Caribbean* (London, 1997), p. 94; see Dawson, *Undercurrents of Power*, pp. 20–21.

3 Mark Twain, *The Adventures of Huckleberry Finn* [1884] (New York, 1918), pp. 62, 128, 155; Andrew Kahrl, 'On the Beach: Race and Leisure in the Jim Crow South', PhD thesis, Indiana University, 2008, p. 20. See Kevin Dawson, 'Enslaved Swimmers and Divers in the Atlantic World', *Journal of American History*, XCII (2006), pp. 1327–55; Robert Duncanson, *Valley Pasture*, 1857, oil on canvas, Smithsonian American Art Museum 1983.104.1; Dawson, *Undercurrents of Power*, p. 36.

4 *The American Slave: A Composite Autobiography, Supplement 1:1 – Alabama Narratives*, ed. George Rawick (Westport, CT, 1972), p. 112, cited in Dawson, *Undercurrents of Power*, pp. 35–7; Frederick Douglass, *My Bondage and My Freedom* (New York, 1855), pp. 33–7, 40, 42, 60, 70, esp. 65; not knowing how to swim: Frederick Douglass, *Narrative of the Life of Frederick Douglass, an American Slave* (Boston, MA, 1845), p. 64; Francis Fedric, *Slave Life in Virginia and Kentucky* (London, 1863), pp. 1–2.

5 James Mangan, *Europe, Sport, World: Shaping Global Societies* (London, 2001), pp. 87–8 (Zimbabwe was then known by its colonial name); Nicholas Aplin and Quek Jin Jong, 'Celestials in Touch: Sport and the Chinese in Colonial Singapore', in *Sport in Asian Society, Past and Present*, ed. Fan Hong and James Mangan (London, 2002), pp. 72–3; Archive photographs, '100 anos', Clube Naval de Maputo, www.clubenaval.co.mz, accessed 18 May 2021.

6 Jeff Wiltse, *Contested Waters: A Social History of Swimming Pools in America* (Chapel Hill, NC, 2007), p. 78; Stephanie Orfali, *A Jewish Girl in the Weimar Republic* (Berkeley, CA, 1987), pp. 187, 196; Ian Hancock, *Danger! Educated Gypsy: Selected Essays* (Hatfield, 2010), p. 249.

7 Lester Wong, 'Singaporeans Now More Active', *Straits Times*, 30 August 2016; Ngiam Tong Dow, *A Mandarin and the Making of Public Policy* (Singapore, 2006), p. 167, though see p. 69; Ang Mo Kio, 'Swimming in the

Summer Sun of Singapore', *Remember Singapore*, 10 January 2013, https://
remembersingapore.org, accessed 18 May 2021.

8 Nguyen Dong-Chi, *Kho Tang Truyen Co Tich Viet Nam* (*The Vietnamese
Legendary Stories*) (Hanoi, 1982). Quận He is the sobriquet of Nguyễn
Hữu Cầu, a Vietnamese nobleman who led a major farmer rebellion in
what was then called Annam. 'He' is the name of a fast-moving fish, and
the sobriquet reflects Quận He's swimming skills. Popular Vietnamese
stories feature this folk hero swimming as he fights the rich landlords;
the parallels to the Chinese Water Margin stories may not be coincidental.
Swimming contests: Minh Mang Emperor, 'Ten Moral Precepts',
Sources of Vietnamese Tradition, ed. George Dutton et al. (New York, 2012),
pp. 306–7.

9 Truong Buu Lâm, *Colonialism Experienced: Vietnamese Writings on
Colonialism, 1900-1931* (Ann Arbor, MI, 2000), pp. 49, 88; 'Vietnam:
Children Learn to Swim and to Survive', IRIN: *Humanitarian News and
Analysis* (United Nations, 5 May 2010); 'UNICEF Supports Swimming
Instruction to Prevent Child Deaths in Bangladesh', UNICEF *Bangladesh*,
3 September 2009.

10 Rohinton Mistry, 'The Art of Swimming', in *Colonial and Post-Colonial
Fiction: An Anthology*, ed. Robert Ross (New York, 1999), pp. 263–82 (pp.
268–9). See Tarashankar Banerjee, 'Boatman Tarini', trans. Hiren Mukerjee,
in *Indian Short Stories, 1900–2000*, ed. E. Rāmakrsnan (New Delhi, 2005),
pp. 9–23, where swimming once again ends in disaster.

11 Xan Fielding, *Corsair Country: The Diary of a Journey along the Barbary
Coast* (London, 1958), p. 98; Paula Holmes-Eber, *Daughters of Tunis:
Women, Family, and Networks in a Muslim City* (New York, 2002), p. 12.

12 John Lohn, *Historical Dictionary of Competitive Swimming* (Toronto,
2010), p. 139; Julie Masis, 'David Hunt Saves Lives by Teaching Swimming
in Cambodia', *Christian Science Monitor* (21 June 2013).

13 Ngo Vinh Long, *Before the Revolution: The Vietnamese Peasants under
the French* [1973] (New York, 1991), p. 247; William Johnston, *The Life of
General Albert Sidney Johnston* (New York, 1878), pp. 37, 41.

14 *National Museum of Australia: Tangled Destinies*, ed. Dimity Reed
(Melbourne, 2002), p. 116; *Australian Territories*, I (Department of
Territories 1960), p. 24; *Mission Field: A Monthly Record of the Proceedings of
the Society for the Propagation of the Gospel in Foreign Parts*, LVIII (1913), p. 72.

15 Joel Franks, *Crossing Sidelines, Crossing Cultures: Sport and Asian Pacific
American Cultural Citizenship*, 2nd edn (Lanham, MD, 2010), p. 194.

16 Carol Irwin et al., *Constraints Impacting Minority Swimming Participation*
(Memphis, TN, 2008, 2010). Figures vary: the USA Swimming report said
62 per cent of African Americans and 44 per cent of Hispanics could not
swim well, while 68 per cent of White people could. But the Memphis
Report found that 58 per cent of African American children and 56 per
cent of Hispanic children could not swim well, while 69 per cent of White
children could. See Donald Hastings et al., 'Drowning in Inequalities:
Swimming and Social Justice', *Journal of Black Studies*, XXXVI (2006),

pp. 894–917. See also Howard Means, *Splash! 10,000 Years of Swimming* (London, 2020), p. 215.

17 Red Cross data, in Brad Mielke and Robert Balint, 'Why Can So Few American Minorities Swim?', *The TakeAway*, 30 July 2012, n.p.; Gitanjali Saluja et al., 'Swimming Pool Drownings among U.S. Residents Aged 5–24 Years: Understanding Racial/Ethnic Disparities', *American Journal of Public Health*, XCVI (2006), pp. 728–33; World Health Organization, 'Facts about Injuries: Drowning' (Geneva, n.d.), Table 2; *World Report on Child Injury Prevention*, ed. Margie Peden (Geneva, 2008), p. 60.

18 Baba Ahmed and Krista Larson, 'Boat Sinks on Mali River; 43 Dead, Dozens Missing', *USA Today*, 13 October 2013; Elizabeth Rubin, 'How a Texas Philanthropist Helped Fund the Hunt for Joseph Kony', *New Yorker*, 21 October 2013.

19 For example, Li Yuanhong or Yao Chen-Tuan: 'Birth of the Republic', *Free China Review*, XIII/1, 1 January 1973, https://taiwantoday.tw; Yao Chen-Tuan, 'My Adventures during the Boxer War', in *The World's Story: A History of the World in Story, Song, and Art*, ed. Eva Tappan (Boston, MA, 1914), vol. I, pp. 239–47.

20 'The people now living around the site of what we call Assyria, adjacent to the river Tigris, do not swim for exercise or amusement as do Europeans, but only when it is necessary': Ralph Thomas, *Swimming* (London, 1904), p. 78.

21 James Riordan, *Sport in Soviet Society: Development of Sport and Physical Education in Russia and the USSR* (Cambridge, 1977), pp. 335, 341–2; Lyudmila Aristova, 'Russian Facilities for Sports and Leisure: Realities and Perspectives', *Moscow Times*, 4620, 19 April 2011, Christopher Ward, *Brezhnev's Folly* (Pittsburgh, PA, 2009), p. 42; Mary Dejevsky, 'Why Russia's Diplomats Should Learn Swimming-Pool Etiquette', *The Spectator*, 4 May 2013.

22 Rebecca Mead, 'Going for the Cold', *New Yorker*, 27 January 2020, pp. 42–9 (p. 45).

23 Sabine Czerny, 'Warum viele Kinder nicht schwimmen lernen', *Das Deutsche Schulportal*, 2 July 2019, Sally Peck, 'Nearly Half of British Children Can't Swim – and It's Their Parents' Fault', *Daily Telegraph*, 12 September 2013. John McManamon attributes lower British drowning rates in the twentieth century to better swimming abilities, but assiduous fencing and signposting of ponds and rivers have done more. McManamon, *'Neither Letters nor Swimming': The Rebirth of Swimming and Free-Diving* (Leiden, 2021), p. 273.

24 Brian Palmer, 'How Many Americans Can't Swim: The Demographics of Land-Lubbing', *Slate*, 4 August 2010; Irwin et al., *Constraints Impacting Minority Swimming Participation*; Hastings et al., 'Drowning in Inequalities', pp. 894–917; Melissa Korn, 'For Certain College Students, This Test Calls for a Plunge', *Wall Street Journal*, 28 November 2012.

25 Thomas Leeuwen, *The Springboard in the Pond: An Intimate History of the Swimming Pool*, ed. Helen Searing (Boston, MA, 1998), p. 297; Larry

Rohter, *Brazil on the Rise: The Story of a Country Transformed* (New York, 2010), p. 86.

26 Mead, 'Going for the Cold', p. 45; Scott Reyburn, 'Banksy Is a Control Freak. But He Can't Control His Legacy', *New York Times*, 5 February 2020.

27 Margie Peden, *World Report on Child Injury Prevention* (Geneva, 2008), p. 60; Riordan, *Sport in Soviet Society*, p. 335; Michael Wines, 'Russians Drown Sorrows, and Selves', *New York Times*, 28 June 1999.

28 'Drowning', World Health Organization Fact Sheet, 3 February 2020. However, high drowning rates in Japan are due to older women drowning in their bathtubs, often as a form of suicide, and do not reflect people's ability to swim; Ian Rockett and Gordon Smith, 'Covert Suicide Among Elderly Japanese Females: Questioning Unintentional Drownings', *Social Science and Medicine*, XXXVI (1993), pp. 1467–72.

29 Czerny, 'Warum viele Kinder'; Katrin Woitsch, 'Mehr Badetote in Bayern: Das raten die Rettungsschwimmer', Merkur.de, 7 June 2017; Woitsch, 'Kommentar zur DLRG-Studie: Mehr Nichtschwimmer wegen Sparkurs', Merkur.de, 7 June 2017.

30 Roger Duchêne and Jean Contrucci, *Marseille, 2600 ans d'histoire* (Paris, 1998).

31 J. Moth, *The City of Birmingham Baths Department, 1851–1951* (Birmingham, 1951). See also, for Britain, Ian Gordon and Simon Inglis, *Great Lengths: The Historic Indoor Swimming Pools of Britain* (Liverpool, 2009), pp. 109, 123 and *passim*; for the United States, Wiltse, *Contested Waters*, p. 93; idem, 'Swimming Pools, Civic Life, and Social Capital', in *A Companion to Sport*, ed. David Andrews and Ben Carrington (Chichester, 2013), pp. 287–304.

32 Mary Helen Sprecher, 'New Report Provides Insights on What Sports are Growing, Gaining in Popularity', *Sports Destination Management*, 3 October 2018.

33 Christopher Love, 'An Overview of the Development of Swimming in England, *c.* 1750–1918', *International Journal of the History of Sport*, XXIV (2007), pp. 568–85 (p. 585); John Schofield et al., *Archaeological Practice in Great Britain: A Heritage Handbook* [1979] (London, 2011), p. 71; Wiltse, *Contested Waters*, p. 93; idem, 'Swimming Pools', pp. 287–304; 'Nine Birmingham Leisure Centres Face Closure through Council Cuts', BBC *News*, 26 November 2013, though there is now a prospect of opening some new pools.

34 Some people have taken up 'wild swimming' in Britain, but as an eccentricity with its own sets of rules, not a general trend: Mead, 'Going for the Cold', p. 42.

35 Alexandra Heminsley, *Leap in: A Woman, Some Waves, and the Will to Swim* (New York, 2017), p. 3.

36 Bruce Lee, 'Please Stop Peeing in the Pool, CDC Says', *Forbes*, 31 May 2019; Rosie Gizauskas, 'Urine Trouble: Why You Should Never Wee in the Sea when Swimming in these Places', *The Sun*, 18 October 2018; Katie Jennings, 'Is it OK to Pee in the Ocean?', *Business Insider*, 22 August 2014.

37 Bruce Wigo, 'The Importance of Swimming in China', ISHOF
    News, https://ishof.org, accessed 18 May 2021; Michel Pedroletti, *Les
    Fondamentaux de la natation* (Paris, 2000), p. 57; Yannick Cochennec,
    'Pourquoi vous ne savez pas nager la brasse comme aux Mondiaux', *Slate*,
    24 July 2011, www.slate.fr, accessed 18 May 2021; Uwe Rheker, *First Steps:
    Learning by Playing*, trans. Isabel Schmallofsky (Oxford, 2004), pp. 81–7;
    Mead, 'Going for the Cold', pp. 45, 46.

38 William Tullett, 'Grease and Sweat: Race and Smell in Eighteenth-
    Century English Culture', *Cultural and Social History*, XIII (2016),
    pp. 307–22 (pp. 309, 318).

39 Lyall Watson, *Jacobson's Organ: And the Remarkable Nature of Smell*
    (London, 2001), pp. 87, 135; Michael H., review of Spreewaldbad pool
    (16 February 2012), Yelp: 'The changing rooms are often dirty and often it
    does not smell so great . . . obviously because of the location (immigrant
    clientele).' Another Yelp reviewer complained about 'Turkish young
    people' at the same swimming pool; Andrew Kettler, '"Ravishing Odors of
    Paradise": Jesuits, Olfaction, and Seventeenth-Century North America',
    Journal of American Studies, L (2016), pp. 827–52 (pp. 832–3); Kido Takayoshi,
    quoted in William Beasley, *Japan Encounters the Barbarian: Japanese
    Travellers in America and Europe* (New Haven, CT, 1995), p. 216; G. Satpathy,
    ed., *Encyclopedia of AIDS* (Delhi, 2002), vol. I, p. 81; Ann Curthoys, 'The
    Freedom Ride and the Tent Embassy', in *The Aboriginal Tent Embassy:
    Sovereignty, Black Power, Land Rights and the State*, ed. Gary Foley et al.
    (Abingdon, 2013), pp. 98–114 (p. 108); Nicola Caracciolo, *Uncertain Refuge:
    Italy and the Jews during the Holocaust* (Champaign, IL, 1995), pp. 86–7.

40 Om Prakash Goyal, *Nomads at the Crossroads* (Delhi, 2005), p. 126; Tassilo
    Herrsche, *Global Geographies of Post-Socialist Transition: Geographies,
    Societies, Policies* (London, 2006), p. 218; Council of Europe, *Human Rights
    of Roma and Travellers in Europe* (Brussels, 2012), p. 181; *Lonely Planet Russia*
    (Melbourne, 2010), p. 182.

41 Khara Lewis, 'Pa. Swim Club – Accused of Racial Discrimination –
    Agrees to Settlement', CNN *Justice*, 17 August 2012.

42 Joseph Shapiro, *No Pity: People with Disabilities Forging a New Civil Rights
    Movement* [1993] (New York, 2011), p. 176; Jenna Rennert, 'The Memorial
    Day Beauty Countdown: How to Prep in 5 Days or Less', *Vogue*, 20 May
    2019; Elizabeth Narins, 'The Only Workout You Need to Look Sexy AF by
    Summer', *Cosmopolitan*, 8 May 2016; Catherine Saint Louis, 'Bikini-Ready?
    Who's Judging?', *New York Times*, 25 May 2011.

43 Lawrence James, *Raj: The Making and Unmaking of British India* (New
    York, 1997), p. 502; Kahrl, 'On the Beach', p. 7; 'Hawaiian to Swim at
    Olympic Games', *New York Times*, 14 January 1912; Jim Nasium [ha!],
    'Kanaka Swimmer Has No Equal in the Water', *Philadelphia Inquirer*
    (1913), reprinted in the *Salt Lake Tribune*, 2 February 1913. See Franks,
    Crossing Sidelines, pp. 192ff.

44 For example, Portland Parks and Recreation, *Activities for Aquatics
    Programs* (Winter 2020); New York City Parks, *Asser Levy Recreation*

Center Pool Schedule (Winter 2020); Amy Farrell, *Fat Shame: Stigma and the Fat Body in American Culture* (New York, 2011), pp. 5, 8. Pools lose money on open swim hours, and have to make it up on classes.

45 Bonnie Tsui, *Why We Swim* (Chapel Hill, NC, 2020), p. 6; Mead, 'Going for the Cold', p. 46; Elisha Cooper, 'The Winter Surfers of Rockaway Beach', *New York Times*, 23 February 2020.

46 John Stedman, *Narrative of Five Year's Expedition Against the Revolted Negroes of Surinam, in Guiana, on the Wild Coast of South America; from the Year 1772, to 1777* (London, 1813), vol. II, pp. 7, 295; John Warren, *Para: or, Scenes and Adventures on the Banks of the Amazon* (New York, 1851), p. 9; Jonathan Swift, *Gulliver's Travels* [1726], ed. Claude Rawson (Oxford, 2005), pp. 248–9.

47 Franks, *Crossing Sidelines*, p. 191; Dawson, *Undercurrents of Power*, pp. 19–20.

48 Warren, *Para*, p. 9.

49 Rutherford Alcock, *The Capital of the Tycoon: A Narrative of a Three Years' Residence in Japan* (New York, 1877), vol. II, p. 276; Alice Bacon, *Japanese Girls and Women* (Boston, MA, 1891), pp. 256–7; Eliza Scidmore, *Jinrikisha Days in Japan* (New York, 1891), pp. 367–8, 253.

50 Warren, *Para*, p. 102; Gilberto Freyre, 'Social Life in Brazil in the Middle of the Nineteenth Century', *Hispanic American Historical Review*, V (1922), pp. 597–630 (p. 627).

51 Holmes-Eber, *Daughters of Tunis*, pp. 5, 12; Wangari Muoria-Sal et al., *Writing for Kenya: The Life and Works of Henry Muoria* (Leiden, 2009), p. 287.

52 John Pierre Entelis, *Culture and Counterculture in Moroccan Politics* [1989] (Lanham, MD, 1996), pp. 118–19; Martha Hutchinson, 'The Image of Terrorism and the Government's Response to Terrorism', in *Terrorism: The Second or Anti-Colonial Wave*, ed. David Rapoport (London, 2006), pp. 237–77 (p. 240); Alistair Horne, *A Savage War of Peace: Algeria, 1954–1962* [1977] (London, 2006), pp. 52, 185–6; Jamie Grierson, 'Tunisia Attack: How a Man with a Parasol Could Murder 38 People on the Beach', *The Guardian*, 28 February 2017.

53 Jeffrey Bayliss, *On the Margins of Empire: Buraku and Korean Identity in Prewar and Wartime Japan* (Cambridge, MA, 2013), pp. 82, 351, 371–2; Noah McCormack, *Japan's Outcaste Abolition: The Struggle for National Inclusion and the Making of the Modern State* (Abingdon, 2012), p. 72; John Swain, 'Female Bodies Translated Across the Strait of Korea: Corporeal Transformation in Chong Wishin's Plays', *Japanese Language and Literature*, XLIII (2009), pp. 363–82.

54 Shikitei Sanba, *Ukiyoburo* (1809–13), complete with threats to children that *kappa*s will get them; Scott Clark, *Japan: A View from the Bath* (Honolulu, HI, 1994), pp. 1, 4, 66; Lesley Wynn, 'Self-Reflection in the Tub: Japanese Bathing Culture, Identity, and Cultural Nationalism', *Asia Pacific Perspectives*, XII (2014), pp. 61–78.

55 Bartolomé de las Casas, *Brevísima relación de la destrucción de las Indias* (Madrid, 1552); Dawson, *Undercurrents of Power*, pp. 17–18; this idea that women did not swim in the nineteenth century seems to have been

common by the 1940s: Harold Ulen and Guy Larcom, *The Complete Swimmer* (New York, 1945), p. 161.

56 Fatima Faizi and Thomas Gibbons-Neff, 'For Women in Kabul, "It Is Just Me and the Water"', *New York Times*, 22 December 2019; 'Hitting the Beach in Hijab in Iran', *The Guardian*, 11 August 2014.

57 Mead, 'Going for the Cold', p. 42.

58 Vaughn Scribner, *Merpeople: A Human History* (London, 2020), pp. 196, 230.

59 Fiona MacCarthy, *Byron: Life and Legend* (New York, 2002), p. 59 and *passim*; Charles Sprawson, *Haunts of the Black Masseur: The Swimmer as Hero* (Minneapolis, MN, 1992), pp. 118–19.

60 Thomas Eakins, *Swimming*, 1885, oil on canvas, Fort Worth, TX, Amon Carter Museum of American Art 1990.19.1; Michael Hatt, 'The Male Body in Another Frame: Thomas Eakins' *The Swimming Hole* as a Homoerotic Image', *Journal of Philosophy and the Visual Arts: The Body*, ed. Andrew Benjamin (London, 1993), p. 19; Martin Berger, 'Modernity and Gender in Thomas Eakins's "Swimming"', *American Art*, XI (1997), pp. 32–47.

61 Matt Cook, *London and the Culture of Homosexuality, 1885–1914* (Cambridge, 2003), pp. 3, 35–7, 147–9.

62 Gordon Waitt, '(Hetero)sexy Waves: Surfing, Space, Gender and Sexuality', in *Rethinking Gender and Youth Sport*, ed. Ian Wellard (New York, 2007), pp. 99–126 (p. 121); Eddie Kim, 'Straight American Men Hate Speedos for No Good Reason', MEL *Magazine*, 24 May 2018, https://medium.com, accessed 18 May 2021.

63 Keith Tankard, 'The Establishment of a "Native Vigilance Association" at East London (South Africa) to Protect the Interests of the Black Community against Social Manipulation by the Local Municipality, 1890–1923', *H-Urban Seminar on the History of Community Organizing and Community-based Development*, 1996, available at https://comm-org.wisc. edu, accessed 18 May 2021; see Keith Tankard, 'The Development of East London through Four Decades of Municipal Control, 1873–1914', PhD thesis, Rhodes University, Grahamstown, South Africa, 1991, pp. 396–402; Keith Tankard, 'Urban Segregation: William Mvalo's "Celebrated Stick Case"', *South African Historical Journal*, XXXIV–XXXV (1996), pp. 29–38 (p. 37); Kamilla Swart, 'Swimming, Southern Africa', in *Sports Around the World*, ed. John Nauright and Charles Parrish (Santa Barbara, CA, 2012), vol. I, pp. 162–3 (p. 162).

64 Eric Jennings, *Curing the Colonizers: Hydrotherapy, Climatology, and French Colonial Spas* (Durham, NC, 2006), p. 163.

65 The Fairground Pool in St Louis: Wiltse, *Contested Waters*, pp. 78–81.

66 South African MP Edward Brabant [1893], quoted in Tankard, 'The Establishment of a "Native Vigilance Association"'.

67 *New York Voice* [1890], quoted by Monée Fields-White, 'How Racism Tainted Women's Right to Vote', *The Root*, 25 March 2011; Scott Poynting, 'What Caused the Cronulla Riot?', *Race and Class*, XLVIII (2006), pp. 85–92.

68 Mead, 'Going for the Cold', p. 42; Jason Wilson, *Buenos Aires: A Cultural and Literary History* (Oxford, 1999), p. 54; Joe Blakely, *Saving the Willamette:*

A History of Oregon's Heartland River (2020), p. 76; Jeffrey Mindich, 'Intractable River Pollution', *Taiwan Today*, 1 October 1991.

69 Richard Steele, 'Violence in Los Angeles: Sleepy Lagoon, the Zoot-Suit Riots, and the Liberal Response', in *World War II and Mexican American Civil Rights*, ed. Richard Griswold del Castillo (Austin, TX, 2008), pp. 34–48 (p. 35); David Day and Margaret Roberts, *Swimming Communities in Victorian England* (Manchester, 2019), p. 4.

70 Susie Parr, *The Story of Swimming: A Social History of Bathing in Britain* (Stockport, 2011); Phyllis Arnold, 'Always Look for the Light', *Stories from Teachers and Pupils, St Joseph's School*, https://web.archive.org, accessed 23 July 2021; Don Hinrichsen, *Coastal Waters of the World: Trends, Threats, and Strategies* (Washington, DC, 1998), pp. 79–80; Kosonike Koso-Thomas, *Swimming against the Tide: Without Fear or Favor* (Freetown, 2004), p. 18; Olga Kalashnikova, 'Swimming Unsafe in City: More than 25 Percent of all Wastewater in St. Petersburg is Released into the Environment Untreated', *St Petersburg Times* (3 July 2013); Larry Rohter, 'Drawing Lines Across the Sand, Between Classes', *New York Times*, 6 February 2007; Rohter, *Brazil on the Rise*, p. 87.

71 Mistry, 'The Art of Swimming', pp. 268–9.

72 Norman Rockwell, 'No Swimming', *Saturday Evening Post*, 4 June 1921.

73 Mamie Fields, *Lemon Swamp and Other Places: A Carolina Memoir* (New York, 1982), pp. 191–2, cited in Andrew Kahrl, *The Land Was Ours: How Black Beaches Became White Wealth in the Coastal South* (Chapel Hill, NC, 2012), pp. 11–12.

74 Isak Lidström and Ingvar Svanberg, 'Ancient Buoyancy Devices in Sweden: Floats made of Reed, Club-Rush, Inflated Skins and Animal Bladders', *Folk Life: Journal of Ethnological Studies*, LVII (2019), pp. 85–94 (p. 85); Tsui, *Why We Swim*, p. 9; Woitsch, 'Mehr Badetote in Bayern'; Mead, 'Going for the Cold', p. 46; Shozo Makino, 'Long Distance Racing', in *Swimming in Japan*, ed. Shigeo Sagita and Ken Uyeno (Tokyo, 1935), pp. 143–7 (p. 147), available at www.svoemmenoerden.dk.

75 Thomas Cureton, *How to Teach Swimming and Diving* [1929] (New York, 1934), p. ix.

76 Mohammed Salim, *My Mother's Aspirations: My Commitment, Determination and with Allah's Help and Mercy I Became a Doctor* (Bloomington, IN, 2011), p. 82; Kevin Rushe, *Stories from Teachers and Pupils, St Joseph's School*, https://web.archive.org, accessed 23 July 2021.

77 James, *Raj*, p. 502.

78 Chris Ayriss, *Hung Out to Dry: Swimming in Britain* (Morrisville, NC, 2009), p. 8; Tsui, *Why We Swim*, p. 6.

79 John Gribble, *Dark Deeds in a Sunny Land: Blacks and Whites in North-West Australia* [1905] (Perth, 1987), p. 50; Ernest Hunter, *Aboriginal Health and History: Power and Prejudice in Remote Australia* (Cambridge, 1993), p. 41; Penelope Hetherington, *Settler, Servants, and Slaves: Aboriginal and European Children in Nineteenth-Century Western Australia* (Perth, 2002), pp. 157, 160.

80 John Stephens, *Incidents of Travels in Egypt, Arabia Petraea and the Holy Land* (London, 1837), p. 29; Charles Warner, *My Winter on the Nile* (Boston, MA, 1891), vol. I, p. 246; Des Alwi, *Friends and Exiles: A Memoir of the Nutmeg Isles and the Indonesian Nationalist Movement* (Ithaca, NY, 2008), pp. 55, 63.

81 Charles Steedman, *A Manual of Swimming* (London, 1867), pp. 81–6, and his last chapter, where he 'discredits the superior prowess of savages as swimmers', quoted in Thomas, *Swimming*, p. 312; Matthew Webb, quoted in Thomas, *Swimming*, p. 134; Sprawson, *Haunts of the Black Masseur*, p. 20; see also Ulen and Larcom, *The Complete Swimmer*, pp. 1–7. As Steve Mentz says, swimming today has 'a complex history of entanglement with European Romanticism and imperial expansion'. ('Swimming in the Anthropocene', *Public Books*, 17 December 2020).

82 Cecil Colwin, *Breakthrough Swimming* (Champaign, IL, 2002), p. 198; Mead, 'Going for the Cold', p. 45.

83 Fortunino Matania, poster for Southport, Great Britain, *c.* 1930 (London, Victoria and Albert Museum E.189-1968), and a South African airline poster (*c.* 1960s?), Washington, DC, National Air and Space Museum, Smithsonian Institution A19960165000; Daniel Burdsey, 'Strangers on the Shore? Racialized Representation, Identity and In/visibilities of Whiteness at the English Seaside', *Cultural Sociology*, V (2011), pp. 538–9; Noorjehan Barmania, 'This Muslim Life', *The Guardian*, 3 July 2008; see Gurinder Chadha's movie *Bhaji on the Beach* (1993).

84 Duncan McDowall, 'The Colour of Tourism Part 2', *The Bermudian*, 12 June 2012, www.thebermudian.com.

85 Giorgio Miescher et al., *Posters in Action: Visuality in the Making of an African Nation* (Basel, 2009), p. 40; Petri Hottola, 'Coastal Bird Tourism: Postcolonial Resources and Restraints', in *Tourism Strategies and Local Responses in Southern Africa*, ed. Petri Hottola (Wallingford, 2009), p. 113.

86 Gwyn Topham, 'The Politics of Tunisian Tourism', *The Guardian*, 17 January 2011; Mead, 'Going for the Cold', p. 46.

87 Martin Evans and John Philips, *Algeria: Anger of the Dispossessed* (New Haven, CT, 2007), p. 39; Alison Baker, *Voices of Resistance: Oral Histories of Moroccan Women* (Albany, NY, 1998), pp. 50–51.

88 Mohamed Helal, 'Tourism and Development in Tunisia', *Annals of Tourism Research*, 22 (1995), pp. 157–71 (pp. 166–7); Rohter, *Brazil on the Rise*, p. 86; Rohter, 'Drawing Lines'; Benjamin Stora, *Algeria, 1830–2000: A Short History* (Ithaca, NY, 2004), p. 50.

22 EVERYONE OUT OF THE WATER

1 See for example Kawanabe Kyosai's 1863 print 'Repelling of the Mongol Pirate Ships', now at the Houston Museum of Fine Arts.

2 Shigeo Sagita, 'History of Swimming', in *Swimming in Japan*, ed. Shigeo Sagita and Ken Uyeno (Tokyo, 1935), pp. 1–40 (pp. 1–3); François

Oppenheim, *The History of Swimming* (North Hollywood, CA, 1970), p. 3; Fujiyama Dojo, 'Nihon Eiho: Samurai Swimming', *Daito Ryu Aiki Bujutsu Rengokai*, 28 January 2008, Hisashi Sanada et al., 'Reorganization of Suijutsu Led by Kano Jigoro', *Japan Journal of Physical Education, Health and Sport Sciences*, LVII (2007), p. 315.

3 Masao Matsunaga, 'Samurai Styles of Swimming', in *Swimming in Japan*, pp. 41–58 (pp. 49, 51).

4 Eliza Scidmore, *Jinrikisha Days in Japan* (New York, 1891), pp. 367–8, 218, 253; Midge Ayukawa, 'Japanese Pioneer Women', in *Sisters or Strangers: Immigrant, Ethnic and Racialized Women in Canadian History*, ed. Franca Iacovetta et al. (Toronto, 2004), p. 238; Joel Franks, *Crossing Sidelines, Crossing Cultures: Sport and Asian Pacific American Cultural Citizenship*, 2nd edn (Lanham, MD, 2010), pp. 12–13, 201–3; Michael Bourdaghs, *Sayonara Amerika, Sayonara Nippon: A Geopolitical Prehistory of J-Pop* (New York, 2012), p. 111.

5 Hideko Maehata, 'Early Days of Women's Swimming in Japan', in *Swimming in Japan*, pp. 174–85; Ikkaku Matsuzawa, 'The Rise of Japanese Swimmers', ibid., pp. 86–90 (p. 90).

6 Shigeo Sagita, 'History of Swimming', p. 1.

7 Sanada et al., 'Reorganization of Suijutsu', p. 315; Andreas Niehaus and Christian Tagsold, *Sport, Memory and Nationhood in Japan* (London, 2013), pp. 32–3; Niehaus, 'Swimming into Memory: The Los Angeles Olympics (1932) as Japanese Lieu de Memoire', *Sport in Society*, XIV (2011), pp. 430–43; Matsuzawa, 'The Rise of Japanese Swimmers', in *Swimming in Japan*, pp. 86–7.

8 Katsuo Takaishi, 'Crawl Stroke', in *Swimming in Japan*, pp. 91–135 (p. 91); Yasuji Miyazaki, 'Short Distance Racing', in *Swimming in Japan*, pp. 136–42 (p. 138); Shozo Makino, 'Long Distance Racing', in *Swimming in Japan*, pp. 143–7 (p. 143, 145); Yoshiyuki Tsuruta, 'Breast Stroke', in *Swimming in Japan*, pp. 150–61 (pp. 150–51), who attributes Japanese improvement in breaststroke to the work of the Filipino swimmer Teófilo Yldefonso; David Welky, 'Viking Girls, Mermaids, and Little Brown Men: U.S. Journalism and the 1932 Olympics', *Journal of Sport History*, XXIV (1997), pp. 24–50; Niehaus and Tagsold, *Sport, Memory*, p. 33; Cecil Colwin, *Breakthrough Swimming* (Champaign, IL, 2002), p. 204.

9 There are still practitioners of the old Japanese samurai-style swimming today: Bonnie Tsui, *Why We Swim* (Chapel Hill, NC, 2020), pp. 192–212.

10 Atsunori Matsui et al., 'The History and Problem of Swimming Education in Japan', in *International Aquatic History Symposium and Film Festival* (Fort Lauderdale, FL, 2012), pp. 129–37; 'Swimming Lessons Popular for Japanese Children', www.nippon.com, 8 April 2020; Nikki Khanna, *Whiter: Asian American Women on Skin Color and Colorism* (New York, 2020).

11 George De Vos and Hiroshi Wagatsuma, *Japan's Invisible Race* (Berkeley, CA, 1966), pp. 107–8; Jackie Kim-Wachutka, *Zainichi Korean Women in Japan: Voices* (London, 2018), pp. 243–4; John Lie, *Zainichi (Koreans*

in Japan): Diasporic Nationalism and Postcolonial Identity (Berkeley, CA, 2008), p. 8; Sunny Che, *Forever Alien: A Korean Memoir, 1930–1951* [2000] (London, 2011), pp. 57, 60.

12 Koreans did not compete in swimming at the Olympics, for example: Seok Lee, 'Colonial Korea and the Olympic Games, 1910–1945', PhD thesis, University of Pennsylvania, 2016, p. 170.

13 Kyo Nobuko (with Akemi Wegmüller), 'A Perfectly Ordinary Ethnic Korean in Japan: Reprise', in *Transcultural Japan: At the Borderlands of Race, Gender and Identity*, ed. David Willis et al. (Abingdon, 2007), pp. 47–64 (p. 51).

14 Salman Rushdie, *Midnight's Children* [1980] (London, 1991), pp. 104, 210–11; Lawrence James, *Raj: The Making and Unmaking of British India* (New York, 1997), p. 546; 'Club History', *The Calcutta Swimming Club 1887*, Kolkata 2019, www.calcuttaswimmingclub.com, accessed 18 May 2021; Partha Pratim Majumder and Sayantani Roy Choudhury, 'Reasons for Success in Competitive Swimming among Various Human Races', *IOSR Journal of Sports and Physical Education*, I (2014), pp. 24–30.

15 Alison Jefferson, 'African American Leisure Space in Santa Monica: The Beach Sometimes Known as the "Inkwell," 1900s–1960s', *Southern California Quarterly*, XCI (2009), p. 178; *California Eagle*, September 1925 to January 1926, *Santa Ana Daily Register*, September 1925 to January 1925; 'What's the Matter with Bruce's Beach', *California Eagle*, 8 July 1927; Jeff Wiltse, *Contested Waters: A Social History of Swimming Pools in America* (Chapel Hill, NC, 2007), pp. 178–9. Today, the descendants of the owners of the Bruce's Beach resort are still fighting to get back their beach: Jaclyn Cosgrove, 'Black Descendants of Bruce's Beach Owner Could Get Manhattan Beach Land Back under Plan', *Los Angeles Times*, 9 April 2021.

16 Andrew Kahrl, 'On the Beach: Race and Leisure in the Jim Crow South', PhD thesis, Indiana University, 2008, p. 7.

17 John Stephens, *Incidents of Travels in Egypt, Arabia Petraea and the Holy Land* (London, 1837), p. 29; Charles Warner, *My Winter on the Nile* (Boston, MA, 1891), vol. I, p. 246; 'Hawaiian to Swim at Olympic Games'; Nasium, 'Kanaka Swimmer Has No Equal'; Warren Henry, *The Confessions of a Tenderfoot 'Coaster': A Trader's Chronicle of Life on the West African Coast* (London, 1927), p. 109.

18 R. Allen and David Nickel, 'The Negro and Learning to Swim: The Buoyancy Problem Related to Reported Biological Differences', *Journal of Negro Education*, XXXVIII (1969), pp. 404–11 (their bibliography cites many other articles along the same lines); Michael Shermer, *The Borderlands of Science: Where Sense Meets Nonsense* (Oxford, 2001), p. 81; P.F.M. Ama and S. Ambassa, 'Buoyancy of African Black and European White Males', *American Journal of Human Biology*, IX (1997), pp. 87–92; see also Bruce Ettinger et al., 'Racial Differences in Bone Density between Young Adult Black and White Subjects Persist after Adjustment for Anthropometric, Lifestyle, and Biochemical Differences', *Journal of Clinical Endocrinology and Metabolism*, LXXXII (1997), pp. 429–34; Dean Sewell et al., *Sport and*

Exercise Science: An Introduction (New York, 2013), p. 267. Thanks to the blogger Lòt Poto-a for the references.

19 Douglas Booth, *The Race Game: Sport and Politics in South Africa* (London, 1998), p. 6; Sewell et al., *Sport and Exercise Science*, p. 267; Gordon Russell, *Sport Science Secrets: From Myth to Facts* (Victoria, BC, 2001), pp. 21–2.

20 Sundiata Djata, 'African Americans in Sports', in *The Columbia Guide to African American History since 1939*, ed. Robert Harris and Rosalyn Werberg-Penn (New York, 2013), p. 145; Barry Kelly, 'Olympic Gold Medalist Anthony Ervin Gives Up Swimming, Fame and Money', *Daily Californian*, 6 July 2004; Karen Crouse, 'Cullen Jones Sets U.S. Record in 50 Freestyle', *New York Times*, 5 July 2008; Katherine Fominykh, 'Gold-Medalist Olympic Swimmer Cullen Jones Teaches Baltimore Kids the Importance of Swimming', *Baltimore Sun*, 2 June 2018.

21 Kahrl, 'On the Beach', p. 1; Jeff Wiltse, 'Swimming Pools, Civic Life, and Social Capital', in *A Companion to Sport*, ed. David Andrews and Ben Carrington (Chichester, 2013), p. 300; Wiltse, *Contested Waters*, p. 162.

22 Ibid., pp. 172–5; Gilbert Mason, *Beaches, Blood, and Ballots: A Black Doctor's Civil Rights Struggle* (Jackson, MI, 2000), p. 51.

23 Pete Daniel, 'Accidental Historian', in *Shapers of Southern History: Autobiographical Reflections*, ed. John Boles (Athens, GA, 2004), p. 177; Wiltse, 'Swimming Pools', p. 291; Dan Warren, *If It Takes All Summer: Martin Luther King, the KKK, and States' Rights in St Augustine, 1964* (Tuscaloosa, AL, 2008), p. 118; Steven Taylor, *Desegregation in Boston and Buffalo: The Influence of Local Leaders* (Albany, NY, 1998), p. 140.

24 Ann Curthoys, 'The Freedom Ride and the Tent Embassy', in *The Aboriginal Tent Embassy: Sovereignty, Black Power, Land Rights and the State*, ed. Gary Foley et al. (Abingdon, 2014), pp. 98–114 (p. 109); Haleh Afshar, 'Muslim Women in West Yorkshire', in *The Dynamics of Race and Gender: Some Feminist Interventions*, ed. Afshar and Mary Maynard (London, 1994), p. 141; A. Patel, 'Racism in Weymouth', *Dorset Echo*, 29 June 2010; Sussex Police, 'Woman Sought after Racist Abuse on Brighton Beach', 25 July 2013; Karen Fields and Barbara Fields, *Racecraft: The Soul of Inequality in American Life* (London, 2012), p. 31; Khara Lewis, 'Pa. Swim Club – Accused of Racial Discrimination – Agrees to Settlement', CNN *Justice*, 17 August 2012; Azi Paybarah, 'Michigan Man Charged with Hate Crime after Attack on Black Teen', *New York Times*, 13 October 2020.

25 Victoria Wollcott, *Race, Riots, and Roller Coasters: The Struggle over Segregated Recreation in America* (Philadelphia, PA, 2012), p. 28; Wiltse, *Contested Waters*, pp. 182, 192; 'Australia's Swimming Success and Swimming Pools', www.australia.gov.au, 12 January 2009.

26 Rebecca McNeer, 'Virginia Woolf: Natural Olympian: Swimming and Diving as Metaphors for Writing', in *Virginia Woolf and the Natural World*, ed. Kristin Czarnecki and Carrie Rohman (Clemson, SC, 2011), pp. 95–100 (see also the two following essays); James Riordan, *Sport in Soviet Society: Development of Sport and Physical Education in Russia and the*

USSR (Cambridge, 1977), p. 346; Jenny Landreth, *Swell: A Waterbiography* (London 2017), pp. 5–6.

27 James Mangan, *Europe, Sport, World: Shaping Global Societies* (London, 2001), pp. 87–8; Nicholas Aplin and Quek Jin Jong, 'Celestials in Touch: Sport and the Chinese in Colonial Singapore', in *Sport in Asian Society, Past and Present*, ed. Fan Hong and James Mangan (London, 2002), pp. 56–81 (pp. 72–3); Guenter Lewy, *The Nazi Persecution of the Gypsies* (Oxford, 1999), p. 129 (though I do not support all of Lewy's conclusions).

28 Christopher Love, *A Social History of Swimming in England, 1800–1918: Splashing in the Serpentine* (Abingdon, 2008), pp. 48, 136; Ian Gordon and Simon Inglis, *Great Lengths: The Historic Indoor Swimming Pools of Britain* (Liverpool, 2009), pp. 37, 87 and *passim*; Day and Roberts, *Swimming Communities*, p. 171.

29 Trevor Bowen and Ira Reid, *Divine White Right* [1934] (Ann Arbor, MI, 2006), p. 169. See also Nina Mjagkij, *Light in the Darkness: African Americans and the YMCA, 1852–1946* (Lexington, KY, 1994).

30 James Kirkup, quoted in John Walton, *The British Seaside: Holidays and Resorts in the Twentieth Century* (Manchester, 2000), p. 98; Michel Rainis, *Histoire des Clubs de Plage (XXe siècle): Exercices, jeux, concours et sports sur le sable* (Paris, 2001), pp. 24, 5, 10.

31 Mennen, Gerhard, Co., Mennen's Borated Talcum Powder, *Town and Country* (1907), Washington, DC, Smithsonian Institution, National Museum of American History; Chrysler Corporation, 'Plymouth Has It!' (1947–8), Washington, DC, Smithsonian Institution, National Museum of American History; Pepsi-Cola Company, 'Be Sociable, Have a Pepsi' (*c.* 1959), Washington, DC, Smithsonian Institution, National Museum of American History.

32 Annette Kellerman, *How to Swim* (New York, 1918), p. 53; Dawson, *Undercurrents of Power*, p. 38.

33 Melissa Korn, 'For Certain College Students, This Test Calls for a Plunge', *Wall Street Journal*, 28 November 2012; Dorothy Riker, ed., *The Hoosier Training Ground: A History of Army and Navy Training Centers, Camps, Forts, Depots, and Other Military Installations within the State Boundaries during World War II* (Bloomington, IN, 1952), p. 128. The British Navy has required a swimming test since 1879; the British army teaches recruits to swim in basic training.

34 Andrew Kahrl, *The Land Was Ours: How Black Beaches Became White Wealth in the Coastal South* (Chapel Hill, NC, 2012), pp. 90–99.

35 Katerina Capkova, *Czechs, Germans, Jews? National Identity and the Jews of Bohemia* (New York, 2012), p. 111; David Sorkin, *Jewish Emancipation: A History across Five Centuries* (Princeton, NJ, 2019), p. 348; Linda Borish, 'Jewish American Women, Jewish Organizations, and Sports, 1880–1940', in *Sports and the American Jew*, ed. Steven Reiss (Syracuse, NY, 1998), p. 116; Hallie Bond, Joan Brumberg and Leslie Paris, 'A Paradise for Boys and Girls': Children's Camps in the Adirondacks* (Syracuse, NY, 2006), p. 5.

36 Aplin and Jong, 'Celestials in Touch', pp. 72–3; Franks, *Crossing Sidelines*, p. ii (in 1926).

37 Lie, *Zainichi*, p. 8; Che, *Forever Alien*, pp. 57, 60; Pascale Herzig, *South Asians in Kenya: Gender, Generation and Changing Identities in Diaspora* (Münster, 2006), p. 98; Mahmoud Mamdani, *From Citizen to Refugee: Uganda Asians Come to Britain* (London, 1973), p. 68.

38 Richard Moss, *Golf and the American Country Club* (Urbana, IL, 2001), pp. 120–21.

39 Aplin and Jong, 'Celestials in Touch', pp. 72–3; Shehong Chen, *Being Chinese, Becoming Chinese American* (Urbana, IL, 2002), p. 168.

40 Moss, *Golf and the American Country Club*, p. 120; Kahrl, *The Land Was Ours*, p. 99.

41 Zelbert Moore, 'Out of the Shadows: Black and Brown Struggles for Recognition and Dignity in Brazil, 1964–1985', *Journal of Black Studies*, XIX (1989), pp. 394–410 (p. 402); Arilson dos Santos Gomes, 'O Primeiro Congresso Nacional do Negro e a sua importância para a integração social dos negros brasileiros e a ascensão material da Sociedade Floresta Aurora', *Revista Brasileira de História e Ciências Sociais*, I (2009), pp. 1–18; João Batista de Jesus Felix, 'As Primeras Formas de Lutas Contra o Racismo no Brasil Republicano', *Tempo da Ciência*, XVI/32 (2009), pp. 67–80 (p. 75); for the earlier existence of similar clubs, see Kim Butler, 'Up from Slavery: Afro-Brazilian Activism in São Paulo, 1888–1938', *The Americas*, XLIX (1992), pp. 179–206.

42 Mario García, *Mexican Americans: Leadership, Ideology, and Identity, 1930–1960* (New Haven, CT, 1989), p. 88; Richard Griswold del Castillo, 'The War and Changing Identities: Personal Transformations', in *World War II and Mexican American Civil Rights*, ed. Griswold del Castillo (Austin, TX, 2008), pp. 49–73 (pp. 58–61); Julie Gilchrist et al., 'Self-Reported Swimming Ability in U.S. Adults, 1994', *Public Health Reports*, CXV/2–3 (2000), pp. 110–11; Jennifer Pharr et al., 'Predictors of Swimming Ability among Children and Adolescents in the United States', *Sports*, VI, 24 February 2018, www.mdpi.com, with further references.

43 Riordan, *Sport in Soviet Society*, p. 340.

44 Tsui, *Why We Swim*, p. 6; Rebecca Mead, 'Going for the Cold', *New Yorker*, 27 January 2020, pp. 42–9 (pp. 45–6).

45 Mead, 'Going for the Cold', p. 45; Raphaël Le Cam and Adrien Guilloret, 'Histoire des techniques de nage', *Service interuniversitaire des activités physiques et sportives* (Rennes, 2016), n.p., available at www.apprendre-a-nager.univ-rennes1.fr, accessed 19 May 2021.

46 Geoffrey Manning, *A Colonial Experience, 1838–1910: A Woman's Story of Life in Adelaide, the District of Kensington and Norwood, Together with Reminiscences of Colonial Life* (Adelaide, 2001).

47 Photograph by Wilhelm von Blandowski, comment by Gustav Mützel; Thomas Britten, *American Indians in World War I: At Home and at War* (Albuquerque, NM, 1997), pp. 80, 100; Dawson, *Undercurrents of Power*, p. 15.

48   *The Family Herald: A Domestic Magazine of Useful Information and Amusement*, 60 (April 1888); Constance Romanné-James, 'In the Land of the White Elephant', *Chatterbox* (Boston, MA, 1913), pp. 211–12.

49   Sumālī Bamrungsuk, *Love and Marriage: Mate Selection in Twentieth-Century Central Thailand* (Bangkok, 1995), p. 54; Jack Leemon, 'Extracts from *The Body Snatchers*', in *The Thailand-Burma Railway, 1942–1946*, ed. Paul Kratoska (London, 2004), pp. 61–86 (pp. 68, 78); Orapin Larosee et al., 'Child Drowning in Thailand', *World Conference on Drowning Prevention* (2011).

50   James, *Raj*, p. 502; Ruth Ginio, *French Colonialism Unmasked: The Vichy Years in French West Africa* (Lincoln, NE, 2006), p. 49; Steven Wöndu, *From Bush to Bush: Journey to Liberty in South Sudan* (Nairobi, 2011), p. 90.

51   Leslie Paris, *Children's Nature: The Rise of the American Summer Camp* (New York, 2008), p. 220; 'YMCA Camp Opens for Boys', *Afro American*, 15 June 1957.

52   'UNICEF Supports Swimming Instruction to Prevent Child Deaths in Bangladesh', UNICEF Bangladesh, 3 September 2009, Boys learn to swim in Golla Para, Bangladesh (©UNICEF Bangladesh/2009/Crowe)

53   Wiltse, *Contested Waters*, pp. 147, 240, 242, 244, and *passim*; Aplin and Jong, 'Celestials in Touch', pp. 73–4; Kamilla Swart, 'Swimming, Southern Africa', in *Sports Around the World*, ed. John Nauright and Charles Parrish (Santa Barbara, CA, 2012), vol. I, pp. 162–3 (p. 163).

54   *United States Congressional Record* 115.15 (1969), 20299.

55   'Brazilian Swimming Community Bands Together to Save Julio de Lamare', *Swimming World*, 29 August 2013; Annie Murphy, 'What's a Walk in the Park Worth in Peru?', *Christian Science Monitor*, 24 December 2013.

56   Phan Boi Chau, *Tan Viet Nam* (1907), quoted in Truong Buu Lâm, *Colonialism Experienced: Vietnamese Writings on Colonialism, 1900–1931* (Ann Arbor, MI, 2000), p. 107.

57   Martin Alexander and John Keiger, *France and the Algerian War, 1954–1962: Strategy, Operations and Diplomacy* (London, 2013), p. 5; Kosonike Koso-Thomas, *Swimming Against the Tide* (New York, 2004).

58   Sierra Leone: Koso-Thomas, *Swimming Against the Tide*, p. 18; Nigeria: George Basden, *Among the Ibos of Nigeria* (London, 1921), p. 160, cited in Steve Craig, *Sports and Games of the Ancients* (Westport, CT, 2002), pp. 26–7 and Benjamin Chijioke Asogwa et al., 'The Sociological and Cultural Significance of the Argungu International Fishing and Cultural Festival in Nigeria', *International Journal of Humanities and Social Science*, II/II (2012), pp. 243–9 (p. 247); Benin: 'Benin: Firmin Fifonsi, "I told my friends not to go swimming in the river because it is dangerous"', IRIN *Humanitarian News and Analysis*, 15 April 2009; Chad: Caterina Batello et al., *The Future Is an Ancient Lake: Traditional Knowledge, Biodiversity and Genetic Resources for Food and Agriculture in Lake Chad Basin Ecosystems* (Rome, 2004), pp. 100–103; Sudan: Human Rights Watch, *Children in*

Sudan: Slaves, Street Children and Child Soldiers (New York, 1995), pp. 56, 61; Kenya: William Routledge and Katherine Routledge, *With a Prehistoric People: The Akikuyu of British East Africa* (London, 1968), pp. 13–14; Angola: Adebayo Oyebade, *Culture and Customs of Angola* (Westport, CT, 2007), p. 98; Cameroon: John Mukum Mbaku and Nicodemus Fru Awasom, 'Cameroon', in *Teen Life in Africa*, ed. Toyin Falola (Westport, CT, 2004), p. 46; Navajo: James Olson and Raymond Wilson, *Native Americans in the Twentieth Century* (Salt Lake City, UT, 1984), p. 1, and Donna Dehle, *Reflections in Place: Connected Lives of Navajo Women* (Tucson, AZ, 2009), p. 182; Indonesia: Tsui, *Why We Swim*, p. 30; Hawaii: Dawson, *Undercurrents of Power*, pp. 24, 32.

59 'Hanging in Hampi', https://myindiaencounters.wordpress.com, accessed 25 July 2021; 'Grace Itoje's Story' in *Mapping Memories: Reminiscence with Ethnic Minority Elders*, ed. Pamela Schweitzer (London, 2004); Tsui, *Why We Swim*, p. 30.

60 Basden, *Among the Ibos*, p. 184, cited in Craig, *Sports and Games*, pp. 26–7.

61 Asogwa et al., 'The Sociological and Cultural Significance', p. 247; Mwangi Wanderi, *The Indigenous Games of the People of the Coastal Region of Kenya: A Cultural and Educational Appraisal* (Addis Adaba, 2011), p. 89; Dawson, *Undercurrents of Power*, p. 1.

62 Wanderi, *Indigenous Games*, p. 89; Dawson, *Undercurrents of Power*, pp. 24, 32; Basden, *Among the Ibos*, p. 184; Don Hinrichsen, *Coastal Waters of the World: Trends, Threats, and Strategies* (Washington, DC, 1998), pp. 209–10.

63 Mary Seddon et al., 'Freshwater Molluscs of Africa: Diversity, Distribution, and Conservation', in *The Diversity of Life in African Freshwaters: Under Water, Under Threat. An Analysis of the Status and Distribution of Freshwater Species throughout Mainland Africa*, ed. William Darwall et al. (Cambridge, 2011), pp. 92–125 (pp. 123–4).

64 Mead, 'Going for the Cold', p. 45.

65 'Lake Lagano', in *Encyclopaedia Aethiopica*, ed. Siebert Uhlig (Wiesbaden, 2007), p. 502; Nima Elbagir and Lillian Leposo, 'Holidays in Somalia? Mogadishu Hopes to be Tourist Hotspot', CNN *International Business*, 12 June 2013; Edward Denison and Edward Plaice, *Eritrea: The Bradt Travel Guide* (Guildford, CT, 2007), pp. 155–60.

66 International Monetary Fund, Africa Dept, *Guinea: Poverty Reduction Strategy Paper*, 3 July 2013, p. 78.

FURTHER READING

Alpers, Edward, *The Indian Ocean in World History* (Oxford, 2014)

Auberger, Janick, 'Quand la nage devint natation . . .', *Latomus*, 55 (1996), pp. 48–62

Barrett, Caitlín Eilís, *Domesticating Empire: Egyptian Landscapes in Pompeian Gardens* (Oxford, 2019)

Blom, Philipp, *Nature's Mutiny: How the Little Ice Age of the Long Seventeenth Century Transformed the West and Shaped the Present* (New York, 2017)

Chou, Cynthia, *The Orang Suku Laut of Riau, Indonesia: The Inalienable Gift of Territory* (Abingdon, 2010)

Dawson, Kevin, *Undercurrents of Power: Aquatic Culture in the African Diaspora* (Philadelphia, PA, 2018)

Deng, Gang, *Maritime Sector, Institutions, and Sea Power of Premodern China* (Westport, CT, 1999)

Fagan, Garrett, *Bathing in Public in the Roman World* (Ann Arbor, MI, 1999)

Foley, Gary, et al., eds, *The Aboriginal Tent Embassy: Sovereignty, Black Power, Land Rights and the State* (Abingdon, 2014)

Hoss, Stefanie, *Baths and Bathing: The Culture of Bathing and the Baths and Thermae in Palestine from the Hasmoneans to the Moslem Conquest*, British Archaeological Reports International Series 1346 (Oxford, 2005)

Hữu Ngọc, *Viet Nam: Tradition and Change* (Athens, OH, 2016)

Kahrl, Andrew, *The Land Was Ours: How Black Beaches Became White Wealth in the Coastal South* (Chapel Hill, NC, 2012)

Keegan, William, and Lisabeth Carlson, *Talking Taino: Caribbean Natural History from a Native Perspective* (Tuscaloosa, AL, 2008)

Kneebone, Emily, *Oppian's Halieutica: Charting a Didactic Epic* (Cambridge, 2020)

Konstantopoulos, Gina, 'The Bitter Sea and the Waters of Death: The Sea as a Conceptual Border in Mesopotamia', *Journal of Ancient Civilizations*, XXXV (2020), pp. 171–98

McManamon, John, *'Neither Letters nor Swimming': The Rebirth of Swimming and Free-Diving* (Leiden, 2021)

Mason, Gilbert, *Beaches, Blood, and Ballots: A Black Doctor's Civil Rights Struggle* (Jackson, MS, 2000)

Mentz, Steve, *Ocean* (New York, 2020)

Moore, Zelbert, 'Out of the Shadows: Black and Brown Struggles for Recognition and Dignity in Brazil, 1964–1985', *Journal of Black Studies*, XIX (1989), pp. 394–410

Painter, Nell, *The History of White People* (New York, 2010)

Parr, Susie, *The Story of Swimming: A Social History of Bathing in Britain* (Stockport, 2011)

Pitts, Lee, *Black Splash: The History of African American Swimmers* (Fort Lauderdale, FL, 2007)

Ragheb, Ashraf Abdel-Raouf, 'Notes on Diving in Ancient Egypt', *International Journal of Nautical Archaeology*, XL (2011), pp. 424–7

Ray, Sugata, *Climate Change and the Art of Devotion: Geoaesthetics in the Land of Krishna, 1550–1850* (Seattle, WA, 2019)

Sagita, Shigeo, and Ken Uyeno, eds, *Swimming in Japan* (Tokyo, 1935)

Schafer, Edward, 'The Development of Bathing Customs in Ancient and Medieval China and the History of the Floriate Clear Palace', *Journal of the American Oriental Society*, LXXVI (1956), pp. 57–82

Scribner, Vaughn, *Merpeople: A Human History* (London, 2020)

Tsui, Bonnie, *Why We Swim* (Chapel Hill, NC, 2020)

Van Duzer, Chet, *Sea Monsters on Medieval and Renaissance Maps* (London, 2013)

Villa, Paola, et al., 'Neandertals on the Beach: Use of Marine Resources at Grotta dei Moscerini (Latium, Italy)', *PLoS ONE*, XV (2020), pp. 1–35

Wiltse, Jeff, *Contested Waters: A Social History of Swimming Pools in America* (Chapel Hill, NC, 2007)

Yegül, Fikret, *Bathing in the Roman World* (Cambridge, 2010)

ACKNOWLEDGEMENTS

I began to work on the history of swimming a few years ago with a set of articles for the history website Quatr.us Study Guides. Since that time my work has greatly benefited from conversations with Simon Trafford, Torsten Wallina, Kevin Dawson, Richard Strassberg, Sucheta Mazumar, Patrick Bartlein, Ryan Baumann, Margaret Cool Root, Heather Clydesdale, Bruce Wigo at the International Swimming Hall of Fame, George Armantrout, Sarah Scullin, Yung In Chae, Megan Lewis at Digital Hammurabi, Rich SantaColoma, Pietro Montanari, Robert Pappalardo of the Europa Mission at JPL, Carly Silver, Molly Swetnam-Burland, Anne McClanan, Rebecca Futo Kennedy, Dan Martin, Steve Mentz, Bethany Hucks, Sophie Hay and Alex Nice. If I have inadvertently left your name off this list, please forgive me. Carol Burrell convinced me to send off a proposal. Jodi Magness, Jim Haberman, Peter Hess, Baragur Venkatesha and Anandajoti Bhikkhu provided photographs crucial to the argument. I am grateful to early readers (and old friends) Robina Marshall, Robert Schneider, Sam Pottle and Cynthia Sims Parr. Any remaining errors are, of course, my own and not theirs.

Parts of this book were presented at various meetings of the American Institute of Archaeology, at local AIA society lectures, at the annual meeting of the Classical Association of the Pacific Northwest, at the Oregon Regional North African Studies Workshop in 2016, at Gonzaga University's conference on Archaeology and the Humanities in 2017 and at Brown University's Brown Bag lecture series in 2018. In each case I have benefited from the questions and suggestions of the participants, which I hope I have answered sufficiently here.

Two institutions have supported this work by generously extending library privileges. The first is Portland State University, which let me keep full library privileges as an Associate Professor Emerita, even though I resigned tenure before I started work on this book. The second is Brown University, which has extended library privileges to me for the last four years as a Sponsored Scholar in the Department of Classics, and made room for me in the Joukowsky Institute's lovely Archaeology Library in Rhode Island Hall.

Many of the texts and images used to assemble this book were located, conveniently for me, in the British Museum, the Metropolitan Museum of Art, the Boston Museum of Fine Arts and the Smithsonian Institution. Most of these texts and images were made in colonized parts of the world and rightfully belong to them. If they were in their original locations, people who live there would have easier access to them. Part of the privilege colonialism has brought me has facilitated my writing this history, while simultaneously making it more difficult for previously (or currently) colonized people to write it. I hope I have at least spoken for them in a way they will find helpful rather than injurious.

In a book with this wide a chronological sweep, it is impossible to do justice to the deep scholarship in each area, and I make no claim to completeness. In an effort to avoid Eurocentrism, this book refers throughout to Southwest Asia or West Asia, not the Middle East or Near East. Translations from European languages, ancient and modern, are mine unless otherwise noted. English-language sources have been preferred where possible, and sources in other languages are presented in translation. Names of people and places are throughout in the most widely understood form. In a book of this length and breadth, written by someone of my sadly imprecise inclinations, I am sure there must be many small errors, which I hope do not detract from the main points. Michael Leaman, Alex Ciobanu, Amy Salter, David Rose and everyone at Reaktion Books have been indefatigably helpful. Damian Carr deserves the commendation of the reader for finding and improving on many small infelicities in the writing and for drawing the small swimmers at the end of each chapter. Finally, I am most grateful to my parents, who provided a haven where I have written large parts of this book.

PHOTO ACKNOWLEDGEMENTS

The author and publishers wish to express their thanks to the below sources of illustrative material and/or permission to reproduce it. Every effort has been made to contact copyright holders; should there be any we have been unable to reach or to whom inaccurate acknowledgements have been made please contact the publishers, and full adjustments will be made to any subsequent printings. Some locations of artworks are also given below, in the interest of brevity:

akg-images/Nimatallah: 28 (Museo Archeologico Nazionale, Florence); from William Andrews, *Old-Time Punishments* (Hull and London, 1890): 70; Archives Center, National Museum of American History, Washington, DC: 98; photo Crispin Barnham, used with permission: 53; Biblioteca Apostolica Vaticana, Vatican City (Pal.lat.1071, fol. 69r): 71; Bibliothèque de l'Institut de France, Paris (MS 2173 [Manuscript B], fol. 81v): 84; Bodleian Library, University of Oxford (MS Ouseley 381, fol. 166b): 72; Boston Public Library: 88, 89; British Library, London: 59 (Royal MS 2 B VII, fol. 170r), 69 (Add MS 62925, fol. 86r); The British Museum, London: 66; Brooklyn Museum, NY: 47; after Giorgio Buchner, 'Pithekoussai: Oldest Greek Colony in the West', *Expedition Magazine*, VIII/4 (1966): 27 (Museo Archeologico di Pithecusae, Lacco Ameno, Ischia); from E. A. Wallis Budge, ed., *Assyrian Sculptures in the British Museum* (London, 1914): 24, 25; Burgerbibliothek, Bern (Cod. 120.II, fol. 107r): 56; The Cleveland Museum of Art, OH: 36; photo Daderot: 26 (Museum für Asiatische Kunst, Staatliche Museen zu Berlin); photo De Agostini/G. Dagli Orti via Getty Images: 15; after Wolfgang Decker, *Sport und Spiel im Alten Ägypten* (Munich, 1987): 3, 4 (illustration Marcelle Baud/Museo Egizio, Turin); after Eleanor von Erdberg Consten, 'A Hu with Pictorial Decoration: Werner Jannings Collection, Palace Museum, Peking', *Archives of the Chinese Art Society of America*, VI (1952): 10; Forschungsbibliothek Gotha der Universität Erfurt (MS Memb. I 90, fol. 139v): 57; GuoZhongHua/Shutterstock.com: 81; photos © Jim Haberman, all rights reserved/reproduced with permission of Jodi Magness: 41, 42; from *Hainei qiguan* 海⌐奇觀 (1609), photo Harvard-Yenching Library, Harvard University, Cambridge, MA: 11; photo Richard Hansen, © FARES 2019, used with permission: 12; photo Peter Hess, used

INDEX

Numbers in *italics* refer to illustrations